Historical Tapestry: Adele France and John LaFarge in Southern Maryland

By Janet Butler Haugaard, PhD

Margarita Haugaard
Editor, contributor, and map-designer

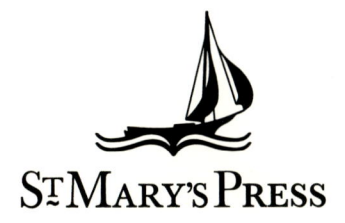

St Mary's Press

St. Mary's College of Maryland

Copyright © 2023 by Janet Butler Haugaard
All rights reserved, including the right to reproduce this work in any form whatsoever, except for brief passages in connection with a review.

Library of Congress Control Number: 2023916546

ISBN 978-0-9787269-1-1

Image on the cover courtesy of Saint Cecilia Catholic Church,
Roman Catholic Archdiocese of Washington.
Photographed by Chuck Steenburgh.

Cover Design: Abigale Larsh

Printed in the United States of America.

Table of Contents and Lists of Photographs and Maps

Foreward 1

Author's Notes: (2008 and 2018) 3

Introduction: Barely Four Days and Four Miles Apart 7
    A. Arrivals of Adele France and John LaFarge   7
    B. Steamboats to St. Mary's County   12
    C. Forging Ahead, in and for, St. Mary's County   15

Chapter 1: Blood, Sweat, and Brains 19
    A. 1840 Painting: a Picture in Time   19
    B. Two Outsiders in St. Mary's County   23
    C. The Triangular Trade   30
    D. The Rise and Fall of Britain's Slave Trade   33
    E. What the 1840 Painting Does Not Reveal   39

Chapter 2: Catholics: Exiled in Place 43
    A. Further Back In Time and In Place   43
    B. Headquarters: London   44
    C. Branch Offices: Maryland in Particular   48
    D. Persecution: "a bad and indirect way to plant Religion"   54
    E. The Cost of Being Catholic in Maryland   72
        1. Governmental Acts   72
        2. Papal Acts   76
        3. Jesuit Schools   77
    F. Again Enacting Religious Freedom: Now the U.S. Constitution   78

Chapter 3: "O Brave New World" 81
    A. Freedom in the Air   81
    B. "One Candle at a Time"   84
        1. Debate   86

  2. Education   88
  3. Literature and Science   91
 C. The Power of the Pens   95
  1. Quest for a National Identity   95
  2. Monument No. 1: Plymouth Rock   97
  3. St. Mary's City and John Pendleton Kennedy   98
  4. Monument No. 2: A School for Religious Tolerance   99
 D. The Female Seminary as Living Monument   106
 E. Turning the Page: Two "Furriners"   114

Chapter 4: Head, Heart–and a Horse Named "Morgan" ... 119
 A. Head and Heart: Adele France   119
  1. Gumption   121
  2. The Woman's Literary Club   129
  3. The Horsey Collection   133
 B. Head and Heart: John LaFarge   135
  1. Reading and Writing   138
  2. Music   140
  3. Flair for Languages   140
  4. Intellect and Empathy   146
 C. Finally, Morgan the Horse   148

Chapter 5: The "Not-Quites" (Women) ... 151
 A. Declaration of Rights and Sentiments   152
 B. The "Dependent and Abject Life"–Not for Adele France   156
 C. "Anatomy is Destiny"   158
 D. Certainly Not Astride   163
 E. "Do Not Rush Your Daughters Through School"   167
 F. No "Unkindness of Feeling"   171

Chapter 6: Slavery ... 179
 A. Lord Baltimore's Maryland Colony   179
 B. Colonial Culture of the West Indies   183
  1. Language   184
  2. Ability to Think Colonially   185
 C. Slavery: Economics Trumps Morality   186

    D. Stirrings: What "The New World" Promised   190
    E. England's "Sea Dogs"   193
    F. From the Ark and Dove: "Anchors Aweigh"   198
    G. "Sooner Than One Might Think"   209
    H. "Morally Acceptable"   211

Chapter 7: Voices from Europe 213
    A. Curiosity and Perspective   213
    B. Hazards of Travel   219
    C. The Issues   224
    D. Travelers from England   224
        1. Democracy: station   227
        2. Women: vacancy of thought   239
        3. Religion: substitute for education   246
        4. Indians and Africans: ejected and subjected   250
            a. Indians   250
            b. Africans   254
    E. Travelers from France   259
        1. Democracy: focus on money-making   260
        2. Women: household as convent   265
        3. Religion: rigor and rigidity   267
        4. Africans and Indians: oppression and genocide   268
            a. Africans   269
            b. Indians   272

Chapter 8: St. Mary's County: Catalyst for John LaFarge's
Mission Against Racism–and the Disappeared Encyclical 277
    A. Précis   277
    B. Growing Up   281
        1. Languages   282
        2. Music   282
        3. Reading and Writing   283
    C. Education   283
        1. Harvard (1897–1901)   283
            a. Music   283
            b. Languages   285

c. Reading and Writing	285
2. Austria (1901-1905)	286
a. Reading and Writing	286
b. Music	288
c. Languages	288
3. Becoming a Jesuit Priest (1905-1911): "Poverty, Chastity, and Obedience"	290
D. Knowledge and Work (1911-1926)	293
1. Assistant Pastor in Leonardtown	293
2. Slavs!	295
3. Establishing Mission Schools	301
a. St. Alphonsus School	303
b. St. James School, later dubbed St. David's School	305
c. Ridge: Dichotomy of Place	308
i. St. Peter Claver Elementary School	310
ii. St. Michael's Schools	313
d. Cardinal Gibbons Institute	315
4. Public Schools of St. Mary's County	322
E. The Disappeared Encyclical	325

Chapter 9: Adele France: "Ornaments No Longer"............333

A. Addie and the Chestertown Years	334
B. Addie Becomes "Miss France"	339
C. Miss France Battles for St. Mary's	344
1. First Battle – Rising from Charred Ruins	344
a. Fire Galvanizes Mettle	344
b. Building on Heritage	346
c. Two-year Junior College	349
2. Second Battle – Overcoming The Great Depression and World War II	350
a. Stock Market Crash and Revitalization	350
b. Maryland's 300th Birthday Celebration	352
c. Four-year Junior College	353
d. Seminary's 100th Birthday Celebration	356
e. World War II	357

  3. Third Battle – Again Triumphing Over Forces
    Intent on Closing St. Mary's   358
    a. Marbury Commission   358
    b. Go bust? No: instead, funding boost!   359
 D. Opening Windows and Modernizing the Living Monument 360
 E. The Junior College as Institutional Catalyst for the
  Liberal Arts College   364
 F. Full Circle   366

Appendix A ***371***
Appendix B ***371***
Appendix C ***372***
Appendix D ***378***

Acknowledgments ***389***

Index ***397***

About the Author ***419***

List of Photographs

The Steamboat Landing at Brome's Wharf, image provided courtesy of St. Mary's College of Maryland Archives, 8

Painting of The 1840 Anti-Slavery Society Convention, image provided courtesy of the National Portrait Gallery, London, 18

The "Living Monument" sign at SMCM, image provided courtesy of Lee Capristo, 25

Students on Brome's Wharf, image provided courtesy of St. Mary's College of Maryland Archives, 120

The Main Building before the 1924 fire with horses in front, image provided courtesy of St. Mary's College of Maryland Archives, 120

The Pieria Literary Society, 1894, image provided courtesy of Washington College Archives and Special Collections, 125

vii

Adele France in 1902 holding her M.A. diploma, image provided courtesy of St. Mary's College of Maryland Archives, 126

The Music Hall (& Main Building) before the 1924 fire, image provided courtesy of St. Mary's College of Maryland Archives, 172

John LaFarge and congregation of St James Church, image provided courtesy of the St. Mary's County Historical Society, 300

The Cardinal Gibbons Institute, image provided courtesy of the St. Mary's County Historical Society, 321

Painting of Adele France in 1948 with her doctoral robe; photo taken by Lee Capristo, image provided courtesy of St. Mary's College of Maryland Archives, 343

The Main Building destroyed by the 1924 fire with car in front, image provided courtesy of St. Mary's College of Maryland Archives, 345

The New Main Building, re-built in 1925, image provided courtesy of St. Mary's College of Maryland Archives, 347

Newspaper-clipping with note attached indicating that published by *The Baltimore Sun*, image provided courtesy of St. Mary's College of Maryland Archives, 348

Adele France wearing flowered dress (1930s), image provided courtesy of St. Mary's College of Maryland Archives, 363

List of Maps

1. Steamboat routes from Baltimore and Washington D.C. 9
2. Towns in Southern Maryland (focusing on inset) 10
3. Towns from Baltimore to Southern Md. (with inset) 11
4. Churches in Southern Maryland (early-to-mid 20th Century) 298
5. Schools in Southern Maryland (early-to-mid 20th Century) 299

Foreward

In June of 1923, the Trustees of St. Mary's Female Seminary unanimously elected Adele France to be the next Principal. A true trailblazer, she soon transformed the Seminary into a Junior College. After her quarter-century leadership, the Seminary-Junior College evolved into St. Mary's College of Maryland, now known as "The National Public Honors College."

This book began as a project on M. Adele France. She was born in 1880 and graduated from college about twenty years before she was even allowed to cast a ballot to vote. Undaunted by society's constraints and inequities, both before and after the passing of the 19th Amendment, she advocated for women's rights to education. Naturally, questions arise about the historical context of her extraordinary life's work.

Research for what was contemplated as a slim book on Adele began in 2009.[1] Over a decade, the book broadened in scope. Why? History. The need to provide context and perspective for the hows and whys.

---

[1] Most of this book had been drafted by 2019. There are references to persons who were living at the time (for example, Queen Elizabeth II), and as such, are still referred to in the present tense.

In addition to women's rights, given Maryland's unique past, religious rights and human rights are also woven into the background of this historical tapestry.

This book also broadened in scope to welcome a contemporary of Adele France: John LaFarge, a Jesuit priest, who served in St. Mary's County and became a prominent voice against racism.

In this tapestry, 1840 was a landmark year. Twenty years later, the Civil War would erupt. Forty years later, Adele France and John LaFarge would both be born.

In 1840, St. Mary's Female Seminary was created by the Maryland Legislature as a "living monument" that would teach girls of different religious faiths to respect each other, thereby reviving Lord Baltimore's original vision for a religiously tolerant Maryland. Two intertwined threads: women and religion.

Also in 1840, the World Anti-Slavery Convention was held in London. Black men were encouraged to attend–but women's participation was forbidden. Two intertwined threads: women and slavery.

In 2012, the author chanced upon a painting (by Benjamin Haydon) of the 1840 Abolitionist Convention held in London. This painting is introduced in Chapter One and reappears here and there.

Like the steamboats that traversed the Potomac River and the Chesapeake Bay, this book zig-zags its course through the rough waters of historical context navigated by its two protagonists–Adele France and John LaFarge. This book does not have to be read in any particular order. It can be sampled at whim.

Margarita Haugaard
June of 2023

Author's Notes (2008 and 2018)

Cultural Snapshot of a Time and Place: St. Mary's Junior College

[After a cold-trail investigation I did in 1992, delving into a student incident that had occurred 40 years ago], for me, the in-depth investigative process was important because it opened up for me the whole world of the old seminary-junior college. Many of its customs (demerits and dance cards, for example) were familiar to me from my own teenage years of the 1940s, and with the encouragement of Dirk Griffith, I decided to get those years and those customs down on paper before they were lost to time. I hit on the quarter-century when M. Adele France was head of the school, and with the help of a 12-woman alumnae committee I set up, we sent out questionnaires to the "girls" who had been here from 1923 to 1948. The returned questionnaires provided what Dirk called "a cultural snapshot" of a time and place. I presented some of the findings at Alumni Reunion in 1993.

But any further work on the project had to be done in my "spare" time, and for years the questionnaires lay pretty much untouched in a file drawer.

[W]hen I hit my early seventies, I suddenly began wondering about Adele France herself. She did not come to St. Mary's until she was 43–and what had she been doing in the preceding two decades? She spoke with a clear voice: "The time is past," she wrote in the 1920s, "when we educated our daughters for ornaments only" and went on to note that they should be preparing to take "an economic place in the world." Washington College awarded her an honorary degree in 1942, and she stood on the platform, next to Eleanor Roosevelt, to receive it.

As time allows, my research into her formative years has taken me to Chestertown where she grew up and where she graduated from Washington College in 1900 with a degree in math and physics. The St. Mary's College of today would have gone out of existence decades ago if it had not been for Adele France's vigorous–and successful–exertions to save it.

Janet Butler Haugaard
January of 2008

How the Quest for a Word Led to the Discovery of Historical Records

In the first week of August 2010, I left the familiar surroundings of St. Mary's College of Maryland (Southern Maryland's public college for the liberal arts) and made a trip up to Washington, D.C. I was going up solely to check on the mysterious word "pilgrim" as it had been used in Maryland in the 20th (not the 17th) century, and I also knew that it would probably be found in the LaFarge collection at Georgetown University.

Up until that point, the writing project had been planned to be relatively brief and focused solely on a former president of what was then called the St. Mary's Seminary Junior College. That subject was Adele France, born in 1880.

Therefore, I saw no need for chapters on colonialism, the slave trade, or Catholicism, for my immediate project in the year I went to Georgetown was simply to discover the origin and use of the mysterious word "pilgrim" and how it pertained to St. Mary's County.

It was only as I was packing my bags to leave Georgetown that it struck me: John LaFarge, S.J., was not only the man who had given special meaning to the 20th-century word "pilgrim" but who had also created–in 1924–the Cardinal Gibbons Institute for educating the almost 50% of blacks living in St. Mary's County.

John LaFarge, like Adele France, had also been born in February of 1880, and his educational resolve was equal to hers.

By 1926, however, LaFarge had been recalled to New York City to function in varying capacities as editor of *America*, a weekly publication of the Catholic Church, specifically of and by the Jesuits.

Once I realized that–at Georgetown–some 40 huge banker's boxes contained much of Father LaFarge's written output, a young curator, Scott Taylor, casually mentioned, "You've got a lot of Father LaFarge's still-unclassified material down there in St. Mary's County."

"No we don't," I answered.

"Yes, you do," he replied. "Hundreds of pages turned up in the empty convent at the parish church of St. Peter Claver. Everything had simply been thrown into one of the empty rooms of the former convent."

Returning to St. Mary's College of Maryland, I contacted Father Scott Wood, at that time in charge of two parishes: St. Cecilia, and St. Peter Claver. He, in turn, contacted Claudette Bennett, who took the initiative and marshalled hundreds of papers. And so, on Saturday mornings a tiny committee of women (including Claudette's mother, Shirley Dickerson)–and I–sorted through them. In 2018, this committee was still navigating those records which go into a strictly "parish" file, as well as those sent to Georgetown to be catalogued with both the John LaFarge and Horace McKenna holdings.[1]

Janet Butler Haugaard
June of 2018

---

[1] As of 2023, this Committee is still going strong–continuing to review and archive historical records.

Introduction:

Barely Four Days and Four Miles Apart

A. ARRIVALS OF ADELE FRANCE AND JOHN LAFARGE

It is 1911. On a September afternoon, Adele France, M.A., boards a steamboat in Baltimore for the long run down the Chesapeake Bay to St. Mary's City in Southern Maryland.

This will be M. Adele France's third year as a popular teacher of math and physics at St. Mary's Female Seminary ("seminary" is an old-fashioned word for school), which was established in 1840. (In 1926, under Adele's leadership, it would evolve into St. Mary's Female Seminary-Junior College. And in 1964, it would become St. Mary's College of Maryland.)

Adele–still a redhead–already knows that the steamer will not arrive at St. Mary's City until the dark hour of 3:00 in the morning when she will disembark at Brome's Landing, also known as Brome's Wharf. The steamboat will then continue on up to its destination in Washington, zigzagging its way along the Potomac River between the shores of Maryland and Virginia.

Brome's Landing is 16 miles south of Leonardtown and the parish of St. Aloysius where John LaFarge is just starting off as assistant pastor.

At 4:00 in the afternoon in that very same month of September 1911, John LaFarge, S.J., M.A., boards a steamboat in Washington, D.C. and, with a fellow Jesuit, starts the 12-hour, zigzagging voyage down the Potomac River to St. Mary's County. At that time, Jesuits posted to Southern Maryland were based in one of three centers. The first was St. Thomas' Manor and St. Ignatius Church in Charles County, and the other two were in St. Mary's County: one in Leonardtown, the other at St. Inigoes, just four miles from St. Mary's City. (See Chapter 8-D at fn 55 & fn 88.) After depositing the two young priests sometime after midnight at the Leonardtown wharf, the steamer continues on up the Chesapeake and is due to arrive in Baltimore 24 hours after leaving Washington.[1]

John LaFarge is just 31, born barely four days before Mary Adele France (February 13th and 17th, 1880).

---

[1] See photo of a steamboat docking at Brome's Wharf. See map of two partial steamboat-routes, meandering between two major cities and Southern Maryland (shown without intermediate and final ports of call). The Southern Maryland map and the regional map identify certain towns that may not be known to "furriners" (see Chapters 3-E and 7-A). A GIS map of Southern Maryland and surrounding areas (during the first part of the 20th century), including towns, schools, and churches may be found at https://tinyurl.com/Historical-Tapestry or at https://www.scribblemaps.com/maps/view/Overview-FINAL-locked/Overview-FINAL-locked

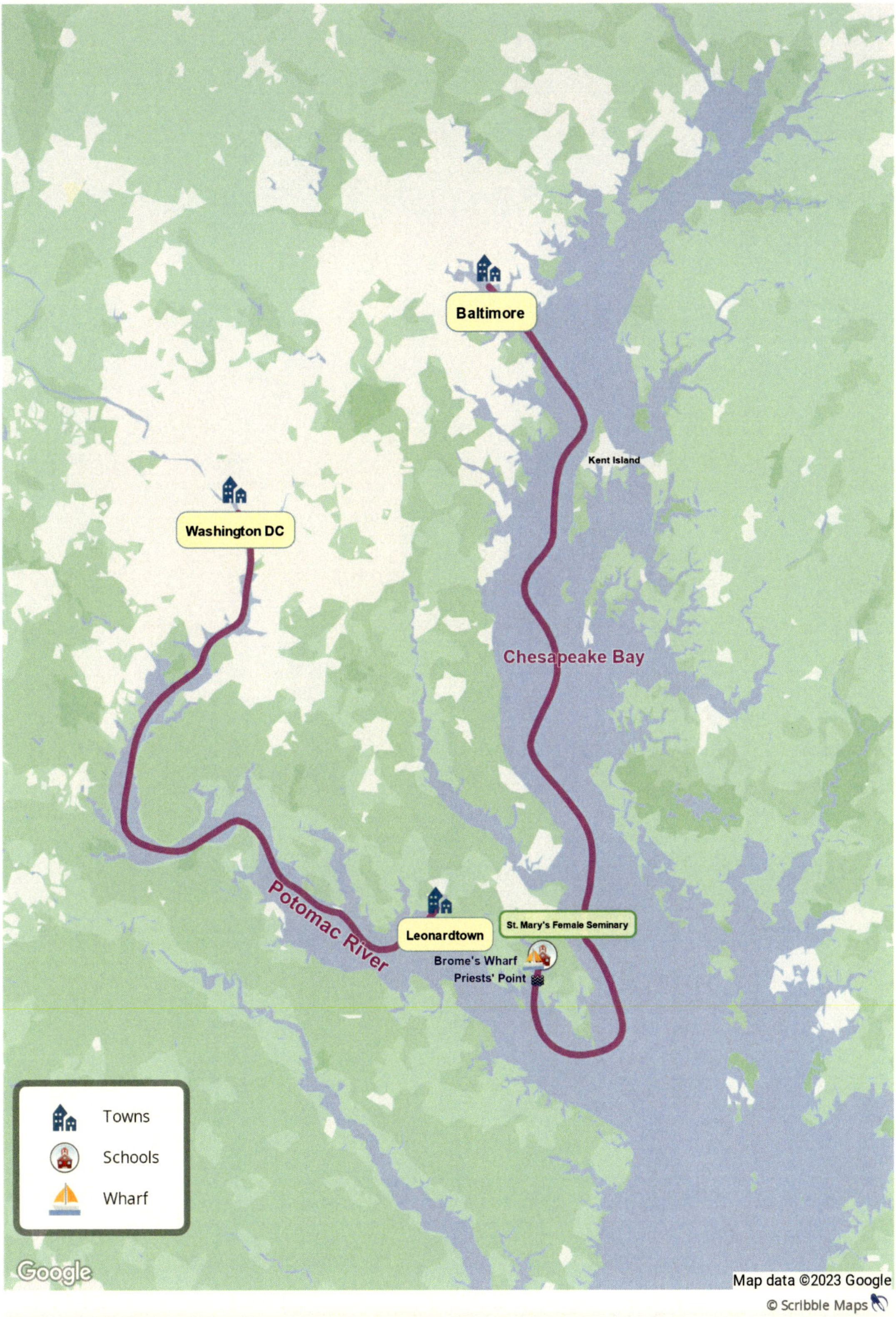
Baltimore
Kent Island
Washington DC
Chesapeake Bay
Potomac River
Leonardtown
St. Mary's Female Seminary
Brome's Wharf
Priests' Point
Towns
Schools
Wharf
Google
Map data ©2023 Google
© Scribble Maps

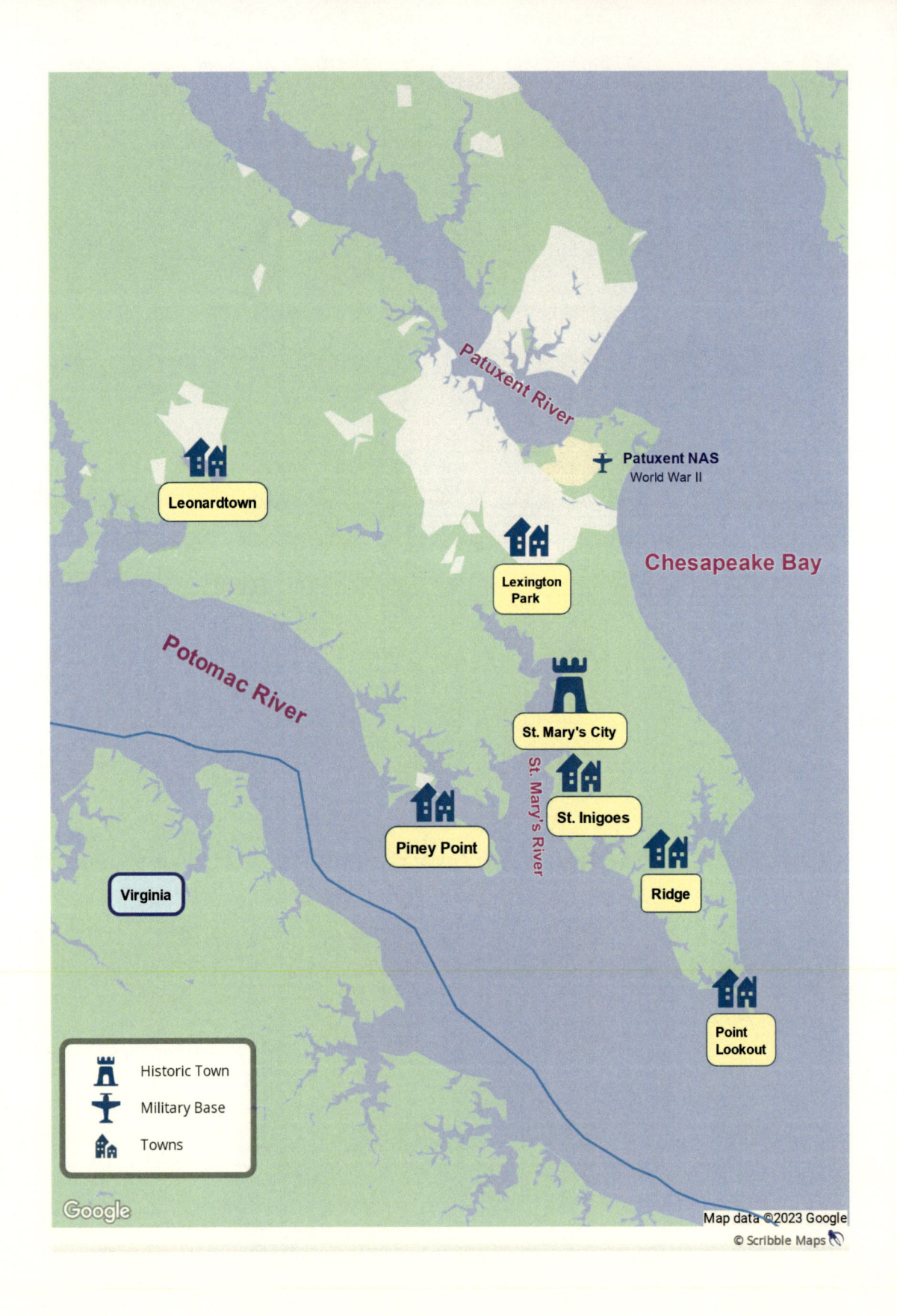

Map of St. Mary's County

Patuxent River

Patuxent NAS
World War II

Leonardtown

Lexington Park

Chesapeake Bay

Potomac River

St. Mary's City

St. Mary's River

Piney Point

St. Inigoes

Virginia

Ridge

Point Lookout

Legend
- Historic Town
- Military Base
- Towns

Map

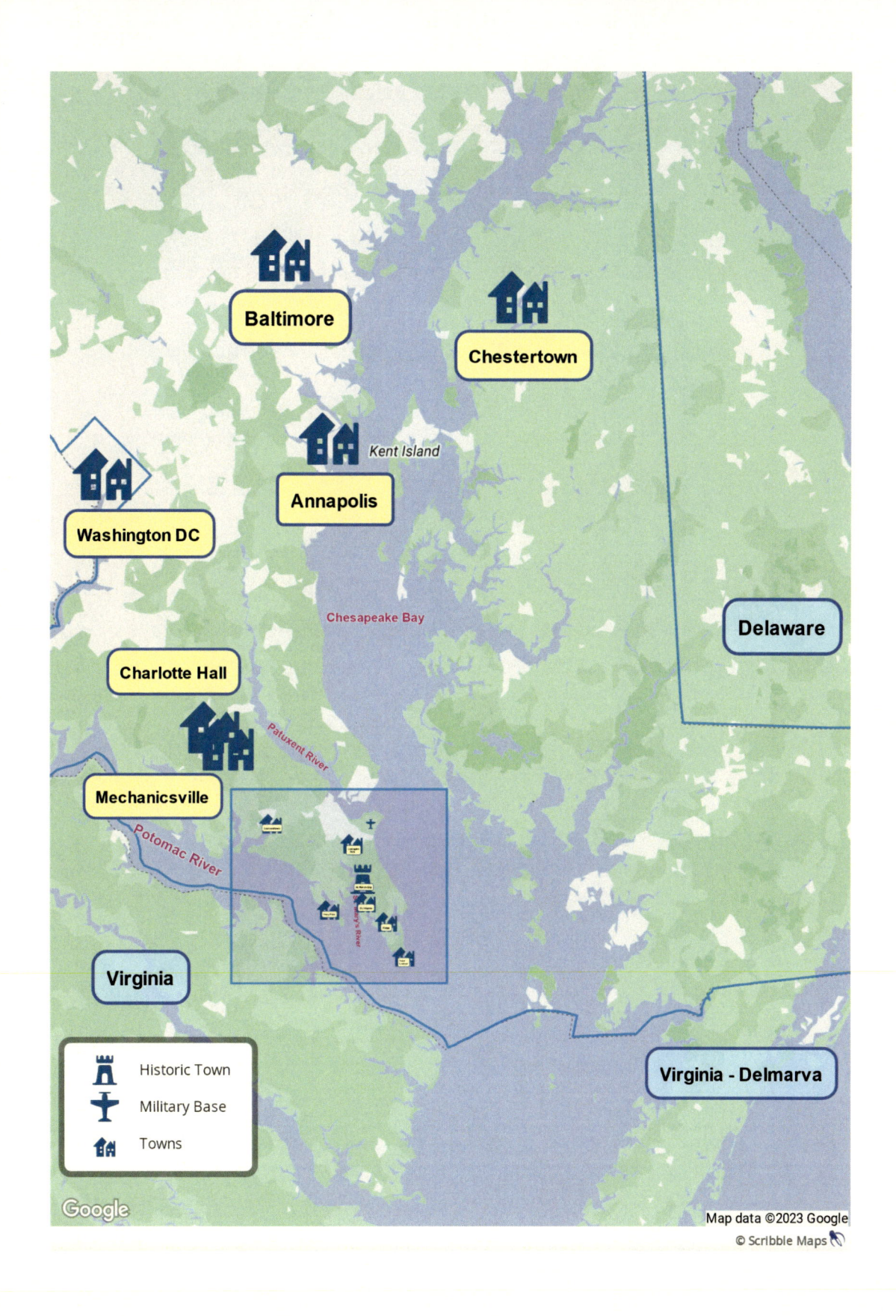

- Baltimore
- Chestertown
- Kent Island
- Annapolis
- Washington DC
- Chesapeake Bay
- Delaware
- Charlotte Hall
- Patuxent River
- Mechanicsville
- Potomac River
- Virginia
- Virginia - Delmarva

Legend:
- Historic Town
- Military Base
- Towns

11

B. STEAMBOATS TO ST. MARY'S COUNTY

No cars. No buses. No paved roads. But steamboats aplenty.

While hindsight may provoke second thoughts, it can also give rise to nostalgia. In his 70s, John LaFarge looked back on the steamboat travel of the early 1900s and later summed it up in his 1954 autobiography:

> Trips on the old Chesapeake [steamboat] line, though tedious if you were in a hurry–which you never could be in that part of the world–were agreeable enough. Accommodations were spacious and comfortable; you were well fed with a fried oyster or crab dinner according to the season, and tolerable weather made the time pass all the more pleasantly.[2]

Similarly, in her late 60s, Mary Blair **Lane** Patterson wrote an article for the *Mulberry Tree Papers* in which she looked back on her life as a high school student at the Female Seminary in the mid-1920s.[3] After graduating from college, she became a social worker, a profession she called upon when writing about the steamboats that once tied up three times a week at Brome's Landing in St. Mary's City:

> We were painfully white (as to skin color) and predominantly female. . . . The boats ran regularly between the school and Baltimore-Washington, and there were connecting lines to the Eastern Shore. The [dirt] roads were poor, and there was no railroad below Charlotte Hall. I remember one group returning by boat after Christmas vacation who were stuck in the St. Mary's River because of dense fog, within calling distance, for two days.

> One of the best shows I ever saw, which included tap dancing and beautiful banjo music was an impromptu one given by ["colored"] deckhands on one of those boats, as we students–who shouldn't have been there at all–sat on the bank, enraptured.[4]

---

2 LaFarge, John. *The Manner Is Ordinary*. New York: Harcourt, Brace and Company, 1954. 155. Print. Hereafter cited as LaFarge, *Manner*.

3 Women's maiden names may be given bold emphasis throughout this book.

4 Lane Patterson, Mary Blair. "A Very Different World." *Mulberry Tree Papers* (Fall 1976): 22. Print. The *Mulberry Tree Papers* has been published by St. Mary's College of Maryland since 1972.

Robert Pogue, a local historian of St. Mary's County, also remembered the steamboats from his boyhood, around 1916, and described from his perspective:

> Our steamboats were not like the Mississippi steamers we hear so much about in song and story. They were built for the rough waters of Chesapeake Bay, and were high-sided and seaworthy with the appearance of ocean-going ships. . . .
>
> Passenger accommodations aboard these steamers were all that could be desired, and the meals were noted far and wide for their excellence and cost only a dollar. . . . The passengers' quarters were usually spotless and always appeared to have been freshly painted. . . .
>
> One of the most enjoyable features of the trip was sitting on the deck and watching the loading and unloading of freight when the boat docked at wharves. The colored deck hands knew the people were watching them, so they always put on a good show. They strutted and danced and used all kinds of body motions as they pushed their two-wheeled hand trucks. Each one had his individual step, and they appeared to be a bunch of comedians rather than stevedores. Sometimes they had trouble getting the livestock aboard, and they really put on a show then, yelling and pushing and twisting the tails of the cattle to make them move along.[5]

And finally, in her beautifully written account of County life at Piney Point, Jean **Tolson** Waikart wrote this of the steamboat-landing near her home, only a couple of stops away from St. Mary's City:

> In those days ladies packed their clothing in steamer trunks, and these were the first freight to be brought down the gangplank by the spry stevedores, always a lively show as they plied the loaded dollies between the boat and warehouse, whistling and sometimes indulging in a few steps of a jig for the pleasure of the assembled spectators who invariably responded with delighted cheers.[6]

---

[5] Pogue, Robert E.T.. *Yesterday in Old St. Mary's County*. U.S.A.: Robert E.T. Pogue, 6th ed. 2008. 255, 257. Print.

[6] Waikart, Jean Tolson. *Piney Point Memories*. N.p.: Braintree Press, 2000. 21. Print.

These steamboats were, of course, racially segregated, as was the railroad that ran from Washington to Mechanicsville (with never-realized plans to extend it farther south to Point Lookout). When John LaFarge described travel by steamboat, he noted in his late-life autobiography (1954), that in the first two decades of the twentieth century "there was no other way to reach St. Mary's County except a tedious and complicated land trip by jerkwater railroad plus horse and buggy."[7] But, true to form, he enjoyed the comical aspects of this train travel, and much later in a letter to Charles Fenwick, at that time president of St. Mary's Historical Society, he noted the following:

> There is a story, somewhere I believe among good Fr. Zwinge's reminiscences ("Woodstock Letters") that Father Brennan, S.J. a former Union army chaplain, was summoned from the train by a sick call. The train waited politely until Fr. Brennan returned, and then continued its journey.[8]

John LaFarge concluded his 1962 letter to Charles Fenwick with the observation that "it was precisely the *absence of rail connections* that differentiated the Southern Maryland peninsula from the Eastern Shore."[9] This difference was–and still is–critical. Just as rural as St. Mary's County, the Eastern Shore nevertheless provided itself with more roads as well as a rail-line up to Baltimore.

The Eastern Shore could also boast Washington College (founded 1782), a liberal arts college in Chestertown that included both a library and pre-college preparatory courses taught by the College's own faculty. Chestertown may not have been John LaFarge's native Newport, but it was an environment that encouraged young Adele France–Chestertown born–to aim just as high as she wanted to go.

---

[7] LaFarge, *Manner* 156.

[8] LaFarge, John. Letter to Charles Fenwick, president of the Historical Society of St. Mary's County. 18 September 1962. Fenwick Collection. Historical Society of St. Mary's County, Leonardtown. Hereafter cited as LaFarge Letter to Fenwick.

[9] LaFarge Letter to Fenwick (emphasis added). The "Eastern Shore" refers to a long stretch of land on the east side of the Chesapeake Bay, comprised of nine Maryland counties nestled on the "Delmarva Peninsula" (a portmanteau of the three states that share this land: Delaware, Maryland, and Virginia).

And high was what she was after. Not that she was looking for fame; neither she nor John LaFarge ever showed any interest in self-promotion.

C. FORGING AHEAD IN, AND FOR, ST. MARY'S COUNTY

By 1911, each person was absorbed in the job at hand: taking up their work in St. Mary's County. John LaFarge would spend four years as assistant-priest in the Leonardtown parish, and Adele France was no more than a faculty member (math and physics) at the Female Seminary.

John LaFarge was not yet awake to the work he would undertake in providing education for blacks–Catholic and otherwise.

Adele France, on the other hand, seems to have been aware since her teens that she wanted to work for women: their education, their sense of self-worth, and their active participation in work that would go beyond the gender confines of the usual "ladies' auxiliary."

Beginning in September of 1909, Adele France taught mathematics and physics/science at the Female Seminary for a total of four years, then left for positions that would broaden her teaching and administrative experience. She returned to the Female Seminary briefly in academic year 1917-1918, but it was not until 1923 (while studying for her *second* Master's degree at Columbia University in New York) that she was unanimously elected by the Board of Trustees to head the Female Seminary. By this time she was 43.

Although John LaFarge was under the direction of the Society of Jesus ("S.J." or the "Jesuits"), in that same year of 1923-24, it was his idea to create the first high school (a non-technical school) for blacks in St. Mary's County. Like Adele France, he was also just 43 at the time.

LaFarge built his school about four miles south of the Female Seminary on the road to Point Lookout and named it the "Cardinal Gibbons Institute" (later changed to Cardinal Gibbons High School). See map of schools in Chapter 8.

In 1926, the Jesuits called LaFarge to New York City, but soon his school was well underway and would eventually come under the leadership of Horace McKenna, S.J., for whom LaFarge had become a friend and mentor.

The two priests saw eye-to-eye on virtually everything they discussed by mail. John LaFarge created a board that could, in theory, run the Cardinal Gibbons Institute from New York City. LaFarge had been called to New York City in order to become associate editor of the weekly *America* magazine, which is still in existence. By this time he was describing himself as "a priest journalist."[10]

From Manhattan, LaFarge would continue to serve on the Institute's board of trustees and make frequent trips back to the County. In a sense, no matter where his writing and travels took him, he never really left St. Mary's County, the lifelong focus of his missionary work.

But woe to the persons who think they can discuss the work of either John LaFarge or Adele France apart from the history of St. Mary's County. One way or another, social attitudes will have to be discussed in order to be understood–but understood they must be. These "attitudes" (understood as "facts") are part of the history of St. Mary's County and were well understood by both John LaFarge and Adele France.

Therefore, before delving further into their lives,[11] historical foundation and framework must first be laid out: Catholicism, education, women, slavery, and social context.[12] These themes are intricately interwoven in this historical tapestry.

---

[10] LaFarge, John. *The Book of Catholic Authors*. Grosse Pointe, Michigan: Walter Romig, Sixth Series, 1960. Print. <http://www.catholicauthors.com/lafarge.html>. See also LaFarge, *Manner* 247, 248.

[11] Mainly Chapters 4, 8, and 9, and also Chapters 1-B, 1-D, & 1-E, 3-E and 5-B, 5-E, & 5-F.

[12] Chapters 1, 2, 3, 5, 6, and 7. Chapter Seven portrays post-revolutionary ways as perceived by five Europeans who travelled to "America" in the 1830s and 1840s. Their perspectives illuminate how Adele France and John LaFarge found Southern Maryland at the dawn of the 20th Century.

Benjamin Robert Haydon. The Anti-Slavery Society Convention, 1840. © National Portrait Gallery, London.

Chapter 1

Blood, Sweat, and Brains

A. 1840 PAINTING: A PICTURE IN TIME

Look carefully at this painting of the World Anti-Slavery Convention, held in Freemasons' Hall, London, in June of 1840.[1] All of the delegates are male, and they will speak in favor of eliminating slavery throughout the entire world. Although Britain had already abolished slavery in her colonies in 1833, the men here have met–just seven years later–to act as a moral force in eliminating it throughout the entire world.

You may have noticed a few women scattered here and there throughout the audience. They are not part of the Convention, however, and are indulged solely as silent witnesses to their husbands' remarks. In fact, *because* they are women, they are not allowed to speak at all.

---

[1] The painting hangs in London's National Portrait Gallery and was painted in 1841 by Benjamin Robert Haydon. (In 1816, Haydon had formed the famous life mask of his friend, the poet John Keats.) The painting of 1841 was finished and displayed at yet a second meeting of the British and Foreign Anti-Slavery Convention, held in London from June 13 to June 29, 1843. See fn 23 below. That second meeting was recorded in *Niles' National Register* for that year, citing accounts from the

Look again at the painting, this time straining your eyes to see a group of people seated far at the back, horizontal to the viewer's eye. They are segregated behind a wooden screen. Most of these are women, forming a small delegation from the United States. They have been led three thousand miles across the Atlantic by Lucretia **Coffin** Mott, a Quaker minister and abolitionist leader who had believed that she would be speaking at the Convention. Elizabeth **Cady** Stanton, a fellow American, is travelling on her honeymoon, but today she meets Coffin Mott for the first time and makes common cause with her: both had mistakenly assumed they were to have speaking privileges at this World Anti-Slavery Convention.

As the first session opens at 11:00 on June 12th, Wendell Phillips of Massachusetts, aware of growing sentiment against the women, makes a motion to accept them, not only as fellow abolitionists, but also as active participants–that is, with rights to speak:

> When the call . . . reached America, we found that it was an invitation to the friends of the slave of every nation, and of every clime. Massachusetts has for several years acted on the principle of admitting women to an equal seat with men in the deliberative bodies of anti-slavery societies.[2]

European correspondent of the *National Intelligencer*, who cited accounts from both the *London Advertiser* and the *London Times*.

The matter of slavery in North America included the Republic of Texas, criticized by a New York delegate who opined it was "the republic of fugitives from justice and bankrupts in character." "[T]he discussions turned mainly on the subject [annexation] of Texas." Lord Aberdeen "promised that no legitimate means should be spared [by the British government] to effect the great object of abolishing slavery in the republic of Texas.'"

To his credit, the delegate who chaired that 1843 Convention, George Howard (Lord Viscount Morpeth) "disclaimed the right on the part of England, so recently relieved from the stain of slavery, to assume a tone of self-righteousness." "Anti-Slavery, or the World's Convention in London." *Niles' National Register*, Fifth Series, No. 23, Vol XIV, 5 Aug. 1843, p.363 (column 3). Print. Available online at the HathiTrust Digital Library: <https://babel.hathitrust.org/cgi/pt?id=nyp.33433081665857&view=1up&seq=379&skin=2021&q1=self-righteousness>.

Lord Morpeth emphasized during his speech on June 21, 1843: "whatever might be the character of our ulterior proceedings with respect to slavery, we could hardly yet consider ourselves qualified to use a tone of unmixed self-righteousness (hear, hear) or of unqualified reproach on the conduct of others...." "Lord Morpeth's Speech." *Niles' National Register*, Fifth Series, No. 23, Vol XIV, 5 Aug. 1843, p.364 (column 2). Print. Baltimore: Jeremiah Hughes. Available online at the HathiTrust Digital Library: <https://babel.hathitrust.org/cgi/pt?id=nyp.33433081665857&view=1up&seq=379&skin=2021&q1=Morpeth>.

Nonetheless, Texas would enter the Union as a slave state on December 29, 1845.

2 Committee of the British and Foreign Anti-Slavery Society. *Proceedings of the General Anti-Slavery Convention [1840]*. London: Johnston and Barrett Printers, 1841. 24. Print. Web. Last accessed

After considerable discussion, Wendell Phillips' motion to include the women is voted down by a significant majority. The Convention will continue for another ten days, and the women will continue to follow the proceedings intently, but silently, from behind the screen.

Elizabeth **Cady** Stanton will later state that it was at this 1840 Convention that she and Lucretia **Coffin** Mott first began to plan a convention in America that would focus on women's rights. The thinking and organizing for it would take another eight years, but the Seneca Falls Convention of 1848 in upstate New York marked the opening salvo in the Women's Movement. To put it more forcefully, the Women's Movement can be said to have had its origins in the rejection experienced by both Cady Stanton and Coffin Mott that June day in London when–because they were women–they were refused participation in the Anti-Slavery Convention.

The 1840 Anti-Slavery Convention offers a delicious irony in the uses of Biblical authority. That is, the men who liked to quote Saint Paul as the authority for not letting women speak were *the same men who had already flouted Saint Paul on the matter of slavery.*

On the one hand, we have St. Paul's anti-female "Let the woman learn in silence, with all subjection. I suffer not a woman to teach, nor to usurp authority over the man, but to be in silence" (I Timothy 2:11-12).

And on the other hand, we have St. Paul's pro-slavery admonition which the Convention was actively flouting: "Slaves, obey your masters" (Ephesians 6:5; 1 Peter 2:18; and Titus 2:9).

During this early pre-Convention debate, the Reverend Henry Grew of Philadelphia warned the women that their participation in the Convention would be "not only a violation of the customs of England, but of the ordinance of Almighty God." Centuries of Christian custom had given St. Paul's views on women a special force, and it was often felt that women who spoke in public were being "indelicate"–or, worse–"promiscuous." (The mere act of standing up in mixed company, in public, subjected a woman to a man's gaze–that is, to sexual assessment.)

---

20 Dec. 2021. <https://atlanticslaverydebate.stanford.edu/module1_library >. Hereafter cited as *1840 Anti-Slavery Convention*.

His motion defeated, an outraged Wendell Phillips observed that:

> this Convention tells us that it is not ready to meet the ridicule of the morning papers, and to stand up against the customs of England. In America we listen to no such arguments. If we had done so, we never would have been here as abolitionists. It is the custom there [the United States] not to admit coloured men into respectable society, and we have been told again and again, that we are outraging the decencies of humanity when we permit coloured men to sit by our side. . . . We think it right for women to sit by our side there, and we think it right for them to do the same here [England].[3]

Also voting against Phillips' proposal to include the women was Samuel Jackman Prescod, a journalist and "colored" abolitionist from the colony of Barbados who, according to the diary kept by Coffin Mott while in London, "thought it would lower the dignity of the Convention and bring ridicule on the whole thing if ladies were admitted."[4]

And what of William Lloyd Garrison, that abolitionist writer and close friend of Wendell Phillips, who co-founded the American Anti-Slavery Society in 1833? His ship had been delayed while crossing the Atlantic, and by the time he reached London, the debate on seating the women had already been concluded in the negative. His response was vintage Garrison: he gave up his seat at the 1840 Convention and, in a gesture of solidarity, went to sit behind the screen with the silenced women. Garrison had founded *The Liberator*, an anti-slavery weekly newspaper in 1831; he would write his last editorial for it in 1865, the year in which the Thirteenth Amendment to the U.S. Constitution formally abolished slavery.

Voting rights for (white) women would finally be assured in August of 1920 when three-quarters of the states ratified the Nineteenth Amendment to the U.S. Constitution. In the same United States, however, voting rights for blacks (men and women alike) would have to wait until the Voting Rights Act of August 1965, a full one hundred years after the end of slavery.

---

[3] *1840 Anti-Slavery Convention*, 36, 36.

[4] "Slavery And 'The Woman Question'. Lucretia Mott's Diary of Her Visit to Great Britain to Attend the World's Anti-Slavery Convention of 1840." Ed. Frederick B. Tolles, *Worcester Women's History Project.* Web. 02 Aug. 2013. <http://www.wwhp.org/Resources/Slavery/mottdiary1840.html>.

B. TWO OUTSIDERS IN ST. MARY'S COUNTY

Two of the ongoing problems revealed at that 1840 Convention in London found particular expression in Southern Maryland: (1) women; and (2) race.

Much later, around World War I, two well-educated outsiders came into St. Mary's County, Maryland. Both had been born in February of 1880. Although they may not have known each other initially, by the 1920s, they both took up positions which addressed these issues via transformational changes. They founded non-traditional schools, spearheading education for women and for blacks.

In the case of M. Adele France, the change was a junior college (1926) which she added on to St. Mary's Female Seminary, already a state-supported school for girls. This junior college was a "first" for Maryland. As a follower of John Dewey, Adele France believed in the radical notion that girls' education should be active rather than passive: "Learn to do by doing."

In the case of John LaFarge, the change (actually a revolution or radical transformation) was the establishment of the County's sole high school for black students, the Cardinal Gibbons Institute (1924). Writing in his late-life autobiography, Father LaFarge observed:

> As I continued in my work of catechizing and home visiting, I became more and more aware of three outstanding problems which lay concealed under the peaceable exterior of the St. Mary's County community. The first was the deplorable condition of the schooling; the second was the condition of the local Negroes; and the third was the rural life problem.[5]

For quite different reasons, each of those two schools closed in the mid-1960s, having outgrown their original purpose.

The Female Seminary-Junior College, Adele France's 1926 institution, formally evolved into a public, four-year, liberal arts college–St. Mary's College of Maryland. In 1964, the name was changed from St. Mary's Junior

---

[5] LaFarge, John. *The Manner Is Ordinary*. New York: Harcourt, Brace and Company, 1954. 177. Print. Hereafter cited as LaFarge, *Manner*.

College to St. Mary's College of Maryland; and in 1966, on paper only, it was elevated to senior college status.

In the case of John LaFarge, his 1924 Cardinal Gibbons Institute in Ridge closed in 1967, when integration of public schools finally became mandatory in St. Mary's County. This avant-garde school was torn down in 1972.

Neither France nor LaFarge lived to witness the closings of the schools where they had labored so energetically.

John LaFarge was posted away to New York in 1926 to become associate editor of the Jesuit weekly, *America*, although he continued to function from afar as treasurer (and *de facto* fund-raiser) on the board of trustees of the Cardinal Gibbons Institute.

In spirit, John LaFarge never quite left Southern Maryland and traveled back to the County often. Born into privilege and unacquainted with both rural life and blacks, he had been jarred awake by his missionary experiences. He learned from them and later made their lessons his life's work in New York, taking the lead for interracial justice long before it was expected–let alone encouraged–of the clergy. He died in November of 1963, just four months after occupying a reserved seat behind Martin Luther King Jr. as he delivered his "I Have a Dream" speech at the Lincoln Memorial.

Adele France, however, was able to stay with her innovative institution for twenty-five years, and she took it through the privations of both the Great Depression and World War II.

During her on-site leadership of a public institution that–by Maryland law–was not allowed to accept blacks,[6] Adele France expanded the school's

---

[6] After ratification of the Fourteenth Amendment to the U.S. Constitution in 1868–which was drafted to address issues of inequality following the American Civil War–many states, including Maryland, nevertheless implemented *de jure* segregation, i.e., segregation that was legally recognized in such states. And on a federal level, the U.S. Supreme Court later ruled that "separate but equal facilities" did not violate the Fourteenth Amendment. *H.A. Plessy v. J.H. Ferguson*, 163 U.S. 537 (1896). More than half a century later, after the landmark decision of *Brown v. Board of Education of Topeka*, 347 U.S. 483 (1954), "the State of Maryland did nothing more than merely lift the rule excluding African-American students from being admitted into and attending TWIs [traditionally white institutions]. Maryland officially ended *de jure* segregation in its public accommodations in response to the Civil Rights Act of 1964. . . . In Maryland, the *de jure* era of segregation in higher education extended through 1969, when the federal government put the State of Maryland on

original focus. Her addition of a junior college meant that its graduates could now enter four-year colleges and universities as upperclassmen, or in the case of girls who had *not* planned on a college education at all, to prepare for a "useful" life of work and citizenship. In this she was very much in step with educational theories about junior colleges then coming out of both Stanford and the University of Chicago.

In January of 1940, as St. Mary's Female Seminary approached the one-hundredth anniversary of its founding, Adele France asked the State Highway Commission to place one of Maryland's historic markers on the narrow state road leading up to the Female Seminary, formerly known as Brome's Landing Road (or Brome's Wharf Road).[7] In her letter to the Commission, she commented informally that the original school had been "a unique monument of flesh and blood and brains."

---

notice that it operated an illegally segregated dual system of higher education. In fact, in a 2005 Maryland Attorney General opinion, the State of Maryland admitted that 'there is no doubt that Maryland operated a *de jure* segregated public higher education system before 1969, when federal officials found the state in violation of Title VI and that some policies, such as program duplication at geographically proximate schools are traceable to the era.'" Pierre, John K. "History of De Jure Segregation in Public Higher Education in America and the State of Maryland Prior to 1954 and the Equalization Strategy." 8 *Fla. A&M U. L. Rev.* (2012). 109. Web. 29 April 2022. <http://commons.law.famu.edu/famulawreview/vol8/iss1/7>. See Chapter 8-D-3 at fn 76 & fn 84.

7 France, M. Adele. Letter to the Office of Director of Historical Markers. 13 February 1940. Office of the President. RG 2.1.1, Box 1 "Correspondence, 1935-1945" [folder title]. St. Mary's College of Maryland Archives. The historical-marker sign remains there to this day; see photo. The sign proclaims that the Female Seminary was established as a "living monument" to "mark the birthplace of the state and of religious liberty."

John LaFarge would have agreed with the sentiment: his Cardinal Gibbons Institute (a private school) had been forced to close from 1933 to 1938 during the worst years of the Great Depression, and it would take not only willpower but brains for him and his successor at the Institute, Horace McKenna, S.J., to get it up and running again as a (day) high school for Catholic (and non-Catholic) students who were black.

Both John LaFarge and Adele France were embarking on uphill battles: he for Catholic schooling, and, increasingly, for education for blacks; she for education for women, *all* women, not just those anxious to continue on after St. Mary's Female Seminary in the hope of finally earning a B.A. degree.

Born and educated in Chestertown, Maryland–with both a B.A. and a M.A. (from Washington College) and a M.A. in Education (from Columbia)–Adele France was forty-three by the time she was unanimously elected Principal of St. Mary's Female Seminary in 1923. She was well-acquainted with Southern ways, having worked as both teacher and school administrator in her native Chestertown as well as in Washington D.C. and Memphis, Tennessee (see Chapter 9-B at fn 27). She had already been "tested in the trenches." Her lifelong habit at the Female Seminary-Junior College was to state her educational philosophy in each year's school catalogue, and in 1924, she got quickly to the point:

> The time is past when we educated our daughters for ornaments only; woman has an economic place in the world, which it is her duty to fulfill to the best of her ability.[8]

Strong words, then and now.

In the end, Adele France was carried out of the Female Seminary-Junior College on a stretcher in December of 1947, following a serious heart attack. As a convalescent, she lived another six years and died in September of 1954, the same year in which LaFarge published his autobiography (*The*

---

[8] France, M. Adele. *Annual Prospectus for St. Mary's Female Seminary for 1924-1925*, at p.12. May 1924. Office of the Provost. Catalogs. RG 3.4.1, Box 1 "Prospectus 1924/1925." St. Mary's College of Maryland Archives.

Manner is Ordinary) that centered on his transformative fifteen years in Southern Maryland.

John LaFarge had been sent by the Jesuits to what, for him, was a daunting environment. A native of Newport, Rhode Island, he graduated from Harvard College in 1901, in the same class as Robert Frost. He had come to Leonardtown, Maryland in 1911, following brief chaplaincies in the State of New York (Poughkeepsie State Hospital for the Insane, as well as Welfare Island). In Leonardtown, his position was that of assistant pastor in the parish of St. Aloysius.

It wasn't until 1915 that John LaFarge was sent twenty-some miles farther south to the more rural environs of St. Inigoes and Ridge where he functioned as a missionary. It didn't take him long to identify the problem he faced

> Imposing as were the Jesuit accomplishments elsewhere, they were, practically speaking, of no aid at all in the problem that faced the Maryland missionary. As far as education was concerned, he worked in a vacuum. The work was to be accomplished not by striking a few heroic poses, not by the bull in the ecclesiastical china-shop. It could only be the fruit of patient and determined and planned effort.
>
> Let me add that there were always men and women among the white population of the parish who showed themselves singularly free of a narrow and prejudiced attitude toward the colored people. Some of these were educated persons who benefitted by outside contacts; but some were just honest Catholics who knew their faith and practiced it integrally in one of its most difficult and sensitive areas. Social disapproval is hard to endure under any circumstances, but it is well-nigh intolerable in an old Southern community of English descent. Only when one has lived in such a community does one realize what stings and barbs can sink into a sensitive soul from a few choice sneering remarks. . . . The bitter and prejudiced people are a minority, small, but noisy and aggressive. The trouble was and still is in such communities that this minority so easily takes the lead and sways a large number of people who are

fundamentally well disposed but simply unable to face any strong form of marked disapproval.[9]

Unlike John LaFarge, Adele France left no autobiography. In fact, as the school's sole administrator she had no time to do so, being supported throughout most of her 25-year presidency by only a housemother. Aside from that, she functioned at once as school president, dean of the faculty, dean of students, and manager of the budget. In the 1930s she did acquire a secretary, Frances "Eppie" Gill, who had graduated from the Seminary high school in 1928. But it was not until then that Adele France's office papers–both incoming and outgoing–were kept at all, and even those few were not in much semblance of order. Today, however, they are clearly catalogued in the Archives of St. Mary's College of Maryland, and invariably this correspondence–largely with parents and others–tells us what Adele France wanted them to know: her school philosophy, and how it was actually playing out in the daily life of the girls.

John LaFarge, by contrast, became a prolific writer of books and articles. Once posted to New York in 1926 to take up his new position as associate editor of *America*, the Jesuits' weekly magazine, he wrote daily and read omnivorously, including books and newspapers in several European languages. By this time he was forty-six, and though his missionary years "in the field" were behind him, for the rest of his life those experiences in Southern Maryland provided the material for his writing efforts in two fields: racism, and rural life.

Racism was by far his greater concern. The matter of slavery has always been connected with the Southern states, and, if asked, most people would center America's slave trade in Savannah, Charleston, or New Orleans. Not so. The answer to the issue of slave trade lies much farther north–actually, in Newport, Rhode Island–but LaFarge did not learn the rudiments of this so-called "triangular trade" until he was in his fifties.

As a boy growing up in Newport, young John LaFarge had been taught to admire an ancestor on his mother's side, Christopher Champlin. Not until his adult years did an older LaFarge learn of the dealings of this

---

[9] LaFarge, *Manner* 192-193, 193.

successful merchant in "the triangular trade." In 1950 LaFarge published *No Postponement: U.S. Moral Leadership and the Problem of Racial Minorities*. He opens Chapter 1 of this book with his recent discovery of Champlin's "business" dealings. His language is corrosive:

> One stormy night, over a hundred years ago, the ocean wind blew strong from out Point Judith and Brenton's Reef into the sheltered streets of Newport, Rhode Island. It shook the old gambrel-roofed houses on Washington Street, with their tunnels under the lawn whereby goods and men could be conveniently and privately transferred to skiffs serving the merchant vessels in the harbor. It rattled the panes in the new house on Mary Street. Mr. Christopher Champlin had recently purchased it from Mr. Cheseborough and found it quite befitting his station as a public-spirited citizen, an exemplary family man, and a vestryman of Trinity [Episcopal] Church. The rattling bothered Mr. Champlin. He rose in the chill of the night and stopped the window-sash with a wad of paper. Thereafter he slept in peace and forgot he had ever tinkered with the window. He would have been considerably surprised had he lived to learn many decades later, around 1896, that this bit of script was read with some interest when his quondam mansion was converted into a club-house for the YMCA.
>
> The memo noted, with New England precision, costs and expenditures incurred and profits gained by a workmanlike trading in and out of Newport Harbor in such matters as sugar, molasses, rum, and the living bodies of African slaves.
>
> In my Newport childhood I had accepted without question the tradition of ancestor Champlin's eminent respectability. The discovery of this trifling memo disturbed the legend. Still, it left the halo clinging to his head by the tenuous thread of ignorance. We charitably assume that this worthy man never suspected how these transactions flagrantly insulted the very elements of that religion which every Sunday he professed in the pleasant privacy of his high-partitioned pew in Spring Street's Trinity Church. Even less did he realize what an enormous mess in human suffering, degradation, injustice

and conflict he and his like were leaving for all the coming generations of Americans to clean up.[10]

C. THE TRIANGULAR TRADE

What Father LaFarge was learning about in mid-life was "the triangular trade": the method of transporting shackled blacks from the west coast of Africa (the "Guinea Coast") to Brazil, the Caribbean islands, and the British colonies up and down the east coast of what today is the United States. It was a prosperous trade, carried on by the empires of England, France, Holland, Denmark, Spain, and Portugal–as well as by the American colonies, both before and after the Revolutionary War of 1776.

This triangular trade generally had three legs.

The first leg was from an established home port–whether English or European–to Africa, where desirable goods were traded for slaves. And, as Father LaFarge was learning, American colonies had also played their own unique role in the Triangular Trade. The first leg had run from his birthplace, Newport, to the Guinea Coast, carrying its own special part of the Trade: rum. Barrels and barrels of rum, all of it made from the juice of sugar cane grown and harvested on Caribbean islands. At various ports along the Guinea Coast, Newport ships had traded this rum for cargos of slaves.

The second leg (commonly known as the "Middle Passage") was from points along the Guinea Coast to Brazil or the Caribbean islands. Here, the slaves were sold off to high bidders and used as forced laborers in the vast sugar plantations, sometimes milling the sugar into molasses.

The third leg of the trip was from the Caribbean back to England and Europe, leaving time to drop off slaves that had been requested for cotton, rice, and tobacco plantations in the southern section of what is now known as the United States. Thus, on the third leg of voyages bound for Rhode Island, slaves were dropped off in the South where they were forced to work in fields of cotton, rice, and tobacco, and often a large part of the cargo

---
10 LaFarge, John. *No Postponement: U.S. Moral Leadership and the Problem of Racial Minorities.* New York: Longmans, Green, 1950. 1-2. Print.

was either the sugar or molasses that had been milled in the Caribbean. In Rhode Island itself, distilleries dotted the coastal areas (especially in the southern part of the state, known colloquially to Rhode Islanders as "South County"). Here the sugar and molasses were turned into rum for the return voyage to Africa.

The American version of the Triangular Trade generally looked like this:

Newport → Africa ↓
Africa → Caribbean ↓
Caribbean → Newport

This trans-Atlantic route allowed for variations, largely made by the several trading companies, whether English, European, or American.

In his late-life autobiography, John LaFarge called attention to the link between Southern states and his own native Newport. Today we think of Newport in terms of the "Gilded Age" and the bastion of "cottages" built by Vanderbilts and Astors, but that end-of-the-1800s building boom was actually a rather late development. LaFarge writes that, well before the Civil War, the rush of summer residents to Newport was not from New York but rather from the South:

> . . . Newport in ante-bellum days was an annex of the deep South, a haunt of Southern summer residents. It was only after the [Civil] war that the summer literary colony was drawn from literary Boston, and eventually from plutocratic New York. In the 1850s and earlier, wealthy plantation owners from South Carolina, Georgia, and Louisiana built palatial homes at Newport and beautified the town by their generosity.[11]

Certainly this invasion by Southern plantation owners would have been accompanied by business negotiations while they summered in Newport's breezy weather. Arrangements would have been made with ship captains travelling to the Guinea Coast, and deals would have been struck with Rhode Island mill owners anxious to play a winning role in the overall slave trade.

---

11 LaFarge, *Manner* 19.

In her ground-breaking, thoroughly researched study, *The Manor: Three Centuries at a Slave Plantation on Long Island* (2013), Mac Griswold writes that: "The North American 'Guinea Trade' indeed centered on Newport, which sent eighteen to twenty-two ships to the west coast of Africa for slaves and gold every year between 1732 and 1764. Most of Newport's top-tier investors bought shares in these voyages." Griswold continues:

> The foundations of Newport's eighteenth-century fortunes rested on the coastal colonial and West Indian trades, which generated steady profits year after year. . . . Because Rhode Island's tiny acreage could not furnish provisions and goods in the huge quantities needed for the West Indies trade, Newport's citizens established complex networks with other continental colonies from whom they purchased what they would then sell south at higher rates.[12]

Northerners who were not sailors were also complicitous in the slave trade, finding provisioning work in small Rhode Island mills. Here, a textile known as "kersey" was designed specifically for slaves on Southern plantations. A blend of cotton-and-wool, kersey was known informally as "negro cloth," and mill owners in Rhode Island contracted for its sale with Southern planters. Another, more linen-like "negro cloth" was "osnaburg" or "oznabrig." To add to this Northern complicity, Rhode Islanders manufactured boots of un-tanned leather, known as "brogans." These were worn by slaves working in plantation fields of the South; brogans extended a little over the ankle and were often part of a Northerner's sale to Southern planters.[13]

---

[12] Griswold, Mac. *The Manor: Three Centuries at a Slave Plantation on Long Island*. New York: Farrar, Straus and Giroux, 2013. 248, 249. Print.

[13] Readers interested in the Triangular Trade are directed to Jay Coughtry's 1981 study, *The Notorious Triangle: Rhode Island and the African Slave Trade, 1700-1807*. Two more works are worth the reader's attention: Adam Hochschild's *Bury the Chains: Prophets and Rebels in the Fight to Free an Empire's Slaves*, 2005, and Charles Rappeleye's *Sons of Providence*, 2006. Also recommended is Christy Clark-Pujara's article on the manufacture of "negro cloth" in *Rhode Island History*, the peer-reviewed journal of the Rhode Island Historical Society. See Volume 71, No. 2, Summer/Fall 2013. See also Mac Griswold's *The Manor: Three Centuries at a Slave Plantation on Long Island*, 2013, p. 256; and Roy and Lesley Adkins, *Jane Austen's England*, 2013, p. 282.

D. THE RISE AND FALL OF BRITAIN'S SLAVE TRADE

What now of that 1840 Anti-Slavery Convention, so clearly captured in the Haydon painting? Aside from their exclusion of women delegates, the two hundred men present did indeed have much to be proud of: their efforts and those of their immediate predecessors, all of them abolitionists, had finally eliminated slavery throughout the British Empire, an enormous–and costly–undertaking. Its history bears repeating.

The slave-trade of Britain and her colonies had been abetted for around two centuries. The Royal Africa Trading Company, established in 1660, merged twelve years later with the Gambia Merchants Company. By the beginning of the next century, slavery was prospering with the full consent of the British monarchy.

As an example, in 1706, Queen Anne turned her attention to Maryland, putting out a proclamation in which she designated those towns that were to be responsible for regulating this lucrative African trade. St. Mary's City was one such terminus. A short section of her (unpunctuated) Proclamation of 15 June 1706 reads as follows:

> An act for advancement of trade and erecting Ports & Towns in the Province of Maryland.
>
> Be it enacted by the Queens most excellent Majesty by and with the advice and consent of her Majesty's Governour Council and Assembly of this Province and the Authority of the same that from and after the end of this present Session of Assembly the Towns Ports and Places herein after mentioned shall be the Ports and Places where all Ships and Vessells trading into this Province shall unlade and put on shoare all Negroes Wares goods merchandizes and Commodities whatsoever (That is to say)
>
> In *St. Maries County Saint Maries Town* Saint Clements Town and a Town on Beckwiths Island in Petuxent river. . . .[14]

By the mid-1740s, Englishmen were lustily singing "Rule, Britannia! Britannia rule the waves! Britons never never never will be slaves!" Not

---
14 Maryland Historic Trust, et al, Chestertown, Maryland, *An Inventory of Historic Sites*, 1981, p. vi (emphases added).

33

mentioned was the fact that they *already* owned slaves in the far reaches of empire, such as the West Indies and the American colonies.

But by the beginning of the 1800s, a movement in England to abolish slavery was gaining strength, and Parliament passed the Slave Trade Act of **1807**. While this Act barred merely the *trade* of slaves–the buying and selling of men, women, and children–it did not banish slavery itself, which had already been firmly established throughout the Empire and its former American colonies.[15]

In England, abolitionists decided that stronger measures were called for, and in 1823, they formed an Anti-Slavery Society to abolish not only the slave trade but all entrenched slavery as well. (Its formal name was "Society for the Mitigation and Gradual Abolition of Slavery Throughout the British Dominions"). The strength of this Anti-Slavery Society was such that by 1833, it had enough clout to force through Parliament the Anti-Slavery Act of **1833**, taking effect in Great Britain and her colonies in 1834. A responsible and carefully documented online article summarizes how many "business assets" the British lost as a result of this 1833 Slavery Abolition Act.

> The Act also included the right of compensation for [English] slave-owners who would be losing their property. The amount of money to be spent on the compensation claims was set at "the sum of Twenty Millions Pounds Sterling." Under the terms of the Act, the British government raised £20 million to pay out in compensation for the loss of slaves as *business assets* to the registered owners of the freed slaves. The names listed in the returns for slave compensation show that ownership was spread over many hundreds of British families, many of them of high social standing. For example, Henry Philpotts (then the *Anglican Bishop of Exeter*), *in a partnership with three business colleagues, received £12,700 for 665 slaves in the West Indies*. The majority of men and women who were awarded compensation under the 1833 Abolition Act are listed in a Parliamentary Return, entitled Slavery Abolition Act, which is an account of all moneys awarded by the Commissioners of

---

[15] As to the United States, the abolishment of slavery would not be proclaimed until 1863 when President Lincoln issued the Emancipation Proclamation in the midst of the Civil War. Although the American Civil War ended in 1865 after four years of bloodshed, as of this writing, Confederate flags still continue to be used as a rallying cry.

Slave Compensation in the Parliamentary Papers 1837-8, Vol. 48. Slavery Abolition Act 1833.[16]

With the bit now between its teeth, it is small wonder that a second anti-slavery group ("The British and Foreign Anti-Slavery Society") was meeting in London in **1840** in an attempt to banish slavery throughout the entire world. It is perhaps less of a wonder that its members should be willing to sit, individually, for Haydon's painting which today hangs in the National Portrait Gallery in London. (See fn 23 below.)

The focus of the 1840 painting is white-haired Thomas Clarkson, much admired in abolitionist circles for his steady, unrelenting condemnation of slavery. The artist, Benjamin Robert Haydon, described his own painting thus:

> [A] liberated slave, now a delegate, is looking up to Clarkson with deep interest, and the hand of a friend is resting with affection on his arm, in fellowship and protection; this is the point of interest in the picture, and illustrative of the object in painting it–the African sitting by the intellectual European, in equality and intelligence, whilst the patriarch of the cause [Clarkson] points to heaven as to whom he must be grateful.[17]

But what was the thinking–not of the abolitionists–but of the average Englishman? For an answer we must go to novels written during the nineteenth century. So-called "historical" novels (written in the present but focusing on the past) are apt to be misleading since we can never fully understand what an earlier historical period actually felt like. But men and women writing about *their own* contemporary life often betray, without realizing it, the customs of the day: its social assumptions, its political nuances, its morals.

---

16 Citation formerly at <http://jamaicanhistorymonth2007.moonfruit.com/>; this platform has been closed since July 2021. However, citation currently available at: "Slavery Abolition Act 1833 - Main Points of The Act." (Emphases added.) <https://www.primidi.com/slavery_abolition_act_1833/main_points_of_the_act>. Web. 16 Dec. 2021.

17 "Description of Haydon's Picture of the Great Meeting of Delegates Held at the Freemasons' Tavern, June 1840, for the Abolition of Slavery and the Slave Trade Throughout the World." 10. National Portrait Gallery, London. Web. July 2012. <https://www.npg.org.uk/collections/search/portraitExtended/mw00028/The-Anti-Slavery-Society-Convention-1840>.

In the case of nineteenth-century England, there appears to have been a kind of double-mindedness with regard to slavery, and this appears in the novels written at the time. On the one hand, we have a socially sophisticated Jane Austen. And on the other, a rurally confined Charlotte Brontë.

Jane Austen (1775-1817) was one of Thomas Clarkson's earliest admirers, and if her most recent biographer, Paula Byrne, is correct, then Jane Austen's upbringing led her to Clarkson's abolitionist point of view. Byrne argues that Jane Austen's *Mansfield Park* (1814) was so named for Lord Mansfield, England's Chief Justice, who had ruled in 1772 that a black slave who escaped to England need *not* be returned to his master in the colony of Jamaica. Slave-holders in the American South were appalled not only by this decision but also by England's social acceptance of black people. Byrne goes on to quote from the diaries and letters of Thomas Hutchinson, colonial governor of Massachusetts during the Revolutionary War. In 1779 he visited in London and–shocked–wrote the following:

> A Black came in after dinner and sat with the ladies and after coffee, walked with the company in the gardens, one of the young ladies having her arm within the other. Lord M [Mansfield] calls her Dido, which I suppose is all the name she has.[18]

Historians Roy and Lesley Adkins also often quote from diaries and letters of visitors to England. In particular, they like to quote from an American abolitionist and professor of chemistry at Yale University, Benjamin Silliman (1779-1864). "Although black people formed a minority of England's population," write the Adkins historians, "they were present at all levels of society, mostly in urban areas." They then go on to quote from an 1805 letter from Silliman to a friend back in the United States:

> A black footman is considered as a great acquisition, and consequently negro servants are sought for and caressed. An ill dressed or starving negro is never seen in England, and in some instances even alliances are formed between them and white girls of the lower orders of society. . . . As there are no slaves in England, perhaps the English have not learned to regard negroes as a degraded class of men, as we do in

---

[18] Byrne, Paula, *The Real Jane Austen: A Life in Small Things*. New York: Harper Collins, 2013. 214. Print.

the United States, where we have never seen them in any other condition.[19]

Yet the double-mindedness concerning slavery (and its sexual by-product, mixing of the "races") did indeed exist in England. Our second novelist to be considered is Charlotte Brontë, best known for *Jane Eyre*, published in 1847. Both Jane Austen and Charlotte Brontë were daughters of Anglican parsons, meaning that they had access to their fathers' personal libraries (largely scholarly) and read omnivorously throughout their girlhoods. But there the resemblance ends.

Jane Austen lived, with her family, in several different locations in the south of England, all of which gave her relatively easy access to Bath and the liveliness of a London that she so much enjoyed. Moreover, two of her brothers, Charles and Frank, were in the Royal Navy, and once the Slave Trade Act of 1807 passed in Parliament, both brothers served on ships actively involved in seizing slave vessels belonging to Great Britain.

In contrast, Charlotte Brontë lived in remote–and rural–Yorkshire, on the moors of the far north. With her sisters, Emily and Anne, she wrote Romantic fantasies while they were all still children. It is possible to argue that later, as an adult, she went right on writing them. In *Jane Eyre*, the heroine's forthcoming marriage to Mr. Rochester of Thornfield Hall is doomed when the parson is informed that Mr. Rochester is already married. The worst that Brontë can say of Jane Eyre's fictional rival, Bertha Mason, is that she is not only a born-and-bred West Indian mulatto (that is, "colored"), but that the very white Mr. Rochester had been lured into marrying her. Bertha Mason is also "a maniac."

The novel does conclude with a "happy ending," but at a cost not entirely realized, even by Brontë herself. In unrelated incidents, the "lunatic" Bertha Mason leaps to her death from a Gothic parapet atop Thornfield Hall, and Jane eventually inherits a small fortune from her "Uncle John." However, neither Jane Eyre nor her creator (Charlotte Brontë) pause to question the source of this inheritance and the happy ending that it provides for the novel. The "happy ending" inheritance has come from a once impecunious

---
19 Adkins, Roy and Lesley. *Jane Austen's England*. New York: Penguin Group, 2013. 199. Print.

uncle, John Eyre, who later made his fortune on the island of Madeira, a Portuguese colony. Madeira was made wealthy not only by its production of sugar but by the slaves who–in order to cut the cane down–had toiled in a permanently stooped-over position.[20]

In contrast to Jane Austen who lived a sophisticated life amongst the realities of her day, which included discussions of slavery, Charlotte Brontë lived a rural life and spent much of it struggling with loneliness, physical isolation, and a love affair that existed only in her mind.

If the cost of ending slavery in the British Empire was high in terms of money (witness the "business assets" of the Bishop of Exeter), it was far higher in America where eventually it would be measured in blood. States in the American South believed in the right to run their own affairs, and since their economies rested predominantly on the labor of slaves, they concluded that secession from the rest of the non-slave-owning republic presented itself as their only option. The result was that more American men died in the ensuing Civil War than in World Wars I and II combined.[21]

It is important to recognize, however, that for all her anti-slavery and abolitionist rhetoric, Britain (unlike the United States) never had to deal with the reality of a vast underclass made up largely of uneducated slaves, whether shackled or "freed." Black-skinned in a white world, purportedly uneducable, and frightened or terrorized into subservience, the large number of blacks was nonetheless increasingly perceived as a threat to whites in the new United States.

It was to the education of this huge American underclass that Father LaFarge dedicated his life. Following his death in 1963, two Jesuits, associate editors at *America*, wrote an appreciation of the man whom they referred to as "this gently doggèd priest." Doggèd he certainly was, wrestling with

---

20 Brontë, Charlotte. In her 1847 novel, *Jane Eyre*, Jane's uncle, John Eyre, is referenced in chapters 10, 21, 24, 30, 33, and 37. For a modern response to Jane Eyre, see *Wide Sargasso Sea* by Jean Rhys (pronounced "Reece"). This 1966 novel defends Mr. Rochester's first wife, the mulatta born in and raised in the Caribbean.

21 See the Wikipedia article, "United States military casualties of war." <https://en.wikipedia.org/wiki/United_States_military_casualties_of_war>.

issues both Catholic and racial, long before either Vatican II or the 1954 Supreme Court decision outlawing racial segregation in public schools.[22]

Although it is unlikely that either John LaFarge or Adele France ever saw Haydon's painting of the 1840 Anti-Slavery Convention, it is almost certain that Adele France–somewhere in her teen years–absorbed the teachings of Lucretia **Coffin** Mott and Elizabeth **Cady** Stanton, widely reported at that time in the press. Both Coffin Mott and Cady Stanton–because they were women–had been refused speaking rights at that Abolitionist Convention, and as a result they now turned their attention to the demands for women's rights, convening the Seneca Falls Convention of 1848. It should not come as a surprise that although Haydon "had intended to give Mott a prominent place in the painting, . . . during a sitting on June 29, 1840, to capture her likeness, he took a dislike to her views and decided to not use her portrait prominently."[23]

From the moment that Adele France entered Washington College as a freshman in the Fall of 1896, she insisted–tactfully–that women had as much right to be educated as men and just as much right to take part in the extracurricular affairs which up until then had been strictly a male preserve.

When Adele finally took over St. Mary's Female Seminary in 1923, she spelled the matter out in annual catalogues, declaring that it was time not only for women to be educated, but for them to take their "economic place in the world."

E. WHAT THE 1840 PAINTING DOES NOT REVEAL

Were there any Catholics among the delegates at that 1840 Convention in London?

Possibly, but most likely not. Only eleven years before, in 1829, Great Britain had finally lifted the penalties for being Catholic in a country (and her

---

[22] Keane, James T. and Jim McDermott, "The Manner is Extraordinary," in *America*, October 27, 2008. (The Second Vatican Council met beginning in 1962 and concluded in 1965.)

[23] See Wikipedia article titled "Lucretia Mott" at <https://en.wikipedia.org/wiki/Lucretia_Mott>. Web. 25 May 2023. A licensed image of the 1840 Painting is printed in this chapter. The website for the National Portrait Gallery in London also provides identification of many of the persons depicted (just hover a digital pen or mouse over the faces). You can also access that link here: https://tinyurl.com/1840-Painting

colonies) that still feared religious and political takeover by a foreign pope. The Roman Catholic Relief Acts of 1791 and 1829 finally allowed England's Catholics to have their own churches and schools and to enter the legal profession–all of which had been denied them following the Popery Act of 1698, at the height of the Protestant Reformation in England. (See Chapter 2-D at chronological table for 1698, 1778, 1791, and 1829.) Nonetheless, a strong anti-Catholic prejudice still prevailed in both Great Britain and her former American colonies.

As discussed, two of the ongoing problems revealed at that 1840 Convention in London were: (1) women; and (2) race.

Yet, focus should also be cast on a third issue that once overwhelmed Maryland, particularly Southern Maryland: (3) the legalization of anti-Catholicism in the 1700s, during the colonial period. Bad enough that the new United States was being forced–mid-nineteenth century–to cope with the problems of both race and gender: Southern Maryland also had to deal with the sensitivities of a people too long scorned for their Catholicism.

In 1634, King Charles I had granted to Cecil Calvert (the second Lord Baltimore) land for a colony that was to be made up of a relatively small number of Catholic gentry as well as an even larger number of Protestant laborers. Cecil (who was never able to leave England to visit his colony) commissioned his younger brother, Leonard Calvert, to serve as leader and governor of the colony that was to be founded on religious tolerance.

Difficulties–both religious and political–erupted only a few decades later however, with the result that England imposed a virulent anti-Catholicism on the American colonies during the 1700s. Up until the Revolutionary War of 1776, Protestants lost no time in enacting legislation that deprived Maryland Catholics not only of their religion but also of their civil liberties. By the 1800s, the American colonies had finally fought themselves free of Great Britain, but bitter memories of religious persecution affected St. Mary's County and, in a sense, as we shall see, led to the creation of St. Mary's Female Seminary in 1840. The original Female Seminary was designed as a school that would try, once again, to bring to fruition Lord Baltimore's hope for religious tolerance.

Neither the work of John LaFarge nor that of Adele France can be understood apart from the specifics of time and place, and for that reason Chapter 2 ("Catholics: Exiled in Place") gives a quick overview of what it meant to be Catholic in Maryland before the Revolutionary War.

Chapter 2

Catholics: Exiled in Place

A. FURTHER BACK IN TIME AND PLACE

A good friend of mine was astonished recently to hear that persecution of Catholics had once taken place not only in England but also in the American colonies. "I thought persecution was the reason that Catholics left England and that when they came to Maryland they found religious freedom," she said.

Not quite. Catholics in the 1700s and since have tended to put the blame for their miseries on Maryland's *local* agents (the governor, the legislature, or the sheriff who locked the door of the Catholic chapel at St. Mary's City). However, John LaFarge, with his strong academic background, pinpointed the real source of the problem: little-to-zero knowledge of English history.

> They [Southern Marylanders] had no sense of any past European background. In fact, the absence of historical sense among the Maryland Catholics, except with a few educated persons, was disturbing. St. Mary's County was just "home,"

where they grew up, where their ancestors had lived, and their mental perspective reached no further back.[1]

"Further back" would have had to involve knowledge of England's century-and-a-half-long convulsion known as the English (sometimes "Protestant") Reformation. In the American colonies, the English Reformation, which began in 1534, had a lasting impact–including the period when, a century later, English Catholics first arrived on Maryland shores in 1634. As Father LaFarge assessed the situation, his parishioners were (1) generally "educationally handicapped" and (2) didn't realize the toxic source of their miseries: England herself.[2]

Unfortunately, it is always easier to blame a *local* authority than to understand the source of the problem, a source which may lie not in the Americas but in England, on the opposite shores of the Atlantic, over three thousand miles away. Out of sight, out of mind.

B. HEADQUARTERS: LONDON

School children may have heard of Henry VIII who defied Pope Clement VII in order to divorce Catherine of Aragon (his widowed sister-in-law) so that he could marry Anne Boleyn. The pope, of course, refused permission, and Henry's solution to this impasse was to declare *himself* supreme head of the Catholic Church in England via the 1534 Act of Supremacy. The result was the freshly named Church of England ("Anglican"), and to this day, the official state religion in England is Anglican, headed not by the pope but by the reigning monarch. This means that, as of this writing,[3] Queen Elizabeth

---

1 LaFarge, John. *The Manner Is Ordinary*. New York: Harcourt, Brace and Company, 1954. 157. Print. Hereafter cited as LaFarge, *Manner*.

2 LaFarge, *Manner* 162, 157.

3 See Foreward, fn 1 (most of this book had been drafted by 2019).

II is Supreme Governor of the Anglican Church, while the Archbishop of Canterbury is the church's spokesman and senior bishop.[4]

It may help to think of the England of that era as something familiar to us today: a transnational corporation, such as Mercedes-Benz (headquartered in Germany), McDonald's (headquartered in the United States), or BP (British Petroleum, headquartered in London). Such corporations have logos, policies about wording in advertisements, and most important, CEOs to make sure that branch offices, scattered all over the world, do not fall out of line.

For all the former English colonies–including Maryland–"corporate headquarters" was the monarchy headquartered far across the Atlantic in London, and orders issuing from there had to be obeyed by the little colonial "branch offices." (While American colonists rebelled against Great Britain in the Revolutionary War of 1776, most of England's African, Caribbean, Asian, and Near Eastern colonies were not freed until the mid-20th century.)

As the kings and queens of England succeeded each other during the era of the English Reformation, so too did their religious loyalties. With each new monarch, there was the possibility of a Catholic or Protestant reversal in the official state religion, and monarchs were closely watched. With each such reversal came a royal mandate to either force out–or wipe out–those citizens of the opposing religion. (One wit has referred to these Catholics and Protestants in England as "equal opportunity victims."[5])

During these reigns that were both political and religious, Englishmen with dissenting religious views fled to the eastern seaboard of North America

---

[4] Francis Walsh, Catholic missionary and local historian, presents an interesting point of view. In his 1997 book about the St. Inigoes Mission, he reminds us that Henry VIII rejected Luther and penned a defense of the seven sacraments that won him the title "Defender of the Faith." Walsh comments further: "Pope Pius V's misguided policy of using political means to fight the Reformation only served to fan the flames of nationalism and undermined the position of the Catholic Church in England. By attempting to release English Catholics from their obligations to render allegiance to the monarchy, Pius succeeded in planting deep within the English psyche the notion that to have allegiance to the Pope was to be a traitor to England." Walsh, Francis Michael. *Resurrection: the Story of the Saint Inigoes Mission: 1634-1994*. 1997. Part I, p.12/191. Web. Available online at The Wayback Machine. <https://web.archive.org/web/20160304205306/http://www.reocities.com/RainForest/vines/6480/inigoes1.html>.

[5] Simon, John. "The World of Christopher Marlowe': A Brawler and a Spy." *New York Times Book Review*, Jan. 2, 2005. <https://www.nytimes.com/2005/01/02/books/review/the-world-of-christopher-marlowe-a-brawler-and-a-spy.html>.

where they could practice their beliefs in the wildernesses of the "New World": the Separatist group ("Pilgrims") emigrated to Plymouth in 1620; Puritans (who called themselves "the godly") settled in Massachusetts Bay in the 1630s; Catholics aboard the *Ark* and the *Dove* landed in the Province of Maryland in 1634; and Quakers settled the Province of Pennsylvania in 1682.

The Society of Jesus, founded by Ignatius Loyola ("Iñigo" as he had been known in his Basque childhood) had been outlawed in England in 1584 during the early era of the English Reformation. During two centuries of this accelerating Reformation and beyond, Jesuits were either in hiding or had migrated to the more welcoming environs of European countries. The Reformation's finale may be traced as around 1689, when the Toleration Act of 1688 gave Protestant dissenters freedom of worship–yet it would not be until a century later that Parliament finally passed the first Roman Catholic Relief Act in 1791.

Getting back to headquarters: this London-based "corporation" (that is, the monarchy) was far from stable. From about 1534 to 1702, England and her Parliament were rocked by religious and political dissent. Ever present during these back-and-forth shifts and sways were two queries.

- → Which major party–Catholic or Anglican–would become the state religion of England and all her colonies?

- → Who (Catholic, Anglican, or even the radically Protestant Puritans) would rule the transnational corporation and also make sure that its far-flung branch offices toed the party line?

Ever since the Maryland colony was founded in 1634, each English ship plying the Atlantic from the Eastern seaboard down to the Caribbean brought news of the latest in palace gossip, political intrigue, and anticipated reversals in government.

Before the English Reformation, sparked in 1534, had finally fizzled out by 1689, citizens of England and her colonies had endured the following reigns that lurched from Anglican or Protestant to Catholic and back again:

Henry VIII	1509 – 1547: Catholic, then Anglican
Edward VI	1547 – 1553: Anglican
Mary I	1553 – 1558: Catholic
Elizabeth I	1558 – 1603: Anglican
James I	1603 – 1625: born Catholic, raised Protestant, Anglican leanings
Charles I	1625 – 1649: Anglican (beheaded)
1st English Civil War (1642 – 1646)	
2nd English Civil War (1648 – 1649)	
3rd English Civil War (1649 – 1651)	
Interregnum	1649 – 1660: Rule by (a Presbyterian/Protestant) Parliament (1st Commonwealth, three Protectorates/Cromwell, 2nd Commonwealth)
Charles II	1660 – 1685: Anglican, then Catholic on his deathbed
James II	1685 – 1688: Anglican, then Catholic (conversion in 1668 not disclosed until 1676) (deposed)
Wm & Mary	1689 – 1702: Protestant (William) and Anglican-raised (Mary)

Thus, after a century and a half of infighting kindled by the Reformation–including *three* English civil wars–Protestantism "won" in the so-called Glorious Revolution when James II, a Catholic, was deposed from power. In the Glorious (that is, "bloodless") Revolution that followed, William of Orange (a Protestant, from the Netherlands) and Mary II (Anglican daughter of James II, a Catholic convert) were crowned together in 1689. Their coronation was performed by the Bishop of London because the Archbishop of Canterbury refused to do so.

From then on, until America's Revolutionary War of 1776, to be a practicing Catholic in the "branch office" of the Maryland colony was not only to be in danger but, more ominously, to be suspected of treason as well. For it was the London "headquarters"–not Baltimore, Philadelphia, New York, or even Annapolis–that was calling the shots.

Always, it was London.

C. BRANCH OFFICES: MARYLAND IN PARTICULAR

The colonial problem in America was that, increasingly, colonists saw themselves as "American," while in actual fact they were still English citizens whose presumed loyalty was to the English monarchy, "the Crown." Colonists inhabited wilderness outposts of the expanding English empire, the center of that empire (London) being over three-thousand miles and a minimum of six weeks away on the opposite side of the Atlantic.

While the English monarchy see-sawed back and forth between Catholicism and Anglicanism or Protestantism, the colonies were expected to snap-to and fall in line behind whichever religious denomination was then in power.

In 1632, Charles I as "King of England, Scotland, France and Ireland" granted a Charter for the Province of Maryland to Cecil Calvert (the second Lord Baltimore).[6]

The Maryland colony was a mix of Catholic gentry, yet outnumbered by Protestants who generally had signed on as indentured servants. The colony had been founded in 1634 during the reign of Charles I. During this period, Cecil Calvert never travelled to his Maryland colony, but he appointed his younger brother, Leonard, to govern the colonial experiment. It was meant to be a Catholic haven for about seventeen *younger* sons of the aristocracy (who, by law, could not inherit either property or title in England; see Chapter 7-E-1) as well as an economic opportunity for an even larger group of Protestant hopefuls.

---

[6] "The Charter of Mary Land." 20 June 1632. *A Relation of the Successefull beginnings of the Lord Baltemore's Plantation in Mary-land*. Maryland State Archives SPECIAL COLLECTIONS (Huntingfield Corporation Collection). London: 1635. MSA SC 1399-526. Web. 04 May 2022. <https://msa.maryland.gov/msa/educ/exhibits/founding/html/charter.html>

Throughout this chapter, there are numerous references to records provided by the Maryland State Archives or the MSA, and each should be read as including: "Courtesy of the Maryland State Archives."

The reigning Anglican monarch at that time, Charles I, was careful to impress the fragility of a Catholic haven upon Cecil Calvert (Lord Baltimore); and Cecil, in turn, made certain that his younger brother, Leonard, understood the political delicacy of this mixed Catholic-Protestant journey across the Atlantic in the *Ark* and the *Dove*:

> His Lo[pp] [Lordship; Cecil Calvert, the second Lord Baltimore] requires his said Governor and Commissioners th[t]. in their voyage to Mary Land they [the Catholics] be very carefull to preserve peace and unity amongst all the passengers on Shipp-board, and that they suffer no scandall nor offence to be given to any of the Protestants, whereby any just complaint may heereafter be made, by them, in Virginea or in England, and that for that end, they cause all Acts of Romane Catholique Religion to be done as privately as may be, and that they instruct all the Roman Catholiques to be silent upon all occasions of discourse concerning matters of Religion; and that the said Governor and Commissioners treate the Protestants wth as much mildness and favor as Justice will permitt. And this is to be ordered at Land as well as at Sea.[7]

Their voyage to the New World lasted several months, from late November of 1633 to late March of 1634, including stopovers in Barbados, St. Christopher (today's "St. Kitts"), and Virginia. The *Ark* and the *Dove* entered a river off Chesapeake Bay, and passengers planted a cross on an island which they named St. Clement's. Weighing anchor, however, the two ships retraced this river route and eventually tied up below an advantageous bluff which they named St. Mary's City, somewhat more Catholic-sounding than "Avalon." ("Avalon" had been the name given by George Calvert, the first Lord Baltimore, to his failed settlement in Newfoundland, about a decade earlier.)[8]

It would be a mistake to imagine that those first settlers, Catholic and Protestant alike, were free of strong religious bias. As Maryland historian James Foster noted of these first settlers:

---

[7] Hall, Clayton Colman. *Narratives of early Maryland, 1633-1684*. 1910. New York: Barnes & Noble, Inc. 1946, reprinted 1953. 16. Print.

[8] St. Mary's City is named for the Virgin Mary, but Mary-land was tactfully named for the wife of King Charles I, Queen Henrietta Maria, a French Catholic.

> Whether religion was the rhetoric of their thought or whether it was their thought, seventeenth century Englishmen were surrounded by religion and absorbed in it. Governments acknowledged and attempted to enforce the medieval ideal of a Christian commonwealth, but neither governors nor governed could consistently agree about what was Christianity.[9]

If each settler had not actually chosen whether to be Catholic, Anglican, or Protestant, his family background had usually chosen it for him. As he struggled ashore in St. Mary's City, he was carrying more than his clothing, his bedding, his tools, his livestock, his seeds, and his weaponry. He was also carrying his assumptions and his memories of family history, dating back to the 1500s.

A settler's religion *was* his identity.

If on the one hand, he was Catholic and a "recusant," he naturally dwelt on the persecutions suffered under Henry VIII and Henry's daughter, Elizabeth I, persecutions which had been related to him in lurid detail, including the 1587 beheading of Mary, Queen of Scots (Mary Stuart; 1542–1587).

If, on the other hand, he was Anglican or Protestant, he could point to the reign of another Mary: Queen Mary I. Also known as Mary Tudor (1516–1558), she briefly made Catholicism the state religion of England after her brother, Edward VI, had followed the example of their father, Henry VIII, and banned it. She was called "Bloody Mary" for persecuting Protestant heretics, hundreds of whom were burned at the stake.

Then there was Guy Fawkes, a young English Catholic who travelled to Spain, fought for that Catholic country, and there became known by the name "Guido." Later, as Guy Fawkes, he would be remembered for hundreds of years later on November 5th, known as "Guy Fawkes Day," when masked effigies of him are raucously burned amidst fireworks and bonfires.[10] This annual event commemorates the day in 1605 when

---

9 Foster, James W. "George Calvert: The Early Years." USA: The Museum and Library of Maryland History, Maryland Historical Society, 1983. 3. Print.

10 Nowadays, in the 21st Century, stylized plastic masks of Guy Fawkes with upturned moustache and goatee are often used in political protests, and these are sometimes referred to as "Anonymous" masks.

Fawkes and fellow conspirators (all Catholic) acquired thirty-six barrels of gunpowder in order to blow up Parliament at the very moment when King James I–then an Anglican–was scheduled to make a state visit to both the House of Commons and the House of Lords. It is often referred to as the "Gunpowder Plot." In literature, Guido Fawkes would reappear as the sinister villain in English Gothic novels of the late eighteenth century. This villain would be presented as Catholic and evil, playing not only to a growing English nationalism but also to its suspicion of foreigners, particularly those from Mediterranean countries who did not speak English.

Although the 1634 colony had originally been seen as a haven for Catholics, it didn't take long for trouble to erupt. In fact, it took only ten years. In 1644, about a year after the first English Civil War had flared up, Protestant pirates began plundering the property of landowners in Maryland who had not sworn allegiance to the English Parliament. This invasion, known as Ingle's Rebellion or the "plundering time," was quelled in 1647 by Lord Baltimore.[11] Yet it proved to be the harbinger of an even more devastating, long-distance involvement in England's second and third Civil Wars (1648-1651) and the latter phase of the *Interregnum* (the Latin term for "between reigns"). This *Interregnum* generally means the monarch-less period between the 1649 execution of Charles I and the 1660 coronation of his son Charles II.

In Maryland, this latter involvement was called "the Puritan Uprising." Political and religious trouble had arrived in Lord Baltimore's little colony in 1649 when Puritans–expelled from the largely Anglican colony in Virginia–had been *invited* to cross the Potomac to find a haven in Maryland. At the point of Lord Baltimore's hospitable but disastrous invitation to these Puritans, the outpost at St. Mary's City was capable of being described by modern-day historian Owen Stanwood as "a powder keg."[12]

---

[11] Captain Ingle primarily pursued wealthy Catholics as well as priests. In 1645, he arrested Jesuit priests Thomas Copley and Andrew White and took them to England in chains to be prosecuted under the 1585 "Act Against Jesuits, Seminary Priests and Other Such Disobedient Persons." Father White's role in Maryland history is discussed at Chapter 6-B-1, close of 6-E, & 6-F.

[12] Stanwood, Owen. *The Empire Reformed*. Philadelphia: University of Pennsylvania Press, 2011. 62. Print. In 1648, Lord Baltimore had appointed a Protestant, William Stone, as Governor; and in 1649, Governor Stone signed Maryland's Religious Toleration Act.

Maryland's much-vaunted "Act Concerning Religion" of 1649, also known as the "Religious Toleration Act"–an attempt to pacify all the members of Lord Baltimore's colony–is often touted for its "tolerance." But its underlying orientation is heavily Christian, and the Maryland Toleration Act (as it came to be called) does not include tolerance for Quakers, Jews, Muslims, or for that matter, agnostics and atheists. Thus, as Catholic historian Edwin Beitzell expressed it, "the Act formally limited the complete freedom of conscience established by Lord Baltimore with the founding of the Province [of Maryland] in 1634 . . . ."[13]

Typical of its time, this Act is written in one dauntingly long paragraph, thereby making it difficult for the modern reader to pull out its essential demands, and our eyes are apt to glaze over with the effort. But the aim of the Act becomes clearer if we modernize the language and then take the liberty of re-arranging portions of it *according to its penalties for disobedience*, moving from most severe to least. Re-arranged, these are some of the key sections of Maryland's Religious Toleration Act of 1649.

1. **On penalty of death as well as forfeiture of lands to Lord Baltimore and his heirs:** No blaspheming against God, or denial that Jesus is the son of God, or that the Trinity (Father, Son, and Holy Spirit) is a unity of Godhead.

2. **On penalty of five pounds sterling, paid to Lord Baltimore and his heirs:** No "reproachful words" against the Virgin Mary or the Apostles.

3. **On penalty of ten shillings sterling:** "And be it also further enacted by the same authority, advise, and assent that whatsoever person or persons shall from henceforth upon any occasion of offence or otherwise in a reproachful manner of way declare, call, or denominate any person or persons whatsoever inhabiting, residing, trafficking, trading, or commercing within the Province or within any [of] the ports, harbors, creeks, or havens to the same belonging: *an*

---

13 Beitzell, Edwin W. *The Jesuit Missions of St. Mary's County, Maryland.* 2nd ed. Abell, MD: E.W. Beitzell; sponsored by St. Mary's County Bicentennial Commission, 1976. 26. Print. Hereafter cited as Beitzel, *Jesuit Missions*. This book is an excellent source on Maryland history, particularly as to religious matters.

heretic, schismatic, idolator, Puritan, Independent, popish priest, Jesuit, Jesuited Papist, Lutheran, Calvinist, Anabaptist, Brownist, Antinomian, Barrowist, Roundhead, Separatist, or any other name or term in a reproachful manner relating to matter of religion shall for every such offence forfeit and lose the sum of ten shillings sterling or the value thereof to be levied on the goods and chattels of every such offender and offenders. . . ."[14]

This last offense, Number 3, suggests that back-biting and name-calling had already been reaching unacceptable levels in the colony.

From 1654 to 1656, the newly arrived Puritans gained enough power in the legislature at St. Mary's City to be able to change the name "St. Mary's County" to the less Catholic-sounding "Potomac County."[15]

And these same Puritans were also able to swiftly abolish the Religious Toleration Act of 1649 and enact a new one which stated that "no one who professed or exercised the Popish religion, commonly known by the name of the Roman Catholic religion, can be protected in this Province."[16] The Puritans in Lord Baltimore's colony included their Anglican neighbors in this prohibition. While Anglicans did not practice "popery," they *did* retain "prelacy," claiming (with Catholics) an Apostolic Succession of bishops.

By 1660, with the English Restoration (of the monarchy) and the coronation of King Charles II, Lord Baltimore managed to regain control of his colony just after this decade-long upheaval (England's third Civil War, followed by two Commonwealth periods, and the Cromwell Protectorates).

Lord Baltimore's Catholic haven struggled on until 1690, but at that point, religious and political maneuvers of English Parliamentarians and Puritans in Maryland would cause the Calverts to lose their propietary colony. William of Orange ("Dutch Billy") and Mary II came to the throne

---

14 *An Act Concerning Religion*, 1649, April 21. GENERAL ASSEMBLY, UPPER HOUSE (Proceedings) Maryland State Archives S 977-1, ff.354-59 (emphasis added). Web. 25 May 2022. <https://msa.maryland.gov/megafile/msa/speccol/sc2200/sc2221/000003/000002/html/toler01r.html>).

15 Combs Hammett, Regina. *History of St. Mary's County, Maryland: 1634-1990*. 2nd printing. Ridge, Md: R.C. Hammett, 1994. 40. Print. Hereafter cited as Combs, *History*. This book provides an excellent focus on the historical importance of St. Mary's County.

16 Beitzel, *Jesuit Missions* 24.

in 1689, and with that, the English Reformation–exhausted–sagged to its conclusion.

England was now stabilized under the Anglican "transnational corporation" which required its colonial "branch offices" to toe the line in all matters, religious and political.

D. PERSECUTION: "A BAD AND INDIRECT WAY TO PLANT RELIGION"
(Sir Thomas Browne, *Religio Medici*, 1643)

It–the English Reformation–had been an exhausting century and a half, not only for England but also for a small colony such as Maryland. Those years of turmoil are recorded in a series of laws passed by Parliament in London's "transnational corporation." These laws are usually referred to as Acts, and at points during the Reformation, they may also have incorporated an Oath–an oath which a Catholic (whether in England or Maryland) would not have been able to sign in good conscience.

During the English Reformation, whenever a political regime changed its religious orientation, members of Parliament would often rise to their feet to create an angrily worded Act that would reverse the religious policy of the previous administration. Then, several weeks later, this Act, Oath, or Declaration would slowly cross the Atlantic and find a place in England's little colonial governments.

Here, it would be carried out on the local level: in Maryland, the legislature had originally met in St. Mary's City, first named for the Virgin Mary. But as years went by and the English Reformation increasingly became law, "St. Mary's" began to sound unacceptably Catholic. The legislature moved the capital north to Annapolis by 1695. Thus, governmentally, St. Mary's City lost out to "Anna-polis" (city-of-Anne), named for Princess Anne of Denmark and Norway, younger daughter of King James II and eventually the Queen of Great Britain (1702–1714).

Some Acts dealt with "allegiance," that is, simple loyalty to the king or queen, while other Acts dealt with the king or queen as "Supreme Head" of the Church of England (Anglican). At Historic St. Mary's City, Henry Miller, director of research, has helped to make clear the bottom-line distinction between the two:

> The first [Oath of Allegiance] was of loyalty to the King, and the second [Oath of Supremacy] stated you believed the King [not the Pope] was head of the church. It is this latter one that caused so much trouble for English Catholics.[17]

Listed on the following pages is a sampling of some of the Acts enacted by Parliament during the century and a half of the English Reformation, 1534-1689 (and three more Acts after the reign of William III, who died in 1702, which were directed at Catholics), as well as certain laws enacted in Maryland. These back-and-forth Acts had to be obeyed in the colonies, and confusingly, some of them are known by other names. The table set forth below is selective and by no means exhaustive. (See, for example, fn 11 above and Section 2-E-1 below.)

Year	Monarch or Authority	Law or Event	Content
1534	Henry VIII	Act of [royal] Supremacy	Any person taking public office or church post must swear allegiance to the King [not the pope] as "the only supreme head on Earth of the Church of England."
1534	Henry VIII	Treasons Act	It is treason to refute the 1534 Act of [royal] Supremacy. Sir Thomas More is executed for treason, and monasteries are dissolved.
1555	Mary I	Repealed: Act of [royal] Supremacy of 1534	The pope is, once again, head of the Church in England. (In 1554, she married King Phillip II of Spain).

---

17 Miller, Henry M. The quoted material comes from an earlier email draft of November 2, 2012 (received by Janet Haugaard). Also, I am mightily indebted to Silas Hurry, Curator of Collections and Director of the Archaeological Laboratory at Historic St. Mary's City, who provided specific online locations where the oaths in question can be found.

Year	Monarch or Authority	Law or Event	Content
1558 [enacted 1559]	Elizabeth I	[second] Act of [royal] Supremacy	Replaces the 1534 Act; and the Queen is "supreme governor . . . in all spiritual or ecclesiastical things or causes." The Oath includes: ". . . I do utterly renounce and forsake all foreign jurisdictions . . ." (including that of the pope).
1584 [enacted 1585]	Elizabeth I	The Jesuits, etc. Act 1584 (27 Eliz. 1. c. 2)	Includes a mandate that all Catholic priests leave England within 40 days unless they were to swear an oath to obey the Queen. Failure to do so would be deemed high treason.
1593	Elizabeth I	The Act Against [Popish] Recusants	Includes penalties for refusing to attend services in Church of England [Anglican]. Provides for forfeiture of properties of Catholic recusants who move more than five miles from their houses.
1605	James I	Popish Recusants Act	In response to the "Gunpowder Plot" (to blow up Parliament and assassinate the king), this law makes it high treason to obey the pope and requires a new oath of allegiance (denying the power of the pope to depose monarchs). This Act requires all "Papists" to attend the Lord's Supper once a year in Anglican church and prohibits them from entering the fields of law and medicine and from becoming trustees/guardians.

Year	Monarch or Authority	Law or Event	Content
1606	James I	Oath of Allegiance	The Oath includes: "I will defend to the uttermost of my power against all conspiracies . . .and make known unto His Majesty, his heirs and successors, all treasons and traitorous conspiracies. . . . And I do further swear that I . . . abhor, detest, and abjure, as impious and heretical this damnable doctrine and position,—that princes which be excommunicated by the pope may be deposed or murdered by their subjects or by any other whatsoever."
1625	Charles I	Oath of Allegiance	The Oath includes: "That I do from my heart abhor, detest and abjure as impious and Hereticall this damnable Doctrine and Position, That Princes which be Excommunicated or deprived by the Pope, may be Deposed or Murthered by their Subjects, or any other whatsoever."
1632	Charles I	The Charter of Mary Land	Charter for the Province of Maryland is granted to Cecil Calvert (the second Lord Baltimore).

Year	Monarch or Authority	Law or Event	Content
1634	Founding of Maryland by English colonists	Settlement of St. Mary's City	After English colonists aboard the *Ark* and the *Dove* land in the Province of Maryland and sign a treaty of peaceful coexistence with the Yaocomico (Yaocomaco) people, they build St. Mary's City, which will be the capital of Maryland for 61 years. The colonists are led by Leonard Calvert (Lord Baltimore's brother), first governor of Maryland.
1638	Maryland Assembly (colony)	"An Act for Swearing Allegeance" [aka as Maryland Oath of Allegiance]	Maryland Assembly requires all citizens to swear an Oath of Allegiance to Charles I, including disclosure of all "Treasons and traiterous consperacies . . . ." (*Proceedings and Acts of the General Assembly January 1637/8-September 1664*. Maryland State Archives Vol. 1, Page 40.)

Year	Monarch or Authority	Law or Event	Content
1643	Charles I	"An Ordinance for Explanation of a former Ordinance for Sequestration of Delinquents Estates with some Enlargements" (aka as the 1643 Oath of Abjuration)	The oath provides in part that the pope has no authority over the Catholic Church. The affiant must swear that there is: no Transubstantiation; no Purgatory; no Salvation by Works. It prohibits the worship of Crucifixes, the Consecrated Host, and Images. Any person 21 years of age or over reputed to be a Papist (and those who harbor them) who fails to take this oath "[s]hall forfeit as Papists" "two third parts of all their Goods and Estates Real and Personal." Also includes a "Reward for discoverers" - i.e., a bounty for those turning in suspected "Delinquents and Papists."
1642-1646	Charles I	1st Civil War in England.	Acts passed by Parliament between 1642-1649 generally did not receive the king's approval, so this period may also be considered part of the *Interregnum* for purposes of archiving recorded laws.
1644-1646	Maryland (colony)	"The plundering time." (aka Claiborne and Ingle's rebellion)	Protestant pirates plunder the property of landowners who had not sworn allegiance to the English Parliament. Jesuit priests are arrested and sent to England for prosecution. Captain Richard Ingle, a Puritan, takes over St. Mary's City; and William Claiborne takes over Kent Island.

Year	Monarch or Authority	Law or Event	Content
1648-1649	Charles I	2nd Civil War in England.	Acts passed by Parliament between 1642-1649 generally did not receive the king's approval, so this period may also be considered part of the *Interregnum* for purposes of archiving recorded laws.
1649	Charles I	Beheading of Charles I after being convicted of high treason for putting his personal interests above those of the nation.	Charles I argues that no court had jurisdiction over him (or any monarch) based upon the principle of "divine right." The court rejects this doctrine of sovereign immunity and holds that "the King of England was not a person, but an office whose every occupant was entrusted with a limited power to govern 'by and according to the laws of the land and not otherwise'."
1649	Maryland Assembly (colony)	"A Law of Maryland Concerning Religion" (aka as the Act of Religious Toleration or as the Maryland Toleration Act)	While this law makes it a crime to blaspheme God, the Holy Trinity, the Virgin Mary, saints, and the Apostles, it also forbids the disparagement of another's religion. Specifically refers to "the free exercise" of religion–for Christians.
1649-1651	Commonwealth	3rd Civil War in England.	War begins when Charles II tries to regain the throne of the Three Kingdoms, but is ultimately defeated by Cromwell's forces.

Year	Monarch or Authority	Law or Event	Content
1649-1653	Commonwealth	"An Act declaring England to be a Commonwealth"	With the abolishment of the monarchy, the Commonwealth of England is established as a republic. Parliament appoints "Officers and Ministers under them for the good of the People... without any King or House of Lords". The Rump Parliament exercises legislative powers. The Council of State exercises executive powers.
1650	Commonwealth	"Certificate of Engagement to the Commonwealth of England"	All adult males must declare their loyalty: "I do declare and promise that I will be true and faithful to the commonwealth of England as it is now established without a king or House of Lords."
1650-1657	Maryland (colony)	Puritan uprising and control of the Colony.	Religious and political disputes. The Puritans (who left Virginia after being invited to settle in Maryland by Protestant Gov. Stone in 1649) revolt against Maryland's proprietorship-type government. In 1654, Gov. Stone tries to impose an oath of fidelity by citizens to Lord Baltimore. In 1655, an army under Gov. Stone is sent by Lord Baltimore (Cecil Calvert) to quell the Puritans' revolt. In the Battle of the Severn, the Puritan army defeats the Catholic army. The Puritans then set up a new government prohibiting both Catholicism and Anglicanism.

Year	Monarch or Authority	Law or Event	Content
1653-1655	Protectorate (Oliver Cromwell)	"Instrument of Government"	First constitution of the Commonwealth of England, Scotland, and Ireland. Oliver Cromwell is installed as Lord Protector.
1654-1657	Maryland Assembly (colony)	Repealed: Maryland Toleration Act of 1649.	Puritans take control of Maryland's colonial government and bar Catholics from the Assembly. "None who profess the exercise of the Popish Religion, commonly known by the name of the Roman Catholic Religion, can be protected in this Province."
1655-1657	Rule of the Major-Generals under Protectorate	Orders (by Oliver Cromwell) to army.	Military rule, after Oliver Cromwell dissolves the first Protectorate Parliament.

Year	Monarch or Authority	Law or Event	Content
1657	Common-wealth	"An Act for convicting, discovering and repressing of Popish Recusants" (aka as the 1657 Oath of Abjuration)	This Oath of Abjuration is based upon the 1643 Oath, yet significantly expands and strengthens it. Any person 16 years of age or over "suspected or reputed to be Papists, or Popishly affected" who failed to take this oath (4 times a year) "shall be adjudged a Popish Recusant convict to all intents and purposes whatsoever." Also includes language similar to the 1625 Oath of Allegiance. Justices are to issue warrants for each "Quarter Session" (four times a year). Numerous penalties include the confiscation of 2/3 of the estate of convicted persons (excepting the "mansion," perhaps akin to a homestead exemption).
1657-1659	Protectorate (Oliver Cromwell; Richard Cromwell)	"Humble Petition and Advice"	Second constitution of England, providing for hereditary monarchy; yet Oliver Cromwell declines to be named as monarch. After his death in 1658, his son, Richard Cromwell, becomes Lord Protector.
1658–1692	Maryland Assembly (colony)	Reinstated: Maryland Toleration Act of 1649.	Cecil Calvert (2nd Lord Baltimore) regains control after political negotiations with the Puritans, his "proprietorship" is restored, and there is a general amnesty agreement.
1659-1660	Common-wealth		After the army removes Richard Cromwell, the Rump Parliament is reinstated.

Year	Monarch or Authority	Law or Event	Content
1660	Charles II: monarchy restored	The "Restoration": Charles II proclaimed king of England, Scotland, and Ireland.	With the House of Commons divided between Royalists and Parliamentarians and Anglicans and Presbyterians, Parliament considers the "Declaration of Breda," wherein Charles II made promises, including general amnesty, religious tolerance, and if throned, to rule in cooperation with Parliament. Parliament then passes a resolution that "government ought to be by King, Lords and Commons" and invites Charles to return to England as king, proclaiming that he has been the lawful monarch since the execution of Charles I in 1649.
1661	Charles II	Restored: Oath of Allegiance. Restored: Oath of Supremacy.	Parliament requires an oath of allegiance and an oath of supremacy, acknowledging the king as having complete power.
1661	Charles II	Corporation Act of 1661	All public office-holders and all members of corporations are required: to take Oaths of Allegiance and Supremacy; and within a year of election to receive sacrament of the Lord's Supper according to the rites of the Church of England.

Year	Monarch or Authority	Law or Event	Content
1673	Charles II	"An Act for Preventing Dangers Which May Happen from Popish Recusants" (aka as the Test Act of 1673)	"Test Act" additionally requires all public office-holders (civil, military, church) to deny "transubstantiation in the sacrament of the Lord's Supper, or in the elements of the bread and wine, at or after the consecration thereof by any person whatsoever." Also requires them to receive the sacrament within three months after admittance to office.
1678	Charles II	Test Act of 1673 expanded and made more restrictive.	In response to rumors of a "popish plot," the Test Act of 1673 is expanded to include all peers and members of Parliament (except Charles's brother, the Duke of York, the future James II), thus excluding Catholics from Parliament. Further expanded to condemn veneration of the Virgin Mary and the saints, as well as "the Sacrifice of the Mass" as being "superstitious and idolatrous."
1685-1688	James II	Short reign until deposed.	James II is at first secretly, and later openly, Catholic. His removal from power, at the behest of English aristocrats, confirms the increasing authority of the Parliament over the monarch.

Year	Monarch or Authority	Law or Event	Content
1687-1688	James II	"Declaration of Indulgence" (aka the Declaration for Liberty of Conscience)	In 1687, James II issues the Declaration to negate the effect of laws punishing Catholics and Protestant dissenters. A few months later, he dissolves Parliament. In 1688, the Archbishop of Canterbury and six bishops are arrested for seditious libel for refusing to have the Declaration read aloud in Anglican churches. Queen Mary (of Modena) gives birth to a Catholic male heir (James Francis Edward Stuart), thus raising fears among some of a potential Catholic dynasty.
1688-1689	William III & Mary II	The "Glorious Revolution."	After the acquittal of the seven bishops in mid-1688, English aristocrats invite William of Orange (a Protestant Prince of the Dutch Republic) and his wife Mary (raised as an Anglican and daughter of James II) to take the throne. In 1689, the Convention Parliament declares that James II had abdicated the throne and then offers the crown to William and Mary.

Year	Monarch or Authority	Law or Event	Content
1688 [enacted 1689]	William III & Mary II	"An Act for exempting their Majesties' Protestant Subjects Dissenting from the Church of England, from the Penalties of certain Laws" (aka the Toleration Act of 1688)	Parliament provides freedom of worship to Protestants ("nonconformists") who pledge the Oaths of Allegiance and Supremacy and reject transubstantiation. This act does not apply to "dissenters," such as Catholics and Jews, who are excluded from holding political office.
1689	William III & Mary II	"An Act Declaring the Rights and Liberties of the Subject and Settling the Succession of the Crown" (aka the Bill of Rights of 1689)	The Bill of Rights of 1689 sets forth specific constitutional and civil rights. It gives Parliament power over the king and queen, limiting certain of their rights, thus ushering in a constitutional monarchy. (Its precursor, the *Magna Carta*, had also limited certain rights of the monarchy–way back in 1215.)
1689	William III & Mary II	Provision barring Catholics as monarchs (in the Bill of Rights of 1689).	Parliament declares that no future monarch may be a Catholic or be married to a Catholic. This restriction is later reaffirmed in the "1701 Act of Settlement"; and it remains in force.

Year	Monarch or Authority	Law or Event	Content
1689	William III & Mary II	Royal Declaration against Transubstantiation (in the Bill of Rights of 1689).	Parliament also requires every monarch at coronation (or at the opening of his first Parliament, whichever occurs first) to make the following declaration: "I do believe that in the Sacrament of the Lord's Supper there is not any Transubstantiation . . . by any person whatsoever . . . and that the invocation and adoration of the Virgin Mary or any other Saint, and the Sacrifice of the Mass, as they are now used in the Church of Rome, are superstitious and idolatrous." This Declaration Against Transubstantiation would be binding on all monarchs till 1910.
1690-1692	Maryland's Protestant Revolution of 1689	Interim government established by the Protestant Associators.	After Maryland's "Glorious Protestant Revolution," the capital, St. Mary's City, is taken over by the Puritan army; and the Protestant Associators sets up an interim government.
1694	Maryland Assembly (colony)	Capital moved from St. Mary's City.	The Assembly votes to move the capital from St. Mary's City up north to "Anne Arundell Towne" (named after Cecil Calvert's wife); in 1695, it is re-named Annapolis (for Princess Anne, daughter of King James II).

Year	Monarch or Authority	Law or Event	Content
1695	William III [in 1694, Queen Mary II died]	"An Act for the better Security of his Majestys Royall Person and Government"	Enacted in 1696 after the discovery of a Jacobite conspiracy to kill the King, backed by an invasion from France, this Act has 21 anti-Catholic proscriptions. It requires all officers to pledge the Oaths of Allegiance and Supremacy Act of 1688 or be disenfranchised. It also makes it an offense for anyone: to say that William III was not the lawful king; or to support the restoration of the senior line of the House of Stuart to the British throne (including James Francis Edward Stuart–the "Old Pretender"–or his father, former King James II).
1698	William III	"An Act for the further preventing the Growth of Popery" (aka the Popery Act of 1698)	Enacted by Parliament in 1700, this law in effect places a bounty on Catholic priests, by payment of £100 (from a county sheriff) to anyone who turns in a "Popish Bishop, Priest or Jesuite" who is convicted of "saying Mass" or performing Catholic church functions. This Act also prohibits Catholic schooling, inheritance, and purchase of land.

Year	Monarch or Authority	Law or Event	Content
1778	George III	"An Act for relieving His Majesty's subjects professing the popish religion from certain penalties and disabilities imposed on them by an Act made in the eleventh and twelfth years of the reign of King William the Third, intituled 'An Act for the further preventing the growth of popery'" (aka the Papists Act of 1778)	Eighty years later, this Act reflects a shift. However, although this Act does not grant freedom of worship, and it imposes an oath declaring loyalty to the reigning monarch and contains an abjuration of the "young" Stuart Pretender, "Bonnie Prince Charlie" (son of James Francis Edward Stuart, the "Old Pretender" *and* grandson of James II), and of certain doctrines attributed to Roman Catholics (*including the lawfulness of murdering excommunicated princes and the pope's temporal and spiritual jurisdiction*), those taking this oath are exempted from some of the provisions of the Popery Act of 1698. It allows such oath-taking Catholics to join the army and purchase (and inherit) land. It repeals certain penalties as well as the bounty provision.

Year	Monarch or Authority	Law or Event	Content
1791	George III	"An act to relieve, upon conditions, and under restrictions, the persons therein described, from certain penalties and disabilities to which papists, or persons professing the popish religion, are by law subject" (aka the Roman Catholic Relief Act of 1791)	This Act gives Catholics freedom to worship. It "relieves" Catholics of certain political, educational, and economic disabilities. For example, although Catholics are now allowed to practice their religion and to establish schools, all such chapels, schools, officiating priests and teachers must be registered. It requires an oath similar to that of the Papists Act of 1778, and also a pledge for the Protestant Succession under the 1701 Act of Settlement. Those taking this oath are no longer be subject to prosecution for being a Papist, receiving Catholic education, hearing or saying Catholic Mass, or belonging to any ecclesiastical community in the Church of Rome. Catholics are <u>no</u> longer required to take the Oath of Supremacy. It also allows Catholics to live in London.
1829	George IV	"An Act for the Relief of His Majesty's Roman Catholic Subjects" (aka the Roman Catholic Relief Act of 1829 or as the Catholic Emancipation Act)	Although this Act is initially opposed by the House of Lords and King George IV, a Catholic movement in Ireland demanding political rights raises concerns that British rule in Ireland may be in jeopardy. Thus, Parliament passes this Act, allowing Catholics to vote in elections, to be members of Parliament, and to hold most senior public offices.

As an observant physician in Norwich, England had commented back in 1643, "Persecution is a bad and indirect way to plant Religion." [18]

E. THE COST OF BEING CATHOLIC IN MARYLAND

In short, the 1700s were a bad century in which to be both colonial and Catholic.

After more than a century and a half of conflict, Protestantism and Anglicanism had finally "triumphed" over Catholicism in the English Reformation, and a succession of Anglican monarchs ruled the American colonies from 1689 (the "Glorious Revolution") until the colonies broke away during our Revolutionary War of 1776.[19]

Nonetheless, the early Christian church had survived persecution many hundreds of years before, and Catholicism would survive yet again in the Province of Maryland–but hardly anyone could have reasonably predicted this during the 1700s, which was Maryland's own "Dark Age."

1. Governmental Acts

For most of the 1700s, once Anglicanism became the official religion of England's "transnational corporation" and therefore of Maryland's own colonial "branch office," this is how matters stood in both St. Mary's City and Annapolis.

- → **Lord Baltimore's[20] original charter (1632) was "vacated" in June of 1691 by King William III**, who declared Maryland a royal colony, rather than a proprietary province. However in 1689, before this royal declaration, an army of 700 Puritans (called "Protestant Associators") had defeated an army of the province (led by a Catholic).

---

18 Thomas Browne, *Religio Medici* (1643), Part I, Section 25.

19 Those Anglican monarchs were: William III and Mary II (1689–1702; although Mary died in 1694); Anne (1702–1707), after the Acts of Union of 1707, Queen of Great Britain (1707-1714); George I (1714–1727); George II (1727–1760); and finally George III (whose reign was from 1760–1820). However, his rule over the 13 colonies was challenged in 1776 with the adoption of the Declaration of Independence by the Second Continental Congress, and it was finally severed in 1783, when the Treaty of Paris ratified the independence of those colonies.

20 "Lord Baltimore" was the title held by Cecil Calvert. Upon his death in 1675, his son Charles inherited his estate, which included the Charter of Maryland. (In 1633, as Lord Baltimore, Cecil Calvert had appointed his brother, Leonard Calvert, as Governor of the Province of Maryland.)

Thus arising from Maryland's "Glorious Protestant Revolution," the interim government of Protestant Associators installed itself from 1690 to 1692. The interim government outlawed Catholicism, thus forcing Catholics to maintain secret chapels in their homes in order to celebrate Mass. The Protestant Associators also appealed to William and Mary to make Maryland a royal colony, which was declared in 1691. Then in 1692, the king appointed Sir Lionel Copley as the first "Royal Governor" of Maryland, thus replacing the Protestant Associators' interim government. Copley's first act as such was to recognize William and Mary as monarchs and to thank them for "redeeming us from the arbitrary will and pleasure of a tyrannical popish government under which we have so long groaned."[21]

→ **Copley's second act was to establish the Church of England (that is, Anglican) as the Church of Maryland**, requiring all "tithables"[22]– Catholic and Protestant alike–to support the Anglican Church with a tax of 40 pounds of tobacco per year.[23] King William refused to allow this, ordering instead "liberty of conscience" for all.[24]

→ **Under William and Mary**, however, there began a series of laws whose aim was to eliminate Catholicism in Maryland to the extent possible.

---

21 Beitzel, *Jesuit Missions* 43. Maryland's delay in proclaiming William and Mary as new sovereigns in lieu of James II may have been an additional factor in the vacating of the Charter of Maryland and the establishment of a royal colony. The other colonies had timely recognized William and Mary as sovereigns. However, the first messenger whom Lord Baltimore had sent to the new sovereigns to express his support had died during the journey, and it is unclear whether a second messenger was sent (as Lord Baltimore had represented). "Protestant Revolution (Maryland)." *Wikipedia*. Web. 10 May 2022. <https://en.wikipedia.org/wiki/Protestant_Revolution_(Maryland)>. See Combs, *History* 42.

22 "A tithable was defined as all free males over the age of 16, and all slaves, male or female, over the age of 16." "From the Archives: Part II, Religious Toleration in Colonial Maryland" *Maryland Episcopalian*. Web. 11 May 2022. <https://marylandepiscopalian.org/2019/08/06/from-the-archives-part-ii-religious-toleration-in-colonial-maryland/>.

23 "An Act for the Service of Almighty God and the Establishment of the Protestant Religion within this Province." Proceedings and Acts of the General Assembly, April 1684-June 1692. Vol 13 p. 429, 1692.; Maryland State Archives. Web. 11 May 2022. <https://msa.maryland.gov/megafile/msa/speccol/sc2900/sc2908/000001/000013/html/am13--429.html >.

24 Beitzel, *Jesuit Missions* 44.

a. In 1692, Catholic lawyers were disbarred; and
b. the Test Oath of 1699 barred Catholic office-holders from their positions. (This was the same oath which denied Transubstantiation during the Mass.)[25]

→ **Under Queen Anne, who succeeded William and Mary in 1702**, the screws were further tightened in Maryland.

c. In 1704, the Act to Prevent the Growth of Popery detailed the following.

 1. It was a penal offense to practice the Catholic religion in public.
 2. Priests could not say Mass in public or otherwise practice as priests.
 3. Priests could say Mass only in an ell contiguous to a private home (commonly known as a "chapel-house" or "Mass-house").
 4. It was a penal offense to keep a Catholic school or teach in it.
 5. Catholics were not permitted to sit in either House of the Maryland Assembly.[26]

d. Catholics were not permitted to vote for Representatives to the Assembly.[27]
e. Catholics were not permitted "to act as Magistrates or to enjoy any Place of Publick Trust or Profit."[28]
f. Governor Seymour ordered the local sheriff to lock the door of the Catholic chapel in St. Mary's City and keep the key.[29]
g. A 20-shilling penalty was imposed on Irish servants entering Maryland.[30]

---

25 Beitzel, *Jesuit Missions* 44.
26 Beitzel, *Jesuit Missions* 44.
27 Maryland State Archives, Volume 9, Correspondence of Governor Sharpe, 1757-1761, pp. 315-16.
28 Maryland State Archives, Volume 9, Correspondence of Governor Sharpe, 1757-1761, pp. 315-16.
29 Beitzel, *Jesuit Missions* 52. Presumably, this was Sheriff John Coode, Jr.
30 Beitzel, *Jesuit Missions* 45.

→ **Under George I, who succeeded Queen Anne in 1714:**

　h.　the tax on Irish servants (presumed to be Catholic) was doubled in 1717; and

　i.　in 1715, a child was to be removed from its mother if she either became or married a Catholic.[31]

→ **Under George II, who succeeded George I in 1727:**

　j.　in 1746, Governor Bladen issued a proclamation against priests who converted Protestants to Catholicism; both priest and convert were to be imprisoned;

　k.　in 1756, a double tax was imposed on Catholics for the support of the militia; and

　l.　in 1754, an unsigned letter was sent to the publisher of the *Maryland Gazette*: "Does Popery increase in this Province? The great number of Popish Chapels [the Mass-houses] and the crowds that resort to them, as well as the great Number of their Youth sent this year to foreign Popish Seminaries for education, prove that it does".[32]

In effect, Catholics were now exiles-in-place.

In the Province of Maryland (as well as in England, Scotland, Ireland, and all of the empire's colonies), Catholics were not allowed to vote nor participate in public life.

It is tempting to think that at least one member of the Upper House of the Maryland Assembly must have worried that this decision barring Catholics from the vote might be "repugnant to the laws of England." But William Bladen, Maryland's attorney general in 1718, was quick to reassure him:

> "Relateing to Papists voteing at Elections be Repugnant to the Laws of England or not; I have Consulted Authoritys and find the same no ways Repugnant but Consonant to the law of

---

[31] Beitzel, *Jesuit Missions* 45.

[32] Beitzel, *Jesuit Missions* 45. Thomas Bladen, first Maryland-born governor, was son of English-born William Bladen, attorney general in Maryland.

England Especially the Act of Parliament of the 7th and 8th years of King William the 3d of Glorious memory, Entitled An Act for the better Security of his Majestys Royall Person & Government [1695]."[33]

Adding insult to injury, Catholic Marylanders were not only taxed more than most but were *also* required to pray for the Anglican king and queen overseas in London. Thus, the sheriff who so famously (or infamously) locked the door of the Catholic chapel in St. Mary's City had no sober choice but to obey the orders from Governor Seymour and the legislature, all of whom by now were Protestant. To be fair, however, it is important to remember that these orders had originated across the Atlantic and had traveled to Annapolis from London. **It is a truism that–just as with the military–neither corporations nor empires allow for disobedience. "Just following orders, ma'am."**

2. Papal Acts

Worse was to come. In 1773, on the very eve of the American Revolutionary War, Pope Clement XIV suppressed all missionary work of the Jesuits that had been undertaken throughout Europe and its colonies in America and the West Indies. Actually, this came as no surprise. The Suppression of the Society of Jesus, levied by the pope himself, was a political action undertaken in an attempt to make peace with the Bourbon monarchs in Europe, all of whom were Catholic but who–for political reasons–were also strongly anti-Jesuit. Writing for the *Catholic Encyclopedia*, John Hungerford Pollen commented:

> The Suppression [of the Jesuits] is the most difficult part of the history of the Society. Having enjoyed very high favor among Catholic peoples, kings, prelates, and popes for two . . . and a half centuries, it suddenly becomes an object of frenzied hostility, is overwhelmed by obloquy, and overthrown with dramatic rapidity. Every work of the Jesuits–their vast missions, their noble colleges, their churches–is all taken from them or

---

[33] Maryland State Archives, Volume 33, 29 April 1718, p. 48.

destroyed. They are banished, and their order suppressed, with harsh and denunciatory words even from the pope.[34]

Edwin Beitzell's observation about Pope Clement XIV is even stronger: "What the Ingle Invasion, the Puritan uprising, and the Protestant rebellion had failed to accomplish over many bitter years of persecution and suffering was accomplished almost overnight by the machinations of European politics."[35]

In Maryland, during this period of a Suppression that was not Protestant but instead Papal, the nine *former* Jesuit priests (of whom John Carroll was one) were not drastically affected; they were more or less able to function as "secular" priests, that is, as non-Jesuits officiating in the "Mass-houses" permitted in Maryland.

If, however, they *were* Jesuit priests and therefore illegal, hunted down by Protestant authorities, they could escape to the "priest hole" provided by larger homes.[36]

The Papal Suppression of Maryland Jesuits would not be completely lifted until Pope Pius VII did so in 1814.

3. Jesuit Schools

For those Catholics who were privileged enough to get a formal education during the 17th and 18th centuries (white males), there were Jesuit schools in Maryland as well as colleges in Europe. In the 1957 *Chronicles* survey, Edwin Beitzell quotes Governor Nicholson's 1697 report describing a Jesuit brick school at St. Mary's in the earliest years of the Maryland colony, but by the time of Nicholson's actual term as (Anglican) Governor of the Maryland Province (1694-1698), such Catholic schools were outlawed. As early as the 1670s, two boys (Robert Brooke and Thomas Gardiner) had graduated

---

34 Pollen, John H. "The Suppression of the Jesuits, 1750-1773." *The Catholic Encyclopedia,* Vol. 14. New York: Robert Appleton Company, 1912. 65. Print. See also<https://www.newadvent.org/cathen/14096a.htm>.

35 Beitzel, *Jesuit Missions* 65.

36 "Woodlawn," a house near Ridge, Maryland, provided such a "priest hole" in the dining-room. It was discovered in the 1980s when then-owners Tom and Ginny Cox came upon the hiding place while restoring the old colonial home. When this chapter was first written in 2014, the house was owned by Jim Grube and has become a bed-and-breakfast.

from the Jesuit school at Newtown and gone from there to the College of St. Omer in northeastern France.[37]

St. Omer's was founded in 1593 by Robert Persons, S.J. It was launched as an English-language high school in France where older boys could get a Catholic education. From Maryland, the future founder of Georgetown University, John Carroll (along with his brother, Daniel, and his cousin, Charles) had not only been a student at St. Omer (in the mid-18th century) but had also gone on to teach there. The town of St. Omer, with its own cathedral, is about twenty miles from the port of Calais, a French town on the English Channel, directly opposite the English town of Dover.[38]

As Beitzell notes, "The law [in the last decade of the 1600s and on into the 1700s] provided severe penalties for a Catholic to keep or teach school and forced the more wealthy Planters to send their children abroad for an education." Beitzell further notes that from 1704 to 1772, the Jesuits were able to carry on their educational activities only "for brief periods and by stealth."[39]

F. AGAIN ENACTING RELIGIOUS FREEDOM: NOW THE U.S. CONSTITUTION

Our Revolutionary War of 1776 is usually presented by historians as a refusal by American colonies to subject themselves any longer to Great Britain[40] and her *economic* policies. In modern times, this rebellious refusal

---

[37] See Edwin Beitzell's "Early Schools of Southern Maryland" in the March 1957 issue of *Chronicles of St. Mary's*. Much of that article later appeared in Beitzell's second edition of his landmark *The Jesuit Missions of St. Mary's County*, 1976.

[38] However, in 1762, almost two centuries after its founding, political events caused the school to re-locate to Bruges (northwest Flanders) and again, in 1773, to Liège (Belgium). In an historical irony, it finally moved to England in 1794, where it still exists today as Stonyhurst, a Jesuit-run boarding school for boys and girls in Lancashire.

[39] Beitzell, Edwin."Early Schools of Southern Maryland." *Chronicles of St. Mary's*, Vol. 5 (March 1957). 31. Print. Without providing dates, Beitzell offers the names of thirty-five families whose sons were sent to Europe. Yet even going abroad for a Catholic education was risky, and on p. 45 of his 1976 edition of *The Jesuit Missions*, Beitzell quotes from the *Maryland Gazette*: "On November 1, 1753 . . . Turner Wooton, High Sheriff of Prince George County, denied, after being accused, that Basil Waring had persuaded him to send his son to St. Omer's to be educated" (p. 39). In the *Chronicles* version of this incident, Beitzell goes on to comment, "He [Sheriff Wooton] would have lost his position and suffered other penalties if the charge had been proven."

[40] In 1707, the Kingdom of Scotland united with the Kingdom of England and Wales to form the Kingdom of Great Britain. In 1801, the United Kingdom of Great Britain and Ireland was established.

is celebrated every year by "tea parties" held in Boston, Massachusetts and in Chestertown, Maryland, where enthusiastic re-enactors hurl casks of tea overboard in memory of that economic defiance.[41]

Yet, independence also provided freedom from Great Britain and her *religious* policies.

Maryland, be it noted, took early action in the Revolutionary War of 1776. In October of that year, the legislature met and passed the "Maryland Declaration of Rights" in which the Anglican church was finally dis-established, and colonists who as recently as 1770 had been required to pray for the health of the king and queen of England were abruptly–a mere six years later–considered traitors if they were to continue to do so.

Prudently, or in modern parlance, in a re-branding effort, the Anglican Church in the new United States now changed its name from the hated "Anglican" to "Episcopal," meaning "governed by bishops."

By war's end, Catholics could now practice their religion under the new U.S. Constitution which guaranteed–in two places–the freedom to do so.

The first guarantee was written into **Article VI of the 1787 Constitution** and refers indirectly to the "Test Acts" (those oaths which England, as the center of a "transnational corporation," had once formerly required): ". . . no religious Test shall ever be required as a Qualification to any Office or public Trust under the United States."

The second guarantee took place four years later when Congress addressed the question of religion head-on in the **First Amendment of the Bill of Rights**: "Congress shall make no law respecting an establishment of religion, or prohibiting the free exercise thereof . . . ."

---

41 Adam Goodheart, historian at Washington College in Chestertown ("this strenuously picturesque village on the Eastern Shore of the Chesapeake Bay") doubts the historical accuracy of Chestertown's annual Tea Party. See p. 21 of his reprint from *The American Scholar*, "Tea and Fantasy," Vol. 74, No. 4, Autumn 2005.

Finally, finally, America and its colonies–now freshly named the United States–had become the core of what Lord Baltimore had so radically attempted back in 1634: a start to religious freedom.[42]

---

[42] The following books also provide historic photographs as well as maps of the Jesuit missions in Maryland: Beitzel, *Jesuit Missions*; Combs, *History*; and LaFarge, *Manner*.

Chapter 3

"O Brave New World"

(William Shakespeare, *The Tempest*, 1610-1611)

In 1950, my senior year of high school, a scientist by the name of Immanuel Velikovsky published his theory that–hundreds of millions of years ago–planet Earth had turned completely upside down before righting itself once again. The theory has since been discredited, but at age seventeen I was transfixed with what this might mean in terms of continental coastlines and their histories. There was a brief period when I turned my little globe, as well as family atlases, upside down. I wondered what it would be like to experience an upside-down world.

A. FREEDOM IN THE AIR

This strange feeling of upside-down-ness might well have been felt by Southern Marylanders right after the Revolutionary War of 1776. Family meals would still have been served at the regular hour. Professionals such as doctors, lawyers, and judges would have gone about their business as usual. Tobacco was still being harvested by arduous slave labor, and plantation owners continued to send large shipments of it to England and other European ports.

But the world of daily living had changed, and in ways that could not even have been imagined only a few decades before. The relief may have been greatest for Catholics, who were still the historic bedrock of Southern Maryland–despite the earlier persecutions of the British Empire's state-run Anglican church. For Southern Marylanders, the relief was twofold: (1) the Bill of Rights of 1789 guaranteed freedom of religion; and (2) in 1814, Pope Pius VII lifted the earlier papal ban on Jesuit activity (see Chapter 2-E-2).

Persecution creates tension in its victims, but when that persecution disappears, muscles relax and relief sets in. At least, to an extent. What, then, does one do with relief? What does one do with the energy which once kept people on guard and which now can be let loose for other ends?

For Protestants–now freed from compulsory Anglicanism–historians have a word for such cultural release: the "Great Awakening." This new religious movement (actually, two, and originally Methodist) emphasized personal Bible study, fervent congregational singing, and good works. Critics from other denominations scoffed at these movements for being so visibly "enthusiastic," but the forces of the Great Awakening lasted from the 1740s through the 1840s, a solid century of religious, social, and political vitality that helped push the new republic into a proud sense of its American-ness.

Leonardtown in particular–the legislative seat of St. Mary's County– experienced what Aleck Loker, author of *A Most Convenient Place: Leonardtown, Maryland*, has described as a "boom." An impressive new courthouse was built in 1832 (the earlier one having burnt down, along with its historical records). Paddle-wheel steamboats now included Leonardtown as one of their ports of call, covering the Chesapeake from Philadelphia to Norfolk. But perhaps the greatest knitting of the social and political fabric took place with the creation of the *Leonard Town Herald* in 1839, undergoing a name-change a few years later to the *St. Mary's Beacon*. In his history of Leonardtown, Loker quotes this 1839 promise from its founder and first editor, Francis M. Jarboe:

> The *Herald* will be conducted on a neutral principle in politics, whether of a general or local character – and the insertion of articles that may have the smallest tendency to produce

personal excitement or angry feeling among [the] community, will be guarded against by the editor.[1]

Clearly, a new spirit of fairness–both political and religious–was being expressed.

For others in Southern Maryland, however, the solution for unexpected release was geographical, a matter of pulling up stakes and heading west for a new beginning. These westward migrations were known at the time as "fevers," and in Chapter 7 of her *History of St. Mary's County, Maryland*, Regina **Combs** Hammett describes the fever which overtook a sizeable portion of the County as early as 1790, shortly before Kentucky's admission to the Union in 1792. "Between 1790 and 1810," she writes, "the population of St. Mary's County decreased from 15,544 to 12,794."[2] This meant that every citizen who remained in Southern Maryland would surely have known at least one other family that had decided to "go west." [3]

The mountain chain of the eastern United States runs from north to south and is variously known as Adirondack, Allegheny, and Appalachian. On a few old maps, this barrier is labelled "The Endless Mountains," and St. Mary's families crossed over them into Kentucky. In Chapter 7 of her *History of St. Mary's County*, Regina **Combs** Hammett cites several possible reasons for this migration of Countians to the Kentucky "frontier": (1) availability of western land that was sometimes offered by the federal government to veterans of the Revolutionary War; (2) newspaper ads and lottery tickets that extolled frontier acreage; (3) anti-Catholicism; (4) severe property damage suffered by Southern Marylanders during the Revolutionary War; and (5) property debts run up when local Countians–who had been former lease-holders–bought the land they had previously farmed after the government

---

1 Loker, Aleck. *A Most Convenient Place: Leonardtown, Maryland*. Commissioners of Leonardtown and Solitude Press, 2001. 48. Print. Hereafter cited as Loker, *Leonardtown*.

2 Combs Hammett, Regina. *History of St. Mary's County: 1634-1990*. 2nd printing. Ridge, Md: R.C. Hammett, 1994. 92. Print. Hereafter cited as Combs, *History*.

3 New England was also part of the "fevers" that took place just after the Revolutionary War. In an article by Ralph Crandall (who cites Stewart Holbrook), we learn that "One winter's day in 1795 an observer [in Albany, NY] counted 500 sleighs passing westward through that town between sunrise and sunset. During the following summer an average of twenty boats daily went up the Mohawk River." Crandall, Ralph J. "New England's Migration Fever: the Expansion of America." *Ancestry Magazine*, Vol. 18, No. 4 (July/Aug 2000). 17. This east-west route later became the Erie Canal, completed in 1817.

had "confiscated" Lord Baltimore's old proprietary manors and sold these lands to the farmers, who later could not meet the purchase-payments.

Moreover, there was the likelihood that John Carroll, newly elected as bishop of Baltimore in 1789, would send a parish priest to Kentucky to minister to Catholic League migrants from Southern Maryland. One researcher writes that by 1796, there may have been "300 Catholic families in Kentucky."[4]

When families "owned" slaves, they were taken along, too. Two generations later, after Emancipation, the Catholic grandson of one of these Kentucky slaves, Daniel Rudd of Springfield, Ohio, founded the *American Catholic Tribune*, "The only Catholic Journal Published by Colored Men in America."[5]

But not everyone chose the physical relief of pulling up stakes and heading west. The majority stayed in St. Mary's County, and for them the relief–the feeling of unexpected freedom–had to find outlets in other ways. What were these expressions of release, of confidence and cordiality that so characterized Southern Maryland in the few decades before the Civil War?

B. "ONE CANDLE AT A TIME"

"They were the movers and shakers of their day." So wrote researcher and writer Alfred Gough in 1992,[6] referring to the men who–beginning in the late 1830s–created the St. Mary's Reading Room and Debating Society of Leonardtown ("RR&DS"). For the next three generations, men met regularly in Leonardtown to debate issues of the day, agitate for education, and discuss current books–which they bought and shelved in their Society-owned library. One might have expected that the Civil War would have discouraged all this public-spiritedness, but, as Gough discovered, many RR&DS members were Confederate veterans who found fresh voice

---

4 Malone, Mary Franceline, SBS (Sisters of the Blessed Sacrament). "Daniel Rudd: Catholic in More than Name." *Mission*, 78.1 (2012): 10. Print. Hereafter cited as Malone, *Daniel Rudd*.

5 Malone, *Daniel Rudd* 10.

6 Gough, Alfred. "The St. Mary's Reading Room and Debating Society." *Chronicles of St. Mary's*, Vol. 40 No.4 (1992). 162. Print. Hereafter cited as Gough, "Debating Society."

immediately after the war, in the 1870s and '80s. During these decades, the RR&DS was at its most active, well before the fray of World War I and the coming distractions of movies and radio in the 1920s.

When did these men first form themselves into a group? In his groundbreaking study, Gough has estimated that it must have been sometime between 1836 and 1839. The minutes from the first fifteen or twenty years have been lost,[7] but a copy of the 1869 "Articles of Incorporation" exists today in Annapolis at the Hall of Records, a copy of which is held in Leonardtown as part of the St. Mary's County Historical Society.[8] In the Preamble to the original Articles of Incorporation of the RR&DS, we find the general intent of these men:

> Whereas, we the undersigned in convention assembled, being desirous of mutually contributing to the improvement of our minds, are of the opinion that a literary society having for its primary objects the discussion of questions and the formation of a library and reading room, will in great measure conduce to that end.[9]

"The improvement of our minds." Gough's assessment of the RR&DS stands as the lasting legacy of this remarkable group of men: "It was this acceptance of change, toleration of those who thought differently, desire for progress and love of education forged with common sense that is the legacy of the membership of the St. Mary's Reading Room and Debating Society."[10] As for the founding members, Gough writes that "It is almost certain that James T. Blackistone, Vincent Camalier, George Combs, A. F. Fenwick, Henry G.S. Key, George J. Spalding and Benjamin G. Harris numbered among the founding members of the Society."[11] James T. Blackistone appears to have played a significant role in the RR&DS, and before long, we will come across his name in another context.

---

7 Gough, "Debating Society" 168.
8 Gough, "Debating Society" 195.
9 St. Mary's County Historical Society: Edwin W. Beitzell Collection; 1985.002.0164.
10 Gough, "Debating Society" 162.
11 Gough, "Debating Society" 168.

Married women were not allowed in the RR&DS, which however, did permit the library to be used by the unmarried few. Tongue in cheek, Gough comments that "The Society had in the finest 19th century traditions addressed the matter of female participation in a very matter-of-fact way: that is, after marriage there was to be no frittering around the library reading books."[12] The place of a married woman was not to be in the public arena but in the home of her husband and children. This conviction was obviously shared by the Englishmen who, as shown in Haydon's painting of that 1840 Abolitionist Convention in London, had decided by an overwhelming vote that–although black *men* were welcome–women would not be allowed to participate.

Alfred Gough has suggested that by "Lighting one candle at a time," the membership of the Society, "individually and collectively, laid the foundation for the present library and educational amenities enjoyed in St. Mary's today."[13]

In order of presentation in this present survey, these "candles" are (1) debate, (2) education, and (3) literature and science.

1. Debate

That these men did indeed debate is clear from the rules written into their "Articles of Incorporation." Two or three times a year, officers were elected to seven prescribed committees, one of which was "Questions," that is, matters for debate. Gough writes that: "It was the duty of the committee on questions to select and report to the Society at each regular meeting no less than three suitable questions for debate," noting further that "the question receiving the majority of votes would be the question for discussion at the next regular meeting."[14]

Unfortunately, because the minutes of the RR&DS have been lost, there is scant record of what the debates were about. Gough, however, spent considerable time searching microfilm records of newspapers, discovering that in 1885, *The Baltimore American* reported that Leonardtown's Reading

---

12 Gough, "Debating Society" 165.
13 Gough, "Debating Society" 167.
14 Gough, "Debating Society" 167.

Room and Debating Society "will decide whether or not 'a Russian advance on Herat is a justifiable 'casus belli' on the part of England'."[15] The *Beacon* newspaper in Leonardtown yielded three more examples: the issue of April 24, 1879, reported that a recent topic for debate had been taxation on mortgages, and that the next scheduled topic was to be "Is the majority party in Congress justified in insisting upon the repeal of the election laws as a consideration of the passage of the army bill?"[16] Roughly twenty years later, the question for debate was "Should convicts be required to work on public roads?"[17] Before the Civil War, just possibly the men of the RR&DS might also have debated abolition and the vote of England's Parliament in passing the Slave Trade Act of 1807, later hardened into the Anti-Slavery Act of 1833. And finally, these men of the RR&DS might also have debated the lack of a county-wide system of public education.

But there was one issue explicitly *not* open for debate: religion.

Under the RR&DS's By Law Number 16, titled "Subject Not Debatable," the wording tersely states that "No religious subject shall be discussed by the society."[18] This bylaw from the late 1830s seems to be part and parcel of Francis Jarboe's pledge while editor of the *Leonard Town Herald* in 1839: that is, not to print articles "that may have the smallest tendency to produce personal excitement or angry feeling." The previous century under British rule had taught Marylanders the divisiveness and inherent brutality of an enforced state religion.

It should be noted, however, that in the 1830s and '40s, remarkable attempts were being made by Protestants in an outreach to Catholics. All of them centered around the construction of a new church building (1846-1847) for St. Aloysius parish in Leonardtown. Aleck Loker has described this outreach as showing "surprising ecumenical tone."[19] Edwin Beitzell noted that "The land for the new church was given by Mr. and Mrs. James T. Blackistone, members of the Episcopal Church, which was part of their

---

15 Gough, "Debating Society" 177.
16 Gough, "Debating Society" 176.
17 Gough, "Debating Society" 180.
18 Gough, "Debating Society" 167.
19 Loker, *Leonardtown* 50.

estate, Rose Hill.[20] Margaret Fresco notes further that James T. Blackistone married Ann Thomas in 1840, whose father, Dr. William Thomas (of "Cremona") deeded Rose Hill to his daughter in 1847.[21] Henry G. S. Key (Episcopalian) gave to St. Aloysius the clay from which the bricks were to be made[22] and, as Gough quotes from the *Beacon*, "otherwise aided materially in the building of the church."[23] Capt. Ben Foxwell (a Methodist) gave a $20 gold piece towards the building of the new St. Aloysius.[24] It's almost as if these Leonardtown Protestants remembered the religious persecution of the previous century and were saying, "We're sorry."

2. Education

In addition to their interest in a good debate, our "movers and shakers" lit a second candle in Leonardtown, and that was for public education. As Gough writes, "In an era when there was little formal education, they were the heralds of education."[25] As a concern, however, public education *per se* may have been a latecomer, owing much of its existence to the Census of 1850, a good dozen years after the RR&DS had held its first meeting.

By the time of that 1850 census, Gough writes, there were only twenty-four "primary" (elementary) schools in St. Mary's County, and beyond that "a uniform state system of public schools did not come into existence in Maryland until 1865"[26]–that is, until just after the Civil War.

Articles have been written about small private schools, many of them Catholic, often held in a private home, but such schools were short-lived,

---

20 Beitzell, Edwin W. *The Jesuit Missions of St. Mary's County, Maryland*. 2nd ed. Abell, MD: sponsored E.W. Beitzell; sponsored by St. Mary's County Bicentennial Commission, 1976. 198. Print. Hereafter cited as Beitzel, *Jesuit Missions*. Gough elaborates further by noting that other parts of the Rose Hill plantation were given to the old St. Mary's Academy. (Gough email to Father Rory T. Conley of 26 May 2012; also received by Janet Haugaard).

21 Fresco, Margaret. *Marriages and Deaths, St. Mary's County, Maryland, 1634-1900*. Ridge, MD: M.K. Fresco, 1982. 26. Print. Hereafter cited as Fresco.

22 Gough, "Debating Society" 169. However, Beitzell credits Vincent Camalier with providing the clay. Beitzell, *Jesuit Missions* 198.

23 Gough, "Debating Society" 169 n1.

24 Gough, "Debating Society" 169.

25 Gough, "Debating Society" 162.

26 Gough, "Debating Society" 166.

and they were not free.[27] St. Mary's County fared badly: there would be no public high school at all until 1927. George King, a member of the RR&DS as well as editor of the *St. Mary's Beacon*, was outraged by what the Census of 1850 revealed, and he made certain to bring the matter to his readers' attention in the *Beacon* issue of April 21, 1853:

> Do our good people know what a miserable figure St. Mary's County cuts in the census returns (1850) on the score of education? They can't have noticed it else we are sure we would have some demonstration on the subject before this. Let us give a few of the figures. The total white population of the county is 6,223 allowing one third of this number to be children (a small estimate perhaps) there remains an adult white population of 4,149. Out of this number the census has it 1,855 or half cannot read or write!! . . . Saint Mary's is the place of ignorance par excellence! . . . We are sure these returns are erroneous–we would certainly be loath to believe them accurate. But there they stand published–in large as life like letters they confront the reader as part of the accurate return of the official census of the United States–and as such are scattered over the country and world to our discredit, our reproach, our disgrace! Citizens of St. Mary's! How like you the aspect in which your beloved County is held up to the world![28]

Actually, a public school system had been established in Maryland during the colonial period when George I was king not only of England but of all her colonies. As Roy Guyther reported in his 1992 *Charlotte Hall School*, the year when public schools were first established was 1723. Maryland's colonial Assembly stipulated that there was to be a free school in all of the twelve counties, as close to the geographic center of each as possible, and with facilities for pupils who needed to board.

In 1774, shortly before the Revolutionary War, the colonial Assembly in Annapolis revisited the issue and decided to consolidate the free schools of the Southern Maryland Counties–Charles, St. Mary's, and Prince George's– and erect one free school, a boarding institution for boys, at Cool Springs, in

---

27 Beitzell, Edwin."Early Schools of Southern Maryland." *Chronicles of St. Mary's*, Vol. 5 (March 1957). 32-33, 35, 36. Print.

28 Gough, "Debating Society" 166.

northern St. Mary's County. Each of the three Southern Maryland counties was to supply seven trustees.[29]

The colonial Assembly in Annapolis further stipulated that this school at Cool Springs was to be named the Charlotte Hall School, an unctuous tip of the hat to Charlotte, wife of King George III, the English monarch whom the colonists detested and against whom they would wage a revolutionary war in less than two years' time. The school–for somewhat older boys–opened in January of 1797, and the initial curriculum included English, French, Latin, Greek, grammar, writing, and mathematics.[30]

The curriculum at Charlotte Hall also encouraged debate, and to this end, the school's Washington Society was founded in 1797, during the school's first year of operation. (After the Civil War it was re-named the Washington and Stonewall Literary Society.) Roy Guyther, the school's historian, writes that debate "train[ed] students to analyze issues, to respond to other points of view, and to talk on their feet."[31] Did this boyhood training of future men have any effect on the founding of Leonardtown's Reading Room and Debating Society in the late 1830s? Possibly.

At the back of his 1992 volume on Charlotte Hall's history, Guyther has listed the surnames of all the students who ever attended this public

---

[29] Guyther, Roy. *Charlotte Hall School 1774-1976*. Charlotte Hall, MD: Charlotte Hall School Alumni Association, 1992. 3-4. Print. Hereafter cited as Guyther.

However, there had been a prior attempt in 1695 to establish free schools in Maryland–presumably for white males only. A manual by the Maryland Department of Education explains: "The General Assembly, in 1695, assessed a tax on the export of furs to raise funds for these schools. . . . Yet, only one school was founded—King William's School (later St. John's College) in Annapolis. In 1717, another financing act taxed importation of Irish Catholic servants and Negro slaves to support public education (Chapter 10, Acts of 1717)." "Origin & Functions." *Maryland Manual 1996-1997 State Department of Education*, Volume 187, Page 237. Web. 13 May 2022 <https://msa.maryland.gov/megafile/msa/speccol/sc2900/sc2908/000001/000187/html/am 187--237.html>. Thus, the 1717 public-schools act was to be funded by taxes on the "importation" (not used in the bill, but reflects the fact that these taxes were commercial in nature, to be contrasted with the immigration of people) of "Irish Servants being Papists and Negroes." *Proceedings and Acts of the General Assembly, October 1720-1723*, Volume 34, Page 388. 3 Nov. 1722. Maryland State Archives . Web. 13 May 2022. <https://msa.maryland.gov/megafile/msa/speccol/sc2900/sc2908/000001/000034/html/am34--389.html>.

Throughout this chapter, there are numerous references to records provided by the Maryland State Archives or the MSA, and each should be read as including: "Courtesy of the Maryland State Archives."

[30] Guyther 5.

[31] Guyther 31.

boarding school, from 1797 to 1976 (although dates are not provided). Nevertheless, several of the listed surnames are the same as those listed by Gough at the end of his long article on the RR&DS. This correspondence of names does not mean that the families were exactly the same, but it does suggest that Leonardtown's "movers and shakers" undoubtedly knew of the curriculum at Charlotte Hall and were impressed that their male cousins, nephews, and sons were learning to take sides in an argument and debate a topic cogently.[32] According to the research of Margaret Fresco, it appears that (Dr.) Joseph F. Shaw–a friend and Seminary ally of James T. Blackistone–had gone to Charlotte Hall,[33] as one day would George Blackistone, the youngest son of James T. Blackistone.[34]

Actually, the RR&DS can be seen as Leonardtown's own version of the nineteenth-century "lyceum" movement. Unlike the travelling "chautauquas" which generally took place *after* the Civil War (see Chapter 9-A, fn 13), town-centered lyceums were enormously popular in the three decades *before* the Civil War. In some American towns, a lyceum even had its own building–witness that of Leonardtown's RR&DS. To these lyceums–very often in the North and Midwest–came well-known men who spoke on science or gave public readings from their own published works.

In Northern towns, pre-Civil War abolitionists spoke against slavery, and–for the first time–American women felt emboldened enough to stand on a public platform and speak not only about their right to own property but also their right to vote.

3. Literature and Science

In the years before education became a concern for the RR&DS, the entire emphasis–as expressed in the founding "Articles of Incorporation"– had been on the "promotion of literature and science and the security and protection of the library and other property belonging to the organization."[35]

---

32 See Appendix A for County surnames that are identical in the lists of both Gough and Guyther.

33 Fresco 264.

34 Fresco 340. On November 7, 1881, Col. James T. Blackistone died in Baltimore. *The Aegis and Intelligencer*. Bel Air, Md. Nov. 11, 1881.

35 Gough, "Debating Society" 162.

In short, a library. Gough not only describes the various locations occupied by the RR&DS but also provides the number of its holdings as well. By 1853–about fifteen years after its founding–this library held two hundred and fifty volumes, a decent number for a library, especially considering that it was the only one in town. By 1870, the RR&DS library could boast eight hundred volumes, and by 1879, over two thousand.[36]

During his lifetime, philanthropist Andrew Carnegie established three thousand libraries in the United States, Canada, Great Britain, and the West Indies. In 1909, Francis V. King, then editor of Leonardtown's *Beacon* (and also a mildly affronted member of the RR&DS), decided to set the record straight and expressed himself in print:

> We read in the papers great brag of libraries founded by rich men in different cities and towns but right here in Leonardtown is one of the oldest and best libraries in the country, built up by contributions of generations of our citizens. We have several thousand good books and they represent not the benefaction of any one man but the small monthly contributions of generations of St. Mary's Countians who started their library before Carnegie's father was born.[37]

Finally, the RR&DS's Articles of Incorporation had specified "promotion of literature and science." But, what literature? And which science?

Possibilities: Benjamin Franklin's work in electricity had been well known since before the Revolutionary War, and now the geological theories of both Louis Agassiz and Charles Lyell were commanding attention. Lyell himself had become a good friend of Charles Darwin after the return of the *Beagle* in 1836. But that the works of these scientists were included in the library is by no means certain.

However, the readership of the RR&DS was made up of men who were remarkably well-educated, either privately, or at Charlotte Hall, or at St. Omer (in French Flanders; see Chapter 2-E-3, fn 38). As adults, such men continued to be well-read. As archivist Carol Moody has expressed their choice of reading material, "The books were not about Maryland,

---

36 Gough, "Debating Society" 163, 176.
37 Gough, "Debating Society" 170.

but all the subjects educated men were supposed to know about in the 19th century."[38] A good number of the men were lawyers and judges. As one might expect from such judicially inclined members, the emphasis was on providing balance of subject-matter in the books chosen for the RR&DS's ever-expanding bookshelves. In his comprehensive write-up of the RR&DS, for example, Gough noted that John Campbell's *Lives of the Lord Chancellors and Keepers of the Great Seal of England* (in ten volumes) was a recent acquisition,[39] as were subscriptions to four English quarterlies, among which was the highly esteemed *Blackwood's*. *Blackwood's Magazine*, a British journal that published from 1817 to 1980, could be expected to have held the same anti-slavery position as did Parliament. But at the same time, the RR&DS was also subscribing to Albert Bledsoe's *Southern Review*, a states'-rights journal founded in 1863 by a well-educated colonel in the Confederate army.

In addition to scientific works, what literature might the men have purchased for their library? It appears that we will never know for certain, but novelists–both British and American–abounded in the nineteenth century.

In addition to well-publicized trips to America made by Frances Trollope and Charles Dickens, much-admired British writers of the mid-nineteenth century included not only Dickens but also Anthony Trollope, William Makepeace Thackeray, and Charlotte **Brontë** (whose work had been preceded by Jane **Austen**'s first novel, published just before 1800).[40]

American writers were increasingly confident in their voice, and after the early productions of James Fennimore Cooper and Washington Irving, popular writers–who might well have been represented on the RR&DS's bookshelves–were Ralph Waldo Emerson, Henry David Thoreau, Nathaniel Hawthorne, Walt Whitman, Herman Melville, and, later, Mark Twain. For writers with a Southern voice, there were books by Edgar Allan Poe and

---

38 Moody, Carol; St. Mary's County Historical Society. Email received by Janet Haugaard, 9 May 2013.

39 Gough, "Debating Society" 174.

40 Both Austen and Brontë, however, took pains not to use a feminine name: Austen's novel was written by "A Lady"; and Charlotte Brontë used her own initials but converted them into the masculine name of Currer Bell.

John Pendleton Kennedy. As yet, with the exception of Emily **Dickinson** and her poetry, none of these popular American writers was a woman.

According to Gough, the *Beacon* reported in 1878 that an appropriation had been made for all books that needed re-binding to be rebound.[41] We assume that this was done, but as the century turned and America entered the Great War, there was less and less interest in debating societies such as the RR&DS and more and more interest in the social and visible aspects of becoming modern: for example, cars, usually referred to as "machines."

In 1952, the RR&DS held its last meeting and decided to give its holdings–roughly two thousand books–to the new Leonardtown Memorial Library. The RR&DS, now quite moribund, met for the last time on December 4th. Only a few months before, those few who were interested in the County's history had formed the St. Mary's County Historical Society. By 1954, librarian Eloise Pickrell wrote in the *Chronicles of St. Mary's* that the books of the defunct RR&DS "are now housed in the St. Mary's County Memorial Library."[42]

Yet today's Leonardtown library has none of the RR&DS's books, and there is a puzzling confusion over what may have happened to them. The RR&DS's "Articles of Incorporation" had covered individual responsibilities of its elected members, and Article 8 had been titled "Duties of the Librarian":

> It shall be the duty of the librarian to keep a register of all books, magazines and newspapers belonging to the library, and to preserve the same in good order, safe keep all papers deposited in the library, report as to its condition at the expiration of his term of office, and faithfully perform the duties required of the librarian by the 23rd by law.[43]

But even this list or "register" no longer exists, and one hesitates to think what those old RR&DS books might now be worth: 2,000 strong, and some of them perhaps first editions. Out of the 2,000 books, only one (in two volumes) still remains and is carefully preserved at the Historical Society

---

41 Gough, "Debating Society" 176.
42 Gough, "Debating Society" 165.
43 St. Mary's County Historical Society: Edwin W. Beitzell Collection; 1985.002.0164.

in Leonardtown. It is Boswell's *Life of Johnson*, including also Boswell's *A Journal of a Tour to the Hebrides*, edition of 1857.

C. THE POWER OF THE PENS

1. Quest for a National Identity

One item remains for discussion because it points not only to tensions expressed by Americans in their relations to Great Britain, but perhaps also to incipient tensions between North and South in the new United States. That is, the men of the RR&DS might also have discussed Noah Webster's quite revolutionary volume on spelling–spelling that was aggressively American in style, rather than British (for example, "color" instead of "colour"). Webster, a schoolmaster and Yale graduate, Class of 1778, had put out in 1783 what was known colloquially as *Webster's Blue-Backed Speller*.[44] In today's parlance, the speller was "a hit," appealing to America's new nationalism and the invigorating upside-down-ness of its recent release from Great Britain. Webster claimed that by 1837 his book had sold *fifteen million* copies, and surely some of these would have come to Leonardtown.

Noah Webster, however, saw beyond the relatively minor question of spelling. In the 1958 "Introductory Essay" to Webster's work, Henry Steele Commager enjoyed quoting from a preface written by Webster himself as far back as 1803:

> This country must in some future time be as distinguished by the superiority of her literary improvements, as she is already by the liberality of her civil and ecclesiastical constitutions. Europe is grown old in folly, corruption and tyranny. For America in her infancy to adopt the maxims of the Old World would be to stamp the wrinkles of decrepit old age upon the bloom of youth, and to plant the seeds of decay in a vigorous constitution.[45]

Again, the problem went beyond simple spelling. In this same "Introductory Essay," Commager wrote that "A nation needs not only

---

44 The proper title was *A Grammatical Institute of the English Language: Part 1*.

45 Commager, Henry Steele. Preface "Schoolmaster to America." 1831. Webster, Noah. *Noah Webster's American Spelling Book With an Introductory Essay by Henry Steele Commager*. USA: Teachers College, Columbia University, 1962. 1-2. Print. Hereafter, cited as Commager.

a common language; it needs, even more, a common past, and a sense of that past."[46] This was something that the thirteen disparate American colonies seemed *not* to share. Commager continues:

> How does a country without a past–without, in any event, a common past– provide itself with a usable past, or with a substitute for it? How does a country without history, traditions, legends, or symbols create them? And how does it find substitutes for those institutions and symbols which customarily served to unify Old World peoples: the Monarchy, the Aristocracy, the Church, the Army, the University, and others?[47]

The first solution to this problem of no "common past" was to write about whatever was familiar or personally fascinating to the author, be it the Manhattan of early Dutch colonists (Washington Irving), or the Indians of the frontier and upstate New York (James Fennimore Cooper). The earlier experiences of (white men) being second-class citizens in England's first-class world were rapidly disappearing. For the first time, as we have seen, Americans were being invited not only to imagine new possibilities for themselves but to appreciate whatever in their background was already uniquely American, not British.

A second solution to the problem of no common national background was to open oneself to the emotionalism known throughout England and Europe as Romanticism. The earlier, strong statements of both the Declaration of Independence and the American Constitution now became an impervious wall against which writers could bounce their Romantic forays into the non-intellectual and mysterious. In doing so, they were delving into different forms of experience.

These new American writers could (and sometimes did) claim that they were only passing on what had supposedly come to them–quite accidentally, not by reasoning–but instead from sources perceived as valid as Reason itself. For example, in 1809, Washington Irving published a "manuscript" history of Manhattan which he said was–accidentally–discovered among

---

46 Commager 9.
47 Commager 10.

the left-behind papers of a traveler named Diedrich Knickerbocker. In 1833, Baltimorean Edgar Allan Poe wrote an emotional tale of a ghostly shipwreck and a manuscript that had been placed in a bottle and then tossed into a "whirlpool." And, in 1850, Nathaniel Hawthorne described in loving detail his vision of what an embroidered scarlet letter ("A" for Adultery) actually looked like; he wrote that it had been found–by accident– in a pile of "heaped-up rubbish."

In other words, Truth (with a capital T) was now regarded as residing not only in the dictates of Reason but equally so in the Romantic with its admiration for the mysteries and coincidences of personal experience.

Irving, Hawthorne, and Poe were not the only ones to base their writings on mysteries suggested by the accidents of history and experience. For example, John Pendleton Kennedy based his 1838 novel about St. Inigoes and St. Mary's City on the (yet again, accidental) discovery of "a sadly tattered and decayed [manuscript] volume–unbound, without beginning and without end, coated with the dust which had been gathering on it. . . . It lay in the state of rubbish, in an old case, where many documents of the same kind had been consigned to the same oblivion."[48] These documents, Kennedy wrote, were records of Lord Baltimore's Provincial Council, laying bare the Calverts' ambitions for a colony that was not only a haven for persecuted English Catholics but equally a society that was tolerant of Protestants.

2. Monument No. 1: Plymouth Rock

Thus, as newly minted Americans looked back over their brief history, they began to look for what Commager would one day describe as an essential element in a new nation: "a sense of a [common] past," or, as he also put it, "How does a country without history, traditions, legends, or symbols create them?"

It didn't take long for New England to create a symbol: Plymouth Rock. Just south of Boston, in the little town of Plymouth, New Englanders

---

[48] Kennedy, John Pendleton. *Rob of the Bowl: A Legend of St. Inigoe's*. 1838. Ed. William S. Osborne. New Haven, Conn.: College & University Press (1965) 12. Print. Hereafter, cited as Kennedy, *Rob of the Bowl*.

erected a protective fence around the granite rock believed to be the spot where the Pilgrim colonists had first stepped ashore in 1620. More was to come: in 1832, a Pilgrim descendant, James Thatcher, published his openly adulatory *History of the Town of Plymouth*.

Plymouth Rock, however, was problematic. While it was handy in teaching schoolchildren about the first English settlers, too often the Pilgrims of 1620 were (and still are) confused with the later Puritans of 1630. Both groups were Protestant, but there the similarity ends.

The Pilgrims of 1620 were Separatists who wished to completely "separate" from the Church of England (Anglican), but the Puritans of 1630 wished to stay within the Church, take it over, and "purify" it.

Pilgrims came ashore at Plymouth in 1620 and are remembered today for the following: Thanksgiving; Governor William Bradford; and Native Americans, Samoset and Squanto.

However, the Puritans who settled the 1630 Massachusetts Bay colony in Boston and Salem: owed their loyalty to Governor John Winthrop; believed in Calvinist theology; expelled both Roger Williams and Anne Hutchinson from the colony; and conducted witchcraft trials in Salem.

In addition to the confusion which Plymouth Rock unwittingly created between Pilgrims and Puritans, the Rock was also pointedly Protestant, thereby making it problematic for other religious groups, such as Quakers and Catholics. More importantly, Plymouth Rock was located "up north" in New England, perhaps signaling what was perhaps the first North-South divide in political and social relations in post-Revolutionary America.

By 1832, when James Thatcher wrote his book on Plymouth Rock, two hundred years had elapsed in which distinct cultures had developed locally up and down the Eastern seaboard. In Maryland, one of these with a distinctive culture–a Catholic culture–was St. Mary's County.

3. St. Mary's City and John Pendleton Kennedy

John Pendleton Who? John Pendleton Kennedy was a Baltimore-trained lawyer who nevertheless found the law "crabbed, unamiable and indigestible."[49] He graduated from Baltimore College in 1812, immediately went to fight at the Battle of Bladensburg in the War of 1812, and was admitted to the Maryland state bar in 1816. For relief from "indigestible" law, he turned to history–Southern history–and produced three books about the South (two of them novels) in that decade of the 1830s. An inheritance from an uncle enabled him to give up law completely, but that legal training had served him well as a Federalist member of Maryland's House of Delegates in the early 1820s and, later, as a Representative to Congress from 1838 to 1845.

Kennedy went on to be elected Speaker of Maryland's House of Delegates (1846 to 1847) and in the mid-1850s served as Secretary of the Navy in the Cabinet of President Millard Fillmore. In 1850, he was elected Provost of the University of Maryland, and in 1866, he was made president of the Board of Trustees of the recently founded Peabody Institute in Baltimore. In his late sixties, he was elected a Fellow of the Academy of Arts and Sciences and also received an honorary Doctor of Laws from Harvard.

A Whig in politics, in religion, Kennedy was Protestant (either Episcopalian or Presbyterian, depending on one's source). Yet his third and final novel, *Rob of the Bowl*, was a tribute to a Catholic: it was a tribute to Lord Baltimore and his long-ago experiment in religious tolerance at the little 1634 colony in St. Mary's City.

That experiment, Kennedy now realized, had foreshadowed the First Amendment of the Bill of Rights, enacted only forty-nine years before he wrote his novel: "Congress shall make no law respecting an establishment of religion, or prohibiting the free exercise thereof . . . ."

4. Monument No. 2: A School for Religious Tolerance

If James Thatcher published and put forward Plymouth Rock as a binding symbol for Americans, John Pendleton Kennedy did the same with *Rob of the Bowl*, his 1838 novel that looked back at Lord Baltimore's plan for religious tolerance. Thus, in one fell swoop Kennedy: (1) provided an early moral value for colonial America–religious tolerance in the St. Mary's

---

[49] Kennedy, *Rob of the Bowl* 6.

City of 1634; and (2) at the same time, pitted a Southern setting against a Northern one.

Rob of the Bowl: A Legend of St. Inigoe's produced a small uproar when Kennedy published his historical novel in 1838. The uproar came from Georgetown, a Catholic college (later, university) in Washington, D.C. The college was Jesuit and included a debating (or "Philodemic") society, established as recently as 1830. Once the men of this youthful debating society at Georgetown College read Kennedy's novel, they were visibly stung, and their overriding emotion was one of Southern embarrassment:

> Why are we so late in the proud ceremonial of this day? Why so far behind our brethren in Massachusetts in testifying veneration for the founders of this time-honored community?[50]

This "time-honored community" was, of course, St. Mary's City, which Kennedy had actually visited and described in his emotional–and Romantic–introduction to *Rob of the Bowl*.

Because of the publicity, the novel would most likely have been read by James T. Blackistone and his friends at the RR&DS in Leonardtown. Not that it is a good book: in fact, it is tiresome reading due to Kennedy's insistence on trying to re-create English dialogue from the 1600s. But Kennedy had already written *Horse-Shoe Robinson*, a best-seller about the South during the period of the Revolutionary War. Well researched, that 1835 novel dealt with the final years of the Revolutionary War in South Carolina, an area in which insurgent Southerners aligned themselves against other Southerners who were "Tory"–that is, pro-British. Kennedy's full title for his popular work was *Horse-Shoe Robinson: A Tale of the Tory Ascendancy*. It went through an astounding four editions in one year, and in 1836 was adapted for a stage performance in New York City.

---

[50] Fausz, J. Frederick. *Monument School of the People: A sesquicentennial history of St. Mary's College of Maryland, 1840-1990*. St. Mary's City, Md.: St. Mary's College of Maryland; 1st Ed., 1990. 29. Print. Hereafter cited as Fausz. See also Beitzell, *Jesuit Missions* 171: "The Philodemic Society of Georgetown College inaugurated in 1842 the celebration of Forefathers Day by a pilgrimage to the cradle of the Colony. The event took place on May 10th . . . ."

On the strength of Kennedy's reputation, therefore, readers were eager to pick up *Rob of the Bowl*–not the least because of its revealing sub-title: *A Legend of St. Inigoe's*.

St. Inigoe's? St. Inigoe's! Catholics at Georgetown College instantly spotted St. Inigoe's–in St. Mary's County–as having been the center of Jesuit activity in the olden days of colonial Maryland. Moreover, Catholicism was now enjoying a resurgence, an emboldening of missionary work, all of it owed to Pope Pius VII and his lifting (in 1814) of the earlier papal ban against Jesuit activity.

The time was now ripe for a remarkable confluence of social forces at work in and around Leonardtown. Laid out chronologically, we see the following:

1797	Charlotte Hall School established, along with its debating society;
1830	Debating Society ("Philodemic") also established at Georgetown College;
1832	New courthouse built in Leonardtown;
1832	*Swallow Barn* ("A Sojourn in the Old Dominion") by John P. Kennedy;
1832	*History of the Town of Plymouth*, by James Thatcher;
1835	*Horse-Shoe Robinson* ("A Tale of the Tory Ascendancy") by J.P. Kennedy;
1838	*Rob of the Bowl* ("A Legend of St. Inigoes") by J.P. Kennedy;
1836-1839	St. Mary's Reading Room and Debating Society established;
1839	*Leonard Town Herald* promises not to produce "angry feeling" in readers;
1840	Three men of St. Mary's County travel to Annapolis to establish a public seminary for girls, operated on principles of religious tolerance, and to be governed by

	trustees of three faiths: Catholic, Episcopal, and Methodist;
1842	Georgetown's debating society makes the first of many "pilgrimages" to St. Mary's City;
1846	St. Aloysius (Catholic) is re-built with contributions from Episcopalians and Methodists; and
1850	Federal census points to relative lack of education in St. Mary's County.

James T. Blackistone, a lawyer, was captivated by what he had read in *Rob of the Bowl*–as were William Coad (of Cherry Fields Plantation) and Joseph Shaw of Charlotte Hall, a physician-farmer who had graduated from both the Charlotte Hall School and the medical school at the University of Pennsylvania. All three were Whigs, but of the three, apparently only Blackistone was a member of Leonardtown's RR&DS. Blackistone was Episcopalian, as was Shaw. Coad was Catholic.

What transpired next can only be conjectured, but Frederick Fausz has hazarded a good guess in his history of St. Mary's College, particularly Chapter Two. According to Fausz, a reliable legend has it that James T. Blackistone, William Coad, and Joseph Shaw met at Coad's Cherry Fields Plantation sometime in 1839 and planned a historic memorial for the freshly recognized–and reverenced–St. Mary's City. By 1839, the City itself was now quite deserted, its only two buildings being Trinity Episcopal Church and the just-built plantation of Dr. John Brome. Aside from that, there was nothing. Unlike Plymouth Rock up in Massachusetts, a memorial to Maryland's past glory could not be a hefty slab of granite, as no rocks were to be found in the marshy sands of St. Mary's City. Did the three men then possibly consider a huge statue of Governor Leonard Calvert on horseback, urging the citizens of his 1634 colony to "play fair" in matters of religion?

Conjecture suggests that while a statue of Calvert might have been tempting, what the three men finally decided on was a *living* monument, a school that would carry out Lord Baltimore's vision of religious tolerance. It would succeed where–for political reasons–Lord Baltimore's plan had finally been forced to fail. It must be built right atop St. Mary's City, the very ground where the Calverts' little colony had once stood. In deference to the City, it would be called St. Mary's Female Seminary ("seminary" being an older name for "school" or "academy"). The proposed seminary would be financially accessible, that is, public, and it would be for girls only, a sister institution to Charlotte Hall. Unlike other, short-lived private schools in the area, the seminary would not introduce "parlor arts" for young ladies but instead present an academic curriculum similar to that of a boys' school. As with Charlotte Hall, the emphasis was to be on academics, not gentility.

Generations of girls would later giggle at the founding legislation which specified that as "the mothers of future generations" they were to instill in their children the "education and early impressions at a place so well calculated to inspire affection and attachment to our native State."[51] Giggles aside, however, it is true that mothers are indeed the ones who send subliminal messages to their small children: either to distrust those of another religion or to put up with them, thereby practicing a religious tolerance. A hundred years later, Rodgers and Hammerstein would encode this problem of early, supper-table prejudice in "South Pacific":

> You've got to be taught, before it's too late,
> Before you are six, or seven, or eight,
> To hate all the people your relatives hate –
> You've got to be carefully taught.©[52]

The girls of St. Mary's Female Seminary of both elementary and high school age, were to live together in one big building and enjoy studying, eating, and playing together. In a relaxed setting, they would learn not to demonize each other's religion. The precepts of their particular religious denomination would be taught to them only by a teacher of that same faith. Grace before meals would be required, and the girls would also be required to attend church on Sunday. Episcopalians had only to cross the Seminary driveway to attend Trinity (Episcopal) Church, but Catholics and Methodists were taken by buggy or carriage up to Leonardtown where they would attend either St. Aloysius Church (Catholic) or St. Paul's (Methodist).

---

51 Fausz 31.

52 *South Pacific*. Music by Richard Rodgers. Lyrics by Oscar Hammerstein II. Book by Oscar Hammerstein II and Joshua Logan. Adapted from *Tales of the South Pacific* by James Michener. New York. 1949. Performance.

Strict care was to be taken in the hiring of teachers from the three denominations, similar to the system of quotas already required on the Board of Trustees. At the outset, the Board was made up of a mixture of thirteen Catholics, Episcopalians, and Methodists, the three white denominations represented in the County at that time. By 1904, the total number of Trustees was raised by the Maryland legislature to fifteen, and Methodists–along with Catholics and Episcopalians–now numbered five.

Over time, these Seminary Trustees, carefully controlled by quota, would speak of their "seat" on the Board, and when, say, a Catholic died, his "seat" was given to another Catholic. The men were all from St. Mary's County and generally from the areas of Leonardtown and Chaptico.[53] This system of quotas survived for a hundred years, until 1941, when Governor Herbert O'Conor did away with the quota requirement, broadened the scope of the Board to include women, and, mercifully, required that henceforth Trustee minutes were to be typed.

But this is to anticipate, and we need to return to the proposed establishment of a girls' school in 1840. In January of that year, three men–Blackistone, Coad, and Shaw, all of them newly elected delegates to the Maryland legislature–set off for Annapolis to present their idea for a girls' boarding school to the General Assembly. Because the state of Maryland was still in the Depression that began in 1837 (aka as the Panic of 1837)–and also $15 million in debt–the three men had agreed to propose that money for both the land and the construction of the large school in St. Mary's City was to be raised *only* by lottery, without a cent coming from the State. Apparently the three delegates had gone so far as to secure the names of three additional men, all local in St. Mary's County, who had agreed to act as commissioners and be responsible for this lottery gamble: John White Bennett, Cornelius Combs, and Caleb M. Jones.

Historian Fausz has reproduced the "Preamble" to the Act of 1840 in his history of St. Mary's Female Seminary, and it is worth noting that Romantic phrases were now being used in order to entice the general public into buying a lottery ticket: St. Mary's City was being described (probably for

---

53 See Appendix B for Willma Reeves's tribute to these two geographical groups.

the first time) as a *"sacred place,"* "the *ancient capital* of the State, the *sad remains* of which cannot but recall to *mind the transient nature of things sublunary* and the *Melancholy reflection* that nothing now remains but a few mouldering [sic] bricks to point out to the antiquarian the spot where civilization and christianity [sic] were first introduced into our State. . . ."[54]

If the other Delegates to the Assembly had not actually read Kennedy's book about St. Mary's City, they were nonetheless enthusiastic[55] at the prospect of bringing a kind of renaissance to St. Mary's City, benighted and abandoned since shortly before 1700. In 1840, the House passed the bill for the proposed Female Seminary on February 26th, the Senate did so on March 4th, and Governor William Grason signed it into law on March 21st. It took an additional four years to raise the necessary funds, but once cash from the lottery was in hand, the Trustees bought six acres from little Trinity Church in 1844. On August 21st, they deeded the Female Seminary property over to the State of Maryland, thereby assuring its future as a state institution.[56] Shortly thereafter, the Trustees also bought a right-of-way from the edge of the Female Seminary property down the hill to Brome's Landing, the steamboat wharf at St. Mary's City, at that time just about the only viable way of reaching St. Mary's City.

In November of 1845, the Trustees organized themselves into two committees: one to plan for ongoing school governance by the Board; and the other to create operational policies.[57] Two months later, they met again and decided on three overall policies for the new school: (1) it was to have a "liberal" and "extensive" course of study; (2) it was to be affordable; and (3) it was to practice religious tolerance "on the consecrated spot where free toleration of the subject of religion was first promulgated."[58]

---

54 Fausz 31 (emphases added to excerpts).

55 See Fausz 29.

56 Fausz 33. Technically, the sale was made by the Parish of William and Mary, of which Trinity Church is a part.

57 Fausz 34.

58 Fausz 35. Combs, *History* 338.

St. Mary's Female Seminary finally opened its doors in the late Spring of 1846.[59]

It had been a long ride from concept to reality, encompassing a full decade between the mid-1830s and the mid-1840s. As we have seen, by the time *Rob of the Bowl* was published in 1838, the decade had become ripe for the remarkable emergence of social forces outlined earlier: a new generosity of religious viewpoint, generosity of action, and generosity in public education.

All of these forces were a response to what Commager would one day (in the 20th Century) portray as a problem for the new American republic: "How does a country without history, traditions, legends, or symbols create them?"

Thanks to James Thatcher, in 1832, latter-day Pilgrims had created one such symbol at Plymouth Rock, and just six years later, in 1838, thanks to John Pendleton Kennedy, Marylanders found a second symbol in the early religious tolerance at old St. Mary's City.

Better yet (and a far cry from Plymouth Rock up in Massachusetts), the original notion of religious toleration–first promulgated in St. Mary's City– had by now become part of America's new Constitution. And St. Mary's Female Seminary, soon to be created by the State as a living monument, would seek to embody this ideal.

D. The Female Seminary as Living Monument

The title for this chapter is "O Brave New World" largely because it sums up the hopes and aspirations of a colonial people newly freed from the British Empire (yet still inequitable for those bound by legal restrictions, such as Native Americans, slaves, and women). The quotation itself comes from the lips of Miranda, young daughter of Prospero in one of Shakespeare's late plays, *The Tempest*. In full, she exclaims:

---

59 Fausz, 37. When the Seminary was founded, "St. Mary's County had the highest illiteracy rate among white adults in Maryland." Fausz, 28.

Fausz's comprehensive history of St. Mary's College of Maryland includes many photographs.

> O, wonder!
> How many goodly creatures are there here!
> How beauteous mankind is! O brave new world,
> That has such people in't![60]

Miranda, however, is a very young fourteen and for the past decade has lived with her father on a remote island. In fact, she is naïve, and Prospero's response to her optimistic outburst verges on the dry and somewhat sardonic, "'Tis new to thee."[61]

Similarly, James T. Blackistone can be forgiven if he imagined that a school dedicated to religious tolerance could immediately succeed in what Christian theologians call "a sinful world." Born in 1814, Blackistone was only 26–apparently an energetic and enthusiastic 26–when trouble erupted at the new Female Seminary in the very late 1840s. The RR&DS, of which he was almost certainly a co-founder in the late 1830s, had seen to it in their by-laws that "No religious subject shall be discussed by the society." A similar warning was now drawn up for the Female Seminary (of which Blackistone was a founder) when it finally opened for instruction in 1846: "No spirit of proselytism, no clashing of conflicting creeds, or controversial questions of churches shall be permitted within the walls of this institution, an institution founded on the consecrated spot where free toleration on the subject of religion was first promulgated."[62]

But while religious safeguards at the Female Seminary did indeed exist, they failed to deal with the consciences of individual teachers who undoubtedly felt that they were "saving" students from a slippery slope to perdition. For example, Eliza M. Ohr, an Episcopalian and Seminary Principal from 1847 to 1851, was fired by the Trustees when she was caught "loaning

---

60 Shakespeare, William. *The Tempest*. 1610-11. Ed. Barbara Mowat, Paul Werstine, Michael Poston, and Rebecca Niles. Folger Shakespeare Library, August 23, 2021. <http://shakespeare.folger.edu/shakespeares-works/the-tempest>. (5.1.2179-2182). Hereafter cited as *The Tempest*.

61 *The Tempest* (5.1.2183).

62 Fausz 35 (citing Trustee dictum).

and even selling" anti-Catholic literature to students.[63] Trustees soon began to mistrust each other, discovering that although they could indeed "talk the talk" of religious toleration, they could not "walk the walk." Attendance fell off, affecting the school's economic base. Finally in 1857, the Trustees threw up their hands and asked the state legislature to close the state-supported Female Seminary and sell all six acres of its land.

It was beginning to seem as if Lord Baltimore's old hope for religious tolerance in St. Mary's City was going to fail–for the second time.

The Annapolis legislature, however, had other ideas: it refused to close the Seminary, chastised the board for its "perversion" of the founding legislation, and on April 24 of 1858, passed "An Act to Preserve the Existence of the St. Mary's Female Seminary." A scant three weeks later, a completely new Board of Trustees was in place: five Catholics, five Episcopalians, and four Methodists.[64] Their first action, in 1858, was to try to persuade a Baltimore school (Madame Despommier's French and English Academy) to come down to St. Mary's County and merge with the Female Seminary. When that proposal failed, the Trustees resorted to what Fred Fausz describes as "hyperbolic" advertising. That, too, elicited nothing. According to historian and archaeologist Silas Hurry, in 1861, an advertisement ran thirteen times throughout August and September: in the *Daily National Intelligencer* of Washington, D.C., the ad announced that the Seminary building could be *rented out*.[65] This, too, failed to happen.

The question must be asked: why did not the General Assembly let this small boarding school simply die? It was–and still is–far away from any town or city and woefully situated on a dead-end peninsula that does not connect with the Eastern Shore.

---

63 Fausz 40. The Trustees concluded that "the conduct of the Principal in giving [the books] circulation in this school is highly censurable...[and] that it would be exceedingly difficult to select books more calculated to excite *unkind feelings* among the pupils on the subject of religion..." St. Mary's Female Seminary Board of Trustees. *Minutes 1845-1854*. Adopted 8 May 1851. Page 76 (emphasis added). MSA S 231-1, MdHR 12962. Manuscript (handwritten). Gratitude is owed to Claire Lattin (MSA Archivist Trainee) for her initiative in scrutinizing these handwritten ledgers.

64 For names of the original Board plus the Reconstituted Board, see Fausz 153.

65 Hurry, Silas; St. Mary's College of Maryland. Email received by Janet Haugaard, 19 April 2012.

First, the legislature most likely saved St. Mary's Female Seminary because it was an academically oriented school, founded at a time in the nation's history when education was beginning to become a serious concern. St. Mary's was academically in line with the private schools established by the Hart sisters: Almira **Hart** Phelps had established the Patapsco Female Institute in Ellicott City in 1834, and her sister, Emma **Hart** Willard had founded the Troy (New York) Female Seminary back in 1821. The Baltimore Academy of the Visitation (Catholic) was another serious school that the Trustees had investigated while drawing up their original plans. St. Mary's offered an education to girls that had customarily been given only to boys (such as at Charlotte Hall), and the Trustees had set tuition at the Female Seminary at as low a cost as possible. In addition to arithmetic, composition, and grammar, St. Mary's offered courses in mathematics, natural philosophy, Latin, French, algebra, chemistry, geology, astronomy, etc.

St. Mary's spearheading of academics for women is showcased in the 1878 Report by the State Board of Education: natural philosophy (eight students); chemistry (four students); algebra (four students); geometry (four students); botany (four students); rhetoric (10 students); logic (two students); drawing physiology (two students); French (12 students); English literature (two students); and instrumental music (16 students).[66]

What the Female Seminary did *not* offer, however, was a "finishing school" education, designed for girls of the upper (rather than the middle) class. In finishing schools, the overall emphasis was not academic but social: young ladies were taught the "parlor arts" of dancing, drawing, etiquette, running a household of servants, and preparing for entrance into upper-class society at age eighteen. Such an entrance was usually signaled by a "coming out" début or, at the very least, a tea. One wit has described the education of a finishing school as "teaching young girls how to sit in a chair." (Answer: posture erect, ankles crossed, spine not touching the back of the chair.)

---

[66] Fausz 47.

A second reason the legislature saved the school was that the Seminary–this "living monument"–had put Maryland on the map of colonial history, a prestige hitherto claimed chiefly by Northerners. St. Mary's City and its early principle of *religious tolerance* had finally raised Maryland to a place of importance in colonial history. Yet, as elsewhere throughout the United States, there was still institutional racial discrimination, which would persist for another century and beyond. Reflecting in part the "Three-Fifths Clause" of the U.S. Constitution (Article 1, § 2, Cl. 3, in force until repealed in 1868 by § 2 of the 14th Amendment), the Trustees resolved on May 3, 1854, that the carpenters to be employed for the Seminary would be at the rate of "fifty cents for white men and thirty-seven and ½ cents for Negroes."

The Seminary seems to have been closed during the Civil War (1861-1865), although some instruction was perhaps taking place in academic year 1864-65. We know this from textbooks in both mythology and natural philosophy signed and dated by student Lucy Dunbar.[67] In 1864, Whig governor Augustus Bradford bailed the Seminary out financially, as did his successor, Thomas Swann, in 1867.

By 1868, the Seminary was finally re-established, undoubtedly owing to its promise to provide ten full scholarships in exchange for State support. In 1898, the number of legislatively-required scholarships increased to twenty-six, offering a free education to one girl from each Maryland county as well as to one from each legislative district in Baltimore City. By 1933, competitive examinations for the scholarships were advertised in local newspapers by state senators, thus eventually becoming known as "senatorial scholarships." (See Chapter 5-C at fn 18.) These lasted until the 1990s and were often mentioned by the "girls" (now elderly women) who recalled having won a senatorial scholarship, describing it on their questionnaire in 1995. For example, Bertha **Moreland** Kerby, Class of 1920:

> Yes, I had a scholarship. It was the Charles County scholarship. Every county had the right to grant a scholarship to one person. The county paper printed a date for the test for the girls who wanted to try for the scholarship. There were seven

---

[67] Fausz 44.

girls–thank God I received the highest grade and therefore I received the scholarship.[68]

But this is to anticipate. Largely due to the new system of "senatorial scholarships," the Female Seminary was now on firm ground and would remain so for another hundred years.[69] In 1846, it had begun as a school for all grades, from elementary through high school.[70]

Cecilia **Coad** Roberts (daughter of Col. William R. Coad, one of the Female Seminary's three original founders) started at eight years old and recalled her early education in a 1924 conversation with Father John LaFarge.[71]

Similarly, Peggy **Clark** Wetherill, Class of 1927, recalled being sent to the Seminary at age ten and sitting on the floor while Lucy **Lancaster** Maddox (Principal from 1900 to 1923) rocked in a chair nearby and tutored her until she was academically ready for the higher grades.[72]

The original Female Seminary never again had to deal with religious intolerance. For a hundred years–between 1846 and 1948–each day began and ended with prayers that were generally Christian in content but free of denominational input. The Lord's Prayer was required at the evening prayers, which immediately followed study hall. A brief grace was said before each meal: "Bless us, O Lord, & these thy gifts which we are about to receive, through Jesus Christ our Lord"; followed by thanks at the end of the meal: "We give Thee thanks, Almighty Father, for these and all thy benefits,

---

68 Typewritten answers to Questionnaire of Bertha **Moreland** Kerby, Class of 1920, answer to question 24 at p.2. RG 20 Janet Haugaard collection. St. Mary's College of Maryland Archives. Hereafter, cited as Moreland Questionnaire.

69 Fausz, 47. "On a consistent basis between the 1860s and the late 1940s, at least half of the annual student body was attending the school on full scholarship. In 1875, the Trustees' annual report to the General Assembly, required under the legislation of 1868, indicated that thirteen of twenty-three students had all of their expenses paid by scholarships, ten funded by the state allocations to the school, and three provided by the Board from other sources." Fausz, 47.

70 See Fausz at Chapter II, including 34-35.

71 Cecilia **Coad** Roberts was present at the laying of *two* Seminary cornerstones: in 1844 and 80 years later, in 1924, when the burned building was replaced under Ms. France's tenure. LaFarge Collection, Box 25, Folder 3, "Items from My Diary: August 1915 to 1926," Georgetown University Library; pp.19, 17 (of what appears to be a typed transcription of a taped recording, p.8).

72 Interview of Peggy **Clark** Wetherill, Class of 1927, by Janet Haugaard. Recordings on cassette tapes during Reunion Weekend on 14 June 1997 and also on 7 August 1997. RG 20 Janet Haugaard collection. St. Mary's College of Maryland Archives.

through Jesus Christ our Lord." Catholic students ate at a separate table, and on Fridays they were supplied with fish.

Before M. Adele France took over in 1923, there were no Jews, Muslims, or even avowed agnostics at the Female Seminary. The "register containing the rules & bylaws" of the Female Seminary had been destroyed by fire in the family-home of one of the Trustees, but in 1872, the Trustees reconstructed the initial "Rules" and once again wrote out in full ten "Fundamental Rules."[73] For example, the Rule 2nd observed that it was "the duty of every officer of the Institution to check [put a stop to] the introduction or discussion among any of the members of the Institution of such religious subjects as would be calculated to produce unkindness of feeling in a household that ought to be harmoniously united." The Rule 3rd required that each day was to open and close with a brief prayer.[74]

The girls were required to go to church on Sunday, but the choice of denomination was up to them and their parents.

Before the advent of cars, girls going to church in Leonardtown (sixteen miles to the north) were taken there in a horse-drawn wagon. A stable once stood overlooking the river where the little red-brick cottage now stands on the campus. According to College historian Fred Fausz, this stable was "reportedly constructed with bricks from the State House of 1676."[75] In 1911, a carriage and harness were bought "for church going."[76] Trustee Minutes for 1912 specifically mention that horses were rented out from one William Dyer for $1.00.[77] There are also stories of Trustees taking the girls up to Leonardtown in their own family buggies.

---

[73] St. Mary's Female Seminary Board of Trustees. *Minutes*. "Report of Committee on Rules." Preamble. Adopted 17 September 1872. MSA S 231-3, MdHR 12963-2. Manuscript (handwritten). <http://guide.msa.maryland.gov/pages/series.aspx?ID=S231>. See also Fausz 42, 50.

[74] St. Mary's Female Seminary Board of Trustees. *Minutes*. "Report of Committee on Rules." "Organic Rules 'A'." Rule 2nd, Rule 3rd. Adopted 17 September 1872. MSA S 231-3, MdHR 12963-2. Manuscript (handwritten). <http://guide.msa.maryland.gov/pages/series.aspx?ID=S231>. See also Chapter 5-F.

[75] Fausz 37. Fausz further explains that, after the fire of 1924, this stable was converted into a cottage which was re-built, paid for, and then donated to the Female Seminary by the Alumnae Association in 1924. Fausz 68. It has since been re-named the Russell-Lyons House. See Chapter 9-C-1-b, including fn 42.

[76] Fausz 52.

[77] St. Mary's Female Seminary Board of Trustees. *Minutes 1912*. Adopted June 13, 1912. Pages 157-58. MSA S 231-4, MdHR 12964-1. Manuscript (handwritten).

Mildred **Spedden** McDorman (Class of 1914) wrote, "We went to nearby churches of our choice each Sunday (required) in carriages. In freezing weather we bundled up in robes and rode to church in wagons filled with hay. The weather never got cold or blustery enough to keep us home from church."[78]

When interviewed, Bertha **Moreland** Kerby (Class of 1920) confirmed what she had reported in her answers to the questionnaire sent out to alumnae:

> Every girl was obliged to go to church on Sunday. The state hired a gentleman from nearby to take the Catholics to church on Sundays [in Leonardtown] and all the other girls went to Trinity Episcopal Church across from the school. One exception: the Methodist girls were taken to Leonardtown Methodist Church the fourth Sunday of every month.[79]

Once automobiles arrived in significant numbers during the 1920s, church-going became much simpler. Questionnaires mailed out to alumnae in the mid-1990s revealed what "the girls" (now elderly women) remembered from their old Female Seminary days. They remembered that once the church-goers arrived in Leonardtown, Catholic girls went to Mass at St. Aloysius. An alumna who graduated in the late 1940s commented in her 1995 questionnaire, "I always thought we picked up some temporary Catholics as one *did* get a ride to Leonardtown–and a little change of scenery."[80] Other girls attended St. Paul's Methodist Church, and one alumna from the mid-1930s recalled the following:

> On alternate Sundays some of us attended the Methodist church in Leonardtown . . . a small rural church . . . the organist was a little girl of elementary school age. The heat was by a pot belly stove up front . . . the stove was refueled by a young

---

78 Spedden McDorman, Mildred. "Study and Fun at the 'Monument School" *Baltimore Sunday Sun Magazine*. 10 March 1963, 2.

79 Moreland Questionnaire, answer to question 4 at p.1. Additionally, see Interview (by Janet Butler Haugaard on 16 Nov. 1995; transcribed Oct. 2007) of Bertha **Moreland** Kerby, Class of 1920, at p.3. RG 19 SlackWater Oral History Collection and Southern Maryland Folklife Project, SMAO10002. St. Mary's College of Maryland Archives. Hereafter, cited as Moreland Interview.

80 Handwritten answers to Questionnaire of an alumna [name redacted], late 1940s (emphasis in original). RG 20 Janet Haugaard collection. St. Mary's College of Maryland Archives.

boy . . . who, when things were dull, would hustle up and put another log on the stove.[81]

By the time Adele France–with two Master's degrees–became Principal in 1923, the Female Seminary was generally seventh and eighth grades plus the high school. Over time, grades seven and eight were gradually phased out, and Ms. France was able to launch her innovative junior college in 1926. By the mid-1930s, she was able to focus on a junior college that had only four levels: junior and senior years of high school, plus two years of junior college.

Under Adele France, the Seminary was indeed proving its old mandate for religious tolerance, adding two Jews to its original mix of inter-denominational Christians: Eleanor ("Ella") **Klobusicky** Perlman, Class of 1926; and Benjamin Weiner, Class of 1930.

In 1938, a writer from *The National Geographic Magazine* included St. Mary's Female Seminary in his tour of Maryland and met Adele France. Ms. France breezily remarked to her guest, "Our teachers–they're of many creeds–come from everywhere. Girls must worship, but as they like. We would accept Mohammedans or Buddhists. I wish we had some."[82]

When May **Russell**, M.A. became president in 1948, she encouraged young men to attend the junior college and dropped the word "Female" from its name.

Finally, about two decades later, the Seminary-Junior College became a traditional four-year college for the liberal arts (St. Mary's College of Maryland), and Renwick Jackson, Ph.D., its first president in 1968.

E. Turning the Page: Two "Furriners"

We turn now to what can only be called the "educational resolve" of two "furriners" (foreigners, outsiders) who came into St. Mary's County just before the 1920s. See Chapter 7-A for an explanation of "furriner.")

---

81 Helen Boughton, A.A. 1935, quoted in "Remember When? ... at St. Mary's, 50 Years Ago," a Reunion circular for that year.

82 Patric, John. "Roads from Washington," *National Geographic* (July 1938, Vol. 74, No.1): 25. Print.

114

Both Adele France and John LaFarge were born in February of 1880, and both were highly educated. Both suffered physical ailments, but neither allowed personal infirmity to stand in the way of their educational plans. In fact, infirmity may have acted as a spur, perceived simply as the first of many barriers to be overcome.

The work of both Father LaFarge and Ms. France cannot be understood apart from the history of St. Mary's County where they had come to teach and work. For this reason it has been necessary to create a background introduction in the first three chapters, each dealing with the complex web of historical backgrounds in St. Mary's County.

To recapitulate before moving on: Chapter One, "Blood, Sweat, and Brains," introduced readers to the apparent anomaly of an 1840 painting: while black men were welcomed at the 1840 World Anti-Slavery Convention held in London, women–whether black or white–were not. The outrage that this engendered eventually led women to public platforms and protest. Chapter One also included a brief summary of the so-called "Triangular Trade" and its "Middle Passage" which had first brought slavery to all of Great Britain's colonies, including Maryland.

Chapter Two, "Catholics: Exiled in Place," dealt not only with England's Protestant Reformation but also with Lord Baltimore's decision to create a colony of religious tolerance in Maryland, to be governed by his younger brother, Leonard Calvert. Within a few decades, however, England's monarchy changed, and as a result Catholics became *persona non grata* both there and in England's American colonies. The resulting loss of civil liberties–whether in London or Leonardtown–has often been ascribed to the legislature in Annapolis, but this answer has been too easy–even simplistic–and ignorant of English history. To ascribe the Catholic sufferings of St. Mary's County to Annapolis is understandable, but–because Maryland was a mere colony–the real culprit was superpower England. As a result, Catholicism in St. Mary's County had to go underground for several decades. Later, as with other persecuted religions, Catholicism rose again and prospered. St. Mary's County is (and always has been) bedrock Catholic.

And this Chapter Three, "O Brave New World," introduced the reader to the new freedoms–religious among others–won by the Revolutionary War of 1776 against Great Britain. The next eight decades, between the Revolutionary War and the Civil War, were years of cordiality and courtesy (among gentry and bourgeois) in St. Mary's County. They saw the formation of a library and debating society in Leonardtown; they saw the establishment of the first County newspaper; they saw the help that a small town gave to a newly built Catholic church; and they also saw the creation of a state-supported girls' school in St. Mary's City, specifically designed to combat religious intolerance.

We are now ready to turn to the work of both Adele France and John LaFarge as they entered St. Mary's County as "foreigners" shortly before the 1920s.

The Reverend John LaFarge (S.J., B.A., and an M.A. in philosophy) was a Northerner, having grown up in Newport, Rhode Island. Ms. Adele France (B.A., and two M.A. degrees, the first from Washington College, the second from Columbia's Teachers College) was a Southerner who had grown up in Chestertown, Maryland, on the Eastern Shore of Chesapeake Bay.

While a large, uneducated population of black workers was a tacit part of Adele France's upbringing, for John LaFarge, these impoverished descendants of slaves–and their lack of education–came as a shock. It was not until mid-life that he finally learned the role that his own hometown of Newport, Rhode Island had played in transporting those slaves from Africa to the American colonies. And while Adele France understood that Maryland's history of school segregation forbade her from admitting black girls to the public Female Seminary, John LaFarge understood no such race-based impediment and undertook to educate–girls and boys alike, all black–in the Catholic schools that he created specifically for them. This became his mission.

Despite its occupation by despised Union troops during the Civil War, and despite the presence of the Patuxent River Naval Air Station since 1943, a significant portion of today's "white" Maryland remains Southern in its outlook. Politically, it is more progressive than Virginia, its neighbor to the south, immediately across the Potomac River. But memories of perceived injustices die hard, and some don't die at all. Marylanders (primarily white males), particularly those on the Chesapeake peninsula known as St. Mary's County, crossed the Potomac by boat and fought on the side of the Confederate States of America. Memories of the Civil War (known locally as "the War between the States" or even "the War of Northern Aggression") are recalled not only in articles published in the *Chronicles of St. Mary's* (quarterly magazine of the St. Mary's County Historical Society) but also in annual outdoor tributes paid to the memory of those who fought and died in that war.

Adele France's edge was that she was a Southerner. She well understood that there were two St. Mary's Counties: one black, one white. Racism, however, was not her battle.

What concerned Adele France were the limitations that society generally placed on *women*, limitations which girls of school age too often accepted (as had their mothers and grandmothers). At the very least, she wanted her students to become all that they could possibly be, and her mission became that of teaching and encouraging girls during their formative years.

Southern womanhood, however, had for some years been otherwise understood and defined. Al Gough, in his 1992 article on the RR&DS of Leonardtown, called his readers' attention to a brief notice that had run in the *Beacon* for May 27, 1880. The newspaper referenced a Martha Washington Tea Party that had just taken place in the RR&DS's hall, "tastefully ornamented" for the occasion. The stage, it was noted, had "presented a scene of surprising sweetness and beauty." The women at that 1880 Tea Party had chosen a man to speak to them, a man whose views were reassuringly "sound in doctrine":

> The literary feature consisted of an address by Col. Crane, gracefully and even eloquently delivered, on the subject of Woman's sphere. The speaker's conception approximated much nearer the Southern than the Eastern [that is, Northern] ideal of this and put him at once, and naturally enough, in thorough accord with the feelings of his audience.[83]

---

[83] Gough, "Debating Society" 165.

Here, we need to look to John Pendleton Kennedy and his view of girls' education as he expressed it in his three books of the 1830s. Kennedy, in fact, would have agreed with Col. Crane, particularly in the concept of "woman's sphere." He certainly would not have agreed with Messrs. Blackistone, Coad, and Shaw in their 1840 notion of building an academic "Female Seminary." While Kennedy was undoubtedly flattered that his *Rob of the Bowl* had impelled those three young men to build a memorial to Lord Baltimore's notion of religious tolerance, he would most probably have been upset when he learned that the memorial was to be a *girls' school*.

In 1832, Kennedy had published the first of his three books, a series of vignettes describing his brother's plantation home in Virginia *(Swallow Barn; or A Sojourn in the Old Dominion)*. In that book, he described two cousins: Lucy, age 15, and Victorine, one year younger. Kennedy described them warmly as "educated entirely at home, and . . . growing up together in the most confiding mutual affection." He tells us further that "No over-stimulated ambition is likely there to taint the mind with those vices of rivalry which, in schools, often render youth selfish and unamiable, and suggest thoughts of concealment and strategem as aids in the race of preeminence." Kennedy concluded his educational philosophy with the following tableau of the two girls: "They pursue the same studies, and I see them every morning at their tasks, often reading from the same book with their arms around each other's waist."[84]

To sum up and anticipate: John LaFarge's social concern (education for blacks) was not limited to St. Mary's County, and in only a few decades that interest would envelop the entire United States of America. Similarly, Adele France's social concern (the education of young women) would also turn into a national laboratory for "the woman question."

In both cases, there is still much work to be done.

---

[84] Kennedy, John Pendleton. *Swallow Barn; or, A Sojourn in the Old Dominion*. 1832. Baton Rouge and London: Louisiana State University Press,1986. 44-46. Print.

Chapter 4

Head, Heart—and a Horse Named "Morgan"

As foreshadowed in the Introduction and Chapter 3-E, M. Adele France and John LaFarge were what psychologists call "self-starters." Yet both were born with physical problems that would have deterred almost anyone else from what turned out to be the educational work of a lifetime.

A. HEAD AND HEART: ADELE FRANCE

While John LaFarge was stepping aboard that Leonardtown-bound steamer out of Washington in 1911, Adele France was climbing aboard a Washington-bound steamer that would drop her off at Brome's Landing in St. Mary's City. She, too, would be met at 3:00 a.m., in the dead of night, and her trunk would be wheeled by a black employee of St. Mary's Female Seminary up the steep hill to the main building.[1]

---

[1] The Census of 1910 suggests that this was Ernest Barber. Alumna Mildred **Spedden** McDorman (Class of 1914) recalled: "We rode practically all night, from Pier 3 . . . . The steamers, leaving Baltimore at 4:45 PM, arrived at St. Mary's at 3 AM the following day, and Ernest, the school's handyman, met the students at the pier and hauled their luggage to the dormitory by wheelbarrow." **Spedden** McDorman, Mildred. "I remember . . . Study and Fun at the 'Monument School.'" *Baltimore Sunday Sun Magazine*. 10 March 1963. See photo of students at Brome's Wharf.

Female Seminary, St. Marys City.

Today we call this building Calvert Hall, but in 1911–a dozen years before it burned to the ground–it was only two stories high and all the windows had shutters. It was pretty, and looked to be the very essence of what has been called "Plantation Greek." (See photo of main building before 1924 fire.)

Adele had already been teaching at the Seminary for two years and would teach for two more. She would then move on to the Bristol School in Washington for city experience, but whether that was in teaching or administration we do not know.

During her four years at St. Mary's (1909-1913), she was popular with the girls, even though she taught the "hard" courses of math and physics.

Helen Dent, who expected to graduate with the Class of 1914, moaned in a 1912 letter to her mother: "I feel sorry for myself, now that Miss France is coming back because she gives such hard exams."[2] In 1912, Helen Dent also wrote to one of her sisters, indirectly attesting to Adele France's initiative:

> You know we are getting very athletic down here, all of a sudden, and commenced a game of base-ball. But that has gone up into smoke and we are getting up a real basket ball team, which is twice as good. And better still we are going to get the whole out-fit, bloomers, canvas shoes, etc. . . . I really think I have the best team, taken as a whole, because I had first choose [sic], and took the best girls every time. . . . In order to pay for the ball and baskets, each team has to give a play, and charge ten cents admission. And because I had the first choose [sic], I give the first play. Miss France is going to help me with it. She is going to give us a small prize to the one that has the best play.[3]

By the time Adele (and another departing teacher) left the St. Mary's faculty at the end of four years, she was described in the Trustee minutes of June 12, 1913, as one of the two "highly valued teachers."

But Adele was not new to teaching and, in a sense, had actually been doing it most of her young life.

1. Gumption

"Gumption" is a word not often heard these days. According to the dictionary, it means "courage and initiative; enterprise and boldness." It was a value, an attitude toward life which Theodore Roosevelt learned well in his childhood–and then passed on to others. Roosevelt was already a close friend of young John LaFarge's older brother, Grant, and it was Roosevelt who had encouraged John to apply to Harvard. Roosevelt gave his "Strenuous Life" speech on April 10, 1899, the occasion being his appointment as

---

[2] Helen Dent died of appendicitis in her junior year. She was the daughter of Dr. Walter Benjamin Dent who had married Eleanor Grace Blackistone in 1884. Dent, Helen. Six-page handwritten letter addressed to "Mama" dated "Monday" [1912] at p.6. RG 20 Janet Haugaard collection. St. Mary's College of Maryland Archives.

[3] Dent, Helen. Nine-page handwritten letter addressed to "Nellie" [her sister] dated "Sat. Night" [1912] at pp. 2, 5. RG 20 Janet Haugaard collection. St. Mary's College of Maryland Archives.

Assistant Secretary of the Navy. This was one year before charging up San Juan Hill (in Cuba) and two years before becoming president in 1901.

Both Adele and John were in college at the time of this widely reported speech and were no doubt impressed: young John LaFarge and the equally young Adele France were both beset by physical problems, and for each of them, Roosevelt's 1899 speech on "The Strenuous Life" would have become a philosophy for dealing with genuine physical impediments. It opens:

> . . . I wish to preach [T.R. wrote], not the doctrine of ignoble ease, but the doctrine of the strenuous life, the life of toil and effort, of labor and strife; to preach that highest form of success which comes, not to the man who desires mere easy peace, but to the man who does not shrink from danger, from hardship, or from bitter toil, and who out of these wins the splendid ultimate triumph.[4]

Theodore Roosevelt knew well what he was talking about. Biographers stress his asthma, his sickliness in childhood—both of which were impediments that his father had refused to accept. Young Theodore did get into Harvard, but his preparatory schooling had all taken place at home and had been overseen by his father, who also insisted on a strict regimen of daily exercise.

Roosevelt may well have had men–not women–in mind when he preached "the strenuous life." But it was a call which Adele France obviously took to heart. She seems to have been born with both "head and heart" (intellect and empathy). Like Roosevelt, she had "gumption," a necessary component of "the strenuous life," and she would use it on behalf of the girls and young women who came to St. Mary's Female Seminary for an education. As a Southerner, she already knew that, in Maryland at that time, blacks could not be educated at a state-run high school in St. Mary's County. Instead, she focused on a cause that was–just barely–more socially acceptable: education for women. But she wanted it to be education with teeth in it.

---

[4] "The Strenuous Life." *Wikipedia.* Web. 17 August 2021. https://en.wikipedia.org/wiki/The_Strenuous_Life>.

St. Mary's Female Seminary, a state-supported school for girls, had been founded back in 1840. There was nothing quite like it in Adele's native Chestertown. Washington College (private, for the liberal arts) had been founded in 1782, but it was designed for men only. However, it began admitting young women a hundred years later, in 1891; and then went further by offering a preparatory program for younger students of promise, regardless of gender. Better yet, this Preparatory Department was taught by the faculty at Washington College.

A preponderance of Washington College girls went through what was then called the "Normal" program: a popular two-year program which, all over the United States, trained girls to teach in elementary schools–but not beyond.

Adele, however, decided against limiting herself to the Normal program and instead chose to focus her studies on the four-year liberal arts program, majoring in mathematics and physics.[5] At her graduation in 1900, she ranked second in her class, gave the valedictorian's oration, and was one of two women in an otherwise eight-student program devoted to the liberal arts (six men and two women, including Adele). She did take the precaution, however, of also obtaining a Teaching Certificate through the Normal program (two men and seven women, including Adele). See Chapter 9-A at fn 6–10. (She would later earn two Master's degrees.)

Of young Adele's mother, Emma Price "Pricie" **DeCorse** (pronounced in three syllables as "De-COR-see") France we know little, except that she was of Chestertown stock. On the other hand, Adele's father–Thomas "Tom" Dashiell France–had gone through school in Baltimore, and his family connections in that city included two Methodist ministers. Tom's own mother, Sarah **Sanner**, had been born in St. Mary's County, and an Alfred G. Sanner would one day serve on the Seminary's Board of Trustees from 1904 to 1941.

---

5 The private, so-called "Seven Sisters" colleges had already been formed in the Northeast: Mount Holyoke, 1837; Vassar, 1861; Smith, 1871; Wellesley, 1875; Radcliffe, 1879; Bryn Mawr, 1885; and Barnard, 1889. None of these colleges gave the two-year "Normal" program, and all were steeped in the liberal arts.

In Chestertown, Tom France was well-known and liked. He seems to have given up farming in Quaker Neck and moved his young family into Chestertown proper in 1884 when he and his wife, "Pricie", bought the five-bay Dougherty-Barroll house on High Street. At that time "Addie"–as she was known to family and friends–was four years old.[6] This move into town enabled Tom France to take over a wood-and-coal business with his brother-in-law, James DeCorse. Located at the corner of Cannon and Queen Streets, the business was close to the France's home on High Street.

Tom France was not of the high-born in Chestertown, yet he proved to be a leader in the community: he became a justice of the peace, and in 1902 the governor expanded the position so that France might also be able to function as the Police Justice.[7] Today, however, he is most remembered as the man who helped organize and then became president of Chestertown's very first Volunteer Fire Department. Was this gumption? His photo-portrait was done at the same time (1908) and hangs in today's firehouse; it is also reprinted in Kevin Hemstock's 2009 *History of the Chestertown Volunteer Fire Company.*

Although young women were finally admitted to Washington College's undergraduate program in 1891, male students refused to allow them entrance into either of their debating clubs: the Mount Vernon Literary Society, and the Philomathean Society.

In response to this exclusion, the women organized their own debating group in 1894 and called it the Pieria Literary Society. They took as their motto Alexander Pope's famous lines, "A little knowledge is a dangerous thing; drink deep, or taste not the Pierian spring." (See photo of Pieria Literary Society members in 1894.)

In 1896, 16-year-old Addie France entered Washington College to major in mathematics and physics. It is likely (but not known for certain) that earlier

---

[6] Interestingly, the deed is conveyed from Joseph Wickes and his wife *only* to "Emma P. France, wife of Thomas D. France." Tom and Pricie bought the house with a mortgage that was paid off early in 1990, and they continued to own the farm out on Quaker Neck. MDLANDREC.NET, Kent County, SB 5 145-46 & 147-48. See also MDLANDREC.NET, Kent County, SB 3-212. Web. 13 Dec 2021. <https://mdlandrec.net/main/dsp_search.cfm?cid=KE>.

[7] "Justice France Appointed by Governor Smith–Some Provisions of the Law." *The Enterprise* (Chestertown). 7 May 1902. Front page. Print.

Pieria Literary Society in 1894. Landskroener, Marcia C., ed. and Thompson, William L., comp. *Washington: The College at Chester*. Chestertown, MD: The Literary House Press at Washington College, 2000. 74. Print. Courtesy of Washington College Archives and Special Collections.

she had been part of the Preparatory Department–for "sub-freshmen"–run by the college faculty. The curriculum of this high-school-age department was at that time divided into two years: in what would otherwise have been the junior year of high school, the curriculum for Washington College's sub-freshmen covered science, math, English, Maryland history, and penmanship. The following year was devoted to science, math, English, penmanship, with the addition of United States history and Latin.

Once Adele was admitted to the College proper, she was quick to take on leadership roles, being elected president of the Pieria Literary Society in 1898 and 1899, then its vice president until she graduated a few months later with a B.A. in 1900.

The college newspaper, *The Washington Collegian*, was formed as a male enclave in 1898, but Adele managed to insert herself onto its editorial board and was put in charge of the area known as "Social." As a college junior, she was elected secretary-treasurer of the just-formed women's sports club. (This was an interest she would call on a decade later when she formed the basketball team down Chesapeake Bay at St. Mary's Female Seminary.)

Continuing on at Washington College after graduation, Adele went even further in academia, studying for–and receiving–her Master's degree in 1903. She was twenty-three. (See photo of Adele holding this M.A. diploma.) From 1900 to 1904, as a bona fide alumna, she inserted herself onto the College Alumni Association as Recording Secretary. Adele's relaxed personality trait–cheerful assertiveness, head and heart–would have gone far in reducing friction when she simply up and joined the formerly male preserves of editorial boards.[8]

In contrast to John LaFarge, who did describe his poor health in his autobiography (although he had evidently not mentioned it to his parishioners), Adele France never wrote anything about her growing-up years or even of life as the first president of her junior college. She had scant time for personal letter-writing, and what little we do know comes from her voluminous correspondence with the parents of her Seminary students.

It appears, however, that she did have two physical problems: weak eyes and weak legs.

Except for her portrait which hangs today in the library of St. Mary's College of Maryland, Adele France was almost always photographed wearing eyeglasses. In the 1930s, she underwent eye surgery of an unspecified nature, but any eye surgery in those days required the patient to lie still in bed, surrounded by sandbags in order to offset sudden movement.

Her second physical problem was far more serious. It must have happened either at birth or during very early childhood. As Mary Blair **Lane** Patterson expressed it in her 1976 brief memoir of the Seminary, "She had a bad hip."[9] Adele's legs were enough of a problem that they discouraged her from climbing up to the third floor of the new Seminary building in the mid-1920s in order to see what the commotion was all about. (The commotion was a boxing match which the girls had deliberately scheduled for the third

---

[8] "Washington College . . . Meeting of Alumni." *The Chestertown Transcript.* 18 June 1904. Front page. Print. This article states in part that Adele France was then acting as the Secretary of the College Alumni Association at a meeting where a committee was appointed "to revise the Constitution." (Speculation: *if* that alumni association actually had a regular publication at that time, then it is likely that Adele would have also played a role on the editorial board of any such alumni magazine, which would have been a precursor to *The Washington Alumnus*, which was launched in 1931.) However, no further records have been uncovered by this researcher about the Washington College Alumni Association during those four years at the dawn of the 20th Century.

Yet there is no doubt that Adele did indeed have social skills–in today's parlance, emotional intelligence. In 2008, I had the good fortune to meet Carrie Schreiber, a retired teacher in Montgomery County for whom Adele France had been something of a mentor. "She [Adele] was a well-rounded person," said Ms. Schreiber. "She was very friendly and could always remember your name." Meeting in June 2008: Carrie Schreiber (retired teacher) and Janet Haugaard (author).

[9] Lane Patterson, Mary Blair. "A Very Different World." *Mulberry Tree Papers* (Fall 1976): 23. Print.

floor, knowing "Miss France" was not likely to make the effort to climb up and investigate). From snapshots that the girls took of Adele, we see that her dresses were somewhat longer than those generally worn in the 1920s, '30s, and '40s. Her skirts generally fell below the calf and about three inches above the ankle, effectively concealing any leg problem.

Most telling of all, however, was that she did not drive. For a woman of "gumption" during that period, the ability to drive a car during her period as Principal would have been a necessity, especially in remote Southern Maryland. Yet driving was a problem that Adele turned over to a student, to another teacher, to a friend, or to a handyman. Nor is she ever mentioned (as was John LaFarge) as climbing into a sailboat; if there had been any problem with her legs, climbing into a dinghy or rocking vessel of any kind would have been almost impossible. If the problem with her leg(s) was neither genetic nor congenital, it might have been caused by a brief episode with polio during very early childhood. Often called "infantile paralysis," polio frequently struck children between the ages of six months and four years. But this is all speculation.

After receiving her M.A. (presumably in a "scientific" course of study, since her forte was math and physics) from Washington College in 1903, and either at that time, or a little earlier, Adele started her own small school. Joan Andersen, of the Kent County Historical Society, suggested that this may have been a kindergarten as there were no public kindergartens at that time in Chestertown. Yet historian Margie Luckett states that in the early 1900s, Adele "established and was headmistress of a select private school."[10] While the exact location of Adele's school is not documented, her parents' quite large Dougherty-Barroll house on High Street–with its own yard–seems a likely setting for such a small school. See Chapter 9-A at fn 2 & fn 12.

In scattered writings throughout her life, Adele obliquely referred back to this small, private school. A letter written in 1936 finally turned up in the Archives of St. Mary's College of Maryland (successor to the original Female Seminary-Junior College). Joseph Wickes, a law professor at the University

---
10 Luckett, Margie H. *Maryland Women*, Vol. 2. Baltimore, Md: King Bros., Inc., Press, 1937. 120. Print.

of Texas, wrote "Miss France" to ask if his daughter, Adelaide (a graduate of St. Mary's Academy in Leonardtown), might enroll in Adele's new Junior College. Joseph was the son of Judge Joseph Wickes and his wife, Ann, of 102 High Street, Chestertown.[11] Simple arithmetic says that young Wickes (born late December 1896) had been anywhere from seven to 13 years old when he attended Adele France's little school.

In her response to Wickes, Adele addressed him warmly as "My dear Joseph" and referred to him as "one of my first pupils."[12] His daughter, Adelaide **Wickes** (now deceased) did indeed attend Miss France's junior college and graduated with an A.A. degree in 1939.[13]

2. The Woman's Literary Club

At age twenty-three, Adele France must have looked around and realized that–with her Master's degree–she was probably one of the more highly educated women in Chestertown. The year was 1903. Her college education, however, did not mean that either she–or her mother–had been included in the Ladies Improvement Society of Chestertown. By that time, the Society had just finished creating a park and fountain for the center of town (1899). Inclusion in the Ladies Improvement Society belonged chiefly to women whose husbands had achieved a certain social standing by virtue of their university educations and subsequent professional positions within the community. Respected though he was, Tom France was still only a farmer who had gone no further than high school in Baltimore.

Not given the right to vote until 1920, a woman without either a good education or a successful husband was at the mercy of forces beyond herself. A successful social standing could only derive from that of a husband, although a prominent father would also do.[14] Pricie DeCorse (Adele's mother) had neither. Generally speaking, in the derivative function of wife and mother, a woman could not vote, and, in many states, she could

---

[11] Judge Wickes and his wife had sold the Dougherty-Barroll house to Tom and Pricie France back in 1884.

[12] France, M. Adele. One-page typed letter to Joseph A. Wickes. 5 Aug. 1936. RG 20 Janet Haugaard collection. St. Mary's College of Maryland Archives.

[13] Alumni Student Records. RG 5.2.2, Box 3. St. Mary's College of Maryland Archives.

[14] See, for example, Henry James's short novel, *Washington Square*, published in 1880.

not own property. If divorced, her children would usually be given over to the husband. As a wife, she was also expected to agree with her husband's political views, not being considered educated enough to have views of her own. A young girl's negligible sense of her own self-worth made her complicit in all this, and Biblical scripture seemed to confirm the values of the masculine world into which she had been born.

When a family had to choose between sending a daughter or a son to college for a liberal arts education, naturally it was the son–the future provider for his own family–who would benefit; he would learn how to think critically and write cogently.

But there were rumblings–rumblings that had been accelerating both before and after that 1840 abolitionist convention in London when women had not been allowed to speak and had been generally relegated to a position behind the fenced-off area.

Girls' academies–as well as coeducational schools–were springing up in the new United States, and for many, these were the gateways into the equally new women's colleges.[15] Well known at the time were the female "seminaries," or high schools: Emma **Hart** Willard founded the Troy Female Seminary of Troy, New York, in 1821, and her much younger sister, Almira **Hart** Phelps, became president of the Patapsco Female Institute of Ellicott City, Maryland, in 1841. And then, of course, there was St. Mary's Female Seminary, founded in 1840, down in Southern Maryland.

But a college education was quite another matter. Most girls came from families where tuition money was spent on the college education of a young man rather than on that of a young woman. Worse, perhaps, was the young woman's ensuing realization that she didn't count, that any education would be wasted on her. This was precisely the group of girls and young women whom Adele targeted, and sometime just before 1904 (perhaps 1903) she set up The Woman's Literary Club ("WLC") in Chestertown. (See Chapter 9-A.)

---

15 See fn 5 above on women's colleges.

Adele France must have realized that women's suffrage would soon be coming, and she wanted these women–young or not–to be ready and thinking on their feet. At some point in her own M.A. education, she would have learned of what today we call the "distance learning" courses then being offered by the University of Chicago. The University had only just been founded in 1890 by John D. Rockefeller, who appointed as its first president a dynamic young academic, William Rainey Harper.

Harper created "distance learning" courses which, however, could not lead to a college degree unless one actually spent part of the time on the Chicago campus. But it was still possible to sign up for the courses, and all that was required was (1) incorporation and (2) money. In Chestertown, the money for the courses came from the modest dues paid by the members of the WLC. The letterhead on the surviving papers and envelopes from Chicago's distance-learning courses indicate that they came from what was then called the "Correspondence-Study Department" of the University of Chicago (University Extension Division).

On a correspondence basis (just as on a resident-student basis), one could study the following: philosophy, political economy, political science, history, sociology, anthropology, household administration, comparative religion, Semitic languages, classical languages, Romance languages, English (both literature and composition), mathematics, astronomy, physics, chemistry, geology, library science, anatomy, biology, bacteriology, etc.

Several years later, in January of 1909, Chestertown created a time capsule; and when it was opened almost one hundred years later, in 2008, there–in Adele's own handwriting–was a sheet of vellum on which she had noted that "The Woman's Literary Club of Chestertown was organized December 2, 1904." This was followed by a list of the members and officers of the WLC in 1909. (The use of the term "organized" suggests that the actual incorporation of the WLC as an entity took place in 1904; and it likely existed as an association before then.)

There is more. The members of the WLC must have made considerable demands on the library at Washington College: where else were they to find the prescribed books on Shakespeare, or the Columbian Exposition of 1893 (see fn 22 below), or Charles Dickens, or the French Revolution–or that Franco-American artist, John LaFarge? So the WLC decided to provide some relief for the Washington College Library and went on to create a library for Chestertown itself in February of 1907. This, too, was noted on Adele's sheet of vellum in the 1909 time capsule. She further wrote that a subscription to the library cost $.50 (fifty cents) a year, entitling the borrower to one book per week. This vellum page in the time capsule further explained that "The Club members act as Librarians, one each week."[16]

Not until 1909 did Adele France leave Chestertown for her first paid position as a teacher of math and physics at St. Mary's Female Seminary. During those Chestertown years, she had not only founded but also taken charge of the WLC for at least five years (1904-1909). From assorted papers in the Horsey Collection (see below), we learn that–even when she was working in Washington, D.C. or Memphis, Tennessee–she returned often to Chestertown and made sure that the format she had developed for the group was still in place. After the death of her mother (1914) and her father (1918), it appears that she once again lived in Chestertown and led the WLC while working for the Kent County Board of Education from 1918-1920. Then she traveled West to work as Supervisor of Shelby County Schools in Tennessee from 1920-1922. (See Chapter 9-B, fn 27.)

In 1922, she moved to New York City where she lived on the campus of the new Teachers College at Columbia University. Here she studied for her second Master's degree, this time in Education.

But once the Trustees of St. Mary's Seminary elected her as the school's new Principal in 1923, her oversight of the WLC came to an end, and she rushed from New York down to St. Mary's City to start hiring a new (and well-educated) faculty. From then until 1948, her position as Principal, as well as her creation of something new (called a "junior college") occupied all her time.

---

16 The time capsule of 1909 had been first placed in the new building erected on Cross Street by the Volunteer Fire Department, and the entire contents of the capsule were finally opened in the Fire Department's even newer building. This is where I saw them in 2009. Presumably they are still there, unless they have been moved to the town library or the library of Washington College.

As for the WLC in Chestertown: by the 1930s it had developed into a book club, a vibrant reading group, and so it remains to this day, over one hundred years later.

3. The Horsey Collection

What, exactly, were the girls and women of the first WLC actually studying?

In a word, Western civilization. Individual reading topics selected by Adele France from the University of Chicago included the following: "The Church and the Early Drama"; "A Critical Analysis of Richard III"; "Art of the Primitive Peoples of South America"; "Charles Lamb as an Essayist"; "Martin Luther and the Reformation"; "Martin Schongauer: Printing and Engraving before Dürer." And so on.

Adele's study group met twice a month, each member presenting a paper. The study questions that guided the writing of each paper were specific: "In what respect does Shakespearean drama differ from the early church play?" Or this: "What did Chaucer do for the English language? What did Tennyson say of him?" Sometimes one large topic, such as Shakespeare's *Hamlet*, was divided into eleven manageable sub-topics, presented at separate meetings. For example, in 1905, Adele wrote and presented fifteen pages on the topic she had assigned to herself, "Was Hamlet mad?" Finally, each presenter had to include a list of works she had consulted, a bibliography of sorts. The University of Chicago would expect no less.

This revelation of the first WLC would never have come about had it not been for the archival instincts of Joan Horsey in the decade immediately following the year 2000. Our histories–whether individual, family-related, or national–are often lost because someone has thrown papers out, meaning no harm, but simply not knowing what to do with them. Joan Horsey, of Chestertown, knew exactly what to do with those long-ago papers from the WLC, even though they appeared to have been ruined in a rain-storm.[17] Carefully, one by one, she laid all the water-logged papers out

---

17 This is so often what history relies on: a single individual who decides to save–or perhaps decides to throw out–a piece of paper, or a set of papers, that in no way look important.

on her garage floor, and once they were dry, bundled them into cardboard boxes and plastic barrels.[18]

The Horsey papers are invaluable, a glimpse into the ways in which the women of Chestertown were educating themselves–in effect, trusting their own abilities–in the years just before they got the right to vote in 1920.[19]

Most striking about Adele's WLC was her insistence that the members also report briefly on "current events." Yet what place could news reports possibly have in a group that was so obviously geared toward academic knowledge?

From Adele's point of view, the twice-monthly reporting of new inventions, disruptive politics, and social change would act as an antidote to the timelessness of the literature they were busy studying. "Current events" was about life itself: messy and unpredictable.

On the other hand, literature and the other liberal arts took that mess and re-organized it into a satisfying and understandable whole. The new University of Chicago was now presenting all this by course title, following the customary historical format.

Of even greater value, Adele must have thought, was that these girls and young women were being asked not only to report on a "current event" but also–in the very act of presenting–to avoid parroting back the newspaper's own position. Initially the presenter's position might be identical to that of her husband or father, but if Adele was even half the teacher she thought she was, one or two deft questions on her part could have opened up differing points of view which a woman might consider (and reconsider) by herself during the coming week.

In short, this young member of the WLC was now being invited to think for herself, and just possibly she was beginning to feel more assured. Her husband might poke fun at any opinions she put forth, but once 1920

---

18 This was how I found them in June of 2008, answering her warm invitation to come see them.

19 Appendix C includes a somewhat broader presentation of individual papers in the Horsey Collection.

arrived–and once she entered the privacy of the voting booth–she was her own woman.

From 1904 until 1922, these were just a few of the current events presumably being reported on at The Woman's Literary Club: the Bloody Sunday Massacre in St. Petersburg, Russia; the election of Theodore Roosevelt to a second term; the publication of Albert Einstein's theory of Relativity; and the *Lusitania*'s breaking of a world record on trans-Atlantic crossings (4 days and barely 20 hours). The Wright brothers invented a motor-operated airplane; a new entity called the Ford Motor Company produced the first car; F.W. Woolworth Company was founded; and Archduke Ferdinand was assassinated in Sarajevo, leading most European countries to declare war on each other, thereby setting off World War I. The Panama Canal was opened; Margaret **Sanger** was jailed for writing the first book on birth control; an old law gave way when a new one established an eight-hour workday for striking railroad workers; Czar Nicholas and his family were executed in a basement bunker–and so on. And what did the women of the Literary Club think of all *that*?

B. HEAD AND HEART: JOHN LAFARGE

Today, almost 100 years since John LaFarge started his missionary work in that area of St. Mary's County known as Ridge, those who actually remember him (or know of him by reputation) speak reverentially of "Father LaFarge" and his labors, both pastoral and educational. Yet they look puzzled if asked about any "ill health." They know nothing of it. No one seems to have known that John LaFarge suffered from at least one serious (and undiagnosed) illness for much of his life. Although he wrote about it in his autobiography, in his missionary work he held back, evidently not mentioning it to parishioners.

Although John LaFarge and Adele France were exactly the same age, France graduated from Washington College in 1900, but LaFarge didn't graduate from Harvard until 1901. This disparity in graduation years was due to the fact that, in Newport, LaFarge spent the entire sophomore year of his high school (Rogers High) in bed, "too weak even to do much reading"

135

and felt "generally miserable."[20] His mother moved him to New York for surgery to remove his appendix, took an apartment near her husband's studio, and there young John LaFarge lived for two quite stimulating years of his life.[21]

Young John LaFarge's tendency to physical disability–whether innate or caused at birth–is a thread that runs through both his published autobiography and his "diary" (actually, a log-book) that is now part of the LaFarge Collection in the archives of Georgetown University. The last of eight surviving children, John LaFarge was born in February of 1880, fulfilling the age-old description of "runt of the litter": physically weak, less likely to survive. His mother, Margaret **Perry** LaFarge, was 40 and in "failing" health when her eighth and last child was born. In his autobiography, LaFarge notes that his mother kept her pregnancy from her (generally absent) husband in the expectation that she might not be able to bring the baby to full term.[22]

Of his birth, John LaFarge–with characteristic drollery–writes:

> According to legend, people would stop my mother as she wheeled me in a perambulator and express a word of sympathy when they saw her feeble baby, pale and apparently half-lifeless. It was assumed I would not live, so there was not much bother about formalities at my baptism.[23]

This was a harbinger of a life beset by illnesses, never explicitly defined but which nevertheless give pause to today's reader.

---

20 LaFarge, John. *The Manner Is Ordinary*. New York: Harcourt, Brace and Company, 1954. 54, 55. Print. Hereafter cited as LaFarge, *Manner*.

21 The studio of the elder LaFarge was at 51 West Tenth Street; and over the two-year period, the family lived at 55 Clinton Place (today's Eighth Street) and later at 22 East Tenth Street.

22 John LaFarge, père (biological father), had courted his future wife, Margaret **Perry**, quite intensely, but gradually both his global travel and his work as an artist took him away from home and family to such an extent that "in later years we [children] seldom saw him for more than five or six weeks annually." LaFarge, *Manner* 16. A world-renowned artist, muralist, and stained-glass designer, John LaFarge, père, exhibited in the Tiffany Chapel at the 1893 World Columbian Exposition in Chicago. Some of his work may be seen at the Morse Museum of American Art in Winter Garden, Florida, along with that of William Morris, Frank Lloyd Wright, Louis Sullivan, René Lalique, and Carl Fabergé. He painted portraits of both Henry and William James, and, in Maryland, designed and executed the figure of "Justice" for the Supreme Court Building in Baltimore.

23 LaFarge, *Manner* 34-35.

Young John's mother, Margaret **Perry** LaFarge, came from a line of prominent Protestants, most notable of whom were Commodore Oliver Hazard Perry, Thomas Sergeant, and Benjamin Franklin.

Margaret converted to Catholicism shortly after her marriage to the elder John LaFarge in 1860, and her newfound faith helped her as her husband often left her–and their eight children–for long periods of absence, either to his Manhattan studio, or to Europe, or to the South Seas.[24] In his Manhattan studio, the elder LaFarge designed stained glass and worked on the "decorative arts," which included large murals. Up in Newport, Margaret LaFarge held her peace until young John reached adolescence:

> When I was about fourteen I remember walking with Mother along Easton's Beach. It was a dull, gray day and Mother had been a bit silent. Then she said, "There is something I think you ought to understand. You ought to know that your father does not properly look after us. He means well, but nevertheless I am at times forgotten, and there are times when I must turn to almighty God for help." It was a simple thing simply stated, but it made a tremendous impression on me. I had a feeling of pride, a quiet satisfaction. I had vaguely sensed something of the sort, but Mother had never complained. From that time on I was to be a partner with her and share her problems, her anxieties and heartaches. I felt manly and protective.[25]

For young John LaFarge, his enervating illnesses–plus his father's remoteness and his mother's questionable confidences–might constitute what is sometimes known as "a double whammy." His illnesses alone could have excused him from productive life as an adult, but if those illnesses were part of his constitution, so too were his responses. Young John LaFarge was born with immense curiosity and (1) enjoyed reading and writing; (2) loved music; and (3) had an inborn flair for languages. Affection and empathy, however, were somewhat lacking; they would come later, far into his adult years.

---

24 Or to women. In his autobiography, John LaFarge notes–of his father's love affairs–"And the women were not the coarse, seductive and sensual type, but women of intellect, of high social standing. . . ." LaFarge, *Manner* 29.

25 LaFarge, *Manner* 30.

1. Reading and Writing

Young John was given good schooling, his mother unexpectedly deciding not to send him to the local parish school but instead to the public schools. Of these, LaFarge would write later in his autobiography: "Teaching in the Newport public schools was of a high order. The teachers were strict, of the good old New England variety, showing full consideration for my religious beliefs."[26]

Part of the public-school curriculum was given over to the memorizing of poetry–especially Longfellow–and this was supplemented in evenings at home when his mother read aloud to the children "most of Dickens, Trollope, and Jane Austen."[27] Young LaFarge was doing his own reading as well, and he was doing it on the deserted back porch of the town's Redwood Library: "I discovered this magical hiding place myself and spent long summer afternoons there sitting on the floor of the porch, poring over sea stories and biographies":

> One day in August when I was about thirteen, I finished devouring Boswell's *Life of Johnson*, and a feeling of desolation came over me as I turned the last page. I debated with myself for some time what I should read next, and listened to the katydids in the horse-chestnut trees for advice. Then the bright idea occurred to me, why not read the two fat volumes through again? It was a wise choice and I shall never forget it.[28]

Interest in reading led quite naturally to writing. At age ten, he and a couple of other boyhood friends found weeks of delight in a book of woodcuts as well as in a small, hand-printing press. On the printing-press, they ran off monthly issues of *The Sunlight* and sold them to friends and relatives for two cents a copy. *The Sunlight* featured installments of young John's "A Trip to Mars"; the woodcuts illustrated what he and his friends thought the red planet might actually look like. "The only way to utilize the cuts was to build a story about them. I was commissioned to undertake this, and solved the problem by anticipating Buck Rogers and contributing

---

26 LaFarge, *Manner* 37.
27 LaFarge, *Manner* 40.
28 LaFarge, *Manner* 40.

a story of 'A Trip to Mars' in monthly installments. Since no one could dispute what might be found on Mars, one was always able to insert one of the woodcuts." In his autobiography, he writes that after ten or twelve installments, "all the woodcuts and possibilities of the planet Mars were exhausted."[29]

Like most boys, he had dreams about what he wanted to be when he grew up. "My father rather hoped I might become a professor . . . and so confided to his friend, Henry Adams." He also had boyish dreams of commanding "one of the procession of vessels that passed through Newport harbor." If such a life was too impractical, however, he thought of another possibility: "since I was a bookish type of boy there was always room for something in the field of scholarship or libraries."[30]

When it came time to go to college, his first choice, as a devout Catholic–and already headed for the priesthood–was Georgetown University, but he had been told that the food there was bad. "This touched a very sensitive point, for at the time I was laboring with a sort of recurrent nausea and immediately Georgetown became associated in my mind with certain physical sensations."[31] Theodore "Teddy" Roosevelt (not yet president) was a close friend and hunting companion of John's very-much-older brother, Grant. Roosevelt urged young John to go to Harvard, and this he did in 1897.[32]

In his first year at Harvard, John LaFarge was obliged to take freshman English with Charles Copeland ("Copey"). In his autobiography, LaFarge recalls that Copeland "encouraged me to some [further] writing, and as a result I was elected to the editorial board of the Harvard monthly." He was also part of an after-hours group that met once a week, guided by

---

[29] LaFarge, *Manner* 44.

[30] LaFarge, *Manner* 52.

[31] LaFarge, *Manner* 49.

[32] Grant LaFarge was born in 1862, making him eighteen years older than young John, born in 1880. Next in line was Bancel (born 1865), who often supplied young John with help that was both personal and financial. Bancel also taught young John how to sail. "It was Bancel in many ways who took Father's place as a parent, playing the role with me that a young father might assume with his children." LaFarge, *Manner* 3.

a professor of English to read the English Romantic poets, "particularly Wordsworth whom we plowed through from beginning to end."[33]

2. Music

Young John had been unusually homesick during his first weeks at Harvard and had turned to the one activity that he knew would raise his spirits: music. In the years before taking his vows as a Jesuit (poverty, chastity, obedience), he had been able to live without being overly careful about money. According to his log-book in the Georgetown archives, he was now able to buy–outright–an upright piano (an Ivers & Pond) for his room at Harvard. As he had already been classically trained in music, apparently this did the trick. He took private lessons in both piano and organ and found that "it was grand fun practicing the organ in Appleton Chapel."[34] And beyond that, "I had picked up enough to read off a score of a quartet or symphony and hear it in the mind just as if the instruments were playing. This to me was a great satisfaction and joy."[35]

3. Flair for Languages

Music and such literary pursuits as reading and writing are not all that unusual. A flair for languages, however, *is*, and young John LaFarge possessed that inborn talent to an unusual degree. French, of course, was taught at his public school in Newport, and his mother had arranged for further lessons on the side (his famous father was of French extraction.) Given young John's aptitude for language, it is quite likely he would have recognized that some of the French vocabulary he was learning at school bore a distinct resemblance to the Latin he was hearing at Mass. (French developed from Latin in the Middle Ages.)

But his unusual interest in languages first showed itself when he was about ten. The idea that the Norse Vikings had sailed to New England was popular during LaFarge's boyhood, and as LaFarge wrote in his autobiography, "I was curious about the Norse and all the more so when

---

33 LaFarge, *Manner* 62.
34 LaFarge, *Manner* 63-64.
35 LaFarge, *Manner* 47.

at the age of ten I examined in our library at home a collection of books in Danish, Swedish, and Icelandic that my father had gathered . . . I saw no reason why I shouldn't learn to read these books" and found someone to teach him a few words in Danish.[36] (A neat trick, since the Nordic languages are only remotely related to French and English.) Later in his life, he referred back to this boyhood time as his "Norse period":

> The most glorious day in my Norse period was the arrival of a Viking ship in Newport Harbor in 1893. . . . As soon as school was out, I rushed down to the Mill Street wharf, untied a skiff and paddled out to meet the sailors, try a few Danish words on them . . . and learn of their experiences.[37]

During his junior and senior years of high school (when his mother took him to New York for his health as well as for surgery on his appendix), he demonstrated once again his fascination with languages. Through a family friend, he met a small group of elderly, Gaelic-speaking Irishmen:

> [These men] met every week or so over beer and cheese somewhere around Second Avenue and Thirty-fourth Street and cultivated the mysteries of the Gaelic language. I was initiated into their group, picked up quite a little Gaelic, and was elected as secretary.[38]

At Harvard, he did well in his studies. Theodore Roosevelt knew of young John's plans to become a priest and urged him to study Greek and Latin his entire four years as an undergraduate. "In later years I never regretted T.R.'s suggestions," LaFarge wrote in his autobiography.[39]

LaFarge also decided that, as a priest, he ought to be able to read the Bible in its original tongues, and in his last three years at Harvard, he studied the relevant Semitic languages: Hebrew, Syriac, and Aramaic. He became a member of the Hasty Pudding Club and made friends.[40]

---

[36] LaFarge, *Manner* 38.

[37] LaFarge, *Manner* 38-39.

[38] LaFarge, *Manner* 55.

[39] LaFarge, *Manner* 59.

[40] One day in 1962–far into his future–he would publish a slim volume, *Reflections on Growing Old*, which he dedicated to these old friends: "Jim Lawrence, Joe O'Gorman, Bill Reid, and Other Honored Survivors of H.C. [Harvard College], '01, The First Class of the Century." These were undoubtedly "members of the class that year [who] astonished and moved me more than I could

Obviously talented in language study, young John LaFarge–now with a Harvard B.A. in hand–decided to leave the United States and take the required four years of seminary studies at Innsbruck, Austria.

John LaFarge's mother waved him off with a "Don't let them make you a Jesuit!" to which he replied, "Mother, dear, nothing can ever make me a Jesuit."[41]

But once installed in an off-campus apartment in Innsbruck, he became "appallingly homesick ... and felt as if I had been dropped to the bottom of a well. My homesickness led me to desperate measures: I rented a grand piano, a Blüthner, for less than I had paid at Harvard for an upright Ivers and Pond, and somehow got it into the apartment, to the amazement of the landlady."[42] Once again, music helped.

He became fluent in German, made friends, "and enjoyed during those four years a health I had never known before." His decision to study at Innsbruck, rather than in the United States, had been a decision to immerse himself in another language and its culture. He seems to have picked up German quickly, yet all his courses–except for those in church history–were actually taught in Latin.

He would hardly have had any use for his own native English. Every day he heard a babble of voices around him; at the seminary, "the Austro-Hungarian Empire accounted for some twelve different national groups." One of his friends was a Pole who did not speak English, and while LaFarge could have conversed with him in German or French, he decided instead to pick up "a certain amount of Polish." So they chatted in Polish.[43]

Later, during his 1903 summer vacation, he was joined by his mother and sister, and the three made a few days' stop in Brittany, visiting his father's relatives (members of minor French aristocracy). Here, LaFarge determined to learn some Breton. He "struck up an acquaintance with the

---

say by collecting [in 1921] a substantial sum to aid in building my church of St. Nicholas in St. Mary's County near Patuxent, Maryland." LaFarge, *Manner* 75.

41 LaFarge, *Manner* 76-77.
42 LaFarge, *Manner* 84.
43 LaFarge, *Manner* 103.

curé and picked up a few phrases of the Breton language" (a subset of the Gaelic he had learned at age fifteen while at high school in New York City).[44]

He was ordained in the summer of 1905 and returned to the United States in order to enter the Jesuit seminary at St. Andrew-on-Hudson. Here, from 1906 to 1908, he studied for his M.A. in philosophy. But he was "unusually thin," and in his autobiography he notes–with a poker face–that this thinness "blessed me with a very ascetic appearance and secured for me that respect which seems to be the privilege of thin ecclesiastics."[45]

In 1908, he and a fellow priest left for Woodstock, near Baltimore, and of this period LaFarge wrote that "Those two years at Woodstock were for me the time of the greatest natural intellectual satisfaction that I have ever experienced."[46] During his second year, however, he was asked to translate– for the esteemed *Catholic Encyclopedia*–an article originally written in German. "I toiled pretty hard at [it] at a time when I was not feeling any too well, for I still had to struggle with some of my interior organism."[47]

It was during those Woodstock years–still a student, though ordained– that he first became acquainted with Southern Maryland. For three weeks in the summer, he and his Woodstock group "pilgrimaged" in a steamer down to St. Mary's County and were treated to a holiday known as "Villa." This was in the days well before air-conditioning, and for John LaFarge, Villa was not a success:

> There we camped out in a four-story frame building enjoying sun-scorched outdoor life, which was splendid for the vigorous but trying on the less robust. The second year of my villa plus the heat and the examinations left me pretty well weakened.[48]

Once his studies as a Jesuit were completed in 1911, he was assigned as assistant pastor at St. Aloysius in Leonardtown, and once again he showed a talent for music:

---

44 LaFarge, *Manner* 109.
45 LaFarge, *Manner* 126-27.
46 LaFarge, *Manner* 142.
47 LaFarge, *Manner* 143.
48 LaFarge, *Manner* 143-44.

> The musical studies of my youth served me in good stead in my parish work, especially with the children. With the help of a cultivated and enthusiastic young couple who had recently settled in our neighborhood, Mr. and Mrs. Ralph Cullison–he Irish, she Mexican–I managed to get organized the St. Aloysius Choral Club, a dramatic and musical society. Unexpected talent turned up among the young folk, and we gave some creditable performances.[49]

He taught chant to the altar boys at St. Aloysius and was "surprised to see how readily they could pick it up." If they made a mistake, his advice to them was "do it with grace and dignity."[50] Later, at a sodality meeting of blacks near St. Inigoes, he observed that "they sang the familiar hymns," but he wrote later that "the spirituals were unknown."[51] In the chapel at St. Inigoes, the Mass was perhaps less pleasing musically: ". . . in general the Negroes had been content to sit in silence while the white choir did its best in the organ loft."[52] The decades since Father LaFarge wrote those words have seen the rise of spirituals during Mass, and black Catholics are no longer quite so "content to sit in silence."

In 1915, LaFarge left Leonardtown and was posted farther south to St. Inigoes, the old seventeenth-century colonial center of Jesuit activity.[53] It may be that this was originally his own idea, for he had recently heard of Slavic immigrants, Catholic, who did not yet know enough English to make their confessions or understand a sermon. But back in his student days at Innsbruck, when he had been assigned to spend time occasionally with his Polish friend, he had picked up the rudiments of the language. Polish is one of the Slavic languages, and LaFarge was now able to learn enough Slavic so that he could not only hear confessions from this group of Catholics, but also preach to them in their own language. This all took place at the new, one-room St. James Chapel, near St. Mary's City.[54]

---

49 LaFarge, *Manner* 173.
50 LaFarge, *Manner* 289, 291.
51 LaFarge, *Manner* 163.
52 LaFarge, *Manner* 163.
53 See fn 55 in Chapter 8-D-3 about St. Inigoes Manor at Priests' Point.
54 See fn 71 in Chapter 8-D-3-b as to St. James Chapel/Church.

LaFarge's physical problems, however, did not diminish as he grew older. In January of 1916, he recorded in his log-book that he had begun trying to sleep on the porch of the old Villa building at St. Inigoes, "an outdoor [winter] treatment."[55]

Two months later, in the same log-book, he noted that he had just spent *five weeks* at St. Agnes Hospital in Philadelphia "where I was cured of a head trouble that had bothered me for five years."[56]

In 1926, just two years after the opening of his Cardinal Gibbons Institute, the Jesuits re-located him to Manhattan where he was made associate editor of *America* magazine, a Jesuit weekly. Here he lived at Campion House, the recently purchased headquarters on West 108th Street. The Jesuit staff of *America* actually produced the magazine at this site and lived together in community.[57] "*America*," LaFarge wrote in his autobiography, "was frankly designed for those who were interested in the issues and were willing to do at least a little thinking with some possibility of reaching thought-out conclusions."[58] It was just his cup of tea. *America* would also prove a vehicle for his writings on the need for education for blacks.

LaFarge's facility with languages made him the obvious person to attend the International Eucharistic Congress in Budapest, and his senior editor sent him to Europe to report on political events that were soon to lead into World War II. It was now June of 1938. His months-long journey took him to England, France, Germany, Czechoslovakia, Bratislava, Hungary, Slovenia, Croatia, Switzerland, and, of course, Italy.

In Rome, Pope Pius XI had requested a private conversation with him concerning what LaFarge called his work on "interracial justice." LaFarge memorized twenty-five Italian verbs ahead of time, but this proved unnecessary as the pope spoke both French and German.[59] By the time

---

55 LaFarge Collection, Box 25, Folder 3, "Items from My Diary: August 1915 to 1926," Georgetown University Library; p.2 (of what appears to be a typed transcription of a taped recording, p.8). Hereafter cited as LaFarge, *Desk Diary*.

56 LaFarge, *Desk Diary*, p.2.

57 See Chapter 8-A, fn 1.

58 LaFarge, *Manner* 304.

59 See Chapter 8-E.

LaFarge returned to New York, he had lost thirty-five pounds. He was now made editor-in-chief of *America*, but in his 1954 autobiography he noted that:

> ... during my four years of editorial chieftanship[,] I managed some ten months away from my desk in the hospital or during convalescence. As part of my bodily habitation started coming apart in the spring of 1945, I enjoyed a nice repair operation with subsequent repose from August to November of that year. . . . This time, to my surprise, I might say to my bewilderment I did . . . actually stay repaired.[60]

But in 1947, he learned that he would need a second major operation, and then what sounds like yet a third, following which he was "rewarded by lasting health" and allowed to step back into his earlier, less-demanding role as associate editor of *America*.

John LaFarge stayed in this position as associate editor of *America*. He worked and lived at the Jesuits' Campion House in Manhattan until he died in his sleep in 1963, just after watching President Kennedy's funeral procession on television. He was eighty-three.

4. Intellect and Empathy

By the time he wrote his autobiography at age 74, John LaFarge's own assessment of his growing-up years was that in his youth he had been overly intellectual and "priggish."[61] Today, the slang word might be "brainy" or "nerdy." On an intellectual level, this was something he had been made aware of as a boy and a student, yet he had not been so alarmed as to have made any effort to correct it. During his two teenage years in New York, he had pestered Herman Heuser, a social acquaintance of the family and Professor of Scripture at Overbrook Seminary, with "a hundred and one questions." Out of patience, Heuser finally rounded on him:

> Look out, young fellow. You are merely cultivating your intellect and neglecting your heart. What you need is less brains and more heart.[62]

---

60 LaFarge, *Manner* 310.
61 LaFarge, *Manner* 52.
62 LaFarge, *Manner* 56.

LaFarge wrote in his autobiography that he "began to see there was danger in mere braininess and that disaster lay ahead if I were overbalanced in that direction." Nevertheless, he paid little attention, and later, at Harvard, his organ teacher "gave me good advice, and [also] told me bluntly that I was introspective."[63] Yet another warning came from John Ropes, Harvard's Napoleonic historian:

> Mr. Ropes, in his kindly way, explained to me that what I needed for the good of my soul was to forget my rather select companionship, summer in a plain country hotel, and learn to know the common crowd. I saw the logic of his idea but somehow never got around to it.[64]

In fact, LaFarge might never have learned about the human heart–and empathy–if he had not been forced to. But once he entered the Jesuit noviceship at St. Andrew-on-Hudson, he was given a wide variety of assignments, what today we would call "internships." One of these was at the Poughkeepsie State Hospital for the Insane. Here he preached, began to develop a rudimentary knowledge of psychiatry, and–because he was already ordained–heard confessions. His stay there was brief, but five years later, in 1910-1911–just before he was sent to Leonardtown–he was posted to yet another internship at Blackwells Island, later called "Welfare Island" (since 1973, Roosevelt Island), in New York harbor:

> In this capacity I experienced eight of the most tremendous months of my life, for they opened up to me a vast vision of the tragic as well as the human side of life. I had had a glimpse of this in Poughkeepsie State Hospital, but Blackwells Island was the real thing.[65]

On Blackwells Island, he ministered to 900 in the Work House, one of the three administrative divisions. He visited the wards, heard confessions, celebrated Mass, administered Extreme Unction some 3,000 times, and began to see life as he had never known it:

> Gloomy and depressing as the institutions were, another side to life began to dawn. A hospital . . . is also a family, with a life

---

[63] LaFarge, *Manner* 64.

[64] LaFarge, *Manner* 70.

[65] LaFarge, *Manner* 148.

of its own and a spiritual fellowship. . . . One had the distinct feeling of living in a great and rather jovial family. The nurses were a wonderful group, and Father Casey had organized a flourishing nurses' sodality for which we held special services in the little wooden chapel. . . . Even the women prisoners with their bedraggled careers revealed to me much that was hopefully human beneath a forlorn exterior.[66]

John LaFarge concluded his chapter on "eight of the most tremendous months of my life" with this one-sentence summation: "Innsbruck and Woodstock were schools of knowledge, but Blackwells Island was a school of life and death."[67]

Then, with his heart finally–or at least partially–opened to the crucible of life, in September of 1911, John LaFarge stepped aboard that steamship that would carry him down the Potomac River and to his future in St. Mary's County.

C. FINALLY, MORGAN THE HORSE

As previously foretold, it was September of 1911, when the young John LaFarge and the equally young Adele France disembarked from the steamboats that had brought them–in the middle of the night–to their first real jobs in Southern Maryland. Both were thirty-one. The steamboat from Washington was delivering John LaFarge to his first position, assistant pastor at St. Aloysius parish in Leonardtown; the steamboat from Baltimore was delivering Adele France to her third year as instructor of mathematics and physics at St. Mary's Female Seminary in St. Mary's City.[68]

As the crow flies, Leonardtown and St. Mary's City are only sixteen miles apart, but in the very early 1900s, a hefty amount of travel time separated them from each other. The first automobiles had not yet arrived in the County, so the general mode of land-travel in 1911 was by horse and buggy.

---

[66] LaFarge, *Manner* 151.

[67] LaFarge, *Manner* 152.

[68] "The steamboat age came to a sad and sudden end by 1935, due to company bankruptcies, increased competition from automobiles and improved state roads, and a fierce storm on 23 August 1933 that destroyed many of the region's wharves." Fausz, J. Frederick. *Monument School of the People: A sesquicentennial history of St. Mary's College of Maryland, 1840-1990*. St. Mary's City, Md.: St. Mary's College of Maryland; 1st Ed., 1990. 73. Print.

As Father LaFarge would later note in his autobiography, most of the roads between Leonardtown and Mechanicsville "were mere dirt roads, impassable in winter and anything but easy in summer, so that much travel in olden days was by water."[69] Yet a goodly amount of horse-and-buggy travel was still necessary, and he wrote further that "Only after the coming of the auto and good roads did we appreciate the amount of time and energy formerly used up in merely getting around the county."[70]

For Miss France, there was no problem with local travel: her classroom, bedroom, and dining room were all in one building, what today we call Calvert Hall.[71] Once ensconced at the Seminary, she would have had little occasion to travel away from it.

But for Father LaFarge, the situation was entirely different: as he describes it in Chapter Nine of his autobiography, he spent the years from 1911 to 1915 travelling widely throughout Southern Maryland, particularly the area around Leonardtown. In his position as assistant pastor at St. Aloysius, he took his turn at celebrating daily Masses, calling on the sick, attending the dying, baptizing babies, confirming converts, establishing new catechetical centers, writing sermons, giving a weekly talk to the boys at Leonard Hall, and overseeing both the Leonardtown Holy Thursday cavalcades and the Corpus Christi Processions. He made home visits and taught the boys at St. Aloysius to sing the chant of Holy Week.

During those four years in Leonardtown, there is no mention of any illness. Moreover, his recent experience as an intern on Blackwells Island was leading him to both personal insight and outreach. His "braininess" and introversion were beginning to give way to an increasing ability to develop his heart, to reach out to other people. "Once more," he wrote in his autobiography, "I could apply to myself the advice that good Father Heuser had given me in my boyhood, that my heart and not my head must find its due place."[72] For this new extroversion, John LaFarge had Morgan to thank. Who was Morgan?

---

69 LaFarge, *Manner* 156.
70 LaFarge, *Manner* 167.
71 See Chapter 9-C-1-c, including fn 45.
72 LaFarge, *Manner* 159.

Morgan was a horse.

Morgan was a 25-year-old sorrel. For a good twenty-one years before John LaFarge entered the County, Morgan had belonged to a previous Jesuit, Father Clem Lancaster. Good horse that he was, Morgan had quickly adapted himself to Father Lancaster's ways. But Father Lancaster was deaf–stone deaf–and he attempted to overcome this deficiency by halting the buggy each time he met someone he knew, shouting a one-sided conversation at him.

Morgan was now passed on to Father LaFarge, and, as the young priest observed, Morgan "took care of himself":

> He knew his way back if you were on the homeward stretch, and even if you were leaving home, as a rule he had a pretty good idea where you were heading. In fact, it was sometimes a bit embarrassing, because old horses became so acquainted with the habits of their masters that you could guess where your predecessor spent his time. They liked to turn in at certain gates. . . . Morgan would come to a dead stop when we met anyone [on the road], expecting a little conversation to be started up.[73]

This could be, as Father LaFarge expressed it, "a bit embarrassing," but he also began to understand what was expected of him in St. Mary's County:

> Stopping on the road] was a good suggestion and I found myself falling into the same habit. After all, if you stopped, the passer-by always thought that you really did want to talk to him, so I found myself in a little while stopping and conversing with half the countryside.[74]

"It was," John LaFarge concluded, "one of those ways in which you can learn something from a horse." What he was learning, at long last, was personal outreach. And to "half the countryside" at that.[75] Thanks in part to Morgan.

---

73 LaFarge, *Manner* 169-70.

74 LaFarge, *Manner* 169-70.

75 LaFarge, *Manner* 170.

Chapter 5

The "Not-Quites" (Women)

Obviously a lady, the woman was escorted to the podium to deliver her speech to the New York State Legislature. The year was 1860, and by now she was forty-five years old. Her name was Elizabeth **Cady** Stanton, and this is the oft-quoted part of her speech to the assembled men:

> The prejudice against color, of which we hear so much, is no stronger than that against sex [gender]. It is produced by the same cause, and manifested very much in the same way. The negro's skin and the woman's sex [gender] are both prima facie evidence that they were intended to be in subjection to the white Saxon man.[1]

The last time we saw Elizabeth Cady Stanton was back in Chapter 1, when she had just been denied participation in the Abolitionist Convention in London. That year was 1840. Men, both white-skinned and black-skinned, had been invited to participate in this convention that was to

---

[1] Elizabeth Cady Stanton's address on January 1, 1860 in Albany, New York, to the Judiciary Committee of the New York State Legislature. <https://awpc.cattcenter.iastate.edu/2017/03/21/a-slaves-appeal-1860/>.

eradicate slavery worldwide. But when a delegation of women arrived from the United States, they were voted down as participants. Not permitted to speak, they were led, albeit courteously, to a roped-off area at the rear of the hall where they sat in silence during the ten-day-long proceedings. (Elizabeth Cady Stanton, however, took notes.)

This refusal to seat the women was one of those historical mishaps that leads to unintended but far-reaching consequences. Lucretia **Coffin** Mott, a Quaker minister and leading abolitionist in the United States, had also assumed that she would be speaking at this Anti-Slavery Convention and had just led a group of seven other delegates across the Atlantic. The British, however, were appalled: little in their culture (except for the Quakers' belief in expressing an "Inner Light") had prepared them for the public inclusion of women.

At age 25, Elizabeth Cady Stanton (1815-1902) had actually been on her honeymoon when she and Lucretia Coffin Mott (1793-1880) met for the first time at that 1840 convention in London. Though they had not known each other until then, Coffin Mott and Cady Stanton, both abolitionists, and both ejected from participation in the Anti-Slavery Convention, made common cause and decided to make a slight turn away from abolitionism and instead address the question of women's rights. (See Chapter 1 at fn 23.) It would take another eight years, but the battle was joined at the famous Seneca Falls Convention of July 19-20, 1848. Here, Cady Stanton presented her "Declaration of Sentiments."

A. DECLARATION OF RIGHTS AND SENTIMENTS

The document is unrivaled in both challenge and tone. Cady Stanton titled her proposal "The Declaration of Rights and Sentiments," modeling it after the 1776 Declaration of Independence: "When, in the course of human events, it becomes necessary . . ." etc. But she inserted into her second paragraph of resolutions the word "women": "We hold these truths to be self-evident: that all men *and women* are created equal." (Emphasis added.) She then followed this preamble with a layout of some fifteen grievances against men's assumption of power over women, all of them based on English Common Law:

Declaration of Rights and Sentiments
(ratified 1848, Seneca Falls, N.Y.)

1. He [a male] has never permitted her [a female] to exercise her inalienable right to the elective franchise [the right to vote].

2. He has compelled her to submit to laws, in the formation of which she had no voice.

3. He has withheld from her rights which are given to the most ignorant and degraded men–both natives and foreigners.

4. Having deprived her of this first right of a citizen, the elective franchise, thereby leaving her without representation in the halls of legislation, he has oppressed her on all sides.

5. He has made her, if married, in the eye of the law, civilly dead.

6. He has taken from her all rights in property, even to the wages she earns.

7. He has made her, morally, an irresponsible being as she can commit many crimes with impunity, provided they be done in the presence of her husband. In the covenant of marriage, she is compelled to promise obedience to her husband, he becoming, to all intents and purposes, her master–the law giving him power to deprive her of her liberty, and to administer chastisement.

8. He has so framed the laws of divorce, as to what shall be the proper causes, and in case of separation, to whom the guardianship of the children shall be given, as to be wholly regardless of the happiness of women–the law, in all cases, going upon a false supposition of the supremacy of man, and giving all power into his hands.

9. After depriving her of all rights as a married woman, if single, and the owner of property, he has taxed her to support a government which recognizes her only when her property can be made profitable to it.

10. He has monopolized nearly all the profitable employments, and from those she is permitted to follow, she receives but a scanty remuneration. He closes against her all the avenues to wealth and distinction which he considers most honorable to himself. As a teacher of theology, medicine, or law, she is not known.

11. He has denied her the facilities for obtaining a thorough education, all colleges being closed against her.

12. He allows her in church, as well as [in] state, but a subordinate position, claiming apostolic authority for her exclusion from the ministry, and, with some exceptions, from any public participation in the affairs of the church.

13. He has created a false public sentiment by giving to the world a different code of morals for men and women, by which moral delinquencies which exclude women from society, are not only tolerated, but deemed of little account in man.

14. He has usurped the prerogative of Jehovah himself, claiming it as his right to assign for her a sphere of action, when that belongs to her conscience and to her God.

15. He has endeavored, in every way that he could, to destroy her confidence in her own powers, to lessen her self-respect, and to make her willing to lead a dependent and abject life.[2]

Cady Stanton was well aware of possible consequences to this "Declaration" which she and Coffin Mott had written, and in her closing remarks at that Seneca Falls Convention of 1848, she gave this call to action:

> In entering upon the great work before us, we anticipate no small amount of misconception, misrepresentation, and ridicule, but we shall use every instrumentality within our power to effect our object. We shall employ agents, circulate tracts, petition the State and national Legislatures, and endeavor to enlist the pulpit and the press in our behalf. We hope this Convention will be followed by a series of Conventions, embracing every part of the country.[3]

Unlike their contemporary, Susan B. Anthony, both Cady Stanton and Coffin Mott were married and had children (seven and six children respectively) and each considered this work her first priority. Nevertheless, Cady Stanton–the better writer of the two–made time for herself and Coffin

---

[2] Cady Stanton, Elizabeth. *A History of Woman Suffrage,* Vol. 1. Rochester, N.Y.: Fowler and Wells, 1889. 70-71. Print.

[3] Cady Stanton's remarks at the close of the 1848 presentation of her "Declaration of Rights and Sentiments," Seneca Falls, New York.

Mott to draw up the document whose resolutions were passed at the Seneca Falls Convention of 1848.

From her list of grievances, Cady Stanton was outlining the several ways in which women of the nineteenth century were, legally speaking, "not quite" on a par with men.[4] For the next several decades of the 19th century what was known as "the woman question" would become a central matter for discussion.

It was not resolved until women achieved the right to vote in 1920, three years before Adele France–fresh from her M.A. studies in New York at Columbia University–was called to become the next Principal of St. Mary's Female Seminary. She was also the first Principal of the Female Seminary to have been college-educated.

In her 1848 "Declaration of Rights and Sentiments," Cady Stanton attacked the legal system of "Couverture." This French word, meaning "covered," had arrived in England with the Norman Conquest in 1066 and–as part of English Common Law–was eventually brought by England to her American colonies in the 1600s.[5] Today, known in certain jurisdictions as "marriage by the entirety," "coverture" (English spelling) meant that a married woman was legally "covered" by the simple act of marriage and therefore excluded from any public responsibility, including the ability to vote.

Once married, a woman was, as Cady Stanton put it in Grievance # 5 of her "Declaration of Rights and Sentiments," "civilly dead." She and her husband were now considered one person, and, legally, her identity was subsumed under his. If we pause a minute to think back to the creation of

---

[4] Maryland, however, was slightly ahead of the curve in that the law concerning the property a woman brought with her to marriage had already been changed in 1843. "The property of the wife is exempt from liability for the debts of the husband," the change in legislation read. "States of the Union. Maryland. Law Relative to Married Women." *Niles' National Register*, Fifth Series, No. 17, Vol XIV, 24 June 1843, p.261 (column 3). Print. Baltimore: Jeremiah Hughes. Available online at the HathiTrust Digital Library: <https://babel.hathitrust.org/cgi/pt?id=nyp.33433081665857&view=1up&seq=277&skin=2021&q1=husband>.

[5] For a brief and excellent explanation of the predominant role that common law continues to play in Maryland, see the following review. Liebmann, George. Rev. of *The Common Law in Colonial America: Volume I: The Chesapeake and New England, 1607-1660*, by William Nelson (Oxford University Press, 2008). *Law and Politics Book Review*, Vol. 19 No. 2 (2009):148-50. Web. Last accessed 17 Dec. 2021. <http://www.lpbr.net/2009/02/common-law-in-colonial-america-volume-i.html>.

Leonardtown's Reading Room and Debating Society in the late 1830s, we can better understand its ruling that married women could not qualify for membership: they were, after all, under the law of coverture and therefore "not quite" equal to men. The sole responsibility of a married woman was domestic, within the home. As Alfred Gough so well put it–tongue in cheek– "after marriage there was to be no frittering around the library reading books."[6]

B. THE "DEPENDENT AND ABJECT LIFE" – NOT FOR ADELE FRANCE

In Cady Stanton's 1848 "Declaration of Rights and Sentiments," Grievance # 15 reads as follows: "He [a male] has endeavored in every way that he could, to destroy her confidence in her own powers, to lessen her self-respect, and to make her willing to lead a dependent and abject life."

Never could M. Adele France be described as having led "a dependent and abject life." At some point in her growing-up years she must have encountered "the woman question," and most likely she knew of Elizabeth **Cady** Stanton's publications. Born in 1880, Adele France would have been halfway through her undergraduate studies at Washington College when an elderly Cady Stanton (age 83) published her controversial *Woman's Bible* in 1898.[7] Adele was 22 when Cady Stanton died in 1902, and 26 when Susan B. Anthony died in 1906: in a sense, Adele was carrying forward their beliefs and prescriptions for the emancipation of women.[8]

Throughout her life, Adele was embroiled in "the woman question." How else to explain her quiet insistence, as an undergraduate at Washington College, in joining the editorial board of what had always been a male preserve? How else to explain her decades-long leadership of The Woman's Literary Club in Chestertown–the club that introduced housewives to some of the college education they were otherwise missing? How else to

---

6 See Chapter 3-B at fn 12.

7 Elizabeth **Cady** Stanton lived a long life. She was born in 1815, when the new United States was only thirty-eight years old. She died in 1902 at the age of eighty-seven. She did not live long enough to see women get the vote in 1920, but it is surprising when one looks over the fifteen grievances she had listed back in 1848 to see how many of them were already undergoing changes by the time of her death.

8 Research at Washington College, at St. Mary's College of Maryland, and in Chestertown itself has failed to disclose (as of yet) any remnants of Adele France's personal library.

explain the push to establish the first little library in Chestertown? How else to explain her initiative in writing up much of the historical material that went into Chestertown's time capsule of 1909?[9] And how else to explain her determination to create that radically new institution for women, the junior college in St. Mary's City?

Long before she became its Principal, Adele France had taken the steamer down Chesapeake Bay to St. Mary's Female Seminary in order to teach math and physics from 1909 to 1913–and again for the school year 1917-1918. Ever since it opened its doors in 1846, the Seminary (what today we think of as middle school and high school) had enjoyed the same academic rigor as the boys' academy at Charlotte Hall: including Latin, French, arithmetic, algebra, history, and geography. At the Female Seminary, sewing may have replaced the military drills at Charlotte Hall, but aside from that, the academic curriculum was the same.

Except for one thing. The Female Seminary never had a debating society, as did its male counterpart, Charlotte Hall. Why, the Seminary Trustees might have wondered, why would one want to teach young girls the fine points of argument? Certainly a well-bred young woman of the South would never have had the bad taste to stand on a public platform and debate in public. Moreover, in her future life as a married woman, her husband was "master" and his word would prevail, making any opposition on her part poor judgment. In Grievance # 7 of her "Declaration of Rights and Sentiments," Cady Stanton had noted that "In the covenant of marriage, [the wife] is compelled to promise obedience to her husband, he becoming, to all intents and purposes, her master– the law giving him power to deprive her of her liberty, and to administer chastisement." Not until the 20th century did the word "obey" generally disappear from a bride's marriage vow.

There was a related problem. The Seminary had been founded in 1840 on the principle that it would: (a) teach girls of different religious faiths to respect each other, thereby reviving Lord Baltimore's original vision for a religiously tolerant Maryland; and (b) put this mandate in the hands of *mothers*, but not of fathers. The founders were ascribing to women the role

---

[9] Much of the handwriting in that time-capsule is that of Adele France.

they would be expected to play in teaching very young children what we might call "supper-table" tolerance. It was certainly not the founders' intent to extend this to 20th-century racism (as a word, "racism" did not exist until the first decades of the 1900s), but religious tolerance was designed to combat the suspicion and rancor which at that time characterized how one practiced one's religion on Sunday morning in Southern Maryland:

> You've got to be taught, before it's too late,
> Before you are six, or seven, or eight,
> To hate all the people your relatives hate –
> You've got to be carefully taught.©[10]

C. "ANATOMY IS DESTINY"[11]

We would give a great deal to know something of the excited conversations that–according to legend–took place out at William Coad's Cherry Fields plantation. Based on at least one member's reading of John Pendleton Kennedy's *Rob of the Bowl* (the 1838 tribute to Lord Baltimore's religiously tolerant colony),[12] a decision was made at Coad's plantation to create a girls' seminary as a *memorial* to that colony, and to do it precisely on top of Leonard Calvert's legislative base in St. Mary's City. However, there is no record of what William Coad, James Blackistone, and Joseph Shaw actually said. What we do have, though, is the wording from their "Preamble" to the bill designed to finance the state-wide lottery that was going to pay for the construction of the girls' school. The "Preamble" prescribes that:

> the citizens of St. Mary's county . . . desire to establish on that sacred spot [St. Mary's City] a female seminary, that *those who are destined to become the mothers of future generations* may receive their education and early impressions at a place so

---

10 *South Pacific*. Music by Richard Rodgers. Lyrics by Oscar Hammerstein II. Book by Oscar Hammerstein II and Joshua Logan. Adapted from *Tales of the South Pacific* by James Michener. New York. 1949. Performance.

11 Sigmund Freud, quoting Napoleon Bonaparte. Freud, Sigmund. "On the Universal Tendency to Debasement in the Sphere of Love (Contributions to the Psychology of Love)." 1912. Ed. James Strachey. London: Hogarth Press and the Institute of Psycho-analysis, 1957. *The Standard Edition of the Complete Psychological Works of Sigmund Freud*, Vol. 11, 189. Print.

12 See Chapter 3-C-1 and Chapter 3-C-3.

well calculated to inspire affection and attachment for our native State. . . . [13]

Here, the operative word is not "fathers" or even "parents," but "mothers." The idea of the three founders was that if a young girl had gone to the Female Seminary and had absorbed the fact that her best friend spent Sunday mornings worshipping at a church entirely different from her own, then one day, as a mother, she would pass that observation–supper-table tolerance–on to her own children. The assumption here, of course, is that, as a woman, she would marry and have children.

As a theory of religious tolerance, this plan seems to have worked, and Messrs. Coad (Catholic), Blackistone (Episcopalian) and Shaw (Episcopalian) are to be recognized for their vision of religious tolerance in public education. By 1858, the Board of Trustees also included Methodists, and in 1904, a slight increase in apportionment was strictly observed: henceforth the Board was to be made up of five Catholics, five Episcopalians, and five Methodists. This management-by-quota survived until 1941 when Governor Herbert O'Conor deemed it no longer necessary and further shocked the Trustees by stipulating that *women* should join the Board.

Consternation! Yet women–the governor might well have argued–had been voting in national elections for the past twenty-odd years, ever since 1920. Moreover, the Female Seminary, a state-supported school, since 1926 had been supporting a junior-college program for women. Clearly, O'Conor must have argued, it was time for women to join the Board of Trustees. The historically all-male Board was dismayed, but–in gentlemanly fashion–decided it would be "unbecoming" to oppose the governor's decision.

By the time Governor O'Conor put forward his decision, almost a hundred years had passed since Elizabeth **Cady** Stanton had written that male dominance in many areas of life destroyed a woman's "confidence in

---

[13] Laws of Maryland, Legislature of 1839, Chapter 190. "An act to authorise the drawing of a Lottery to establish a Female Seminary in Saint Mary's County, on the site of the ancient City of Saint Mary's." *Session Laws, 1839*. Volume 600, Pages 178-79, Preamble (emphasis added). (See attached pdf at Archives of Maryland Online because the web-version inadvertently omits certain text.) Maryland State Archives. Web. 25 Sept. 2022. <https://msa.maryland.gov/megafile/msa/speccol/sc2900/sc2908/000001/000600/html/am600--178.html>. Throughout this chapter, there are numerous references to records provided by the Maryland State Archives or the MSA, and each should be read as including: "Courtesy of the Maryland State Archives."

her own powers, lessen[ed] her self-respect, and . . . [made] her willing to lead a dependent and abject life." Today, around the globe, women actually do continue to accept (or even seek out) lives that are "dependent," "not quite" equal to those of men and–when culturally necessary–lives that may even be "abject."

The reverse side of the coin, however, rejects the phrase "abject dependency," and as a result, in the United States today one seldom hears the words "spinster" or "old maid." Today's new variant, "unmarried woman," indicates that a young woman–for whatever reason–has chosen to go it alone. She may decide to live by herself or with another woman. Alternatively, if purposeful, she can rely on friends in her profession, or become part of a political community, or–if Anglican/Episcopalian or Catholic or Buddhist–commit to a religious order.

This chapter on women (the "not quites") would be badly off-kilter if it ignored those women who opted out of what is known as The Woman Question. For a surprising number of Catholic girls, anatomy was *not* destiny, and especially in Southern Maryland–a haven for English Catholics–young women could choose a respectable life free of marriage.[14] Much like their priest-counterparts, they believed in "vocation" or a "calling" to the religious life. Up until the late 19th and even 20th centuries, women choosing marriage were required by law to deed their assets over to the husband. Similarly, convents relied on a young woman's dowry for her continuing education and lifelong maintenance. Three orders of Catholic sisters came to Southern Maryland in order to provide education: St. Mary's Academy, 1885, with the **Sisters of Charity of Nazareth** (Bardstown, Ky);[15] St. Michael's, St. David's, St. James, 1922, and Little Flower, 1926, with the

---

14 An exceptional historical figure is Margaret **Brent**, born in England, who in 1638 immigrated with her siblings to the Colony of Maryland and its then capitol, St. Mary's City. The annual *Prospectus* for St. Mary's Female Seminary for 1914-1915 describes her as "the most interesting female character in the entire colonial history of the United States. She acted as Governor of the colony on the demise of Leonard Calvert. Some of her contemporaries say 'she was the ablest *man* in the colony.'" *Annual Prospectus for St. Mary's Female Seminary for 1914-1915*, "The Seventy-First Year" at p.11 (italics in original). [1914.] Office of the Provost. Catalogs. RG 3.4.1, Box 1 "Prospectus 1914/1915." St. Mary's College of Maryland Archives.

15 Beitzell, Edwin W. *The Jesuit Missions of St. Mary's County, Maryland*. 2nd ed. Abell, MD: sponsored E.W. Beitzell; sponsored by St. Mary's County Bicentennial Commission, 1976. 227-28, 256. Print.

Sisters of St. Joseph (Hartford, Conn.);[16] and, in 1924, for both St. Peter Claver and the Cardinal Gibbons Institute, the **Oblate Sisters of Providence** (Baltimore, Md).[17]

As best we can tell, during the 1800s, most girls graduating from St. Mary's Female Seminary did indeed choose marriage. Their parents would have encouraged this, anticipating a time when they themselves would no longer be able to support a daughter financially. This explains the format of today's Alumni Directory of St. Mary's College of Maryland: it lists a married woman twice, first by her school name, then by that of her husband.

Up until the Maryland legislature began giving statewide county scholarships in 1868, the Seminary had been very much a County school. Aside from the teachers, the Board of Trustees was local, the Principal was local, and the girls were usually local, all of which resulted in fairly common cultural assumptions and points of view. But the Maryland legislature stepped in and broadened the pool of applicants: in 1898, it increased the number of *required* scholarships from 10 to 26. Instead of using the original draw-by-ballot selection method, school commissioners were to select these scholars without requiring an exam "so that the most worthy and charitable may be selected," thus providing greater geographical (and even cultural) outlook amongst the students. Textbooks were free to every scholarship student. According to Fred Fausz's history, each Maryland county was now *required* to send one girl to the Seminary–plus another from each of Baltimore City's legislative districts. Later, beginning in 1933, all scholarships required candidates to achieve top score on an examination that was given in the girl's home county. If no one applied from a particular county, then girls from other counties were allowed to sit for that county's

---

16 Beitzel, *Jesuit Missions* 277, 293, 303, 284.
17 Beitzell, *Jesuit Missions* 288.

scholarship exam. Thus it was possible for a girl from Calvert County to apply for the scholarship originally designated for Queen Anne County.[18]

"Dear Miss Lizzie" (Annie Elizabeth **Thomas**, later Lilburn) was Principal of the Female Seminary for almost fifteen years, from 1881 to 1895. Obviously popular with the girls, she was only 22 when she became Principal in 1881. She chose not to marry until 1895–at age 36–when she became Mrs. John Lilburn. As an unmarried Principal, she became the role model for a girl from Montgomery County, Emily "Emma" Jane **Griffith**, who spent her junior and senior years at the Seminary. Graduating as valedictorian of her class in 1885, Emma showed off her skills in Latin by quoting from what is known as the *Ubi sunt* motif: "Where are those who have gone before us?"[19]

The Archives of St. Mary's College of Maryland has become the beneficiary not only of Emma's penciled drafts of her valedictory address but also of much later notes sent to her by none other than her former Principal, "Dear Miss Lizzie." Emma had chosen not to marry, setting her sights instead on a career that produced a modest income. In the Government Printing Office, she advanced from the position of clerk to that of assistant trademark examiner. In later years, "Dear Miss Lizzie" fondly wrote in a note to Emma, "I often tell people of your big work in the Patent Office and feel a real pride in once having helped you in the early years of your life, for it is the foundation that allows for a big ending."[20]

---

18 Fausz, J. Frederick. *Monument School of the People: A sesquicentennial history of St. Mary's College of Maryland, 1840-1990*. St. Mary's City, Md.: St. Mary's College of Maryland; 1st Ed., 1990. 45. Print. Hereafter cited as Fausz. See also *Annual Prospectus for St. Mary's Female Seminary for 1904-1905*, "The Sixtieth Year" at p.9 (about "State Scholarships"). [1904.] Office of the Provost. Catalogs. RG 3.4.1, Box 1 "Prospectus 1904/1905." St. Mary's College of Maryland Archives. Hereafter cited as *1904-05 Prospectus*. For 1898 legislation, see Archives of Maryland, Legislative Records, Proceedings, Acts and Public Documents of the General Assembly, Session Laws, 1898 Session, Session 296, Vol. 482, Chapter 379, Pages 989-90. Maryland State Archives. Web. 17 Oct. 2022. <https://msa.maryland.gov/megafile/msa/speccol/sc2900/sc2908/000001/000482/html/am482--989.html>). For 1933 legislation, see Archives of Maryland, Legislative Records, Proceedings, Acts and Public Documents of the General Assembly, Session Laws, 1933 Session, Session 318, Vol. 421, Chapter 241, Pages 432-33. Maryland State Archives. Web. 17 Oct. 2022. <https://msa.maryland.gov/megafile/msa/speccol/sc2900/sc2908/000001/000421/html/am421--432.html>).

19 Griffith, Emily Jane. Composition book (three copies of valedictory speech). 1885. Emily Jane Griffith papers. MSS 003. St. Mary's College of Maryland Archives.

20 Thomas Lilburn, Annie Elizabeth. Handwritten letter to Emma Jane Griffith, from A.E. (Thomas) Lilburn. 28 Dec. 1930. Emily Jane Griffith papers. MSS 003. St. Mary's College of Maryland Archives.

D. CERTAINLY NOT ASTRIDE[21]

> It will require imagination for you, who cannot remember the beginning of the twentieth century, to picture our seclusion, and resourcefulness. There were no radio, no telephone, no automobile, the ox cart a more familiar sight in St. Mary's County than the horse. The horse was for the gentleman, driver or rider, hardly a woman so modern, certainly not astride.[22]

This letter, describing the Female Seminary just before 1900, was written by Mary Gorman, a teacher from that period. When she wrote it in 1934, she was responding to Adele France's request to learn more of what the old Female Seminary had been like, not only before the disastrous fire of 1924, but even before the 19th century had turned the corner into the 20th.

For five years, from 1895 to 1900, Laurel R. **Langley** (unmarried) was Principal. According to Mary Gorman's letter, "[Langley] taught art, her sister and herself having studied abroad. She had classes in drawing charcoal, painting in water color and oil on canvas and on china."[23]

Before the century ended and the new one became 1900, the Seminary's isolation was indeed complete, but it may have resulted in the long-standing (and still current) student tradition of "we make our own fun." Teacher Mary Gorman, a Catholic, noted the following:

> Our communication with the outside world was by boat, which brought the mail and the "Sun Paper" (*Baltimore Sun*) four or five times a week, except during a period of the winter, then twice a week. There were occasional week end trips home for the girls living within driving distance [that is, by horse and buggy], and trips to the churches within driving distance [also by buggy] . . . . The policy of denominational representation

---

21 Viewers of "Downton Abbey" will recall that Lady Mary Crawley wears a full-skirted "riding habit" and always rides "aside" (side-saddle) rather than "astride." On state and ceremonial occasions today, so also does Queen Elizabeth II.

22 This specific, handwritten letter from Mary Gorman is held by the St. Mary's College of Maryland Archives. It arrived at the College about a decade after Fred Fausz had published his history of the College in 1990. Correspondence from former teacher Mary Gorman to then-current teacher Hélène Cau (describing Seminary at the turn of the century) at p.1. 16 March 1934. Presidential Files, M. Adele France (1923-1948). RG 2.1.1, Box 1. St. Mary's College of Maryland Archives. Hereafter cited as Gorman Letter.

23 Gorman Letter, p.3.

on the faculty was adhered to and religion was taught the different groups by a teacher of the same belief. We had in our faculty Episcopalian, Presbyterian, Lutheran, Methodist, Baptist, and Catholic churches represented. The Christian Endeavor Society held weekly meetings for the encouragement of general interest in religious development.[24]

Gorman went on to note the absence of males at the Female Seminary: "Church service at the Episcopal Chapel . . . was very popular and drew the swains from the county and no doubt there were harmless flirtations, *though the students received no men callers at the Seminary.*"[25]

Mary Gorman may have taught science, but she had to do it without the laboratories that came into being only after the 1923 arrival of Adele France: "Our laboratories [Gorman wrote] were in the open, where in rambles we gathered specimens of plant and insect life. It was my job to keep [up] with chloroforming and dissecting the insects."[26] Literature was taught, but "no original French or German novels and very little very modern literature. A few of the most progressive might bring along some from home."[27]

However, the steamboat which–in good weather–arrived "four or five times a week" during the very late 1800s brought not only the mail but also the library's subscriptions to two surprisingly literary monthlies. Gorman mentions that "several good magazines like *Century* [published in New York] and *Youth's Companion*" [published in Boston] arrived by the steamboat. An online search reveals that in the 1890s, *Youth's Companion* was publishing works by Mark Twain, Harriet **Beecher** Stowe, Emily **Dickinson**, and for a black writer, Booker T. Washington. Similarly, *Century Magazine* was also publishing Booker T. Washington as well as Mark Twain, Bertrand Russell, Walt Whitman, Henry James, Kate **Chopin**, and the poetry of black poet Laurence Dunbar. For both publications, this was, academically, pretty steep material and indicated the intellectual caliber of the Seminary at that time.

---

24 Gorman Letter, at pp. 1, 2.
25 Gorman Letter, at p.2 (emphasis added).
26 Gorman Letter, at p.4.
27 Gorman Letter, at p.2.

According to Gorman, the Female Seminary was well attended under Laurel Langley's leadership (1895-1900):

> The school of between fifty and sixty students included about thirty [merit] scholarships, paid by the state. I don't know what amount was charged for tuition, nor what salaries were paid, except my own, which was exceedingly small. I went for the experience.[28]

But if "Anatomy" is indeed "Destiny," then why were a few women *not* choosing marriage and motherhood? The answer may be that young girls were constantly (and wisely) reminded that any sexual contact with males would one day–like it or not–result in pregnancy, and up until the early 1920s there was no such option as "family planning."

Girls were always chaperoned, and when not chaperoned they walked in pairs, there being safety in numbers. Multiple pregnancies within a marriage could be repeated to the point of exhaustion, and if a mother died in childbirth, her husband usually re-married in order to provide oversight for the children by the first wife. For some women, this vision of never-ending exhaustion was bleak, best summed up in the German phrase, "Kinder, küche, kirche" (children, cooking, church–a concept which Adolf Hitler actively promoted during his Third Reich). If a girl–for whatever reason–believed she had talents that went beyond simple fecundity, she might well opt for the single life. Such appears to have been the case with a very young sculptor, Emily Clayton **Bishop**, Class of 1900 at the Female Seminary.

Today, Emily Bishop's sculptures are on view, not only at the Smithsonian's American Art Museum (Renwick Gallery), but also at the Pennsylvania Academy of The Fine Arts. Emily Clayton Bishop (1883-1912) had evidently known from a very early age that she wanted to be an artist. Out of a family of seven children, she sketched "anything and everything

---

[28] Gorman Letter, at pp.3-4.

that interested and challenged her," according to her biographer (and great niece), Suzanne Smith.[29]

It is possible that Emily Bishop entered St. Mary's Female Seminary solely because of (Principal) Laurel Langley's known reputation as an artist who had traveled throughout Europe, accompanied by her sister. Once Emily graduated from elementary school in Smithsburg, Maryland (Washington County), she decided not to attend nearby Kee-Mar Academy in Hagerstown on the grounds that it had a reputation as a "finishing school." Emily's father was a third-generation Yale graduate, and her mother reportedly published an occasional article in *Harper's Magazine*. Shakespeare was part of the family library, and both parents were what might be called "savvy" about schooling and schools. In any event, Emily traveled 160 miles to board at St. Mary's Female Seminary way down in St. Mary's City. She graduated in the Class of 1900, likely at the extraordinary age of 16.

What she did next has not been firmly established: fires at both the Baltimore Institute of Art (1904) and at St. Mary's Female Seminary (1924) destroyed all student records. There is some report that she received a teaching certificate at Johns Hopkins, taking a year or more to do so, and perhaps doing it while studying at the Baltimore Institute of Art. It seems certain that she entered the Baltimore Institute of Art at age 16, graduating with highest honors and a scholarship to continue on at the Pennsylvania Academy of the Fine Arts (PAFA) in Philadelphia. At PAFA she won the Packard Prize in 1904, the McClellan Anatomy Prize (1905) and–for two years in a row–the Cresson European Scholarship Prize, at that time PAFA's highest award.

The Cresson Prize enabled her to travel to Holland, Italy, Greece, and France in the summers of 1907, 1908, and 1909. While in Paris, she studied sculpture under Auguste Rodin. When she returned to Philadelphia, she established a studio with her friend Marjorie Martanet and accepted commissions.

---

29 Smith, Suzanne Miriam. *The story of an artist: Emily Clayton Bishop, from Smithsburg, Maryland*. Self-published, 2010. Print. (This short, illustrated biography is in the Hilda C. Landers Library, at St. Mary's College of Maryland.)

Emily died in March of 1912, at the age of 28. Her obituary in *The New York Times* noted the following:

> Miss Emily Clayton Bishop, one of the most promising graduates in last year's class at the Pennsylvania Academy of the Fine Arts, whose first works are on show in the current annual exhibition, died of heart disease last night at her home in Smithsburg, Maryland. Miss Bishop was regarded as one of the most promising of America's younger sculptors. . . .[30]

Today, St. Mary's College of Maryland has not a single work by Emily Bishop. She undoubtedly studied under artist Laurel Langley, but anything she might have produced would have gone up in the catastrophic fire of early January 1924. Yet it does seem certain that–at the very least–she would have sketched her friends at the Female Seminary: as her biographer has expressed it, this young girl from Smithsburg sketched "anything and everything that interested and challenged her." It is inconceivable that she would not have sketched (or even sculpted) during her years at St. Mary's Female Seminary.

E. "DO NOT RUSH YOUR DAUGHTERS THROUGH SCHOOL"

That is Lucy **Lancaster** Maddox speaking, the woman who, in 1900, followed Laurel Langley as leader of the Female Seminary. As well connected as previous Principals within the County, she was the daughter of John Lancaster and Priscilla Hebb **Blackistone**. She would be the last Principal before Adele France arrived to take over in 1923. Known affectionately as Madame Maddox, Lucy Maddox was married, had five children, served from 1900 to 1923, and–for the sake of impressionable students–kept her husband, George William Maddox, well at bay.[31]

In general, students do not bother reading a school prospectus [catalogue] from beginning to end, focusing instead on the do's and don't's

---

30 Obituary, p.15 (column 3). *The New York Times*, Sunday, March 3, 1912. Print.

31 Bertha Moreland spoke of the students' titillation when, occasionally after the lights-out bell, they would observe George Maddox climbing in through his wife's bedroom window, accessed at that time by the wide front porch of Calvert Hall. Interview (by Janet Butler Haugaard on 16 Nov. 1995; transcribed Oct. 2007) of Bertha **Moreland** Kerby, Class of 1920, at pp.16-17. RG 19 SlackWater Oral History Collection, SMAO10002. St. Mary's College of Maryland Archives. Hereafter, cited as Moreland Interview.

of what is to be their social life. But cautious parents do read carefully, and in the Seminary catalogues put out by Lucy Maddox in the opening years of the 20th century, we find a concern that her students were graduating too young, not yet ready for the mature decisions that society would expect of them. Was she worried that Emily Bishop's early 1900 graduation from the Seminary was setting a trend? Were other parents hoping that their daughters, too, might go into teaching even if they had not reached emotional maturity?

Seminary historian Fred Fausz has estimated that between 1900 and 1910, fully 70% of Seminary girls went immediately into teaching in Maryland's public elementary schools.[32] Because of the Seminary's high academic standards, its young graduates were permitted by the State of Maryland to forgo the required two-year program at the State Normal School at Towson, a practice which held true within Maryland until the mid-1920s.

Yet in the nation's rapidly growing public-school system, a woman's ability to teach in a coeducational setting often did not extend beyond the elementary grades. In those early grades, she functioned somewhat as a mother, but above that level–in the 1800s–she was seen as "not quite" a man. A school*master* would be needed for the higher grades. Most women teachers were not married, thus avoiding any indelicate suggestion of sexual activity. (If married, however, they should at least have had the foresight to become widowed.)

Meanwhile, Lucy **Lancaster** Maddox expressed her concerns in the annual Seminary *Prospectus*, as we see from the catalogue of 1904-1905. The italics are those of Lucy Maddox herself:

> Since most of the students of this Institution are preparing to teach, in public or other schools, it is necessary that the work be very thorough.
>
> Nothing is omitted that will give the pupil a thorough understanding of each subject in order to meet, not only

---
[32] Fausz 55. One of these was Lettie **Dent** Gough, later becoming the first female superintendent of education in St. Mary's County (1928-1957).

the tests of future examinations, but to enable her to impart readily the knowledge of others.

In connection with this subject we plead with those who contemplate making teaching their profession–*do not rush your daughters through school*. It is no special honor to graduate young. Experience has taught us that though such a student may succeed in taking her diploma, she loses much by a certain non-assimilation of knowledge, resulting from immaturity of mind. No young woman should graduate until she is capable of self-support from her education. Parents then who wish to provide for those contingencies which may require the best preparation of mind, *must give us time to do it*. They must choose for their children between the leisure and pleasure of an early entrance into society, and the painstaking and serious task of acquiring an education of such practical worth as will prove a safeguard when the parent no longer can.[33]

This is a remarkable statement. Most conspicuous is the absence of any mention of future husbands–the focus being solely on a young woman's economic ability to provide for herself. While she was still viewed as someone "not-quite" equal to a man, nevertheless social changes were taking place in society as a whole. Women were becoming more conscious of what they perceived as their rights, and social changes would eventually lead–in 1920–to a woman's right to vote.

One of these (pre-1920) social changes was the founding of the Daughters of the American Revolution (D.A.R.), endorsed by Act of Congress in 1898. In less than two decades, during the school presidency of Lucy Maddox, the *Lusitania* was sunk by Germany in 1915, eventually leading to World War I. Aside from the felt need of the D.A.R. women to "do something" patriotic, they seized instead on one of the founding tenets of their organization: historic preservation.

Thus, when the Major William Thomas Chapter of the D.A.R. was organized in Leonardtown in 1915, it didn't take long for the women to turn their attention not only to Leonard Calvert's historic colony of 1634, but

---

[33] *1904-05 Prospectus* 15 (italics in original).

especially to the 1840 "memorial" to that experiment in religious tolerance: St. Mary's Female Seminary.

Not surprisingly, several members of the Leonardtown chapter of the D.A.R. were also wives of Seminary Trustees, and Seminary Principals themselves were soon included in D.A.R. membership (provided they qualified as having descended from a figure in the Revolutionary War). While the women of the D.A.R. chapter in Leonardtown gave several furnishings for the Seminary, by far their greatest contribution was the establishment of scholarships for girls who otherwise would certainly not have been able to attend the school. This concern for the academic welfare of the Female Seminary continued until 1964, at which time the former Seminary-Junior College became St. Mary's College of Maryland.

A second social (and pre-1920) initiative was the founding of the Alumnae Association in 1917. In 1913, Adele France left her four-year post as a teacher of mathematics and physics at the Female Seminary, doing so in order to acquire administrative experience in the education systems of: Washington, D.C.; Memphis, Tennessee; and her own native Chestertown. Leaving the Seminary just three years later was Lucy **Spedden**, Class of 1916, who established an Alumnae Association for the Seminary in 1917. It is just possible that her determination to form such a critical group had come from her science teacher, Adele France–who back at the turn of the century–had boldly inserted herself onto the board of Washington College's Alumni Association (see Chapter 4-A-1 at fn 8). Adele well understood the power that could be wielded by a similar group of Seminary graduates. In later years, as Principal of the Female Seminary and (then, after 1937, as "president") of the Junior College, whenever she become exasperated with slow decision-making on the part of the all-male Board of Trustees, she relied on both the Alumnae Association and the D.A.R. to do what she felt needed to be done. They, she believed, would not only understand but actually help.

F. NO "UNKINDNESS OF FEELING"

What was the Female Seminary like just before Adele France took over in 1923?

The Trustees were doing their job of following the original legislation for religious tolerance, specifically Christian though it was: before 1923, there were no Jews, no Muslims, not even an avowed agnostic. The "register containing the rules & bylaws" of the Female Seminary had been destroyed by fire in the family-home of one of the Trustees, but in 1872, the Trustees reconstructed the essence of canons aimed at fostering religious tolerance (some similar canons had been drafted in prior decades, including in 1846, 1848, and 1851). This time, the Trustees wrote out in full ten "Organic Rules" as such."[34] For example, the Rule 2nd observed that it was "the duty of every officer of the Institution to check [put a stop to] the introduction or discussion among any of the members of the Institution of such religious subjects as would be calculated to produce *unkindness of feeling* in a household that ought to be harmoniously united."[35]

According to that early legislation of August 1848–which still held true under Mrs. Maddox in the first two decades of the 20th century–"It shall be the duty of the steward to provide on Fridays and other days of abstinence suitable articles of diet other than flesh meat for those boarders who do not eat meat on those days."[36] During her interview, Bertha **Moreland** Kerby, Class of 1920, remembered that "The Catholic girls were put at one table and if there was a Catholic teacher she sat with us. . . . The other girls were placed at the other tables by their grade. (A girl was in charge at each

---

[34] St. Mary's Female Seminary Board of Trustees. *Minutes*. "Report of Committee on Rules." Preamble. Adopted 17 September 1872. MSA S 231-3, MdHR 12963-2. Manuscript (handwritten). <http://guide.msa.maryland.gov/pages/series.aspx?ID=S231>. See also Fausz 42. For a description of the historical events since the Seminary's founding (enacted in 1840 by the Legislature of 1939): see Fausz at 29-42 and Appendix D; and see **Combs** Hammett, Regina. *History of St. Mary's County:1634-1990*. 2nd printing. Ridge, Md: R.C. Hammett, 1994. 37-42. Print. "On 26 February 1846, the State of Maryland incorporated St. Mary's Female Seminary and officially made the Board of Trustees an independent 'body politic and corporate,' . . . ." Fausz 34, 50. See also Chapter 3-C-4 and 3-D.

[35] St. Mary's Female Seminary Board of Trustees. *Minutes*. "Report of Committee on Rules." "Organic Rules 'A'." Rule 2nd (emphasis added.) Adopted 17 September 1872. MSA S 231-3, MdHR 12963-2. Manuscript (handwritten). <http://guide.msa.maryland.gov/pages/series.aspx?ID=S231>.

[36] St. Mary's Female Seminary Board of Trustees. *Minutes 1845-1854*. Adopted 1 August 1848. Page 31. MSA S 231-1, MdHR 12962. Manuscript (handwritten).

table and kept the record for Mrs. Maddox.)" She explained that this was a record as to the students' manners, "just good little manners." There were ten girls at each table, so one can speculate that the record-keeper would have been kept busy taking notes.[37]

The Rule 4th of the reconstructed, but well-remembered legislation, stipulated that: a blessing was to be asked before each meal ("Bless us, O Lord, & these thy gifts which we are about to receive, through Jesus Christ our Lord"); and thanks were to be given afterwards ("We give Thee hearty thanks, Almighty Father, for these & all Thy benefits, through Jesus Christ our Lord.")[38] Bertha Moreland also remembered that, in Lucy Maddox's time, the Principal herself said the grace. Finally, each day was to open and close with a brief prayer.[39]

The Trustees–and Lucy Maddox–were keeping a steady hand on the daily workings of the Female Seminary, including what Fausz has called

---

[37] Moreland Interview at pp. 7, 8, 11. Typewritten answers to Questionnaire of Bertha **Moreland** Kerby, Class of 1920, answer to question 9 at p.1. RG 20 Janet Haugaard collection. St. Mary's College of Maryland Archives. Hereafter, cited as Moreland Questionnaire.

[38] St. Mary's Female Seminary Board of Trustees. *Minutes.* "Report of Committee on Rules." "Organic Rules 'A'." Rule 4th. Adopted 17 September 1872. MSA S 231-3, MdHR 12963-2. Manuscript (handwritten). <http://guide.msa.maryland.gov/pages/series.aspx?ID=S231>.

[39] Moreland Interview, at p.7. Moreland Questionnaire, answer to question 9 at p.1.

Music Hall. Main Building, St. Mary's Seminary, St. Mary's City, Md.

"the building boom" of the first decade of the 20th century.[40] Annually, the Trustees paid Mrs. Maddox exactly $750.00 "plus board and garden."[41] From this amount, she was also expected to pay the salaries of her teachers. Little wonder, then, that Mary Gorman had described her teaching salary as "exceedingly small."[42]

The questionnaires sent out by Janet Haugaard in the mid-1990s led "the girls" to remember what life had been like before Adele France was chosen to head the Female Seminary in 1923. According to the oral interview of Bertha Moreland (Class of 1920), "We had a uniform skirt and jacket of blue, and on Sunday we had a cream-colored outfit of the same quality. In late spring and early fall we wore our regular dresses."[43] A photograph on page 59 of Fausz's book shows the girls wearing a neckerchief, loosely knotted in front to suggest a tie.

Girls at that time wore their long hair *up*, in a bun or intricate knot, making them look like miniature versions of their own mothers: the word "teenager" would not emerge until the early 1940s. Until then, middle-class girls (whose parents wanted them to be educated) were called "young ladies."

Classes were held on Saturday, but Monday was always free, unscheduled. The reasoning was simple: if a girl needed immediate medical attention, whether for teeth or eyes, her family would not have been able to get an appointment for her on a Saturday. Thus sprang up the practice of leaving Mondays open in case a medical trip back home was needed. In effect, Mondays replaced Saturdays.

---

40 Fausz 52. This "boom" included the construction of what was then known as the Music Hall (today, St. Mary's Hall). See photo of the Music Hall before the 1924 fire. Bertha Moreland ('20) also recalled: "A very good music teacher came in and taught all the pupils who wanted to study music. Every spring we had a 'Recital.' It was lovely and people came from far and near and enjoyed it. The trustees always came for this and helped to promote it." Three-page handwritten summary titled "Few Thoughts!!" on yellow-lined paper (mailed to the College) by Bertha **Moreland** Kerby, Class of 1920, item 1 at p.1. RG 20 Janet Haugaard collection. St. Mary's College of Maryland Archives. Hereafter cited as Moreland Supplement.

41 Fausz 57.

42 Gorman Letter, at p.4.

43 Moreland Interview, at p.2. Moreland Questionnaire, answer to question 2 at p.1.

Daily life rested to an appreciable extent on good behavior. In a 1998 letter written to her relative, Aleck Loker of Leonardtown, Eleanor **Loker** Sowell (Class of 1918) recalled the following:

> I was a very homesick little girl, a long way from home (16 miles I believe) with horse & buggy transportation. . . . In those days at school a colored man rang a bell in the a.m. & yelled, "Ladies, come on down" to get us up. For our fun[,] if we had no demerits[,] we went to Park Hall in a truck to buy goodies. I had .50 allowance to spend. To earn demerits the only way was to have a midnight feast and get caught. This [the "feast"] was really fun, also toast[ing] marshmallows over [an] oil lamp.[44]

Demerits, however, were not limited to those after-hours "feasts." In an article prepared for the *Baltimore Sun* in 1963, Mildred **Spedden** McDorman (Class of 1914) recalled the following:

> If we didn't get too many demerits through the week for being late to meals or class, for running through the halls, for being untidy or unladylike in any other way, we were rewarded on our day off, Monday, with a trip by oxcart or wagon to Park Hall, 4 miles away. Park Hall's only attraction was a country store, where we bought candy, hair ribbons, black cotton hose, peanut butter, pickles, crackers, cookies and so on. We weren't supposed to eat in our rooms, but most of us had hidden hoards of food for after-hour snacks. We weren't supposed to play cards, either . . . .[45]

Then, as now, girls–but apparently not boys–enjoyed decorating their rooms. Mildred Spedden continued on in the *Baltimore Sun* article referred to by Fausz:

> . . . most of us created . . . what was the rage then–a "cozy corner" . . . [consisting] of a bed decorated as a couch, often

---

44 **Loker** Sowell, Eleanor. Four-page handwritten letter to Aleck [Loker], at pp.2-3 (underlining in original). Jan 17th [1998]. RG 20 Janet Haugaard collection. St. Mary's College of Maryland Archives. Meanwhile, Bertha Moreland (Class of 1920) had a more melodic memory, recalling that Fred rang "the big outside bell . . . at 7:00 A.M. for us to get up, and at this time he also half sang a song that said, 'Get up ladies, get up, ladies, and he [be] ready for breakfast and your classes.' . . . He had other duties in that he cared for any necessity in the building. He was on the go all day." Moreland Questionnaire, answer to question 1 at p.1. The Census of 1910 suggests that this was Fred Biscoe. Additional discussion at p.1 of Moreland Interview.

45 Quoted in Fausz, 54. Citing: Spedden McDorman, Mildred. "Study and Fun at the 'Monument School'" *Baltimore Sunday Sun Magazine*. 10 March 1963, 2.

with a colorful parasol suspended overhead, with pictures, photographs, fans and other souvenirs tacked on the walls nearby.[46]

A windmill behind the Main Building (pictured on page 56 of Fausz's history) operated the pump which provided running water, but, as Mildred Spedden noted in her article for the *Baltimore Sun*, "only when the wind blew. . . . In calm weather we carried our own water and washed in basins." Gas jets illuminated individual rooms and would do so until Adele France hounded the State to finally provide electricity in 1931.

Daily expectations for the Female Seminary would cause today's students to blanch. When Lucy Maddox published her catalogue for the year 1914-1915, she included a schedule. It included the wake-up bell at 6:15 a.m. and breakfast at 7:00. In the evening, girls had to be back in their rooms by 9:00 p.m, and "lights out" was 9:30. Alumna Bertha Moreland (Class of 1920) recalled:

> Our breakfast was at 7:30 A.M., then we returned to our rooms and put them in order. Our rooms were checked and reported to Mrs. Maddox. If your room was not tidy, you had to go to Mrs. Maddox and she gave you a lecture on taking care of your room. [47]

Mrs. Maddox went on to reassure parents that students would be dealing with the following academics: etymology, grammar, rhetoric, reading, American Literature, English literature, mythology, composition, general history, English history, U.S. history, Maryland history, civil government, political geography, physical geography, physiology, astronomy, arithmetic, algebra, geometry, botany, bookkeeping, Latin grammar, and Caesar.

And Mrs. Maddox strove to keep the students up to date on current events and to impress upon them the lessons of history. "About once a month, Mrs. Maddox brought in an interesting speaker to let us know the conditions of the world. . . . On various occasions we had lectures from officers of Maryland." As to World War I (then the "Great War"), she "gave

---

[46] Quoted in Fausz, 54. Such a paper fan is currently located at St. Mary's College of Maryland. Most of the names are from the Classes of 1900, 1901, and 1902.

[47] Moreland Supplement, item 5, at p.2.

us the war situation very often. She was wonderful in keeping us aware of the situation." Mrs. Maddox "also told us the history of Maryland, especially the St. Mary's City history. . . . It was most interesting and educational–this is why I got to love Maryland so and have passed it on to my children."[48]

Athletics balanced academic studying. Exercise and fresh air included: gymnastics, baseball, basketball "in gym bloomers and played out in the open," outdoor games, bicycling, and daily walks. Bertha Moreland confirmed: "Every day we had to take a walk outside – unless it was raining or snowing." As to the basketball teams, see Chapter 4-A, fn 3.[49]

For an overall total of five years, Adele France was part of Lucy Maddox's faculty. As a teacher of mathematics and physics, she watched–with admiration–during the four-year period 1909 to 1913, and then again for school year 1917-1918. No doubt she would have admired the literature assignments in Milton, Tennyson, and Browning.[50]

But Adele would also have been present during the inspection made by William H. Davenport, Secretary of the Board of State Aid and Charities, in April of 1913. His written report called attention to the problems of garbage disposal and sewerage, but it did not stop there. Part of his report is reprinted on page 55 of Fausz's history and calls attention to what would have interested Adele France the most–classroom environment.

> Most of the equipment in the class rooms is very inadequate.. . . The Recitation Rooms are also lacking in maps, pictures and other paraphernalia for properly teaching. . . . The teaching of chemistry and physics without laboratory work is everywhere now regarded as a farce and it is essential . . . that adequate laboratory facilities be furnished.[51]

Chemistry without a lab would indeed be onerous. Although Mina Dirickson **Bell** Tingle, Class of 1913, won the Latin prize at her graduation,

---

48 Moreland Supplement, item 4 at p.1, item 13 at p.3. Moreland Questionnaire, answer to question 25 at p.3.

49 Gorman Letter, p.2. Moreland Supplement, item 10 at p.3.

50 After Bertha **Moreland** Kerby died, her daughter (Mary Kerby) sent the College these books that her mother had used while at the Seminary.

51 Fausz 55.

she also lost no time in slip-sliding down the hill to Church Point where she dug a hole and proceeded to bury her chemistry textbook.[52]

When it came Adele's turn to run the Seminary in 1923, she went to some lengths to create a science laboratory, housing it in the former Delco building just beyond St. Mary's Hall.[53] (See Chapter 9-C-2-a.)

At her interview in 1995, Bertha Moreland, Class of 1920, commented that there was "no contact" between the Female Seminary and the boys' school at Charlotte Hall, although "some girls had brothers there."[54] After the interview, she sent to the College a follow-up summary of 15 points, including the following:

> After dinner we had a little time before the 7:00 p.m. "Study Hall." Mrs. Maddox said that we could do as we liked (orderly, of course). In my time there were two girls from Charlotte Hall (daughters of the head of that school) who played the piano very well. When we wanted to dance at this time we did (it was very enjoyable).[55]

Very enjoyable indeed, and a good time to practice the latest steps. But any interest in ballroom dancing (with young men) was prohibited and instead diverted to a preoccupation with costuming at the Colonial Ball. This activity pushed aside any interest in–for lack of a better word–sex. Mildred **Spedden** McDorman, Class of 1914, wrote the following in her 1963 article for the *Baltimore Sun*:

> We put on plays and minstrel shows, recitals, dances (no male partners), Halloween parties. Our Colonial ball was a tremendous affair, all in costume. At this ball we always had imaginary guests, all of them terribly impressive. James and Dolly Madison, for example; Dorothy Manners, of Carvel Hall; Dorothy Vernon, of Haddon Hall; Mistress Brent, Lady Baltimore, George Washington, Thomas Jefferson. We danced

---

52 This information came to the College from Mina's daughter, Sarah E. Tingle Everding, who also gave the College Mina's 1913 graduation dress.

53 Today this small building has been turned into restrooms for visitors attending concerts in St. Mary's Hall.

54 Moreland Interview, at p.2. Moreland Questionnaire, answer to question 3 at p.1.

55 Moreland Supplement, item 8, at p.2.

the lanciers,[56] the waltz, and the Virginia reel and, with solemn deference to our imaginary guests, our behavior had to be ever so formal.[57]

When the Seminary Trustees unanimously elected Adele France as Principal in 1923, she brought the 20th century to the Female Seminary by (figuratively speaking) raising some long-shut-and-nailed-down windows and thrusting wide open the doors of the Female Seminary. Young girls were now allowed–in fact, encouraged–to go to dances. With male partners. But that must wait for Miss France's own chapter.[58]

---

[56] Lanciers, or the lancers, was a 19th-century quadrille, an early form of square-dancing in which four couples arranged themselves into a square.

[57] Spedden McDorman, Mildred. "I remember . . . Study and Fun at the 'Monument School.'" *Baltimore Sunday Sun Magazine*. 10 March 1963. Print. And as alumna Eleanor Loker Sowell '18 stated: "We were never invited" to dances at Charlotte Hall or Leonard Hall. "It was not permitted before Miss France's time." Loker Questionnaire, answer to questions 2 & 3 at p.1 (underlining in original). RG 20 Janet Haugaard collection. St. Mary's College of Maryland Archives. See also Fausz, 54.

[58] See Chapter 9.

Chapter 6

Slavery

A. LORD BALTIMORE'S MARYLAND COLONY

When did slavery first arrive at St. Mary's City and Lord Baltimore's landmark colony of 1634?

Sooner than one might think–but for reasons which, at the time, were deemed morally acceptable (by the dominant society).

By the time of Lord Baltimore's settlement of St. Mary's City in 1634, Jesuits had been involved in the African slave trade for the past one hundred years. And even though this trade had been focused on the Portuguese missions in Africa and Brazil, "the word was out," so to speak, in Rome, center for the Jesuits. Thus when Leonard Calvert (Lord Baltimore's slightly younger brother and first governor of the 1634 colony) requested slave labor in 1642, he would most probably have been accommodated.

Timothy B. Riordan, head archaeologist at Historic St. Mary's City, dug into old documents; and *The Plundering Time*, published in 2004, documents Leonard Calvert's request for slaves in 1642:

Calvert sold the rest of his patented land on 7 March 1643. This business transaction involved three thousand acres divided into three manors located south of St. Mary's. He sold the land to John Skinner, a merchant or ship's captain, *in exchange for fourteen male and three female slaves to be delivered by March 1, 1644 at St. Mary's*. If the slaves were not delivered, Calvert was to receive 24,000 pounds of tobacco.[1]

This "transaction" took place a mere eight years after the arrival of the *Ark* and the *Dove*. Riordan further writes that:

> the provision concerning slaves suggests that Calvert assumed he would be in the colony to receive them. Nor would he be lacking land on which to seat them. He had more than two thousand acres due him that had not been patented and, if that were not enough, he could easily get a grant from his brother [Cecil Calvert, Lord Baltimore] for more land.[2]

Leonard Calvert was not the only man who owned slaves, although he was one of the very few *rich* men to have acquired them in the earliest years of the 1634 colony. Another wealthy investor, Thomas Cornwaleys (sometimes Cornwallis), as described by Riordan, "lived in a style [Cross Manor] befitting an international tobacco merchant, that is to say a cut above everyone else in Maryland."[3] After Cornwaleys's home had been plundered and reduced to ashes by his one-time friend, Richard Ingle, on February 15th of 1645, a certain Cuthbert Fenwick testified on October 20 of 1646 in London's Chancery (*Cornwaleys* vs. *Ingle*), that Cornwaleys owned three "Negroes."[4] Fenwick himself owned slaves, and, as a widower, wrote them into a 1649 prenuptial agreement (August 1) written prior to his marriage to the middle-aged Mrs. Jane Moryson, widow of Robert Moryson of Virginia:

> The proceedings of the Provincial Court of Maryland show that in 1649, Cuthbert Fenwick (a widower) "in consideration

---

1 Riordan, Timothy B. *The Plundering Time*. Baltimore: Maryland Historical Society, 2004. 104. (Emphasis added.) Print. Hereafter cited as Riordan, *Plundering*. In his footnote to this passage, Riordan cites John W.M. Lee's *The Calvert Papers*, I: 216, Cecil Calvert to his brother, Leonard Calvert, 21 November 1642, p. 140.

2 Riordan, *Plundering* 104-105.

3 Riordan, *Plundering* 191.

4 Riordan, *Plundering* 193.

of the unfayned love & affection that I beare unto Mrs. Jane Moryson" (a widow) agreed prior to their wedding that upon his death, she would receive three Negro servants *and any subsequent children the servants might have*, nine cows *and future calves*, three horses *and future foals*, one half of the household goods, and all of the clothing, rings and jewelry she possessed at that time."[5]

Jane Moryson (the future Mrs. Fenwick) was spelling out for her husband-to-be, Cuthbert Fenwick, what is known as "chattel" slavery, the word "chattel" coming down to us from the Old French word for "cattle." Chattel slavery defined human beings as *things* rather than as people, items that could be spelled out in someone's last will and testament. In the above context, it is clear that the future Mrs. Fenwick thought of slaves in the same breath as livestock.

Riordan notes, however, that this "large investment in bound labor . . . was not present in early Maryland"[6]; and we can therefore be bolstered in deferring large-scale slavery in colonial Maryland until the legislative session of September 1664. In that year, Lord Baltimore's legislative assembly voted that a Negro slave would serve *durante vita*–for life–and his children, and his children's children would live their lives under the same requirement. Both Upper and Lower Houses of the Assembly voted on the new law, suggesting that by 1664, there was already enough support in favor of the Act to ensure its passage.

Nevertheless, Calvert's business-like request of 1642 for 17 slaves (14 male, three female) warrants serious consideration. In 1642, how had Calvert even heard of slaves? When did it happen?

The initial attraction of Lord Baltimore's New World colony of 1634 had not been tobacco. Rather, it was the anticipation of wealth brought about by pelts of–primarily–beaver, although skins of other animals such as muskrat and deer could fetch a good price back in England. Several years earlier, at George Calvert's "Avalon" community in Newfoundland, the goal was not

---

[5] *Proceedings of the Provincial Court, 1658-1662*. Maryland State Archives, Volume 41 (1658): 262. Courtesy of the Maryland State Archives. Emphases added to indicate not only the "thing-ness" of slavery, but also that it could extend to the unborn, whether animals or children.

[6] Riordan, *Plundering* 196.

fur but fish. By 1629, however, a morose Lord Baltimore was writing the following to King Charles I about Newfoundland's Avalon community:

> From the middest of October to the middest of May there is a sad face of winter upon all this land, both sea and land so frozen for the greatest part of tyme as they are not penetrable, no plant or vegetable thing appearing out of the earth until it be about the beginning of May nor fish in the sea besides the ayre so intolerable cold as it is hardly to be endured . . . my howse hath beene an hospital all this winter.[7]

Under English law, it was only the first son who inherited his father's goods and title, leaving younger sons to fend for themselves, whether as officers in the military, or as clergy in the state-supported Anglican church, or even as "gentleman Adventurers" to the New World. Catholics (including, of course, Jesuits) had been disallowed throughout England and her colonies since the Reformation and the late 1500s, but in the first half of the 1600s, both Lord Baltimores had promised religious tolerance to their colonies: first, George Calvert at Avalon (in Newfoundland), and second, his son Cecil Calvert, at St. Mary's City (in Maryland).

Those younger sons who had decided to invest financially in Lord Baltimore's Maryland colony were known as "gentleman Adventurers"–the word "adventurers" suggesting open-ended risk. If we separate the word into its constituent parts (ad-*venture*), we can imagine these younger sons as what, today, we might call "venture capitalists." For these men, the New World–and the pelts of its choicest animals–must have seemed like an open playground, well worth the financial investment in Lord Baltimore's proposed voyage. This financial investment was to be followed by the calculated risk of an ocean crossing, leading to settlement in an unknown– and possibly threatening–"new world."

Better yet, in Lord Baltimore's outpost of religious tolerance, these young men–17 or so in number–would be free to be openly Catholic. The importance of this extraordinary permission cannot be overstated. Catholics who chose to remain Catholic (rather than converting to the state-

---

[7] "Sir George Calvert and the Colony of Avalon." Newfoundland and Labrador Heritage Website. <www.heritage.nf.ca/articles/exploration/calvert-avalon-colony.php>.

run church now managed by Anglicans) had been persecuted throughout the reigns of Henry VIII, Elizabeth I, James I, and now Charles I: in all, roughly one hundred years. True, between Henry and Elizabeth there had been the five-year reign of "Bloody" Mary I, a Catholic who reversed the persecutions and sent Anglicans to the same fate as those previously endured only by Catholics: torture, fire, and hangings (particularly those of the draw-and-quarter variety).

B. COLONIAL CULTURE OF THE WEST INDIES

Several excellent books and articles–scrupulously scholarly–have been written about the Maryland colony at St. Mary's City; these generally focus on the colonial relationship to political events taking place in England, the little colony's mother country. These studies, however, travel on an England-to-Maryland axis, often ignoring the totality of colonial culture in the West Indies, whether Catholic or Protestant.

However, the *Ark* did not sail directly to Maryland: it first spent considerable time sailing among the islands of the West Indies, as did most other vessels voyaging out of England. What the *Ark* saw and learned on the island of Barbados, for example, was a forerunner of what it would learn soon afterwards on St. Christopher (half of which was English-speaking and–like Barbados–Anglican/Protestant). These two islands had only recently been settled: Barbados by 1627, and St. Christopher by 1630 (resettled by the English after battles and power-struggles with the Kalinago, also known as Caribs, France, and Spain).

The climate of the Caribbean favored (and still does today) the cultivation of sugar, that "sweet salt" introduced to the Caribbean by Christopher Columbus in the last decade of the 1400s. Sugarcane, however, requires extensive labor–row after row, plantation after plantation–devoted entirely to its production. Who was going to farm it? Barbados did not turn to sugarcane until the decade of the 1640s; until then it had favored tobacco, thereby placing it in (unfortunate) competition with the colony of Virginia. Tobacco, however, is also labor-intensive, and it was probably in the 1640s that Barbados first began importing slave labor to replace indentured servants, initially Irish who were kidnapped and sold into servitude, and later enslaved Africans.

Two problems await any researcher wanting to delve into the problem which the West Indies present, and it is the first of these two which presents the most problems.

1. Language

As we would express it today, in the 1600s, all the islands of the West Indies were "up for grabs," seizures that often extended to outright warfare. In this, the European countries were expanding the role of "Cujus regio, ejus religio," roughly translated as "Whoever owns the country, it is his to impose the religion."[8]

The Dutch (who, like the English, were also "Protestant" in the broad sense that they were not Roman Catholic) eventually made landfall on the north coast of both Guyana (now Suriname) and Venezuela as well as the West Indian islands of Sint [Saint] Maarten, Aruba, Bonaire, and Curaçao.

The French, however, were Catholic, and claimed, among other islands,[9] Martinique, Guadeloupe, and the French half of St. Christopher. Father Andrew White particularly enjoyed the French portion of St. Christopher–today's St. Kitts–since it was Catholic and, as a Jesuit from the *Ark*, he was well-treated.

From around 1659 to 1804, Saint-Domingue was a French colony on the western portion of the island of Hispaniola. In 1804, after a successful slave rebellion, the Republic of Haiti was established, becoming the first country to abolish slavery in the "new world" *and* the first independent nation and republic of Latin America and the Caribbean.

The Spanish, who were also Catholic, had the best of the West Indies, with the far larger colonies of Cuba, Puerto Rico, Hispaniola (in 1844, after a 22-year annexation by Haiti, the eastern portion of this island–then known

---

8 This pronouncement (also spelled as "cuius regio, eius religio") had first been expressed at the Treaty of Augsburg in 1555.

9 As well as the Caribbean coastal territory in South America, known as French Guiana or Guyane.

as Santo Domingo–became the independent nation of the Dominican Republic), and also Florida.

Therefore, for researchers who speak English, pertinent colonial records can be found on Barbados (as well as in London), but scholars investigating the colonies of Martinique or the Dominican Republic, for example, need at least a reading knowledge of French or Spanish–and probably also Latin, which at that time was the common language of record.

As a group, however, all the various colonies of the West Indies were treated by their European governments in much the same way: whether the output was tobacco or sugarcane, it necessarily involved African slavery.

2. Ability to Think Colonially

American scholars (by which is meant citizens of the United States) tend to think in terms of governments similar to their own: discrete, stand-alone. Men of the 1600s, however, thought not only of home governments, but also of the profit-bearing colonies in the West Indies. Thus, what today we call "the United States" as well as "the Caribbean" requires genuine readjustment in our thinking.

The entire eastern half of the so-called "New World"–always coastal–was described in terms of its *colonies*, including: Hispaniola (Spanish, 1493); Puerto Rico (Spanish, 1493); Havana (Spanish, 1514); St. Augustine (Spanish Florida, 1565); Jamestown (English, 1607); Plymouth (English Pilgrims, 1620); Barbados (English, 1625); St. Christopher (English/French, mid 1620s); Salem (English, Puritans, 1626); Curaçao (Dutch, 1634); **St. Mary's City (English, 1634)**; Providence (English, 1636); Nieuw Amsterdam, the future New York City (Dutch, 1624); St. Maarten (Dutch, 1631, 1648); Annapolis (English, Puritans, 1649); Charleston (English, 1663); Ste. Domingue (French, 1659); and New Orleans (French, 1690s).

The settlements in the West Indies and Florida were not, as we would say today, "West Indian colonies" or even "Caribbean colonies." The men of that time did not think that way. They spoke of "England's colonies," or "Spain's colonies," or "France's colonies," or "the Dutch colonies." And as such, these many islands formed *separate chains of contact within their own language*–especially for home-country news, gossip, and letters.

Inter-island gossip was, of course, carried by ship, and settlers in St. Mary's City knew what was going on in the other English colonies. For example, which colonial governor was being recalled? (Governor Harvey of Jamestown). Who was leaving Barbados for a better position in another English colony? (William Hawley). Who was leaving the Virginia colony in order to marry Cuthbert Fenwick of St. Mary's City? (Jane Moryson). And so it went.

As the 1600s moved on, slave traffic from Africa to Barbados increased. How, and why, did this happen? To understand, we must first take a very quick look–a general overview–of slavery. And to do this, we must first understand that when slavery is the topic, it was considered by the dominant classes as "business as usual."

C. SLAVERY: ECONOMICS TRUMPS MORALITY

If one goes to an online search for the word *slavery*, one quickly discovers that slavery is not uncommon, and that the enslavement of one group by another is predictable, particularly as an outcome of war. As a word, *slavery* is most easily found in online sites devoted exclusively to that topic, but such sites are of varying value.

The following websites are recommended and form the basis of much of the background research for this chapter:

(1) www.historyworld.net/worldhis/plaintexthistories;

(2) www://en.wikipedia.org/wiki/Catholic-Church-and-slavery;

(3) the Mariners' Museum is particularly recommended for students and the general reader at www.marinersmuseum.org; and also

(4) www.brycchancarey.com/slavery/chrono3.

From these sites, one learns that slavery–in various forms–already existed in cultures that pre-date our modern era. During the centuries that we call either "B.C." ("before Christ") or "bce" ("before the common era"), the ancient Babylonian Code of Hammurabi (1750 B.C.) seems to have acknowledged slavery from within its own Mesopotamian ranks. For example, the Code stipulated that if a man was unable to pay his debts, one option available to him was to sell his wife into slavery for three years.

Generally, conquerors enslaved–and sexually exploited–diverse peoples over whom they had been victorious in battle (thereby, incidentally, creating a new gene pool). In ancient Greece, Spartans enslaved Athenians, and Romans, when their turn came, enslaved the Greeks. Alexander the Great boasted that he had made slaves out of the Medes and Persians (today's Iranians). Muslims enthusiastically made slaves out of non-Muslims, a practice revived in the 21st century when Muslim fighters (of the Boko Haram group) captured Nigerian schoolgirls and raped them into pregnancy. Several Christian popes made galley slaves out of captured Muslims. In the 15th century, Czar Ivan the Terrible enslaved Siberian pagans.

During the period when the Roman Empire extended itself as far north as England, Romans generally forbore making slaves of the native Britons (Celts). But once the Roman Empire fell in 476 A.D., Angles and Saxons–from what today we call Germany–overran southern England and enslaved the British Celts. These Germanic invaders spoke a language we now call Anglo-Saxon, and they called their newly conquered territory "Ængle-lond." Hapless Celts fled north to Scotland, or west to Wales, or across the Irish Sea to Ireland, or even across the English Channel to the French peninsula we know today as Brittany. In all of these places, Gaelic–that is, some form of Celtic–can occasionally still be heard, well over a thousand years later.

Enter the Vikings from what is today Norway, Denmark, Sweden, and Finland: it was almost 800 A.D. when they began to enslave the peoples of northern Europe, terrorizing them from open boats called *longships* or *dragonships*. Slaves were made out of the Slavic peoples along the coasts of the eastern Mediterranean, just before the Vikings advanced (overland, from the northeast) into the great land mass of today's Russia. Two matters of interest: the word "slave" comes from the slavery of those ***Slav***ic peoples; and today one can see on television images of contemporary Russians whose reddish-blond hair reveals their long-ago Viking ancestors (DNA tells the truth).

And Christianity? Slavery undertaken by the Christian church has had a checkered history, seldom lacking in what was purported to be "moral" justification. At its root, the economic needs of any given culture will override religious needs. Because Christian theologians were members of specific cultures, they were not immune to the economic needs of their own people and thus attempted to provide "justification" for slave labor.

Proponents of slavery usually pointed to the Bible, not as an amalgam of cultural history and religious precept, but instead as a document divine in origin, *the precise and literal words of God*. Bolstered by this religious fundamentalism, proponents of slavery could find in the Torah (Christianity's Old Testament) the story of Noah's curse upon Ham. Ham, sometimes written as Cham, was portrayed as the forebear of all black-skinned peoples. According to the story in the book of *Genesis* (chapters 6-9), after the rain and floods had receded, and after the ark was opened once again, eight people were still alive to repopulate the entire earth. These were Noah, Noah's wife, and their three sons: Ham, Shem, and Japheth (JAY-feth), plus the wife of each son.

From this point on, the story becomes muddled, but later Israelites made sense out of the varied people they came in contact with by assigning to Shem (and his descendants) all of the Asian peoples, and to Japheth (and his descendants) the race of all white peoples. That left Ham (Cham). Ham (and his descendants) had been cursed by Noah, since Ham had seen his father (Noah) drunken and naked. What then became known as "Noah's curse" was eventually leveled on *all* Africans, particularly from Africa's vast sub-Saharan region. In short, beginning in the 15th century of our modern period, the book of *Genesis* appeared to provide Biblical justification for condemning all black-skinned peoples to slavery. Well before the advent of biblical scholarship in the mid-19th century, such a story would indeed prove to be a curse.

The New Testament of early Christians further hardened the purported legitimacy of slavery, bearing out our observation that economic needs are likely to trump those of morality. Jesus of Nazareth never spoke one way or the other about slavery, but Saul of Tarsus, eventually canonized as Saint Paul, lived in a culture which expected (a) silence from women and (b) obedience from slaves. Throughout his missionary travels, Paul wrote letters ("epistles") in which he urged Christians to be faithful to the new teachings of Jesus, to wait for Jesus's return to earth, and–from Paul's cultural point of view–to maintain a peaceful society until then. According to his epistles, in such a peaceful society, women were expected to obey their husbands, were not supposed to teach, were to remain silent in church (I Timothy 2:11-12; also Ephesians 5:22-24), and, for modesty, to cover their heads while at prayer (I Corinthians 11:2-16). Further, slaves were reminded to "obey your masters" (Ephesians 6:5; I Peter 2:18; and Titus 2:9).

Today, modern historians have little trouble taking a long, hard look at Christian justifications for slavery. One such is Frank E. Smitha (sometimes "Smith"), historian of the very early Portuguese slave trade in Africa. The trade had begun when the Portuguese "claimed" the African coast of Guinea in 1446, and later with the 1479-80 Treaty of Alcáçovas-Toledo, the Catholic Monarchs of Aragon and Castile conceded the Portuguese slave-trade monopoly on the Cape Verde Islands, just off the coast of Africa.

By 1540, Ignatius de Loyola had formed the Society of Jesus, and almost immediately Jesuits turned their early missionary activities to India, Brazil, and Africa. Frank Smitha writes the following about their missionary activity in 1540s Angola and their apologia:

> In Luanda [a seaport in Angola], Jesuits quarreled among themselves but united against those colonial governors who attempted to interfere with their activities. The Jesuits were responsible for education. They trained blacks and mulattos for the clergy and for lower administrative positions in the colony's bureaucracy. . . . While participating in the slave trade, the Jesuits took on the role of protector of the Africans, believing that the best way to convert Africans was to sell them, in order to introduce them to Christianity through the dignity of labor on plantations in the Americas. Ships owned by the Jesuits were engaged in the shipment of slaves from Luanda to Brazil. And before departing, slaves were baptized

en masse. Although wishing to protect the Africans, the Jesuits sanctioned the use of force against them, claiming that Africans were an unreasonable people who responded only to corporal punishment.[10]

A second historian is Raymond Schroth, currently a Jesuit writer for the weekly *America*. In 2007, he published "The American Jesuits: A History," in which he wrote, "Even up to the Civil War there does not seem to have been a consensus among American Jesuits, most of whom were foreign born, that Negro slavery was immoral."[11]

In 2011, Schroth was followed by historian Owen Stanwood of Boston College, who wrote the following:

> Moreover, some of these Africans, it seemed, were already Catholic before arriving in the New World. A large number of slaves in Carolina came from either the Portuguese colony in Angola–where Jesuit priests routinely performed mass baptisms of captives before sending them into slavery–or the Kingdom of Kongo, an independent African state with its own Catholic Church.[12]

D. STIRRINGS: WHAT "THE NEW WORLD" PROMISED

As the late 1400s turned into the 1500s, three European explorers made pivotal voyages across the Atlantic: Christopher Columbus,[13] Amerigo Vespucci, and John Cabot. Also, a Sevillian merchant's son, later turned Dominican friar, would play a pivotal role in the Spanish *encomienda* system of forced labor.

To the end of his days, and even after his four westbound voyages across the Atlantic, **Christopher Columbus** believed that what he had "discovered" was, he hoped, Japan and perhaps the Far-Eastern islands of "the Indies." (Not, however, the land masses which today we call "America.")

---

10 Smitha, Frank E. "Expansion and Slave Trading from Luanda." 16-17th centuries index "EUROPEANS to ASIA and AFRICA in the 1500s (3 of 3)." <www.fsmitha.com>.

11 Schroth, Raymond A. *The American Jesuits: A History*. New York: NYU Press, 2009. 26. Print.

12 Stanwood, Owen. *The Empire Reformed: English America in the Age of the Glorious Revolution (Early American Studies)*. Philadelphia: University of Pennsylvania Press, 2013. 217-18. Print.

13 Cristóbal Colón, in Spanish. He was born in the born in the *Serenissima Repubblica di Genova*.

In roughly the same decade as Columbus, it would be left to the talented–and better educated–**Amerigo Vespucci** to realize that South America was an entire continent, not an island. Around 1502, he wrote his friend, Lorenzo di Pierfrancesco de' Medici, that what we now call South America must be "a new world."

A new world indeed. It is to **Columbus** that we must turn when searching for the introduction of slavery into this "New World" of North America and its islands, the West Indies. Columbus's first voyage in 1492 was generally exploratory and limited to the West Indian islands of the Bahamas, Cuba, and Hispaniola.

In 1493, however, during his second voyage, out of a total of four, he brought sugar cane ("sweet salt") from the Canary Islands, off the coast of Africa, onto the large West Indian island he named "Hispaniola."[14] Because Columbus believed he had reached not only Japan but also the *East* Indies, he designated the natives of Hispaniola with the name of "Indians."

It soon became clear, however, that these "Indians" were not interested in the heavy labor of cutting down sugar cane. The work is messy, labor-intensive, and back-breaking: it is carried out in a permanently stooped-over position as the field-hand, machete in hand, must first whack at the tough base of an eight-foot stalk, bringing it down to ground level, but being careful to ensure that the basal node will re-grow and produce more cane in the future.

Columbus's solution to the problem of recalcitrant Indians was simple: torture them until they either complied or fell dead. Columbus left orders with underlings, but he was forced to wait five more years before making his third voyage in 1498, when he was arrested by the Governor of Hispaniola, who accused him of cruelty and torture. Columbus denied the charges, and the king of Spain ordered his release from jail, the restoration of his assets, and ended up funding his fourth and final voyage in 1502.

In 1502, 18-year-old **Bartolomé de las Casas**, travelled to Hispaniola and became a landowner with his merchant-father, "owning" native Taino

---

14 Today, Hispaniola is divided between French-speaking and Creole-speaking Haiti, formerly Ste. Domingue, and the Spanish-speaking Dominican Republic, formerly Santo Domingo.

slaves. Even though he was ordained a secular priest in Rome in 1507, a few years later, he would join other landowners in Hispaniola who complained to the king about the anti-slavery position taken by Dominican friars who had criticized what they perceived as genocide of the Indians.

In 1513, after participating in the Spaniards' conquest of Cuba, Las Casas was awarded with *encomienda* land and slaves. Perhaps the sheer brutality of that repression of the native Indians was what compelled him, a year later, to give up his lands and his slaves. He decided to preach against the evils of enslaving Indians–much like the Dominican friars, whom he had previously opposed, had done.

In 1515, Las Casas travelled back to Spain to try and persuade the king (who died in 1516) and later the Holy Roman Emperor, King Charles V, to put an end to the *encomienda* system of land and forced labor. Yet the *encomienda* was lucrative to those in power, and in 1516, Las Casas proposed instead the use of *Africans* as slave labor to work the sugar cane instead of indigenous Indians of the "New World." During King Charles V's reign, Las Casas was appointed as the first "Protector of the Indians." It was not until after Las Casas became a Dominican friar in 1523 that he repented of this introduction of black slavery into the West Indies, but by then the damage had been done. In his 1526 *Historia de Las Indias*, Las Casas wrote:

> I soon repented and judged myself guilty of ignorance. I came to realize that black slavery was as unjust as Indian slavery . . . and I was not sure that my ignorance and good faith would secure [save] me in the eyes of God.[15]

As an Englishman, **John Cabot**'s claim to fame was his 1497 "discovery" of Newfoundland (new-found-land). In his second voyage of 1498, he and his ships were lost at sea. If one then wonders why John Cabot is so important to our discussion of slavery, it is simply this: he had set sail from Bristol (at that time England's second largest seaport), located on the southwest coast. The "West Country" counties of Cornwall and Devon, hotbeds of seafaring activity, boasted such coastal names as Plymouth, Falmouth, Bristol, and Exeter. This southwest corner of England was destined to become rife with

---

[15] De las Casas, Bartolomé. *History of the Indies*.1527. *Wikipedia*. Web. <https://en.wikipedia.org/wiki/Human_rights_in_Haiti>.

the lore of sea voyages, including those of John Cabot. From seaports such as these emerged two legendary men: John Hawkins, and Francis Drake. Both learned about African slavery, how it worked, and how it was being rewarded at the topmost level of society.

E. ENGLAND'S "SEA DOGS"

The dictionary is polite about the nautical term "sea dog," describing it simply as "an experienced sailor." But certainly I remember the early 16th-century term "sea dog" from elementary school, when we all thrilled to learn that such men as Francis Drake and John Hawkins (sometimes "Hawkyns") had both earned the title "Sir" before their names because of their sea-dog piracy on the high seas.

Actually, "piracy" is not the right word. Kings and queens used the term "privateering," which meant that piracy was being conducted *under their sovereign's orders* from English and other European monarchs. Privateers carried with them "a letter of marque," a government document which endorsed their piracy.

Such piracy was not only about gold and silver (which was to be expected from privateers) but far more seriously about slaves–which as 5th-graders we certainly hadn't been told about. Never mind that the (pre-Reformation) Archbishop of Canterbury had already banned slavery outright back at England's Westminster Council in 1102, describing it as "that shameful trading whereby heretofore used in England to be sold like brute beasts."[16] Sea-dogs like John Hawkins and Francis Drake (second cousin to each other) came from the southwest, those sea-faring counties of Cornwall and Devon–and were brought up to admire both piracy and "privateering" on the high seas.

The English were late to the slave-trade (as enslavers; see fn 16), following the Portuguese and the Spanish, both of whom shared the vast peninsula that faces Africa, jutting out as it does into the Atlantic Ocean. Initially, what was to become the English slave-trade began as simple "privateering" attacks on silver-and-gold-bearing Spanish galleons of the late 1500s.

---

16 Manco, Jean. "The Saxon Slave Market." *The Bristol Magazine*, July 2006. 15. Print. Archbishop Anselme was referring to the sale of English slaves (to the Irish, among other buyers).

Fortunately for historians, the voyages of both Hawkins and Drake were written up by geographer and chronicler Richard Hakluyt (HAK-loot), whose dates are 1552-1616.[17] In any discussion of slavery, it is to Richard Hakluyt that we are indebted for his writing on John Hawkins, England's first "sea-dog."

In 1562, Hawkins formed a syndicate of wealthy Londoners who invested in his voyages. His initial voyage would prove to be the first of the "Triangular [slave] Trade" of the 16th through the 18th centuries–and even beyond. Armed with "a letter of marque" from Queen Elizabeth, Hawkins's technique was to sail to the west coast of Africa, rob the Portuguese of their slaves, cross the Atlantic, and sell those same slaves in the Spanish colonies–either on Hispaniola or much farther south in Borburata, on the coast of modern-day Venezuela. Hakluyt described all three of Hawkins's voyages in detail, the following quotation (verbatim) coming from his account of Hawkins's first voyage in 1562-63:

> From thence [Teneriffe, in the Canary Islands, just off the coast of Africa], hee [Hawkins] passed to Sierra Leona, upon the coast of Guinea . . . where he stayed some good time, and got into his possession, partly by the sword and partly by other meanes, to the nomber of 300. negroes at the least. . . . With this preye he sailed ouer [over] the Ocean sea vnto the island of Hispaniola [the Dominican Republic and Haiti now share this island] . . . .[18]

On his second voyage to Africa (1564-65), Hawkins was joined by his younger cousin, Francis Drake, also from the seafaring coast of England's "West Country." Although Drake and Hawkins travelled on separate ships, we may conclude that the shackled slaves captured from the Guinea Coast were ill-treated by the crew of both men.

By way of contrast, Hawkins's words to his own crew are humane, even Christian: he urged his men to "Serue [serve] God dayly, loue [love] one

---

[17] Hakluyt was well educated and was appointed Secretary of State to Queen Elizabeth; he was almost certainly read by his contemporary, William Shakespeare, who died in 1616, the same year as Hakluyt.

[18] Hakluyt, Richard. *The Hawkins' Voyages During the Reigns of Henry VIII, Queen Elizabeth, and James I*. London: Printed for the Hakluyt Society, 1878. "The First Voyage of Sir John Hawkins," 6. Print. Hereafter cited as Hakluyt.

another, preserve your victuals [food supply], beware of fire, and keepe good companie." These Christian thoughts, however, accord little with the treatment meted out to the "cargo" of African slaves. On this same second voyage, Hawkins noted that, "we came to Cape Verde [islands off the coast of Africa] . . . these people are all blacke, and are called Negroes; without any apparell, sauing [saving] before their priurities [privates]: of stature goodly men, and well liking . . . ." On this voyage, Hawkins also described the first open canoe he had ever seen, one capable of holding 60 men, who stood up in order to paddle.[19]

According to Secretary of State Richard Hakluyt, John Hawkins's ensuing trade in slaves was brisk and violent: "In this Island [Sambula] we staied certaine daies, going every day a shoare [on shore every day] to take the Inhabitants with burning, and spoiling their townes . . . ."[20]

The Hawkins/Drake third voyage took place from 1567-69 and was headed once again for the Portuguese-dominated Cape Verde Islands. This time, however, certain Africans appear to have been complicit in the slave trade, anxious to sell men whom they had apparently captured in a local war:

> [T]here came to vs a Negroe, sent from a King, oppressed by other Kings his neighbours, desiring our aide, with promise, that as many Negroes as by these wares [wars] might be obtained . . . should be at our pleasure. . . . Now had we obtained between 4. and 500. [400 and 500] Negroes, wherewith we thought it somewhat reasonable to seeke the coast of the West Indies . . . .[21]

Leaving the Guinea Coast, the Hawkins/Drake fleet now "obtained a secret trade" (in Cartagena, Colombia) and did indeed sail north from there, calling in at other islands in the West Indies.

---

19 Hakluyt, "The Second Voyage of M. John Hawkins," 9, 19, 18. The word "negro" is both Spanish and Portuguese; its English translation is "black."

20 Hakluyt, "The Second Voyage of M. John Hawkins," 16-17. Presumably, Sambula was part of the Cape Verde Islands.

21 Hakluyt, "The Third Voyage of M. John Hawkins," 71-72.

Questions: In 1562, what had led Hawkins to set his first course south for Africa (instead of, say, to the west and Newfoundland, John Cabot's earlier goal)? More to the point, how had Hawkins managed to persuade London investors to help pay for that voyage? Was it the economic lure of the slave trade? Just possibly he had heard of a Yorkshire sailor named Martin Frobisher: according to one source, "Before reaching manhood, Frobisher had been on two voyages to the Guinea Coast." If "manhood" means age 18, then Frobisher had become aware of the Portuguese slave trade by the very early year of 1555. (Frobisher was later knighted by Queen Elizabeth following the Spanish Armada debacle of 1588.)[22]

Clearly, England was now keenly aware (as it had not been before) of what Africa provided: dark-skinned men and women who could be captured and "traded" in lands that had been claimed only a few decades earlier by Columbus. Such new knowledge about the spoils of Africa may have come from captured Spanish vessels, or it may have been "scuttlebutt" on ships arriving back home at their English ports.[23]

Francis Drake, the better known of these two West Country "sea-dogs," joined his cousin (on a separate vessel) during Hawkins's two subsequent voyages, not only in seizing-and/or-trading for blacks from the Guinea Coast of Africa, but also in attacking Spanish galleons, heavy with gold and silver from the New World, particularly Mexico and Bolivia. In 1717, a gold coin known as a "guinea" entered England's currency; it was worth one pound (£1) plus one shilling.

King Phillip II of Spain was hardly pleased with the loss of his fortunes from the New World, and his 1588 decision to send the Spanish Armada to England now became a two-pronged goal: (1) stop the English from plundering Spanish vessels; and (2) stop the ongoing heresy of the Reformation by replacing Queen Elizabeth with Mary, Queen of Scots, a devout Catholic. Phillip's Armada was impressive and should have beaten the English: it consisted of 130 ships, 8,000 sailors, and 19,000 solders. But

---

22 <www.encyclopedia.com/people/history/explorers-travelers-and-conquerors-biographies/sir-martin-frobisher>. Web. 27 Oct. 2014.

23 The word "scuttlebutt" refers to the coal-scuttle on ships. A "scuttle" had a wide lip (or "butt") for pouring out coal, and it had become a good place for shipboard gossip or "scuttlebutt." Today, its equivalent as a place for gossip might be the office water-cooler.

the Armada ran into bad weather and, trapped in the Channel between the coasts of England and France, it was defeated by the English who sent "fireboats" (literally, smaller craft deliberately set on fire) in and out among the awkward Spanish galleons.[24]

By contrast, Queen Elizabeth was outright delighted with her three admirals (Hawkins, Drake, and Frobisher) who had been regarded as spectacularly triumphant over the Armada in August of 1588. John Hawkins was rewarded with a knighthood in that same year. *Sir* Francis Drake had already been knighted in 1581 after having circumnavigated the globe on his vessel, the *Golden Hind*. (In knighthood, Sir Walter Raleigh joined his contemporaries–Drake, Frobisher, and Hawkins–but unlike them he was an aristocrat and came from an elite upper class.)

In 1588, the English victory over the Spanish Armada would have been shouted through the streets of London and featured in the "broadsides" of the day–that is, single-sheet newsprint, costing only half a penny (HAPE-nee). England's victory over Spain became part of the national consciousness, much as "D-Day," "Pearl Harbor," and even "9-11" have recently become for the United States.[25] We can be sure that as the very late 1500s turned the corner into the early 1600s, English pride would have swelled at the memory of its national victory over the Spanish, which was embellished by, what today we would call, political spin. Queen Elizabeth's death in 1603 was followed by the ascent of (Anglican) James I to the throne, James being the great-great-grandson of Henry VII and the son of Mary, Queen of Scots.

The naval successes of both Drake and Hawkins would be well-remembered–a scant two generations later–in the little start-up colonies of the (English-language) West Indies as well as Virginia (1607), and now Maryland (1634). West Indian islands revealed (and still do today) their cultural and religious origins: some were Catholic (Spanish and French islands), and some Protestant (English and Dutch islands).

---

24 Before the 1558 death of Mary I of England ("Bloody Mary," an English Catholic), King Phillip II of Spain, also Catholic, had been Mary's long-distance husband and thus *jure uxoris* King of England from 1554-1558. If Phillip's Armada had been successful, England's Protestant Reformation might have been balked. See Chapter 2-B & 2-C. Phillip (1527-1598) was also known as Philip the Prudent.

25 George Calvert, later to become the first Lord Baltimore, would have been a child of eight at the time. (He was the father of Cecil Calvert, the second Lord Baltimore.)

For our purposes, however, the military defeat of Spain's Armada would also be remembered by those Englishmen who would soon struggle ashore in the little Maryland colony of 1634. (Were any of the many Protestants on board the *Ark* just possibly the grandsons of the men who had fought and vanquished the Spanish Armada?)

It is time to look once again at the *Ark* and the *Dove*. Taken together, their 200-plus passengers were undoubtedly divided in their opinions of England's military might. The minority (perhaps 17) of aristocratic "Catholic gentlemen" were under the care of 55-year-old Father Andrew White, a priest who–until becoming a Jesuit at age 26–had completed all his schooling at Catholic (but English-language) schools in Spain. Andrew White had then gone on to teach on the Continent in both Liège and Douay.

These Catholic "Adventurers" on board the *Ark* would have been wary of the English (Protestant) victory over Catholic Spain and its Armada of very recent memory. To offset any trouble, Catholic adventurers had been warned by Cecil Calvert, the second Lord Baltimore, not to, quite literally, "rock the boat" by being too obviously Catholic in their religious devotions.

That first paragraph of Lord Baltimore's instructions to passengers has often been quoted (see Chapter 2-C, including fn 7), but it is important to remember (as Father Andrew White most certainly did) the *ten* paragraphs of shipboard instructions that followed Baltimore's oft-quoted opening paragraph. The entire set of instructions, dated November 15th of 1633, is included in Appendix D, but an important paragraph from Lord Baltimore is also reproduced below in the following section, "Anchors Aweigh."[26]

F. FROM THE *ARK* AND *DOVE*: "ANCHORS AWEIGH!"

It is hard for us to imagine the tension and unease that must have gripped the Catholic voyagers on Lord Baltimore's *Ark*. Our only account of that voyage comes from Father Andrew White, the Jesuit who waited (probably with two other Jesuits) before boarding the *Ark* on November 22nd 1633,

---

26 The second Lord Baltimore (Cecil Calvert) becomes a little more real for us when we learn that he lived in London: "[his] house is in Bloomsberrie, at the upper end of Halborne, in London." See Lemay, J.A. Leo. *Men of Letters in Colonial Maryland*. Knoxville: University of Tennessee Press,1972. "Andrew White, Apostle of Maryland" at 8-27. Print.

when it put into Cowes Harbour, Isle of Wight, in the English Channel. Both the *Ark* and *Dove* had been prepared to sail as early as mid-October, but the ships had been recalled (mid-Thames) until all the passengers had taken the Oath of Allegiance to Charles I on October 29th. That oath stipulated, in part, that "our Soveraigne Lord King CHARLES is lawfull King of this Realme . . . And that the *Pope* neither of himselfe, nor by any Authority of the Church or Sea [See] of *Rome* . . . hath any power or authority to depose the King. . . ."[27]

This enforced stoppage was beyond simple nuisance: it led Lord Baltimore to address an 11-paragraph warning not only to Leonard Calvert (his younger brother/deputy governor) but also to the two appointed commissioners sailing on the "*Ark*": Jerome Hawley and Thomas Cornwaleys. As Father White's account of the voyage would later demonstrate, he was by now acutely mindful of Lord Baltimore's *second* paragraph, that is, the watch-out-for-trouble warnings to Catholics on both the *Ark* and the *Dove*:

> That while they [the Catholics] are aboard, they do theyre best endeavors by such instruments as they shall find fittest for it, amongst the seamen and passengers to discover what any of them do know concerning the private plotts of his Lo[pps]. [Lordship's] adversaries in England, who endeavored to overthrow his voyage: to learne, if they cann, the names of all such, their speeches, where and when they spoke them, and to whom; The places, if they had any, of their consultations, the Instruments they used and the like; to gather what proofes they cann of them; and to sett them downe particulerly and cleerely in writing wth all the Circumstances; together wth. their opinions of the truth and validity of them according to the condition of the persons from whom they had the information;

---

27 "The Oath of Allegiance." *ENGLANDS OATHS. Taken by all men of Quallity in the Church and Common-wealth of ENGLAND.* 1642. London: Published by G.F. for satisfaction of his Parishioners. Print. <http://www.lukehistory.com/resources/oaths.html>. Web. 17 August 2021. See also Chapter 2-D at year 1625 of the chronological grid. A copy of this Oath of Allegiance is included as "Appendix D" in the following book available online at the U.S. Library of Congress. Russell, William Thomas. *Maryland; the land of sanctuary.* Baltimore: J. H. Furst company, 1907. "Oath of Allegiance" at 529-30. Print.

And to gett if they cann every such informer to sett his hand to his informačon. . . .²⁸

An Introduction by Clayton Colman Hall to the above indicates that the phrase "his Lordship's adversaries" refers to the "old Virginia Company" of London, which feared that a new colony to the north of Virginia might prove economically competitive.

In other words, the Catholics were to detect any Protestant subversion and report back.

Father White had good reason for vigilance. Perhaps he kept a personal journal of what he personally experienced on board the *Ark*, referring to it when it came time to write his *three* 1634 accounts of the voyage. One in Latin was sent to his Jesuit superior, then immediately translated by White himself into an English version. Both were apparently written (perhaps in May) of 1634. These two were followed by yet a third account which White wrote in July of 1634, "A Relation of the Successful Beginnings of the Lord Baltimore's Plantation in Maryland." But, in that all-important *first* account of the voyage of the *Ark* (in both Latin and English), Father White describes the outset of the voyage:

> . . . fear was not absent. For the [Protestant] sailors were muttering among themselves that they were expecting a messenger and a letter from London, and for that reason they seemed to be devising delays. But God destroyed their evil plans. . . . In this way the plans that the sailors considered against us were foiled.²⁹

Nor did those on board the *Ark* feel any safer once they left port, despite the *Ark*'s eight cannons. In 1627, Muslim pirates–referred to at that time as

---

28 Hall, Clayton Colman. *Narratives of early Maryland, 1633-1684*. 1910. New York: Barnes & Noble, Inc. 1946, reprinted 1953. 16-17. Print. The Introduction by Clayton Colman Hall to these Instructions precedes them at 13-15. See Appendix D for full set of *Lord Baltimore's Instructions to Colonists*, 15 Nov. 1633. Published by the Maryland Historical Society in Fund-Publication, No. 28. *The Calvert Papers, Number One*. 131-40. Baltimore, 1889. Digitized by the Internet Archive in 2016. <https://archive.org/details/calvertpapersno128leej>. Web. 2 Nov. 2022.

29 White, Andrew, S.J.. *Voyage to Maryland: Relatio Itineris in Marilandiam*. Ed. and trans. Barbara Lawatsch-Boomgaarden and Josef Ijsewijn. Wauconda, Illinios: Bolchazy-Carducci Publishers, Inc., 1995. 23. Print. Hereafter cited as White, *Voyage*. Father White sent the above account of the voyage (in Latin) to the Society of Jesus ("Relatio Itineris in Maryland-iam") and its translation into English as "A Brief Relation of the voyage unto Maryland." Probable date: May of 1634.

"Turks" or "Ottomans"–had invaded Iceland and captured roughly 250 of its citizens, bearing them away to slave markets on the Barbary Coast of North Africa.

Closer to home–and not long after the Iceland incident–Turks had attacked the small port of Baltimore in West Cork, on Ireland's south coast. Moreover, in June of 1631 (only three years before the *Ark* left Cowes Harbour), the Muslim "Turks" succeeded in capturing over 100 Irish men, women, and children, selling them in the slave markets of Tunis, Algiers, and Tripoli on the Barbary coast. (Only two eventually made it back to Ireland.) For this reason, the *Ark* was careful not to lose sight of the *Dove*, a far smaller and less defendable pinnace:

> . . . we did not sail as fast as we could have, so that we would not get too far ahead of the pinnace [the *Dove*] lest she become a prey to the Turks and pirates, who were mainly responsible for making the sea dangerous.[30]

Let us consider: (1) the *Ark* being held up for a month due to (probable) Protestant concerns about Lord Baltimore's proposed colony; (2) a crew of undoubtedly Protestant sailors, "muttering" on board the *Ark*; followed by (3) fear of capture by Muslim/Ottoman ships; and now to these three was added yet a fourth omen, (4) a sudden storm springing up from the north, in which the smaller *Dove* appeared to have been irrevocably lost. Father White took to prayer, reminding his Maker that:

> the purpose of the voyage was to honor the blood of the Redeemer through the salvation of the savages. . . . I had barely finished, when I perceived that the storm had subsided. . . . I felt even more deeply that the will of God was well disposed toward the peoples of Maryland (to whom your Reverence [Lord Baltimore] has sent us).[31]

As it turned out, the *Dove* had not been lost at sea. Under the "convenient guard" of the much larger *Dragon* (out of London, bound for Portuguese Angola, probably to trade for slaves), the far-smaller *Dove* had returned to England's Scilly Isles (pronounced "Silly") until the weather improved. Shortly

---

[30] White, *Voyage*, 24.
[31] White, *Voyage*, 26, 26-27, 27.

thereafter, protected by the large *Dragon* (described by Father White as "a merchant ship of 600 tons"), the little *Dove* (40 tons) finally set sail from the Scilly Isles and eventually met up with the *Ark* in Barbados. The *Dove* would prove useful (still in 1634) in establishing trade with Governor Winthrop's new little English colony up in Boston.[32]

But this is to anticipate. Before reaching the "great gulf" (what we now call the Northeast Trade Winds or North Equatorial Current), the *Ark* first had to pass along the coast of Spain, entrance to the Mediterranean. Once again the passengers on the *Ark* felt themselves to be in danger of Muslim pirates, yet found none. Father White explained that "perhaps they had withdrawn to celebrate their yearly period of fast . . . *sawm* [Ramadhan], for it was taking place at that time of year." Yet an overall wariness never left the *Ark*. It was not long before three ships were spotted in the distance, and Father White reported that "we were getting ready all things needed for battle" (perhaps the crew was readying the *Ark*'s eight cannons?). However, he finally concluded that:

> they were perhaps as much afraid of us as we were of them. As far as I can infer they were merchants who were making towards the Canary Islands, scattered not far from there, and could not, or did not want to catch up with us.[33]

Fear, genuine fear, never quite deserted Andrew White, not even when the *Ark* would later navigate the various islands in the West Indies. The ship did not make port in the large northern islands of the Greater Antilles, all of them Catholic, but Spanish-speaking. Moving from west to east, those Spanish-owned islands were Cuba, Hispaniola, and Puerto Rico. Just east of Puerto Rico, however, the West Indian islands of the Lesser Antilles round a curve and seem to descend, abruptly, into a straight north-south line down to the very coast of Venezuela. Barbados falls short of being the southernmost of these small West Indian islands that run north-south, but it is certainly the most easterly; it lies only about 456 nautical miles from

---

[32] The *Dove*, however, never made it back to England. In 1634, laden with pelts of beaver and other animals, she proved to have had worm-rot and was lost in the Atlantic. Pogue, Robert E.T. *Yesterday in Old St. Mary's County*. U.S.A.: Robert E.T. Pogue, 6th ed. 2008. 56-57. Print.

[33] White, *Voyage*, 27, 27, 27.

the coast of Venezuela. On January 3, 1634, the *Ark* reached Barbados and remained there until January 24th, a three-week layover.

Father Andrew White did not feel safe on Barbados, nor should he have. He does describe the "wonderful things which the island brings forth" by virtue of its tropical location; all of these "wonderful things," however, were fruits and vegetables. But aside from this, the island was–and still is–English, which means that in 1634, it was Protestant/Anglican. Worse, it was a crown-colony, governed by two brothers of the Hawley family, and if Father Andrew White was fated to be put in chains, it would be on Barbados.[34] Father White makes clear that the original destination had not been Barbados but St. Christopher. Slightly farther up that north-south island chain, St. Christopher was at that time divided, by mutual consent, between the English (who were Protestant/Anglicans) and the French (Catholics). Thus, the tiny island of St. Christopher would have been–and actually was–far more to Father White's liking than was Barbados.

It is time to look a little more carefully at the "gentleman Adventurers" aboard the *Ark*, perhaps 17 in number. Cecil Calvert (the second Lord Baltimore) had planned to join the group but at the last minute, worried about Anglican forces ranged against his Maryland charter, he therefore deputized Leonard Calvert, his slightly younger brother, to serve as governor of the proposed Maryland colony. Still another younger brother, George Calvert, had joined this group of "Adventurers." These two Calvert brothers were then joined by two "commissioners" from the same privileged class: Thomas Cornwaleys (sometimes spelled Cornwallis) and Jerome Hawley (sometimes Halley). Jerome's father, James Hawley of Brentford, had been a Member of Parliament and–before he died in 1622–had most likely known King James I (1603-1625).

Jerome Hawley is interesting because he already had "Adventurer" brothers in the little colonial outposts of the West Indies. In 1634, his brother, Captain Henry Hawley, was the governor of Barbados, and when he was off the island, yet another brother, William Hawley, filled in as his

---

[34] Barbados is the most English of all the islands, sometimes still referred to as "Little England."

deputy governor.[35] Reports conflict as to the time of English settlement on Barbados, but there is consensus that it happened during the late 1620s. The island was claimed for England in 1625 by King James I. On February 17th of 1627, an English ship brought to Barbados ten African slaves (most likely from Ghana) and 80 English colonists.

Far to the north, the Anglican colony of Virginia had at least one more of the Hawley brothers: James (a physician), and Gabriel (surveyor general), as well as John. While it is interesting to note that the Protestant island of Barbados seemed not to have been the *Ark*'s original destination, Father White did believe (or was led to believe?) that the goal had instead been the island of St. Christopher (half Catholic/ French, half English). Describing the situation (as he understood it) in his 1634 Latin-and-English *Relation of the voyage unto Maryland*, Father White wrote:

> When we had sailed past the Canary Islands, Lord Leonard Calvert, the commander of the fleet, began to consider which goods should be loaded on the ship for her return, and where they were to be had, so that through this he might take care of the expenses of his brother, Baron Baltimore; for the whole burden fell to him as the initiator of the entire voyage. *We were expecting no advantage from our countrymen in* [Protestant] *Virginia, for they are hostile to this new settlement*. Therefore we were heading toward St. Christopher; fearing, after some deliberation, that in this late season of the year others might have come before us . . . . We had barely covered two hundred miles, when *at someone's suggestion* our plans were changed again, and so that we might not run out of provisions by traveling in such a roundabout way, we turned towards Barbados.[36]

We can speculate that "someone's suggestion" was that of (Commissioner) Jerome Hawley, perhaps interested in meeting up with his two brothers

---

35 Henry Hawley served as governor from June of 1630 to June of 1640 and created the unicameral House of Assembly in 1639. His brother, William Hawley, served as deputy governor from 1638 to 1639.

36 White, *Voyage*, 29, 30 (emphases added).

on Barbados. In any event, the *Ark* stayed in port at Barbados a full three weeks.[37]

We have to sympathize with Father Andrew White, who was ordained as a Catholic priest in 1605. Not yet a Jesuit, in 1606 he had been expelled from England following the 1605 Gunpowder Plot (intended to blow up King James I, a Protestant/Anglican, while the king was addressing Parliament). Andrew White was arrested, imprisoned, and finally expelled from England, on pain of death. This was not because he was directly involved in the Plot but because he had been caught up in the anti-Catholic sweep that quickly followed it. (See Chapter 2-C at fn 11.) Yet this did not quell his Catholicism; on the contrary, in 1607 he became a Jesuit.

By 1633–two and a half decades later–he had become Lord Baltimore's (Cecil Calvert) long-distance writer and publicist for the New World colony that promised freedom of religion.

Yet, aboard the *Ark*, in this early January of 1634, Andrew White now found himself a reluctant visitor to (Anglican) Barbados, perhaps not yet quite comfortable in the company of the two families–Calverts and Hawleys–who probably knew each other or had known of each other while growing up in England. As for ages: the first Commissioner of the *Ark*, Thomas Cornwallis, was a young but promising 29. Both Hawley brothers on Barbados (Henry and William) may have been in their very late 30s. The second Commissioner of the *Ark*, Jerome Hawley, was 44–and Father Andrew White was easily the senior of the group at 55.

Andrew White's unease and expectation of trouble led him to lash out with two warnings that would cause other voyagers to think twice before stopping at Barbados: (1) the high price of provisions, and (2) a slave revolt.

> As we reached it [Barbados] on the third of January, we came expecting many articles of trade from the English inhabitants

---

[37] From 1961 until the end of November 2021, Barbados was an independent state *and* part of the Commonwealth Realm, a constitutional monarchy under Queen Elizabeth II. By December 2021, the first elected president of Barbados replaced the queen as head of state, and Barbados became a republic and a member of the Commonwealth of Nations. The University of the West Indies, founded in 1948, has several campuses on all English-speaking islands of the Caribbean, and students sit for exams that are read and graded in England at the Universities of Oxford and Cambridge.

and the governor, a brother [of one of the participants in the expedition]; but they had *conspired against us* and resolved to sell a bushel of wheat, which normally sold on the island for half a Belgian florin, for five times the amount. . . . They were offering a suckling pig at fifty florins, a turkey for twenty-five, and other small fowl of that kind for three florins; they did not have any beef or mutton.[38]

Added to this "conspiracy" was the fear caused by a slave revolt on Barbados that failed just as the *Ark* was pulling into port.

> The slaves throughout the island [of Barbados] had conspired to kill their masters; then, after freeing themselves, they had evidently decided to get possession of the first ship which landed and take to the sea. . . . [A]nd on the very day we landed we found eight hundred men in arms with the purpose of opposing this most recent crime.[39]

Three centuries later, Father McKenna (John LaFarge's colleague) pointed out that Father White's passenger lists of the *Ark* and the *Dove* indicate there were two "colored people" with Spanish names, suggesting they may have boarded at Barbados.

> Amongst the Ark and the Dove's pioneer passengers was one listed in Father Andrew White's list as "Matthias Sousa, Molato." (The Maryland Act of Religious Toleration Tercentennial pamphlet lists him as a Jew.) Two years later Father White lists another passenger as "Francisco, a Molato." So there was a Negro on the Ark and the Dove and Negroes are among the First Families of Maryland. The Spanish names remind us that the colonists first stopped at Barbados, and that these two colored people were quite probably Catholics.[40]

Never again would Father White describe in writing the unpleasant details of the *Ark*'s journey across the Atlantic. Once the Maryland colony was well and truly established at St. Mary's City, Lord Baltimore must have

---

[38] White, *Voyage*, 30 (emphasis added).

[39] White, *Voyage*, 30. Some historians today dispute Father White's *slaves*, preferring *servants* instead. But Father White himself used *slaves* in translating from the Latin his own umbrella word, *famuli*, meaning *overall household*.

[40] McKenna, Horace B., S.J.. "Colored Catholics in St. Mary's County." *Woodstock Letters*, Vol. LXXIX, No.1 (Feb. 1950). 55. Web. 29 July 2021. <https://jesuitonlinelibrary.bc.edu>.

asked Jerome Hawley to return to London and *re-write* Father White's "Relation of the voyage unto Maryland." With John Lewger's help, it was to be published for an English audience in 1635. John Lewger (B.A., M.A.) had been a classmate of Cecil Calvert (the second Lord Baltimore) at Trinity College, Oxford, and it is doubtless due to both Hawley and Lewger that the fear-ridden voyage of the *Ark* now disappears from Father White's original account.

Bearing the somewhat new title, "A Relation of Maryland" (September 8, 1635), it became a promotional publication, designed to encourage other Englishmen to take their chances and emigrate. As historian Leo Lemay has pointed out, to have described the hazards of an ocean crossing–stormy weather, as well as Muslim marauders–would scarcely have appealed to or encouraged English readers. Instead, the re-written narrative covers the ocean voyage by never so much as mentioning the hazards that the *Ark* had faced. In lieu, it introduces the entire Atlantic crossing *in one, single, breathless, 70-word opening sentence*:

> And so on Friday, the 22. of *November*, 1633. a small gayle of winde comming gently from the *Northwest*, they weighed from the *Cowes* [Harbour] in the *Isle of Wight*, about ten in the morning; And having stayed by the way Twenty dayes at the *Barbada's*, and Fourteene days at Saint *Christophers* (**upon some necessary occasions**) they arrived at *Point Comfort* in *Virginia*, on the foure & twentyeth of *February* following.[41]

We do not know what the phrase "upon some necessary occasions" refers to, but certainly Father Andrew White found this layover on St. Christopher a happy one, a respite from the recent three-week stay on (Protestant/Anglican) Barbados. The *Ark* had left Barbados on January 24th, passing those islands not yet claimed by other European powers, including St. Lucia and Martinique (whose Indians were not only "ignorant of divinity" but were also reported to have developed a taste for cannibalism). Guadeloupe was still unclaimed, but little Montserrat was inhabited by Irish inhabitants who had been "driven out of Virginia by the English because of the profession

---

41 Hawks, Francis Lister. *A Relation of Maryland: Reprinted from the London Edition of 1635.* New York: Joseph Sabin, 1865. 4 (italics in original, bold added). Print. Note: today (2015) there exists a superb reprint, and its paperbound format makes it easily affordable.

of their Catholic faith." Therefore, the two-week stay on tiny St. Christopher (divided by England and France) proved unexpectedly hospitable:

> ...we were invited in a friendly manner by the English governor and two Catholic captains. The governor of the French colony on the same island received me with especial generosity.[42]

In his brief history of American literature, historian Robert Spiller uses the phrase "thickets of circumstance."[43] Father Andrew White was not yet out of his–quite Protestant–thicket of circumstance: Virginia, he knew, was still to come. That English/Anglican colony already had a history pre-dating not only that of Maryland[44] but also the two aforementioned English islands of the West Indies, Barbados and St. Christopher. Father White's personal reaction to (Protestant/Anglican) Virginia was complicated:

> And so, when we finally sailed from here [Saint Christopher], we reached the cape that they call Cape Comfort, in Virginia, on the 27th of February, *filled with fear* that the English inhabitants, to whom our settlement was completely unwelcome, *might contrive some evil against us*. However, the letter which we were carrying from the king [Charles I] and the supreme treasurer to the governor of those regions was very *effective in appeasing their minds*, and enabled us to obtain things that would be useful to us in the future.[45]

White, however, suspected that the governor's kindness to the *Ark* and *Dove* was not heartfelt but instead calculated to enable the Protestant governor to "more easily recover from the royal treasury a great sum of money which was due to him." Nevertheless, with the Maryland destination now almost in sight, White recorded that: "After eight or nine days of *generous treatment* we set sail on the third of March and, having traveled into Chesapeake Bay, we turned our course north, in order to reach the Potomac River."[46]

---

42 White, *Voyage*, 33.

43 Spiller, Robert E. *The Cycle of American Literature: An Essay in Historical Criticism*. New York: The Macmillan Company, 1956. Chapter III, p. 60. Print.

44 In 1607, Jamestown was founded near Chesapeake Bay by London entrepreneurs of the Virginia Company.

45 White, *Voyage*, 34 (emphases added).

46 White, *Voyage*, 34 (emphasis added).

The joy and relief that now filled Father White's heart must surely have been felt by the passengers and crews of both ships as they sailed up the Potomac and finally set foot on Maryland soil. But perhaps almost as important–from Leonard Calvert's point of view–would have been the relief brought about by necessary connections that had been forged with the other three English-speaking colonies (although they were Protestant/Anglican): Virginia, Barbados, and St. Christopher (half English, half French).

Much has been made about the religious and economic rivalry between Virginia and Maryland, but references to Governor Leonard Calvert's occasional trips to Virginia suggest something more complicated. First, he had established good relations with Governor Harvey of Virginia. Calvert received a visit from Harvey in early July of 1634, and in the interests of "reconciliation," Governor Harvey then invited Calvert, Cornwallis, Hawley, and other "gentlemen" to cross the Potomac and visit Virginia.[47] Second, both colonies were adrift in this New World, vulnerable to Indian attack, and therefore somewhat willing (correction: *barely* willing) to forego religious rivalry in the interests of mere survival. Moreover, Anglican Protestants far out-numbered the roughly 17 Catholic "Gentlemen" on the *Ark* and *Dove*.

We now come full circle back to the question that opened this chapter: "When did slavery first arrive at St. Mary's City and Lord Baltimore's colony of 1634?"

We had answered our own question with: (i) "Sooner than one might think"; (ii) but for reasons which, at the time, were deemed "morally acceptable" by the dominant society.

G. "SOONER THAN ONE MIGHT THINK"

As the 17th century wore on, and 1634 turned into 1642, Governor Leonard Calvert's request for black slaves (14 males and three females) was echoed by Commissioner Thomas Cornwallis's ownership of "three Negroes" in the London court case of 1646. Further, Jane Moryson, the middle-aged widow of Robert Moryson, knew exactly what she wanted

---

47 However, this hospitality was ill-regarded by Virginia's more conservative Privy Council (Anglican), and halfway through 1636, Governor Harvey was removed from office and sent back to England.

and had it written into her pre-nuptial agreement with Cuthbert Fenwick in 1649. Mrs. Moryson was from Virginia, suggesting that (a) the practice of chattel-slavery was perhaps already known in that colony, and (b) the Potomac River had become merely a watery divide between the two colonies and was already seeing back-and-forth traffic by boat. In fact, although the original lure of the Maryland colony had been beaver pelt–managed by indentured servants from the *Ark*–Virginia's obvious wealth in tobacco led to Maryland's turning from beaver pelt to smoking pipe. According to historian Henry Miller, as early as 1637, tobacco had become "the official medium of exchange."[48]

The question is, in 1649 was Jane Moryson *ahead* of her time, or simply *of* it? The little information we have is conflicting and suggests that:

> while Africans may in some cases have arrived as slaves, they could have [had] a share in the social mobility of Maryland. . . . The position of blacks, then, much like the position of lower-class whites in Maryland, was fluid . . . . Despite this practical social mobility, the cultural mindset among whites was still that Africans were naturally slaves.[49]

Like the later growth of cotton, rice, and sugar in both Florida and Carolina, tobacco is labor-intensive, and surely–the planters must have argued–who better to farm it than black people who were already accustomed to the heat of Africa? Was it not but a short step from Africa's heat and humidity to the sweltering conditions of summertime in Virginia and Maryland? Originally, the indentured servants of 1634 had helped with beaver hunts, but the large-scale farming of tobacco would prove quite another matter. As the decades of the 1630s and '40s progressed, tobacco increasingly began to take the place of beaver. Fewer indentured servants arrived from England, and those who did often fell ill from "the seasoning"–a colonial phrase for the extremes of summertime temperatures in Maryland and Virginia. Planters may have conjectured that God himself had provided

---

48 Miller, Henry M. "The Lure of Sotweed: Tobacco and Maryland History." *Slackwater: Oral Folk History of Southern Maryland*, Volume III (32-36). Spring 2001: 33. Print.

49 Johnson, Donald F. "Reconstructing Racial Identity in Seventeenth Century Maryland." *Chronicles of St. Mary's*, Vol. 54 No.4 (Fall 2007). 434. Print.

them with the unique opportunities provided by great crops of tobacco–and, if so, then the pretext of who but black slaves could best farm them?

H. "MORALLY ACCEPTABLE"

"Morally acceptable." This phrase ranges anywhere along a spectrum of Biblical precept (Saint Paul's, "Slaves, obey your masters") to a 17th-century version of today's familiar, "But Mom, *everybody's* doing it."

Increasingly, everybody in dominant society *was* doing it: that is, accepting chattel slavery as the solution to a New World problem that would affect Protestant and Catholic alike. That "problem" was both agricultural and economic: the balminess of a Southern climate differentiated it from the life of a Northerner, often beset by snow and cold on his small family farm. Yet Northerners would eventually prove complicit in their agreements with Southern planters by manufacturing items needed on Southern plantations, but it would take several more decades for such agreements to materialize.

In the meantime, there was the great Atlantic Ocean, and in the 1600s, it was increasingly crowded with vessels from major European countries: England, Holland, France, Spain, Portugal–and even little Denmark. All these ships were headed for opportunities to be found only in the New World, but such lures were going to depend on the kidnapping, transport, and unwilling labor of the many peoples of Africa.

This transportation generally took a Caribbean route: first Barbados, then gradually up the island chain of the West Indies. In coming years, the transport of slaves out of Africa would prove so lucrative that the little Northern town of Newport, Rhode Island would also take part in the slave trade; they too, however, generally made their first stop in Barbados.

Was the practice of slave ownership "Christian"? At the time, Protestant and Catholic alike generally assumed so. Jesuits had held slaves since the middle of the 1500s, and it is even possible that Father Andrew White himself suggested the possibility of slave-ownership to Leonard Calvert in 1642. Moreover, Leonard Calvert would already have known of slavery: like his father, George (the first Lord Baltimore) and older brother, Cecil (the second Lord Baltimore), he would have heard of the exploits of such men as Hawkins, Drake, Frobisher, and the East India Company. When the *Dove* first went missing but finally sailed into port in Barbados, she had been under the protection of the *Dragon*, the latter on route to Angola. The two ships parted company somewhere in the Atlantic, but certainly the men on the *Dove* understood that the *Dragon* was headed to buy slaves from the Portuguese in Africa. Leonard Calvert had also recently witnessed the slave revolt on Barbados, and it is possible he had seen the beginnings of slavery in Virginia–just across the Potomac.

By the second half of the nineteenth century, it has been estimated that roughly 12 million men, women, and children were "bought" by slavers and shipped away from their homes in Africa where they had been born. The men who "bought" them and then brought them called the Americas a "New World"–so why would anyone be surprised to learn that they were bringing the so-called "morals" of the Old World with them?

Chapter 7

Voices From Europe

A. CURIOSITY AND PERSPECTIVE

Up in Scotland, Robert Burns sat in church and watched, in fascination, a tiny creature (louse/lice) crawling around the bonnet of an otherwise well-dressed woman sitting directly in front of him. He reflected on the situation and–in 1786–wrote a poem, "To a Louse, On Seeing One on a Lady's Bonnet at Church." The poem's most famous lines, translated from Scottish dialect, are these:

> And would some Power the small gift give us
> To see ourselves as others see us!

Yes. "To see ourselves as others see us."

But across the Atlantic, about a century and a half later, James Thomas Abell, caretaker for the Jesuit community in Newtown, Maryland, expressed a quite different opinion to young Father John LaFarge. No, said Mr. Abell, we are better off just being ourselves ("us folks") and proud of it. Father LaFarge later recorded their conversation:

> I asked Mr. Abell [1837-1914] what he thought of the world in general. The world in general, said Mr. Abell, consists of three kinds of people: first, "us folks" (that is, the people of St. Mary's and Charles Counties, Maryland); second, furriners (people from Maryland's Eastern Shore, Baltimore, California, China or Sweden and other outlying parts); and the third kind of people, said Mr. Abell, are those damned Virginians. Virginians, be it explained, were extremely annoying because they crossed the Potomac River and interfered with the Maryland oyster fisheries.[1]

So the question now becomes: as Americans, do we–or do we not–want to "see ourselves as others see us"? Do we reflexively fire back at our critics ("furriners" from "outlying parts"), or do we listen before we leap?

In the early-to-mid 1800s, five people were curious enough about our new "democracy" to venture forth on trans-Atlantic voyages (under sail, and each voyage of several weeks' duration) to see what "America"–as they called it–was all about. All of them fit Mr. Abell's definition of "furriners"; all of the five were visiting from monarchies that were either French or English.

The decade from roughly 1830 to the early 1840s saw three British citizens and two from France step ashore to see America for themselves.

Two of these five were women, English women: Frances Trollope (in the very early 1830s), and Harriet Martineau (in the mid-1830s). They are included because both women sometimes commented on matters that were apt to escape notice of the three men.

As for two of the men: Alexis de Tocqueville and his traveling companion, Gustave de Beaumont, both were French and quite unaware of the two English writers (Trollope and Martineau) who had not only preceded them but had each also published a book about "America." Tocqueville and Beaumont also arrived in America in the early 1830s, but because of their French nationality they will not be dealt with until the end of the present chapter.

---

[1] LaFarge, John. *The Manner Is Ordinary*. New York: Harcourt, Brace and Company, 1954. 160. Print. Hereafter cited as LaFarge, *Manner*.

Finally, Charles Dickens. The last of the five to arrive (in 1842), he was, of course, English, and already famous for his writings. All five travelers were well educated, and all five, fortunately for us, took notes and later put their experiences into books that sold well, both in their home countries and here in America. All five visitors criticized us, and all five also praised us.

It must have been a happy time for those in dominant society during those few decades following the successful defeat of Britain in our Revolutionary War (1783), but well before the brutal realities of our Civil War (1861-1865). Ostensibly, God was in his heaven, and all seemed hopeful and promising in an America that was now thrusting its way beyond (1) the Allegheny Mountains, (2) the Mississippi River, and finally (3) what would eventually become known as the Rocky Mountains and the even later Gold Rush of 1848.

Locally, it was during this period of the 1830s and '40s that men in the county seat of Leonardtown, St. Mary's County, Maryland decided to form a "Reading Room and Debating Society" (the word *debating* suggesting that there were at least two points of view on any given subject). It was also in the decades of the 1830s and '40s that Francis Jarboe decided it was time to launch a newspaper, *The Leonard Town Herald* (soon to become *The St. Mary's Beacon*). See Chapter 3-A and 3-B.

Some of the same men who launched the Debating Society also entertained the still-radical notion of educating *girls*, establishing the public St. Mary's Female Seminary (in St. Mary's City) as a sister school to the public, males-only boarding academy up in Charlotte Hall. See Chapter 3-C-4 and 3-D.

And finally, in the early 1840s, Leonardtown became a port-of-call for steamboats passing from Philadelphia all the way down to Norfolk.

Nationality–foreign nationality–was to play a key role for our five visitors to America in that single, critical period of the late 1820s to 1842. While three of the five came from England, they were visiting a new nation that– although English-speaking–had just concluded not one but two wars against the "mother country": the Revolutionary War of 1776, and the follow-up War of 1812.

In other words, these three English travelers were voyaging to territory that had only recently belonged to "the enemy," and it would be a mistake for us not to expect them to take issue with some of what they were seeing. For those three British subjects, the America they were seeing was a travesty of much that was still held dear in England.

That was Problem #1.

Problem #2 was that the three visitors from England were also curious about a system that had provided stability in England for centuries: a system in which one was born to a certain "station" (social class) in life and from which one did not–could not–move up to the highest level of all, either the aristocracy or the landed gentry.

Problem #3: our visitors from England wondered how a constitutional "democracy" actually worked. Did it, or did it not, permit slavery, apparently a violation of the much-touted word "democracy," which suggested that *all* (male) citizens could vote?

Once returned to their respective countries, all five of our travelers wrote about their experiences in what they simply called "America."

First to be published among the English travelers was *Domestic Manners of the Americans* in 1832 by Frances Trollope (known as "Mrs. Trollope"). A literary sensation in London, it went through four editions in that first year alone, providing her (by then in her early fifties) with much-needed income and also with the coveted reputation of "writer"–in her case, as both travel-writer and novelist.

Second to be published in England (1838) was Harriet Martineau's *Retrospect of Western Travel*. The year before, 1837, she had actually published a sociological study of America (titled *Society in America*), but happily for us–and for her readers–she had been persuaded to re-write that professional work into a far more enjoyable read-through, *Retrospect of Western Travel*. Her comments in *Retrospect* often contrast with those of her somewhat more excitable predecessor, Mrs. Trollope. Martineau's professional approach to America required a measured outlook that had not been quite within the emotional reach of Mrs. Trollope.

Third, and last, among our English writers was Charles Dickens. Before he left England to tour America in 1842, he enjoyed the advantage of having already read the books of both Trollope and Martineau. This gave him "an edge," and several contemporary critics have commented on the similarities between criticisms made by both Trollope and Dickens.[2]

In 1842, Dickens published his *American Notes*; it was popular in England, but not in America. Dickens felt that he had even more to say, and most of it came out in the middle section of his scathing 1844 novel, *Martin Chuzzlewit*.[3] And yet: Dickens was the only one of our five visitors to *return* to America, waiting till the end of the Civil War to do so. In 1867-68, he faced a post-Civil War generation that was more willing to understand and even appreciate his earlier comments on democracy. (It also helped him professionally that during this second trip in 1867, he generally confined himself to reading publicly from his most popular novels.)

But what of our writers from France, Alexis de Tocqueville and Gustave de Beaumont? As Frenchmen, we need to treat them apart from the visitors from England. English (whether its history, its literature, or even its spoken language) had not quite been among the classically oriented studies of either of these young French lawyers. While they were somewhat ignorant of England's history and even its language, these two young men were curious about "democracy." After six weeks at sea–and not yet three weeks in New York–Beaumont wrote his mother on June 7, 1831: "As for English [language], we are making progress. Still, not a day passes that we don't have some misunderstanding: we're never quite sure what we're being

---

[2] Susan Kissel wrote in 1993 that Dickens was so influenced by Mrs. Trollope's picture of America "that he would find it difficult to see with eyes other than her own." Kissel, Susan S. *In Common Cause: the "Conservative" Frances Trollope and the "Radical" Frances Wright*. Bowling Green, Ohio: Bowling Green State University Popular Press, 1993. 117. Print. See also: Kissel, Susan S. "'What Shall Become of Us All?': Frances Trollope's Sense of the Future." *Studies in the Novel*, vol. 20, no. 2, 1988, pp. 151-166. JSTOR, <www.jstor.org/stable/29532565>. 18 Aug. 2021.

[3] The serious reader would do well to consult a pithy, day-by-day "Journal" of Charles Dickens' short stay in 1842. Those four pages may be found at: <http://www.dickenslive.com/1842.shtml>.

told."[4] Why, then, had Tocqueville and Beaumont bothered sailing to a country where they did not speak (or even quite understand) the language?

The answer is that, politically, the government in France was still in flux following the French Revolution of 1789 (as well as the previous American Revolution of 1776) and would not settle down until almost the end of the nineteenth century. As members of minor French aristocracy, both the larger Tocqueville and Beaumont families had gone to the guillotine in the French Revolution, although the immediate families had been spared. Following the French Revolution, and its predecessor in America, both Tocqueville and Beaumont were naturally curious about America's experiment in "democracy": exactly how did it work?

In 1831, therefore, Tocqueville and Beaumont presented the French government with a proposal that would require a trip to America: this was to be a study of American institutions, specifically, prisons. (Charles Dickens would later use much the same ploy in 1842.) The ensuing report on American prisons prepared by both these young lawyers required them to be about nine months in America, but their report had only been a pretext: the aim of both men had been to see how democracy actually worked. The two wealthy families, of both Tocqueville and Beaumont, paid for their entire stay in America as well as for their voyages over and back in 1831 and '32.

We also need to remember that when the two young lawyers sailed for America on the *Le Havre* in 1831, Frances Trollope had not yet published her 1832 *Domestic Manners of the Americans*, the first of all the English travel books. Enviably, therefore, both Tocqueville and Beaumont were seeing America fresh, head-on. For our purposes, this gives them an advantage over the other three English writers, who, understandably (the issue of slavery notwithstanding) would be judging America according to *English* standards and even as a latter-day *English* province–located in what was still being called "the New World."

---

[4] De Tocqueville, Alexis Charles Henri Clérel. *Letters from America*. 1798. Ed. and trans. Frederick Brown. New Haven, CT and London: Yale University Press, 2010. 65. Print. Hereafter cited as Tocqueville, *Letters*. This book includes letters written by Gustave de Beaumont, his colleague and traveling companion, Later, in 1835, Tocqueville would marry an English girl who had been raised in France; thus her language with him was French, not English.

Where Tocqueville and Beaumont are concerned, all our quotations come not from Tocqueville's hefty, two-volume treatise titled *Democracy in America*, but instead from the more recent (2010) publication of *Letters from America* (see fn 4 above). This small volume, with introduction and index, is the translation of letters sent by both Tocqueville and Beaumont, as they wrote–with considerable excitement–back to their families and friends in France in 1831 and '32. Here, and here alone, are the first reactions of both young men to America. Superb translations of these letters have been made by Frederick Brown, professor emeritus from the State University of New York at Stony Brook.

If we look, somewhat clinically, at those three *men* who came to America between 1831 and 1842 (Tocqueville, Beaumont, and Dickens), we realize that all had what today we would call "jobs" that required a rapid return to their home country. For Tocqueville and Beaumont, their time in America was almost nine months; for Dickens, only five. The two *women*, however, were not bound by any such strictures. Both Mrs. Trollope and Harriet Martineau managed to stay longer: Mrs. Trollope stayed almost four years, and Harriet Martineau, two.

B. HAZARDS OF TRAVEL

A couple of words before we turn to what struck tourists arriving in an America that was post-Revolutionary but pre-Civil War. Before our five ever left the comforts of home in England and France, they understood that there were hazards–specifically, two–to be faced.

First among the possible hazards: one had to cross the Atlantic Ocean. Four of our five travelers (Dickens excepted) had already taken their lives in hand by virtue of crossing the Atlantic in a large sailing ship known as "a packet." As "packet-ship" suggests, these enormous, multi-sailed, ocean-going boats carried both mail and passengers to and from America. (At 48 days, Tocqueville found them "hopelessly slow."[5]) Packets generally ran from Liverpool (England) to and from the lower East River in New York City– as well as to other ports-of-call, as needed: Halifax, Boston, New Bedford, Philadelphia, Baltimore, Savannah, and New Orleans.

---

5 Tocqueville, *Letters* 197.

Passengers on these packet-ships could choose to travel in one of three possible categories: (a) first class; (b) steerage (probably the choice of most of our emigrating ancestors); or even, willy-nilly, (c) "under the bow." The ship's crew (d) was yet a fourth category. Charles Dickens referred to steerage as "a little world of poverty" (Chapter XVI of *American Notes for General Circulation*).

In a letter to his mother dated April 26th, 1831, Tocqueville estimated the following aboard his packet-ship out of Paris, the *Le Havre*: (a) 30 in first class and "at table"; (b) 13 in steerage; (c) 120 "under the bow"; and (d) 18 crew. Those in steerage did not dine "at table" and were required to make their own meals. The category of "under the bow" does not bear thinking about, and readers may be somewhat relieved to hear that all five of our visitors to America traveled first class.

The captains of these mail packets were justifiably proud of their tight schedules. But by today's standards, travel between Europe and America still took weeks, not days. In 1827, Mrs. Trollope was forced to spend a total of *seven weeks* aboard her packet from London to New Orleans. Harriet Martineau later made it from Liverpool to New York in 42 days, a little over a month. Tocqueville and Beaumont sailed on a schooner from Le Havre, France and reached Newport after at least five weeks at sea. Charles Dickens, however, the last to arrive in 1842, sailed on a new-fangled *steam-packet* in just 18 days, steam by now slowly replacing sail on trans-Atlantic voyages. Once in America, water transport was by the new steamboats plying most of the inland rivers as well as the Great Lakes.

Travel by packet-ship was relatively safe. In a letter dated January 20, 1832, Tocqueville reassured his brother just before embarking on the return voyage to France in the dead of winter: ". . . the voyage on American packets is without danger at any time of year . . . during the past decade, a vessel of this kind sails for Liverpool every week, for Le Havre every ten days, and another for London; to date, not one has been lost. . . . Something you didn't suspect is that we ran an infinitely greater risk on steamboats.

Thirty of them exploded or sank during our first six weeks in the United States."6

Charles Dickens reported much the same problem in 1842: having decided to board a steamboat on the Ohio River, he was told that "western steamboats usually blow up one or two a week in the season." Once he had booked passage on *The Messenger*, "we had been a great many times very gravely recommended to keep as far aft as possible, 'because the steamboats generally blew up forward.'"7

Second among the hazards of travel: our five travelers were often forced to travel by stagecoach in order to see what they wanted to see.8 Dickens does refer to brief trips by steamboat or occasionally by train: Hartford to New Haven, and again from New York to Philadelphia. But aside from that, he (and the other four travelers) bumped along in four-horse stagecoaches of varying age and condition. Harriet Martineau was generally pleased with this method of travel and noted, on her way through the South, "[t]he novelty and the beauty of the scenery seemed inexhaustible; and the delightful American stages, *open or closed all round at the will of the traveller*, allow of everything being seen."9

The roof of a stagecoach could also be used for an extra traveler (usually a boy or young man), but more likely it was used for freight. Charles Dickens commented in 1842: ". . . the luggage (including such trifles as a large rocking-chair, and a good-sized dining-table) being at length made fast upon the roof, we started off in great state."10 In another letter to his mother in 1831, Alexis de Tocqueville had described those horse-drawn stagecoaches as "suspended on nothing but leather straps and driven at a fast trot on roads as deplorable as those in Lower Brittany."11 When Charles

---

6 Tocqueville, *Letters* 263.

7 Dickens, Charles. *American Notes for General Circulation*. 1842. Ed. John S. Whitley and Arnold Goldman. London: Penguin Classics; 1985. 200, 201. Print. Hereafter cited as Dickens, *Notes*.

8 Stagecoach is the English translation for the French term for such a public conveyance, diligence.

9 Martineau, Harriet. *Retrospect of Western Travel*. London: Saunders and Otley, 1838. 3 vols. Vol. II, 39 (emphasis added) (Chapter titled "Country Life in the South"). Print. Hereafter cited as Martineau, *Retrospect*.

10 Dickens, *Notes* 186.

11 Tocqueville, *Letters* 125.

Dickens arrived about a decade later, he, too, noted that: "The coaches are something like the French coaches, but not nearly so good. In lieu of springs, they are hung on bands of the strongest leather."[12]

Of course, the roads were not yet paved: on a "corduroy" road, for example, a stagecoach might manage no more than two miles per hour; if the road was well kept, perhaps five or six.[13] Canal barges were little better, and such passengers as Charles Dickens were forced to lie flat when passing beneath a low-lying bridge.

If one needed to nap on those day-long stagecoaches, one was supposed to do so in an upright position so as not to collapse onto fellow passengers, sometimes eight or nine to a coach. Lumbering slowly up the Alleghenies, and then hurtling down the other side: this was not for the faint of heart– but then, not one of our five travelers could be so described.

Harriet Martineau particularly enjoyed her travels through the South– even when the roads were not the best. They had been better, she noted, when approaching the metropolises of Boston, New York, Washington, and Baltimore. Martineau's travel through the South is best described in her (unnumbered) chapter, "Country Life in the South," from her *Retrospect of Western Travel*. This book reads as an overall amalgam of her journeys: first to Monticello and Charlottesville ("Mr. Jefferson's university"); Charleston and Columbia in South Carolina; Augusta, Georgia; Montgomery, Alabama; Mobile, Mississippi; and finally New Orleans, Louisiana, where she stayed at length before taking a steamboat up the Mississippi River to Cincinnati.

In her chapter on travel by stagecoaches in the South, Martineau notes that at every city she had been warned about proceeding farther: "At Richmond we were cautioned about the journey into South Carolina: at Charleston we were met with dreadful reports of travelling in Georgia: in Georgia people spoke of the horrors of Alabama. . . . [But] I do not remember a single difficulty that occurred, all the way. There was much fatigue, of course. In going down from Richmond to Charleston . . . we were nine days on the road, and had only three nights' rest. . . [I]f I could

---

12 Dickens, *Notes* 177.

13 A "corduroy road" was made entirely of wooden slats placed crosswise on the road.

find a bed or sofa [at frequent stops along the route] it was well: if not, I could wrap myself in my cloak, and make a pillow on the floor of my carpet-bag."[14] At these log-cabin stops along the route, Martineau noticed pictures of "the six Presidents who smile from the walls of almost every log-house in America . . . .[15]

Many of the roads and water-crossings were primitive. As Martineau continues, at night:

> [y]ou are sure to come to a creek, where nobody has ever erected a bridge, or where a freshet has carried one away, and no measures have been taken to rebuild it. With drowsy groans, the passengers rouse themselves, and get out at the driver's bidding. . . . The ladies slip on their India-rubber shoes; for their first step may be into soft mud . . . [t]hey stand upon a bank . . . in order not to be run over in the dark; while the scow[16] shows by the reflection of the light at her bow where the river is. When she [the scow] touches the bank, the driver calls to everybody to keep out of the way, cracks his whip, and drives his lumbering carriage down the bank, and into the scow: the passengers follow; the scow is unchained, and the whole load is pushed across the stream. . . . When the expected shock tells you that you have arrived at the other side, the driver again cracks his whip, and the horses scramble. If they should refuse to mount the steep bank, and back a step upon the passengers instead, every one would infallibly be driven into the river. A delicate coaxing is therefore employed; and I imagine the animals must be aware what a ticklish thing any freak of theirs would be in such a situation; for I never knew them decline mounting the bank, without a single back step.[17]

So much for the hazards of travel, whether by a packet-ship of sail, steamboat, or by stagecoach.

---

[14] Martineau, *Retrospect* Vol. II, 37, 37-38.
[15] Martineau, *Retrospect* Vol. II, 42.
[16] A "scow" was a large barge with a blunt nose.
[17] Martineau, *Retrospect* Vol. II, 43.

C. THE ISSUES

It is time now to turn our attention to Mr. Abell's five "furriners": to what struck them about America, and which observations they would publish when they finally returned home to England or France. For our purposes, all five of our travelers, English and French alike, generally wrote about four aspects of the America that they saw, and we touch briefly on these four:

(1) Democracy (every white man a voter);

(2) Women;

(3) Religion; and

(4) Indians and Africans.

Because three of the five travelers were from England (Trollope, Martineau, and Dickens), we discuss their reactions before turning to those of the two Frenchmen, Tocqueville and Beaumont. Those last two, as we have already noted, came from a culture that, historically, was decidedly un-English. This does matter, and the reactions of Tocqueville and Beaumont to both America and "the West" occasionally act as a corrective to those matters which particularly upset the other three travelers from England.

Who were these travelers, and why did they undergo the rigors of crossing the Atlantic in order to see a New World? We turn first to the visitors from England.

D. TRAVELERS FROM ENGLAND

First of the English to arrive was **Frances Trollope**, in 1827. She was also the only one of the four travelers to be economically dependent on what she could (or, in her case, could *not*) find in order to earn her own living in the still-new United States of America. The other four visitors carried "letters of introduction" and were much celebrated once they set foot on American soil (Martineau, Dickens, Tocqueville, and Beaumont). Generally, however, Mrs. Trollope had few such letters of introduction, and the financial difficulties that soon beset her–at the mature age of 47– undoubtedly affected her outlook on America.

Worse, by having decided to disembark at New Orleans and go immediately up the Mississippi River to Cincinnati, Ohio, Mrs. Trollope missed absorbing the older, more genteel history of the East Coast and its original 13 colonies. She had decided to travel directly to "the West" (as the Mississippi River was then called) where she found only raw settlements and rough manners. Their effect on her was profound, and though she would later cross the Alleghenies to the more refined Eastern seaboard, her initial–and long-lasting–shock was that of the Mississippi River and its new settlements (or states) known as "the West."

To this day she is still known as "Mrs." Trollope. In her very late 40s at that time, she was married, with five children, bringing the youngest three (two girls under the age of 12, plus one teenage boy) across the Atlantic with her. Two older Trollope boys were away at English boarding schools. At 47, Mrs. Trollope could easily have been the mother of Tocqueville (age 25), Beaumont (age 30), and Dickens (also age 30). She could even have been a youthful mother to Harriet Martineau, age 32 at the time.

Mr. Trollope remained in England in order to send his wife the goods she planned to sell in Cincinnati at her "emporium" or "bazaar"–what today we would simply call a "department store." Mr. Trollope ventured only once to America, but otherwise sent insufficient funds to his wife and their three younger children. An impecunious lawyer, he had a reputation for arguing with his clients and was generally insolvent. He would die in 1835, only three years after Mrs. Trollope returned to England, thereby leaving her to enjoy her new widowhood, fame, and future travels throughout Europe.

Second of the English to arrive was **Harriet Martineau**, traveling to America in 1834 with a paid companion, Louisa Jeffrey.[18] Pursued, but not married, Martineau was already self-supporting, owing to sociology articles she had been publishing regularly in the British press–and for which she was being paid professionally. She was already well known and had letters

---

18 In her autobiography, Martineau stresses the advantages of her companion: Louisa Jeffrey paid her own way on the trans-Atlantic voyages, but aside from that, Harriet Martineau paid for the rest. Louisa Jeffrey helped supply what Martineau might otherwise have missed in conversation: Martineau was partially deaf and was forced to use an ear-trumpet. Martineau, Harriet, *Harriet Martineau's Autobiography*. Ed. Maria Weston Chapman. Boston: Houghton, Mifflin and Co.,1877. Print.

of introduction to important people in America, including the president of the United States.

Third of the English to arrive was **Charles Dickens** in 1842, bringing with him his wife, Catherine ("Kate") and her maid. Not only had Dickens already written five popular novels that were being well read in America, but–equally important–he had also been able to persuade his publisher to help foot the bill to "America."[19]

Did these three English visitors arrive with preconceptions? Yes. All three were English abolitionists; however, once the Civil War later broke out, Charles Dickens became pro-Confederate, expressing a strong belief in "States' Rights." Which brings us to a question: if these visitors were all anti-slavery, why then had they come to America? Answer: to see how what was billed as a political "democracy" actually worked. For example, where did the slaves 'fit in"? Aside from the obvious problem of slavery, all three from England wrote about their other–more immediate–impressions of America, and these are guaranteed to come as a surprise to today's readers.

All three of our English visitors had left their own shores in the Old World in order to "go West" in the New World of America. "West" did not convey Hollywood's meaning of "Cowboys and Indians": such lands in the Far West were still largely unknown to many Europeans and settlers. In the early 1800s, "the West" referred only to the new states and territories flanking the Mississippi River, all of which were now opening up to settlers and statehood. Before our Revolutionary War of 1776, and even shortly before the Louisiana Purchase of 1803, the Allegheny Mountains had generally acted as a barrier to whatever unknowns lay on their western slopes. Indeed, on some old maps from the colonial era, the Alleghenies bear the discouraging title, "Endless Mountains."

But (1) once the Revolutionary War was over and we had divorced ourselves from Britain in 1783, and (2) once Thomas Jefferson arranged for the new United States, a "democracy," to fund the Louisiana Purchase in 1803, settlers from the former colonies made haste to cross the Alleghenies and settle those lands bordering the Mississippi River.

---

19 Dickens, *Notes* Appendix 301.

Some of these settlers, as described in Chapter 3-A, migrated from St. Mary's County (Maryland) and settled in Kentucky (which Harriet Martineau would one day describe as "the wild woods of the West."). These settlers from St. Mary's County referred to the Mississippi River as "the West," and for them it truly was.

1. Democracy: station

It would be easy to vilify Frances Trollope (1779–1863). She is generally known as *Mrs.* Trollope, ever since she published *Domestic Manners of the Americans* (March, 1832), having completed it shortly after her return to England in 1831. Hers was the first well-publicized survey of life in America by one of Mr. Abell's "furriners," and it would soon encourage both Harriet Martineau and Charles Dickens to make similar forays into the New World and its "Western" frontier along the Mississippi River. They wanted to see for themselves.

The English thoroughly enjoyed Mrs. Trollope's *Domestic Manners*, and it could even be said that they "lapped it up." It went through four editions in the first year alone (1832), harboring every prejudice that the English had felt towards Americans since the Revolutionary War of 1776–as well as its extension into the War of 1812.[20]

Let us imagine, for a moment, that it is 1826 and that Mrs. Trollope–the first of our visitors to arrive–did *not* disembark from her trans-Atlantic voyage at the port of New Orleans. Let us further imagine that she, like our other four travelers, whether British or French, had disembarked on the eastern seaboard in Boston, New York City, or Baltimore. In any of those cities she could have taken note of what she saw and, with few reservations, perhaps even applauded it.

But this is not what happened. Alone of our five visitors, Mrs. Trollope instead disembarked–after a seven-week voyage–at the port of New Orleans on Christmas Day, 1826. At 47, she was already middle-aged. She and the

---

[20] As schoolchildren in the United States, we all learned of lives lost by American soldiers at Bunker Hill, Valley Forge, and Yorktown–but usually we cannot supply the name of a single English soldier who also died during those same battles. They were simply "the enemy." Probably, however, British scholars could do so, even going so far as being able to name the regiment involved.

rest of her party were headed several hundred miles up the Mississippi–not to Cincinnati, but to Memphis. She and her group were specifically headed to a bi-racial commune, "Nashoba," just outside Memphis, Tennessee's largest city. She had with her the founder of that racial utopia, 30-year-old Fanny Wright.

Miss Frances ("Fanny") Wright, born in Scotland, was a British heiress with enviable connections, to which she added her youth, beauty, and idealism. Among her admirers and supporters she could count the aging Marquis de Lafayette ("my paternal father"), Andrew Jackson, Thomas Jefferson, and Henry Clay. Fanny Wright's plan for her commune outside Memphis was to purchase black slaves, free them, and then educate them (as a freed people) within her bi-racial community, which she called "Nashoba." The education she then planned for the freed slaves was to be two-pronged: standard education as given in a grammar school, followed by the latest methods of farming.[21] The freed slaves, now educated, were to help colonize Liberia, or Haiti–or even both–perhaps as part of the recently established American Colonization Society, founded by the U.S. government in 1816.

Fanny Wright had already established her Nashoba commune in 1825, and by 1826 had sailed to England in order to raise funds for it. She stayed with politically sympathetic friends for several weeks, and also with the abolitionist Trollope family in northwest London.

Now, in late 1826, Miss Wright was heading back to Nashoba with a committed Mrs. Trollope in tow. On board the packet-ship *Edward*, bound from London to New Orleans, the entire Trollope-Wright party consisted of the following: Fanny Wright; Mrs. Trollope; three of Mrs. Trollope's children; the emigré French artist, Auguste Hervieu (who would later sketch the Nashoba commune); a footman in livery, William Abbott; and a lady's maid, Hester Rust–at the very least, eight in all. The plan called for Mrs. Trollope to spend a few months at Nashoba, then go farther up the Mississippi and Ohio Rivers to her ultimate destination, the recently settled "Western" city of Cincinnati, Ohio.

---

21 One hundred years later, Father John LaFarge would also encourage much the same type of education at his Cardinal Gibbons Institute in St. Mary's County, Maryland. See Chapter 8-D-3-d.

However, during the period when Fanny Wright had been away from Nashoba (unsuccessfully fundraising in England), her commune had collapsed. Its white members–along with a few blacks–had left, and all that remained were a few freed slaves, a general lack of food and water, and the very real possibility of disease. The roofs either leaked or had fallen in, leaving both Mrs. Trollope and Miss Wright to try sleeping under dripping rain.

After only two and a half weeks of this, Mrs. Trollope decided to leave earlier than planned and head up the Mississippi River on the *Criterion* to Cincinnati, a journey of two and a half weeks by steamboat. That northward journey would, unfortunately, give her considerable insight into life-as-it-was-actually-lived along the American frontier. Many of those insights were unwanted, but once written into her 1832 travel book they caused a sensation–with much tittering and many guffaws–among her readers back in London.[22]

If the utopian community at Nashoba had been Mrs. Trollope's first disappointment, Cincinnati was now the second. Here, she would later write (in her best-selling travelogue, *Domestic Manners*) that garbage was strewn in the middle of Cincinnati streets, and hogs were encouraged to roam freely and eat it up. For two years, Mrs. Trollope labored, with eventual success, to get her "emporium" built, although she would run into difficulties when her hapless husband sent insufficient funds or inadequate goods for sale.

What Mrs. Trollope had found in her steamboat travels up the Mississippi, and what she now encountered in Cincinnati, convinced her that "democracy"–regrettably–played to the lowest common denominator of mankind. In the introduction to her literary sensation, *Domestic Manners*, Mrs. Trollope summed up her two-year stint in Cincinnati (1829-1831) with a warning to her English readers. In brief, this warning amounted to an "Appreciate Your Very English, Non-Democratic Monarchy." In the preface

---

[22] Fanny Wright, however, did not forget her freed slaves, and in 1830, she escorted them, personally, to the Republic of Haiti (formerly part of the French colony of Saint Domingue). With its Declaration of Independence on January 1, 1804, Haiti had already established the first genuine black independent state in the New World.

(written in the third person) she particularly noted that "she [Mrs. Trollope] has endeavoured to shew *how greatly the advantage is on the side of those who are governed by the few, instead of [by] the many*. The chief object she has had in view is to encourage her countrymen to hold fast by a constitution that ensures all the blessings which flow from *established habits and solid principles*. If they [the English] forego these, they will incur the fearful risk of breaking up their repose by introducing *the jarring tumult and universal degradation which invariably follow the wild scheme of placing all the power of the state in the hands of the populace.*"[23]

What was this "jarring tumult and universal degradation"? It can be found in the title of her book, *Domestic Manners of the Americans*, the grammatical subject of that title being "*Manners.*"

Plainly put, Americans didn't seem to have any–not, at least, on the frontier of "the West." They spat. Here, there, every-where, men chewed "plugs" or "quids" of tobacco, and spat them onto the floor, carpeted or not. They ate with their knives and afterwards cleaned their teeth (publicly) with a pocket knife.[24] On the frontier, public spitting may have been seen as an essential part of American manhood, and therefore accomplished without apology. But spittle stained Mrs. Trollope's long skirts, and a decade later spittle also spattered Charles Dickens' topcoat within the crowded confines of a canal boat. Even Harriet Martineau, otherwise blessed with tolerance for American ways, noted that of the 206 male students at "Mr. Jefferson's University" in Charlottesville . . . "[t]heir demeanour was gentlemanly, to the last degree, except in the one particular of spitting. . . ."[25] In "the West," Martineau later met a judge who had "a quid in his cheek whenever I saw him, and squirted tobacco-juice into the fire-place or elsewhere, at intervals of about twenty seconds." This, she later wrote to a friend back in England, was "exclusively American."[26]

---

23 Trollope, Frances Milton. *Domestic Manners of the Americans*. 1832. Ed. Donald Smalley. New York: Alfred A. Knopf, Inc., First Borzoi Ed., 1949. Preface to 1832 lxxvii-viii (emphases added). Print. Hereafter cited as Trollope, *Domestic Manners*.

24 Trollope, *Domestic Manners* 18-19.

25 Martineau, *Retrospect* Vol. II, 21.

26 Martineau, *Retrospect* Vol. III, 213, 213.

Clearly, tobacco was at fault. At that time it was grown almost exclusively in Virginia and Southern Maryland, particularly in the Maryland counties of Calvert, Charles, and St. Mary's. Cigars were becoming popular along the Eastern seaboard and in the original 13 colonies, but leaf-tobacco (and spitting out of same) was now characterizing the new American frontier and its "pioneers" (a novel use of the word) along the Mississippi.

If spitting (#1) played to the lowest common denominator in American society, so, too, did bad grammar (#2), as well as an inflated use of language (#3). For Mrs. Trollope, these were sure signs of little or no education. (Should uneducated people, she wondered, actually *vote*?) Americans, she noted, insisted on using upper-class language (#4) in order to describe people who were–deplorably, she thought–quite lower class. Back in England, such words as *lady* and *gentleman* had applied only to aristocracy and landed gentry, but now, on America's Western frontier, they were being used for common laborers.[27] Mrs. Trollope provided examples of her displeasure: *Lady* Washington, *Lady* Jackson, *Lady* Franklin.[28] She noted further that while her neighbors in Cincinnati referred to her as "the English old *woman*," other neighbors commented on "the *lady* over the way *what* takes in washing," or "that there *lady* . . . *what* is making dip-candles."[29]

Similarly, in order to be a *gentleman* in England, one did not labor with one's hands. Now, however, Americans were beginning to think differently, especially on the American frontier. Mr. Trollope, arriving for a brief stay, was referred to as "the old *man*," but Mrs. Trollope noted that "draymen, butchers' boys, and the labourers on the canal were invariably denominated '*them gentlemen*' . . . ."[30]

Somewhat earlier, while traveling north from Memphis to Cincinnati on the steamboat *Belvidere*, Mrs. Trollope had also noticed the inflated use of military titles for men who had never served in the military: "we heard

---

[27] In England, "aristocrats" generally inherit both land and title; "landed gentry," on the other hand, inherit land but no title.

[28] Trollope, *Domestic Manners* 182.

[29] Trollope, *Domestic Manners* 100 (emphases added).

[30] Trollope, *Domestic Manners* 100 (emphases added).

them nearly all addressed by the titles of *general, colonel,* and *major.*"[31] Once she arrived in Cincinnati, she observed that a surveyor-general of the Cincinnati district was addressed as "*General*" even though he had seen no military service. For Mrs. Trollope, such forms of address would have suggested not only un-truth but also pretension.[32]

For Mrs. Trollope, the word "democracy" now began to include the reality of men who spat, used deplorable grammar, and gave their friends such undeserved titles as "Colonel." Worse, she thought, such settlers actually *voted*. She deplored that "[a]ny man's son may become the equal of any other man's son," observing that it led to "coarse familiarity, untempered by any shadow of respect, which is assumed by the grossest and the lowest in their intercourse with the highest and most refined." Democracy, she decided, was "a *positive evil*, and, I think, more than balances its advantages."[33] She noted, however, that "I once got so heartily scolded for saying, that I did not think all American citizens were equally eligible to [the presidency], that I shall never again venture to doubt it."[34] But she got good innings when she wrote that the present white populations of the United States "were persons who had banished themselves, or were banished from the mother country."[35] Historically, this was true.

As Americans, do we like Mrs. Trollope? Probably not. But no less a person than Mark Twain came to her defense in 1883 (well after the Civil War) while writing his autobiography. Mrs. Trollope had died in 1863, yet Twain's publisher, James Osgood, did not like Twain's defense of Mrs. Trollope and–twenty years later–edited Twain's remarks out from his autobiography. They may be found, however, just before the Introduction to the 1949 edition of *Domestic Manners of the Americans*. In part, Twain wrote: "It was for this sort of [descriptive] photography that poor candid

---

31 Trollope, *Domestic Manners* 100 (emphases added).

32 Trollope, *Domestic Manners* 182. This inflated use of language is still with us today: Colonel Sanders (of Kentucky Fried Chicken) never saw military service but was given his "military" title in 1935 by Ruby Laffoon (who also commissioned as "colonels" almost a dozen Hollywood actors and actresses), then governor of Kentucky; this was later endorsed, in 1949, by Lt. Governor Lawrence Weatherby, also of Kentucky.

33 Trollope, *Domestic Manners* 121 (emphasis added).

34 Trollope, *Domestic Manners* 124.

35 Trollope, *Domestic Manners* 405.

Mrs. Trollope was so handsomely cursed and reviled by this nation. Yet she was merely telling the truth, and this indignant nation knew it. She was painting a state of things which did not disappear at once. It lasted well along in my youth, and I remember it. . . ."[36]

In those suppressed passages, Twain continued: "She lived three years in this civilization of ours; in the body of it–not on the surface of it, as was the case with most of the foreign tourists of her day. She knew her subject well, and she set it forth fairly and squarely, without any weak ifs and ands and buts. She deserved gratitude–but it is an error to suppose she got it. . . . Mrs. Trollope, alone of them all, dealt what the gamblers call a strictly 'square game.' She did not gild us; and neither did she whitewash us."[37]

America's new democracy continued to beckon to hundreds from Britain and Europe. We know that both Harriet Martineau and Charles Dickens had read Mrs. Trollope's 1832 book and then decided to set sail from England in order to see for themselves. (To "Trollopize" became a verb in England, probably much to the delight of Trollope's readers.) Harriet Martineau learned this from her own English publisher when, in the mid-1830s, he urged Martineau to go to America, write even more about it than Mrs. Trollope had, and tempted Martineau further by adding that she could always "'Trollopize a bit'" and thus make her book more "'readable'."[38]

When Harriet Martineau traveled to Cincinnati in June of 1835 (well after Mrs. Trollope's 1831 departure), she pronounced Mrs. Trollope's bazaar/emporium "the great deformity of the city." Martineau wrote that: "Happily, it is not very conspicuous, being squatted down among houses nearly as lofty as the summit of its dome. From my window at the boarding-house, however, it was only too distinctly visible. It is built of brick, and has Gothic windows, Grecian pillars, and a Turkish dome, and it was originally ornamented with Egyptian devices, which have, however, all disappeared under the brush of the whitewasher."[39]

---

[36] Trollope, *Domestic Manners* [v] before Introduction. Mark Twain was born in 1835, and therefore his "youth" might have held true until about 1850.

[37] Trollope, *Domestic Manners* [v] before Introduction.

[38] Martineau, *Retrospect* Vol. III, 219.

[39] Martineau, *Retrospect* Vol. II, 249.

Yet notwithstanding her comment on the emporium's being "squatted down" on a Cincinnati street, Martineau was equally able to appreciate the *cultural intent* of Mrs. Trollope's ugly building. Martineau describes the first-ever concert given there, at which she herself was present in June of 1835. "There was something extremely interesting in the spectacle of the first public introduction of music into this rising city. . . . The thought came across me how far we were from the musical regions of the Old World, and how lately this place [Cincinnati] had been a cane-brake . . . and here was the spirit of Mozart swaying and inspiring a silent crowd as if they were assembled in the chapel at Salzburg!"[40]

Harriet Martineau did not agree with Mrs. Trollope's withering assessment of Americans who followed "the wild scheme of placing all the power of the state in the hands of the populace" (that is, by voting). Instead, Martineau approved of voting and called up George Washington, a commoner, to prove her point: "The kings of Europe would have laughed mightily, two centuries ago, at the idea of a commoner, without robes, crown, or sceptre, stepping into the throne of a strong nation. Yet who dared laugh when Washington's super-royal voice greeted the New World from the presidential chair, and the old world stood still to catch the echo?"[41]

As a well-published sociologist (plus her all-important letters of introduction), Martineau spent several weeks in Washington before heading to the South. She was always welcome at President Jackson's White House and took an active interest in her many visits to the Senate chamber. In the Senate, she noted–with obvious approval–that: "Some [of the Senators] were descended from Dutch farmers, some from French huguenots, some from Scotch puritans, some from English cavaliers, some from Irish chieftans. They were brought together out of law-courts, sugar-fields, merchants' stores, mountain-farms, forests and prairies."[42] Thus, she and Mrs. Trollope differed substantially on the underlying nature of democracy.

---

40 Martineau, *Retrospect* Vol. II, 250.

41 Martineau, Harriet. *Society in America*. New York: Saunders and Otley, 1837. 3 vols. Vol. I, 154. Print. Hereafter cited as Martineau, *Society*.

42 Martineau, *Retrospect* Vol. I, 301.

Somewhat later still, in 1842, Charles Dickens also enjoyed Washington, but he, too, noted that it was "the head quarters of tobacco-tinctured saliva. . . . In the courts of law, the judge has his spittoon, the crier his, the witness his, and the prisoner his . . . ."[43] Dickens found beauty in the new government buildings in Washington but noticed, even in the Senate, that it was strange to see "an honourable gentleman leaning back in his tilted chair with his legs on the desk before him, shaping a convenient 'plug' with his penknife, and when it is quite ready for use, shooting the old one from his mouth, as from a pop-gun, and clapping the new one in its place."[44] Dickens also recommended that his readers "not . . . look at the floor; and if they happen to drop anything, though it be their purse, not to pick it up with an ungloved hand on any account."[45]

But it was not spitting that struck both Harriet Martineau and Charles Dickens as drawbacks to American culture. Nor was it even the bad grammar or inflated language of "Colonel."

No. Rather, what immediately struck both Martineau and Dickens on first arriving in America was: (1) the absence of what was called "livery" (uniforms and other distinctive markers of one's class or "station"); (2) the absence of public display of this permanent "station" on the doors of upper-class coaches; and (3) the absence of wigs and gowns in courts of law. In short, there was little or no display of one's social class in this new America.

In England, livery (the uniformed reminder of one's social class or "station") was expected of English aristocracy as well as of visiting dignitaries from other countries. The coachman of an aristocratic family, for instance, wore his uniform or "livery," and the coach he drove through the streets of London displayed the title (and perhaps the coat-of-arms) of its aristocratic occupant. Bystanders, therefore, could read the situation at a glance: the permanent "station" (social class) of the coach's aristocratic owner, as well as the coachman's "livery" and thus his permanently inferior "station" in life.

---

43 Dickens, *Notes* 160.

44 Dickens, *Notes* 169. Here, Dickens may possibly have relied too much on Mrs. Trollope's description of the House of Representatives and confused it with the better-behaved Senate.

45 Dickens, *Notes* 169.

Charles Dickens noticed the absence of uniforms and coats-of-arms as he disembarked in Boston, remarking on the absence of "liveries and badges we are so fond of at home."[46] So, too, did Harriet Martineau as she noticed much the same when writing her original (1837) sociological study, *Society in America*: "One of the pleasures of travelling through a democratic country is the seeing no liveries. No such badge of menial service is to be met with throughout the States, except in the houses of the foreign ambassadors at Washington."[47]

Therefore, we need to ask why, back in 1827, Mrs. Trollope decided to clothe her manservant, William Abbott, in livery. His uniform would probably have included either a symbol or a word defining his (very English) economic dependence on her. In America, and particularly on the frontier, why did Mrs. Trollope insist on doing this? She may have reasoned that, after all, Abbott was her servant. Once in America, she could easily have changed Abbott's "livery" to a less conspicuous form of dress, but this she did not do—even when the Cincinnati sheriff confiscated most of her goods for failure to pay outstanding debts.[48]

Worse was to come. Mrs. Trollope now discovered that even the word *servant* was no longer being used in democratic America: it was being replaced by more gentle wording–in fact, by a euphemism–the help. On the frontier of the Mississippi, Mrs. Trollope had trouble with a (white) girl who "helped" in the kitchen but was not allowed to eat with the Trollope family. (This social barrier would have been observed in both the former–upper-class–American colonies as well as in the "mother country," England). Mrs. Trollope thought about the situation and decided that the girl must have heard "a thousand times that she was as good as any other lady, that all men were equal, and women too, and that it was a sin and a shame for a free-born American to be treated like a servant."[49]

---

46 Dickens, *Notes* 80.

47 Martineau, *Society* Vol. II, 254.

48 In contrast to our other visitors to America, Mrs. Trollope quite liked any suggestion of social class: once she left Cincinnati and arrived in New York, she noticed that "the want [the lack] of smart liveries destroys much of the gay effect" on private coaches. Trollope, *Domestic Manners* 352.

49 Trollope, *Domestic Manners* 52, 54.

Only a few years later, it was Harriet Martineau who also noted this American aversion to the word *servant*. Once returned to England, she wrote that "[English] servants have been so long accustomed to this subservience; it is . . . the . . . custom for the mistress to regulate their manners, their clothes, their intercourse with their friends, and many other things which they ought to manage for themselves. . . . In America it is otherwise: and may it ever be so!"[50]

In this early period of American life, the White House was open to all visitors, and while in Washington, Charles Dickens availed himself of the popular pastime of visiting it, as had both Mrs. Trollope and Harriet Martineau before him. He noted that President Tyler, while sitting at a desk in the White House office, "looked somewhat worn and anxious, and well he might; being at war with everybody." At the White House, Dickens met his "dear friend," Washington Irving, and here he also allowed himself to see what a democracy looked like. Yet even Dickens could not prevent himself from using the class-conscious English word, "station": "That these visitors, too, *whatever their station*, were not without some refinement of taste and appreciation of intellectual gifts . . . "[51] He noticed that the crowd visiting the White House was "miscellaneous," not "select," and that "every man . . . appeared to feel that he was a part of the Institution [of democracy], and was responsible for its . . . appearing to the best advantage."[52]

"Station" (or what as Americans we call "social class") had been critical to the English way of life. Viewers of the British version of "Antiques Road Show" may have noticed that occasionally an elderly woman offers for appraisal a piece of good jewelry or even a small painting. She explains that her great-grandmother's "station" in life had been that of "in service" as housemaid, nanny, or cook; upon retiring, this former housemaid had been given the expensive item by her aristocratic employers "for devoted years of service." Before the First and Second World Wars, one's "station" was, in general, quite fixed in English society.

---

50 Martineau, *Society* Vol. II, 254, 254, 254.

51 Dickens, *Notes* 172, 173, 173 (emphasis added).

52 Dickens, *Notes* 173.

Now, however, Dickens was beginning to question the fatalism inherent in such a rigid class system. While in Boston, where he had disembarked, he made a day-trip out to Lowell, Massachusetts in order to visit the new manufacturing mills, most of whose workers were young girls, not yet married, many of whom lived temporarily in boarding houses. The mills had been built as recently as 1822 and thus were still somewhat new. (Several years earlier, Harriet Martineau met Ralph Waldo Emerson and noted that "He lectures to the factory people at Lowell when they ask it."[53])

Dickens liked what he saw at Lowell and took the opportunity to inveigh against any possible questioning that his British readers might have of the girls' "station" in life. Once back in England, he wrote, "I am now going to state three facts, which will startle a large class of readers on this [English] side of the Atlantic, very much. Firstly, there is a joint-stock piano in a great many of the boarding-houses. Secondly, nearly all these young ladies subscribe to circulating libraries. Thirdly, they have got up among themselves a periodical called *The Lowell Offering*, 'A repository of original articles, written exclusively by females actively employed in the mills,'– which is duly printed, published, and sold; and whereof I [have] brought away from Lowell four hundred good solid pages, which I have read from beginning to end."[54]

Anticipating objections from his English readers about such defiance of rigid social class, he wrote, "Are we quite sure that we in England have not formed our ideas of the 'station' of working people, from accustoming ourselves to the contemplation of that class as they are, and not as they might be?"[55]

Dickens now decided that education was perhaps the only way to work against the very English consciousness of social class or "station." Traveling from Boston to New York, he noticed from his train window that: "Every little colony of houses has its church and *school-house*, peeping from among the white roofs and shady trees."[56] Later, while in Cincinnati, he also expressed

---

53 Martineau, *Retrospect* Vol. III, 230.
54 Dickens, *Notes* 116-17.
55 Dickens, *Notes* 117.
56 Dickens, *Notes* 119 (emphasis added).

admiration for its free public schools. When it came to colleges, he wrote that he had enjoyed meeting faculty at Harvard, and in New Haven he later thought of Yale College as "an establishment of considerable eminence and reputation."[57]

"Whatever the defects of American universities may be," Dickens wrote, "they disseminate no prejudices; rear no bigots; dig up the buried ashes of no old superstitions; never interpose between the people and their improvement; exclude no man because of his religious opinions; above all, in their whole course of study and instruction, recognise a world, and a broad one too, lying beyond the college walls."[58] Once in Washington, he applauded that: "At George Town, in the suburbs, there is a Jesuit College; delightfully situated, and, so far as I had an opportunity of seeing, well managed."[59]

Ever on the lookout for the education of *women*, however, it had fallen first to Mrs. Trollope to notice that: "At George Town is a nunnery, where many young ladies are educated, and at a little distance from it, a college of Jesuits for the education of young men . . . ."[60]

We now turn to the second issue identified in Section C above: women.

2. Women: vacancy of thought

Always on the lookout for institutions that might work to improve America's new "democracy," Charles Dickens, as we saw, found an answer in the mills at Lowell. In common with Harriet Martineau, he also found hope in Cincinnati's new, free, public schools.

---

57 Dickens, *Notes* 125.

58 Dickens, *Notes* 77.

59 Dickens, *Notes* 170.

60 Trollope, *Domestic Manners*, 231. Both these educational institutions had been encouraged by Maryland's own John Carroll, first archbishop of Baltimore. It appears that the "nunnery" was part of Georgetown Visitation, founded in 1799. "Today it is a thriving college preparatory school, home to a religious community, and a site with 14 buildings on the historic registry, nine of them built before the Civil War. It has laid claim to be the oldest Catholic school for girls in the original 13 colonies, but this is not precisely true since it was founded in the District of Columbia." "History of Georgetown Visitation." *Georgetown Visitation*. Web. 18 Oct. 2022. <https://www.visi.org/our-mission/history-of-georgetown-visitation>.

More tellingly, he also noticed that women–and even younger girls–did not have to be escorted in public by either a man or another woman. In America, women were now able to walk alone and even travel alone.

He first noticed this apparent flouting of English custom in America's new railway cars. In his 1842 *American Notes* he recorded that, "There are no first or second class carriages as with us; but there is a gentlemen's car and a ladies' car . . . in the first, everybody smokes; and in the second, nobody does. As a black man never travels with a white one, there is also a negro car. . . . In the centre of the carriage there is usually a stove, fed with charcoal or anthracite coal. . . . In the ladies car, there are a great many gentlemen who have ladies with them. There are also a great many ladies who have nobody with them: for *any lady may travel alone, from one end of the United States to the other, and be certain of the most courteous and considerate treatment everywhere.*[61] Shortly after his arrival in January of 1842, Dickens had written home to his old friend, John Forster, that: "Universal deference is paid to ladies; and they walk about at all seasons, wholly unprotected."[62]

Aside from these observations, however, Dickens had very little to say about the role of women in America's new democracy.

It would be left to both the women travelers, Mrs. Trollope and Harriet Martineau, to better understand (and sympathize with) the place of women in this new America. Both women might even have wondered: Who, in fact, had designed those American railway carriages that were so different from their counterparts in England? Those American trains–which allowed women to travel unaccompanied? The disappearance of *economic class* on American trains might be seen as an appropriate response to America's recently avowed "democracy," but the *gender issues* (that is, protection by men, "delicacy," and "woman's place") now appeared to be challenged in America's public conveyances.

---

61 Dickens, *Notes* 111 (emphasis added). Dickens is silent as to black women; presumably they were relegated to the "negro car" without differentiation of gender.

62 Dickens, *Notes* 306 (and see 111 therein).

With hindsight, we might even view a woman's new ability to travel alone as the thin end of what would much later be called a "feminist" wedge. "The woman question" would not be answered in the 1800s, but it would swell larger and larger until it was finally addressed by a woman's right to vote in 1920.

In Cincinnati, Mrs. Trollope was probably the first to comment on the nature of the frontier: unabashedly masculine. "In America," she noted, "women are guarded by a seven-fold shield of habitual insignificance."[63] She added later that in America "all the enjoyments of the men are found in the *absence of the women*. They dine, they play cards, they have musical meetings, . . . but all *without* women."[64] She would later travel to the slave states, and even here, she discovered much the same agreement that men and women were to occupy quite separate spheres, women being content with raising children and household management. She observed that "even in the [Southern] slave states . . . the very highest [women] occupy themselves in their household concerns, in a manner that precludes the possibility of their becoming elegant and enlightened companions. In Baltimore, Philadelphia, and New York, I met with some exceptions to this; but speaking of the country [America] generally, it is unquestionably true."[65]

Harriet Martineau carried this one step further. In the sociological study she wrote upon her return from America (*Society in America*) she raised two questions, both of which applied to England as well as to America.

The **first concern** had to do with law. "The question has been asked . . . in more countries than one, how obedience to the laws can be required of women, when no woman has, either actually or virtually, given any assent to any law." She noted further that "The truth is, that while there is much said about 'the sphere of woman,' two widely different notions are entertained of what is meant by the phrase."[66]

---

63 Trollope, *Domestic Manners*, 69.
64 Trollope, *Domestic Manners*, 156 (emphases added).
65 Trollope, *Domestic Manners*, 157.
66 Martineau, *Society* Vol. I, 149, 153.

That first concern of Martineau's would not be settled in either England or America until the early twentieth century, but Martineau's **second concern** possibly contains a familiar problem. She wrote that (in England, as well as in America), "Men do not choose to marry early, because they have learned to think other things of more importance than the best comforts of domestic life." (Such as, for instance, graduate study in order to earn a living that will feed a wife and several children.) But as for women, Martineau wrote: "We are driven back upon marriage as the only appointed object in life: and upon the conviction that the sum and substance of female education in America, as in England, is training women to consider marriage as the sole object in life, *and to pretend that they do not think so.*"[67]

This male-centered society is still with us today. Women often feel it to be a problem; men do not.

Biologically, the female of the species is "gifted" with a body that starts seeping red fluid at about the age of twelve and which does not cease until middle age. This fluid ceases once "seed" meets the egg of a woman (married or not), and thereafter her body becomes what might be called "a walking womb" for children who–unless prevention is exercised–can potentially number ten, twelve, or even sixteen.[68] Children must be nursed (yet another seeping of bodily fluid), and during one of her many childbirths, a woman may die, physically exhausted. A quick glance at census reports before the 20th century reveals that men often needed to marry a second time: after all, who was going to manage a household of twelve or sixteen children?

If the first wife continued to live, she turned for sympathy to the single, public avenue open to her: religion. "Poor, credulous woman!" Harriet Martineau later wrote, as she described a woman's penchant for providing funds to educate men in theological seminaries. "[S]he can be made to think anything a duty. How have we seen her neglecting her health, her comfort, her family, the poor, and, above all, neglecting the improvement of her own mind, that she might earn a few dollars towards educating a

---

67 Martineau, *Society* Vol. II, 242, 229 (emphasis added).

68 The notion that women are more prone than men to hysterics comes from the Greek word hystera: in English, the translation of hystera means womb, or uterus.

young man, who is far more able to do it himself, and who, nine times in ten, laughs in his sleeve at her."[69]

It may therefore come as a surprise to the reader that Harriet Martineau–even if not married–was a happy woman. In addition to her extensive writings, she prided herself on two of her domestic accomplishments: embroidery, and entertaining as hostess. She also enjoyed the pleasure of male friendships (one of which was with Erasmus Darwin, older brother of Charles Darwin). As a Unitarian, she believed in "the improvement of her own mind," having been educated at a Unitarian school during her early years. After that, she educated herself through her own reading and writing. "It must happen," she wrote in 1837, [that] "there are women no more fit to be wives and mothers than to be statesmen and generals; no more fit for any responsibility whatever, than for the maximum of responsibility."[70] But she also realized that hers was a minority opinion: "Wifely and motherly occupation may be called the sole business of woman there [in America]. . . . The only alternative, as I have said, is making an occupation of either religion or dissipation [drink]; neither of which is fit to be so used: the one [religion] being a state of mind; the other altogether a negation [of it] . . . ."[71]

In common with Charles Dickens, Harriet Martineau was a strong believer in the power of education. And like Mrs. Trollope before her, she enjoyed visiting West Point: "I never see the interior of a college without longing to impress upon its inmates how envied and enviable they are."[72] Later, she and her female companion, Louisa Jeffrey, made a point of spending a great deal of time listening to debates in the Senate ("our favorite resort"), all the while deploring that the British (their own countrymen) had burnt the Library of Congress during their "atrocious attack," their "bandit expedition" in 1814 (amid the War of 1812).[73]

Martineau went on to note that back in England there were no public high schools, nor was there any version of America's increasingly popular

---

69 Martineau, *Society*, Vol. II, 416.
70 Martineau, *Society* Vol. II, 416, 245.
71 Martineau, *Society* Vol. II, 245.
72 Martineau, *Retrospect* Vol. I, 63.
73 Martineau, *Retrospect* Vol. I, 242, 274, 316.

"lyceums" (one variation of which–although Martineau didn't know it– was Leonardtown's newly created Reading Room and Debating Society; see Chapter 3-B). She also wrote that, in America, "Their common and high schools, their Lyceums and cheap colleges, are exciting and feeding thousands of minds, which in England would never get beyond the loom or the plough-tail [plow-tail]."[74]

However, where education for women was concerned, Martineau worried about its absence in an America that was still overwhelmingly rural. She had learned that a farm-woman could "bind" a girl from age 11, providing her with food, clothing, and a grammar-school education until she reached age 18, at which point she would be given $50 "or a cow, or some equivalent." That was the theory, but often girls in their mid-teens grew "restless," and Martineau wrote that this seemed to be due to "the fashionable novels which deluge the country from New York to beyond the Mississippi."[75] These "happily-ever-after" novels are what today are known as "romance novels" (or "bodice-rippers"). Gloomily, Martineau concluded that "Readers are plentiful: thinkers are rare,"[76] and decided that women in charity work do "good or harm, *according to the enlightenment of mind . . .* "[77]

Martineau continued: "As women have none of the objects in life for which an enlarged education is considered requisite, the education is not given. Female education is much what it is in England. . . . But what is given is, for the most part, passively received; and what is obtained is, chiefly, by means of the memory." (That is, rote, or memorization.)[78] She saw what she called "religious excitements" as *substitutes* for politics, justice, and philosophy, writing that "I was perpetually struck with this when I saw women braving hurricane, frost, and snow to flit from preaching to

---
74 Martineau, *Retrospect* Vol. III, 24.
75 Martineau, *Society* Vol. II, 250.
76 Martineau, *Society* Vol. II, 256.
77 Martineau, *Society* Vol. II, 255 (emphasis added).
78 Martineau, *Society* Vol. II, 228.

preaching [of religion]; and laying out the whole day among visits for prayer and religious excitement. . . ."[79]

Martineau appeared on firm ground when she specifically advocated for the serious education of women. Invited to visit Montpelier in 1835, home of former-president James Madison, she was delighted to learn that Madison, at age 83, "thought it of the utmost importance to the country . . . that the brain and the hands should be trained together; and that no distinction in this respect should be made between men and women."[80]

Much later, in 1835, she also visited Amherst College in Massachusetts (all male, founded in 1821). She noticed that village girls often sat in on the lectures. "These girls were from a neighbouring [high] school, and from the houses of the farmers and mechanics of the village. . . . We found that the admission of girls to such lectures as they could understand (this was on Geology), was a practice of some years' standing; and that no evil had been found to result from it. It was a gladdening sight, testifying both to the simplicity of manners, and the eagerness for education."[81]

A year after Martineau completed her trip to America, the first of the private "Seven Sister" women's colleges sprang up: Mount Holyoke, in 1837.[82] (See Chapter 4-A-1, fn 5.)

Just a year or two after her visit to Amherst College, Harriet Martineau labeled a feminine condition as "vacuity of thought"–what today we might call "empty-headedness" (not to be confused with "absent-mindedness"). Such psychological "vacancy" (the absence of dedicated thought) served to replace education or any other sense of self-worth. Now, after at least two years in America, Harriet Martineau expanded on her charge that–for too

---

[79] Martineau, *Society* Vol. II, 227, 346.

[80] Martineau, *Retrospect* Vol. II, 10.

[81] Martineau, *Retrospect* Vol. III, 13, 13.

[82] But not all girls had–or still have–the ability, whether intellectual or financial, of furthering their own education. "The woman question" remains a problem to this day. It is partially answered by the community college movement–originally known as the "junior college" movement–of which M. Adele France was such a strong proponent. Ms. France introduced "higher education" courses–first and second years of college–for the first time in Maryland, at St. Mary's [public] Female Seminary in 1926. (See Chapter 9-C & 9-E.)

many women–"vacancy" of thought took over their waking moments and thus turned them to the one public activity allotted them: religion.

3. Religion: substitute for education

Mrs. Trollope, Harriet Martineau, and Charles Dickens all came from England, a country whose state-run religion was Anglican, although by 1829, it had finally become possible to belong to other Protestant groups, as well as to the previously-persecuted Catholic church. Mrs. Trollope was Anglican, but she had a genuine appreciation for Catholicism. Harriet Martineau was originally Unitarian but would soon become a Freethinker. And Charles Dickens would be buried in the Poets' Corner of (Anglican) Westminster Abbey, although in his adult years he often frequented a Unitarian church.

Two of our three English visitors (Mrs. Trollope and Charles Dickens) took the opportunity–while still so far from home–of visiting out-of-the-mainstream Protestant revivals, at that time particularly popular in "the West," that is, along the Mississippi River. Mrs. Trollope, the first to arrive in America, spent all of Chapter 11 of her *Domestic Manners* on the topic of religion, worrying that in a country without a national church "a religious tyranny may be exerted very effectually without the aid of the government."[83]

Just what was this "religious tyranny"? In order to be socially accepted in Cincinnati, Mrs. Trollope wrote that, as a woman, "it was necessary to declare yourself as belonging to some one of these [churches]." She noted–with considerable apprehension–that among the Protestant groups, "each [woman] had a right to choose a creed and mode of worship for herself."[84] On this frontier of the West, no one minded that Mrs. Trollope knew of "a family where [of all the females] one was a Methodist, one a Presbyterian, and a third a Baptist; and [yet] another [family], where one was a Quaker, one a declared Atheist, and another an Universalist. These are all females . . . ."[85] Religion, it seemed, was a woman's concern (and quite possibly the penalty for not having been well-educated).

---

[83] Trollope, *Domestic Manners*, 107.
[84] Trollope, *Domestic Manners*, 108, 127, n.2.
[85] Trollope, *Domestic Manners*, 126.

For some women on the frontier at Cincinnati, religious revivals provided emotional release, and in so doing they took the brunt of Mrs. Trollope's criticism, particularly in Chapter 8 of her *Domestic Manners*. In the burgeoning town of Cincinnati, for instance, religious revivals filled a social void left by (1) no cards, (2) no billiards, (3) no concerts, (4) no dinner parties, (5) "and by far the larger proportion of females deem it an offence against religion to witness the representation of a play."[86]

Where, then, were women to organize, to play a conspicuous role, to dress themselves up and finally become important? Answer: (A) in the Protestant chapels, and (B) at the revivals and organizational activities leading up to them.

As for (A), the Protestant chapels: "No evening in the week but brings throngs of the young and beautiful to the chapels and meeting-houses, all dressed with care, and sometimes with great pretension; it is there that all display is made, and all fashionable distinction sought."[87] All these remarks come from Mrs. Trollope's Chapter 8, partly devoted to religion on the frontier in the late 1820s.

As for (B): If the weekly meetings in "chapels and meeting-houses" were one of two possible religious expressions, the other form of expression was "the revival" with its itinerant preachers. When the "Itinerant" arrived in town, he was usually housed in the home of a follower. At these revivals, women dressed well and called each other, affectionately, "Brother" and "Sister" before being encouraged to openly confess their weaknesses and sins. The congregation as a whole was invited to come forward and sit on the "anxious bench" where they would then whisper their sins to the Itinerant who would urge them to "Come to Jesus." Mrs. Trollope noted that "It is hardly necessary to say that all who obeyed the call to place themselves on the 'anxious benches' were women, and by far the greater number, very young women."[88]

---

86 Trollope, *Domestic Manners*, 74.
87 Trollope, *Domestic Manners*, 74.
88 Trollope, *Domestic Manners*, 77, 79, 81.

Mrs. Trollope admired the stable structures of both the Catholic Church and the Church of England (Anglican, but re-named "Episcopal" in the new United States). Not for her were the camp "revivals" of itinerant evangelists (all male) and their audiences of young, hysterical women, whom she generally deplored. She praised the Catholic Church as appearing to be "exempt from the fury of division and sub-division that has seized every other persuasion." Though Anglican, Mrs. Trollope became increasingly convinced of "the advantages of an established church as a sort of head-quarters for quiet unpresuming Christians," noting that "having a Pope "prevents the outrageous display of individual whim which every other sect is permitted."[89] In Chapter 12 she went on to note that "every young lady claims a right to be her own bishop, and every parent, who ventures to doubt the lawfulness of her calling, is liable to hear himself doomed to eternal perdition by the voice of his child."[90]

Putting Cincinnati behind her in March of 1830, Mrs. Trollope, along with her son and two daughters, decided to cross the Alleghenies and travel to the older, more settled areas along the East Coast. Arriving by steamboat in Wheeling (at that time still in Virginia), she boarded a nine-passenger coach and found the mountain scenery generally delightful. It was when the coach finally pulled up at the inn at Hagerstown that "we became fully aware that we had left Western America behind us."[91]

From Hagerstown, Maryland, the coach traveled to Baltimore, "one of the handsomest cities to approach in the Union"; here she and her family stayed "a fortnight" (two weeks). They attended Mass at the Catholic Cathedral, but for her, the most moving sight was that of St. Mary's Catholic College with a chapel, which she described as "a little *bijou* [jewel] of a thing. . . . There is a sequestered little garden behind it . . . bearing a lofty cross

---

[89] Trollope, *Domestic Manners*, 109, 108, 109.
[90] Trollope, *Domestic Manners*, 127, n.2.
[91] Trollope, *Domestic Manners*, 201.

... [T]here is something of holiness, and quiet beauty about it, that excites the imagination strangely."[92]

For Charles Dickens (as for Mrs. Trollope), religion must have seemed what today we would call "a spectator sport." Shortly before leaving America, Dickens paid a visit to the Shaker village in Lebanon, New York–only to discover that it had been shut down for a full calendar year. He already knew that Shaker agriculture was "highly esteemed" and that Shakers were also "good breeders of cattle . . . kind and merciful to the brute creation."[93]

But (and Dickens used several buts), he wrote that Shakers accepted into their group "persons so young that they cannot know their own minds." All Shakers were devoted to a life of celibacy, and Dickens regretted that it was a "bad spirit" that would "strip life of its healthful graces, [and] rob youth of its innocent pleasures." In true Dickens style, he wrote: "we walked into a grim room, where several grim hats were hanging on grim pegs, and the time was grimly told by a grim clock, which uttered every tick with a kind of struggle, as if it broke the grim silence reluctantly . . . ."[94]

Harriet Martineau did not appear to have visited either a camp revival (as did Mrs. Trollope) or a Shaker community (as did Charles Dickens). But when Martineau met an elderly James Madison in 1835, she enjoyed quoting his remark from Voltaire: "[T]hat if there were only one religion in a country, it would be a pure despotism; if two, they would be deadly enemies; but half a hundred subsist in fine harmony."[95] Martineau had already developed her own ideas about religion and the role it was playing in addressing a woman's "vacuity"–or vacancy–of thought, thereby providing said woman with a publicly legitimatized focus of activity: religious activity.

---

92 Trollope, *Domestic Manners*, 208 (italics in original). The Sulpicians founded St. Mary's College in 1799 as a boys' school, and in 1805, it was chartered as a non-sectarian college by the Maryland legislature. However, because their primary purpose was to train priests, in 1852, the Sulpicians closed the college while maintaining the seminary. Fortunately, the "bijou" chapel and garden have been preserved (located at St. Mary's Spiritual Center & Historic Site, 600 N. Paca Street, Baltimore). See also: Sherwood, Grace H. "Old St. Mary's College." *The Baltimore Sun*, Sunday, 18 Dec. 1927: 8, 14. Print.

93 Dickens, *Notes* 259.

94 Dickens, *Notes* 259, 259, 259, 257.

95 Martineau, *Retrospect* Vol. II, 12.

We can now look back and see that religion (before the 20th century) served as a limited substitute for a good education–but minus education's inclusion of history, philosophy, mathematics, science, and literature.

When, therefore, three men of St. Mary's County (James Blackistone, William Coad, and Joseph Shaw) faced a County population rife with religious factionalism in the late 1830s, they decided to create a public "Female Seminary"[96] in which religious controversies were not to be allowed. The Trustees of the Seminary even went so far as to fire an early principal for the anti-Catholic literature she was passing out to her young girls. (This is discussed in Chapters 3-C-4 & 3-D.)

4. Indians and Africans: ejected and subjected

Indians were being increasingly *ejected* from their tribal lands, and black Africans (whether kidnapped in Africa or "bought" outright from local African tribes) were *subjected* as American slaves. But the wording of "American slaves" poses yet a further conundrum: were these slaves, in fact, actually "American"? Were they considered as "belonging"–as actors–of this new "democracy"? Or were they considered as some form of lesser being? This, in fact, was what our English abolitionists (Mrs. Trollope, Harriet Martineau, and Charles Dickens) wanted to find out.

America promised opportunity, and by the early 1800s thousands upon thousands of [white] men decided to "chance it" in an America where, by report, all men were created equal. Sailing to America, whether "under the bow" or "in steerage," these men and women made their way across the Atlantic. And because America was no longer part of the British colonies, they now had the chance to push their wagons across the Alleghenies and settle what they considered "the West."

Needless to say, all these settlers from England and Europe were white.

a. Indians

And therein lay the problem. Had the Indians been white-skinned and speakers of French, Spanish, or any other European language, new settlers

---

96 In the 1800s, "seminary" = "school."

in America could simply have declared a tidy little war on them–for which there was indeed precedent. Indians, however, of reddish-brown skin, were hunters, living off the land and considering themselves at one with it. Their disputes with each other were almost always territorial and tribal. English and other European settlers who wanted Indian lands made "treaties" with brown-skinned peoples–and then proceeded to break them.

Mr. Trollope, hapless husband of Mrs. Trollope, made a single visit to Cincinnati, and on Saturday, January 24th of 1829, met and shook hands with General Andrew Jackson, at that time on his way to Washington to deliver his first inaugural address. Mr. Trollope reported himself as "pleased by [Jackson's] conversation and manners."[97]

President Jackson, newly elected, proceeded to include Indians in his initial inaugural address: "It will be my sincere and constant desire to observe toward the Indian tribes within our limits a just and liberal policy, and to give that humane and considerate attention to their rights and their wants *which is consistent with the habits of our government and the feelings of our people.*"[98] The rejection of Indians lies in the last 15 words of that address; and during his second inaugural speech in 1833, Jackson, ever judicious, was careful to make no further mention of the Indians.

In a landmark decision proclaimed in 1832, the U.S. Supreme Court recognized the Cherokee as a sovereign nation and ruled that Georgia laws regarding the Cherokee nation were unconstitutional. *Worcester v. Georgia*, 31 U.S. 515 (1832). Yet in 1835-36, President Jackson repudiated this ruling, allegedly declaring, "[Chief Justice] John Marshall has made his decision; now let him enforce it." The damage caused by Jackson's nullification would have irreversible consequences.

As destined by the Indian Removal Act of 1830, the Trail of Tears bore witness to the forced removal of brown-or-red-skinned Indians–by the thousands–who were now forced westward from their tribal lands in North Carolina, Georgia, Alabama, and Tennessee ("Tanasi" in the Cherokee

---

[97] Trollope, *Domestic Manners*, 145.

[98] First Inaugural Address of President Jackson on March 4, 1829. Point 8 (emphasis added). <www.andrewjackson.org/p/inaugural-addresses.html>.

language).[99] Trekking westward–over time–and well beyond the Mississippi River, Indians would either inter-marry with whites or end up on today's "reservations." In 1838, President Van Buren sent 7,000 military men to expedite the removal of Cherokee. During this Trail of Tears, more than 5,000 Cherokee died of disease, starvation, cold, and in some cases, murder.

Although the Cherokee nation was a matrilineal society, by the 1830s, Cherokee governance had been eroded by European ideas of patriarchy. In 1835, the Treaty of New Echota, which led to what became known as the [Cherokee] Trail of Tears, was signed by men who represented a faction of the Cherokee nation and by representatives of the federal government.[100] Like the women silenced and sitting behind the wooden screen at the 1840 Anti-Slavery Convention in London, Cherokee women were sidelined, allowed to observe but not participate. (See Chapter 1-A and fn 23.)

Meanwhile, Mrs. Trollope, as usual, had her own opinions. Following her two-year stint in Cincinnati, she visited Washington in 1830 and made a point of visiting the Bureau of Indian Affairs. She wrote of (white) Americans as being "treacherous and false almost beyond belief in their intercourse with the unhappy Indians." Once back in England, she wrote (in her tell-all book on American "democracy") that "it is impossible for any mind of common honesty not to be revolted by the contradictions in [Americans'] principles and practice. They [proponents of democracy] inveigh against the governments of Europe, because, as they say, they favour the powerful and oppress the weak. You may hear this declaimed upon in Congress, roared out in taverns, discussed in every drawing-room, satirized upon the

---

99 To be distinguished from the Choctaw "Trail of Tears and Death" which began in the winter of 1831, as well as many other forced removals or so-called "relocations" of indigenous peoples, such as the Cherokee, later that decade. Although the term "Trail of Tears" is usually associated with the Cherokee, the term is broader because it "invokes the *collective suffering* those [indigenous] people experienced, although it is most commonly used in reference to the removal experiences of the Southeast Indians generally and the Cherokee nation specifically. The physical trail consisted of several overland routes and one main water route . . . ." "Trail of Tears - United States history." *Encyclopaedia Britannica*, (emphasis added). Web. 14 June 2022. <https://www.britannica.com/event/Trail-of-Tears>.

100 "Historian Theda Perdue explains that 'Cherokee women met in their own councils to discuss their own opinions' despite not being able to participate.[74] The inability for women to join in on the negotiation and signing of the Treaty of New Echota shows how the role of women changed dramatically within Cherokee Nation following colonial encroachment." "Trail of Tears . . . Historical Context, . . . Cherokee forced relocation." *Wikipedia*. Web. 13 June 2022. <https://en.wikipedia.org/wiki/Trail_of_Tears#Choctaw_removal>

stage, nay, even anathematized from the pulpit: . . . You will see them one hour lecturing their mob on the indefeasible rights of man, and the next driving from their homes the children of the soil, whom they have bound themselves to protect by the most solemn treaties."[101]

Fortunately for the readers of today, Charles Dickens reported a long conversation with an Indian chief while the two men were aboard a packet-ship on the Ohio River, traveling from Cincinnati to Louisville in April of 1842. Using italics to show his astonishment, Dickens wrote that Pitchlynn, a chief of the Choctaws, "*sent in his card* to me," and thus began their conversation. Pitchlynn (who spoke English well and enjoyed the poetry of Sir Walter Scott) was returning from Washington where he had spent the past 17 months, negotiating with "the Government."[102]

For these negotiations, however, Pitchlynn had no great hopes, "for what could a few poor Indians do, against such well-skilled men of business as the whites?" On his way back home from Washington, Pitchlynn was still wearing his business suit, and when Dickens remarked that he had hoped to meet an Indian in full Indian dress, Pitchlynn noted "that his race were losing many things besides their dress, and would soon be seen upon the earth no more . . . . There were but twenty thousand of the Choctaws left," Pitchlynn told Dickens, "and their number was decreasing every day. A few of his brother chiefs had been obliged to become civilised, and to make themselves acquainted with what the whites knew, for it was their only chance of existence."[103] Dickens never saw Pitchlynn again, but, before parting, invited him to visit England.

Harriet Martineau spent two years in America (1834-1836), and thus was present for the trails of tears of the Creek and Chickasaw nations (after that of the Choctaw nation in 1831). Martineau became friends with Henry Clay (1777-1852) and–although disappointed with his decision to let Missouri become a slave state–nevertheless admired him for his pleas on behalf of the Indians. She spent several days with Clay at his home in Kentucky ("the

---

[101] Trollope, *Domestic Manners*, 221, 221-22.
[102] Dickens, *Notes* 210 (emphasis by Dickens).
[103] Dickens, *Notes* 210, 210, 211.

wild woods of the West"), and one of their topics of conversation concerned Clay's opinion that Cherokees should have a place on the Supreme Court, which he viewed "as contemplated by the Constitution."[104]

In a separate vein, Martineau wrote: "I often wonder whether it is yet too late to revert to the Indian names [of places],"[105] and she was pleased to see that some New Yorkers still referred to their city by its Indian name, *Manhattan* (perhaps "island of many hills" or a "place for gathering wood to make bows"). She expanded on this theme by writing that Indians still living in Connecticut "must be mourning their lost Quonnecticut." [106]

b. Africans

All three of our English visitors were abolitionists. But then, it is important to remember that black slavery did not exist *visually* in England, and therefore a pro-abolition stance cost an English individual almost nothing in terms of social acceptance. (See Chapter 1-D). England's overall economy was based on slavery–but well beyond any visual reminders of it.

Before Parliament's Slave Trade Act of 1807, much of England's economic success had been based far, far away on the West Indian islands of the Caribbean: these were the English-owned islands of Barbados, Trinidad, Dominica, Montserrat, Jamaica, Antigua, Grenada, and half of St. Kitts. There, in the Caribbean, sugar was either milled into molasses (for rum) or sent to an increasingly sugar-dependent worldwide market. (English abolitionists, however, refused to sweeten their tea with sugar.) Cotton grown on those islands (and in America) was also shipped to Britain, where it was loomed and then sold world-wide.

England herself might remain white–but, overall, her economy depended on black slavery. In Britain's Slave Trade Act of 1807, the simple *trade* of slaves was forbidden (thus impacting St. Mary's County as well as Washington, D.C. in the War of 1812). But *slavery itself* still existed in the British Caribbean until 1834, at which point all of England's slaves,

---

104 Martineau, *Retrospect* Vol. I, 297.
105 Martineau, *Retrospect* Vol. I, 129.
106 Martineau, *Retrospect* Vol. I, 129; Vol. III, 10.

worldwide were declared to be freed after "apprenticeships" which ended in 1838. (Except for certain lands controlled by the powerful East India Company; thus, it would not be until 1843 that slavery would end in the British islands of Saint Helena and Ceylon–now Sri Lanka–respectively off the coasts of Africa and India.)

Before our Revolutionary War of 1776, Jesuit priests (generally pro-slavery) were often faced with having to "justify" the colonial system of slavery to the slaves themselves. So it was with a priest named John Lewis, S.J., who in 1761 was the Superior (head priest) of the Maryland Jesuits. Recently, however, in the year 2001, yet another Jesuit, Thomas Murphy, took the bull by the horns, researching and writing about slavery in the 13 (still British) colonies of "America." Murphy noted (and also published) that Father Lewis preached the following sermon during Mass at an Annapolis plantation in 1761: "He [Father Lewis] told them [the slaves] that they ought to rejoice that they were not rich, for their poverty placed them "in a happy state both in order to ys. [this] life and the next." This condition of slavery meant that they were freed from "innumerable cares of ys. [this] world and so lived in an easy road to eternal felicity in ye [the] world to come." Unlike a master, a slave had "few or none to answer for but yourself," and so "your obligations are both few in number and easily comply'd with."[107]

Almost 70 years after this sermon, Mrs. Trollope disembarked at New Orleans in 1827, immediately following a seven-week voyage across the Atlantic. In New Orleans, she admired the mixed-race Quadroons (each of whom had one white grandfather from the planter class). In addition to "the grace and beauty of the elegant Quadroons," Mrs. Trollope also remarked on "[t]he large proportion of blacks seen in the streets, all labour being performed by them." She further noted, "We were much pleased by the chant with which the Negro boatmen regulate . . . their labour on the river;

---

107 Murphy, Thomas, S.J, *Jesuit Slaveholding in Maryland, 1717-1838 (Studies in African American History and Culture)*. New York: Routledge, 2001. 110. Print. In the Introduction to his book (at xvi), Father Murphy observes that, before the Second Vatican Council in 1962-65 had urged a more impartial analysis of church history, the tone of Catholic historians had been apologetic. Father Murphy criticizes Father LaFarge for an article he wrote in 1935, in which he regretted Jesuit slaveholding, yet argued that Jesuits had a more "benevolent" style than other slave-holders. Yet slavery is slavery–regardless of so-called "benevolence."

it consists but of very few notes, but they are sweetly harmonious, and the Negro voice is almost always rich and powerful."[108]

It may not have been until she left Cincinnati (roughly two years later) and made her way to the Eastern seaboard that Mrs. Trollope's sense of aesthetic beauty (that "sweetly harmonious" Negro voice) finally gave way to a realization of the brutalities of slavery. Condemning hypocrisy and inhumanity, she criticized both the oppression of Indians and slavery: "it is impossible for any mind of common honesty not to be revolted by the contradictions in [Americans'] principles and practice . . . look at them at home; you will see them with one hand hoisting the cap of liberty, and with the other flogging their slaves."[109]

Boarding for some months with a friend in Stonington, Virginia, Mrs. Trollope learned that it was a criminal offense to teach a slave to read. Otherwise, slaves seemed to be "taken care" of in Virginia. "These are the favourable features of their situation. [But] the sad one is, that they *may* be sent to *the south* and sold. This is the dread of all the slaves north of Louisiana. The sugar plantations, and more than all, the rice grounds of Georgia and the Carolinas, are the terror of American negroes; and well they may be, for they open an early grave to thousands; and to *avoid loss* it is needful to make their previous labour pay their value. . . . In what is their condition better than that of the kidnapped negroes on the coast of Africa? . . . Among the poorer class of landholders, who are often as profoundly ignorant as the negroes they own, the effect of this plenary power over males and females is most demoralising . . . ."[110]

Mrs. Trollope concluded her remarks with the observation that: "The idea of really sympathising in the sufferings of a slave, appeared to them

---

108 Trollope, *Domestic Manners*, 7.
109 Trollope, *Domestic Manners*, 221, 222.
110 Trollope, *Domestic Manners*, 246 (all emphases by Mrs. Trollope), 246, 247.

Similarly, Martineau noted that the Alabama Digest stated that while the fine for *torturing* a slave was $200, the fine for *teaching* a slave to read was a whopping $500. Martineau, *Society* Vol. II, 131. Although certainly not in the same horrifying context, fear of the power of knowledge brings to mind the women of the *Pieria Literary Society*, who defying their gender exclusion, took as their motto Alexander Pope's famous lines, "A little knowledge is a dangerous thing . . ." See Chapter 4-A-1.

[the Virginians] as absurd as weeping over a calf that had been slaughtered by the butcher." And what was probably worse: "They talk of [Negroes], of their condition, of their faculties, of their conduct, exactly as if they were incapable of hearing."[111]

Charles Dickens, as we have seen, had previously arranged with his English publisher to tour public institutions in an America now freed from its former colonial rule. In Boston, therefore, he visited a House of Correction (prison) where he found Northern women engaged in the prison's business dealings with the South: that is, making "light clothing, for New Orleans and the Southern States."[112]

Later, traveling down to Baltimore, Dickens noted that we "were waited on, for the first time, by slaves," adding that their presence "filled me with a sense of shame and self-reproach."[113]

By the time he reached Fredericksburg, Dickens had decided he could go no farther south than Richmond: "In the negro car belonging to the train in which we made this journey, were a mother and her children who had just been purchased; the husband and father being left behind with their old owner. The children cried the whole way, and the mother was misery's picture. The champion of Life, Liberty, and the Pursuit of Happiness, who had bought them, rode in the same train; and, every time we stopped, got down to see that they were safe."[114]

Once again, it was Harriet Martineau who gave the most measured response to whatever she saw of both slavery and of the South. Following her mid-February trip (1835) to James Madison at his Montpelier home, and continuing on to the University of Virginia at Charlottesville, she planned to continue traveling through the Deep South by stagecoach. Martineau spent several weeks in the Carolinas, Georgia, and Alabama before reaching New Orleans on April 24th of 1835. Throughout, she made a point of never broaching the subject of slavery. At her original departure from Philadelphia

---

111 Trollope, *Domestic Manners*, 248, 249.
112 Dickens, *Notes* 102.
113 Dickens, *Notes* 161.
114 Dickens, *Notes* 180-81.

in early 1835, she had written that "my determination had been adopted long before, never to evade the great question of colour; never to provoke it; but always to meet it plainly in whatever form it should be presented."[115]

By the time she reached Charleston, Martineau had learned how to disagree without being disagreeable: "I made it a rule to allow others to introduce the subject of slavery, knowing that they would not fail to do so, and that I might learn as much from their method of approaching the topic as from any thing they could say upon it. . . . I met with much more cause for admiration [of the South] in their frankness than reason to complain of illiberality [of the Southerners]."[116] Martineau was, after all, a sociologist, and professional to the core.

Yet even she had her limits, although they seemed to grow the farther south she traveled. While she admired the graciousness of her hosts and hostesses, she wrote that "The sweet temper and kindly manners of the Americans are so striking to foreigners, that it is some time before the dazzled stranger perceives that, genuine as is all this good, evils as black as night exist along with it."[117] No less a person than James Madison (a slave-owning Virginian) had warned her of this: "He [Madison] observed that the whole bible is against negro slavery; but that the clergy do not preach this; and the people do not see it."[118]

One particular problem, Martineau soon learned, was the need for medical students in Baltimore to dissect bodies of the recently deceased. "In Baltimore the bodies of coloured people exclusively are taken for dissection, 'because the whites do not like it, and the coloured people cannot resist.'"[119] In Charleston, she was taken to the slave market and there observed a boy, eight or nine years of age who was being sold by himself. "There was no bearing the child's look of helplessness and shame."[120] In April of 1835, she finally reached Montgomery, Alabama and saw slave

---

[115] Martineau, Retrospect Vol. I, 229.
[116] Martineau, *Retrospect* Vol. II, 67, 68.
[117] Martineau, *Retrospect* Vol. I, 228.
[118] Martineau, *Retrospect* Vol. II, 5.
[119] Martineau, *Retrospect* Vol. I, 230-31.
[120] Martineau, *Retrospect* Vol. II, 85.

quarters that were similar to "a lunatic asylum": "The natural good taste, so remarkable in free Negroes, is here extinguished. Their small, dingy, untidy houses, their [corn] cribs, the children crouching round the fire, the animal deportment of the grown-up, the brutish chagrins and enjoyments of the old, were all loathsome."[121]

Alone of the three English visitors–and as early as 1835–Harriet Martineau seemed to understand that a day would come when slavery would no longer be acceptable in an America that prided itself on its "democracy." Given the climate of her day, Martineau's prescience is astounding, suggesting, as it does, the beginning of the Civil War, still a quarter of a century into the future. Her concern seems to have arisen quite naturally from her visit to the University of Virginia–and as early as February of 1835: "To observing eyes it appears plain that the hour is approaching when these young men must, like all other American men, choose their part, and enter decisively into struggle, to maintain or overthrow the first principles of freedom. . . . . The eyes of the world will be fixed on Jefferson's University during the impending conflict between slave-holders and freemen." Martineau reported that, in 1835, the total number of students was 206: 151 were from Virginia, 50 "from the South and West"–and five "from the Northern States."[122]

One wonders about those few students from the Northern states as well as the Northerners who, in the years ahead, probably would have followed them across the Potomac for their college education. When the Civil War finally did erupt in 1861, did those few Northern men join the Union forces? Or did they, perhaps, make common cause with their brother classmates and follow them into battle?

E. TRAVELERS FROM FRANCE

Decision time: who best understood the new American frontier?

Not the English–although they spoke the same language. Not Mrs. Trollope. Not Harriet Martineau. Not even Charles Dickens.

---

[121] Martineau, *Society* Vol. I, 224.
[122] Martineau, *Retrospect* Vol. II, 30-31, 31, 23.

1. **Democracy: focus on money-making**

Our visitors from England (Mrs. Trollope, Harriet Martineau, and Charles Dickens) could not possibly have seen the United States of America "head-on," as we would say today. For reasons, having to do with history, they were too close to it.

The question therefore remains: what did the two French men notice that had escaped the attention of all three English visitors?

Unfortunately, our three *English* visitors were looking for ways in which "America" had changed from its former status as profitable and reasonably well-mannered British *colonies* to an aggressively "democratic" English-speaking *nation*. That the English and the Americans spoke the same language was, perhaps, misleading, suggesting a history of shared outlook, history, and even belief. But this the two countries did not have. It would fall to our two Frenchmen, not yet fluent in the English language (and truly, therefore, Mr. Abell's "furriners") who would see America in a clearer light, and perhaps, as it actually was at that time.

Once they arrived in New York City from the gaiety of their trans-Atlantic crossing, Tocqueville and Beaumont found–to their astonishment–that conversations with Americans did not dwell on either politics or the subject of "democracy." Instead, conversations dwelt on a related freedom: "make money."

The two Frenchmen disembarked in New York City on May 12 of 1831. This was only a brief four days before **Gustave de Beaumont** sat down to re-assure his father that they had arrived safely: "The only thing that preoccupies everyone is *commerce*," Beaumont wrote his father. "It is the *national passion*. . . . Americans are, as I said, a *mercantile* people. . . . Their sovereign goal is to make money."[123] Later, on July 4th, Beaumont would write his older brother, Jules, that "Money is the universal divinity."[124]

Alexis de Tocqueville, as usual, agreed with Beaumont. A little over two weeks after their first arrival, Alexis de Tocqueville wrote his brother,

---

[123] Tocqueville, *Letters* 29 (emphases by Beaumont himself).
[124] Tocqueville, *Letters* 103.

Édouard, that: "Here we are truly in another world. *Political passions are only superficial.* The one passion that runs deep, the only one that stirs the human heart day in and day out, is the acquisition of wealth. . . . This is a world of merchants who give some thought to public affairs *only when their work affords them the leisure to do so.*"[125]

Our two Frenchmen were young lawyers (prosecutors), born and raised in the aristocracy. Alexis de Tocqueville was 25, and Gustave de Beaumont, 28. Once their ship docked in New York, these two young men were not only sending long, excited letters back to their families in France, but also scribbling notes on what surprised them most about an America where they would spend the next nine months.

Their letters back to France were, of course, in French, and–as noted before–the recent 2010 translations made into English by Frederick Brown have been a godsend to historians. Here, in these letters–and here alone– are the first raw insights that Tocqueville was later to use in *Democracy in America*. Brown's recent (2010) *Letters from America* is a small, slim volume of fewer than 300 pages, plus a good introduction and index (see fn 4 above). All of these letters have the excitement of personal discovery and far surpass Tocqueville's later use of classical prose in his two-volume *Democracy in America*.

Tocqueville and Beaumont were aristocrats by birth and by education. The larger, wealthier families of both men had gone to the guillotine in the French Revolution of 1789. Although both sets of parents had finally been spared, Tocqueville's mother, Louise, had been destined for the guillotine, her death sentence being reprieved only after ten months spent in a prison cell.

The two men first met while practicing law in their offices at Versailles. "The monotony of Versailles was killing me," Tocqueville later confessed in a letter to a cousin while traveling in America.[126] Both had wanted to visit America's new democracy, and again, it was probably both who concocted the idea of persuading the French government to release them briefly from

---
125 Tocqueville, *Letters* 44 (emphases added).
126 Tocqueville, *Letters* 201.

their legal labors in order to make a study of American prisons. (The families of both young men, however, paid all of their expenses.) Beaumont and Tocqueville had studied English "by the book," so neither was anywhere near fluency in the spoken language of the country they were visiting. This was, no doubt, a useful "problem," encouraging the girls they met at society balls in New York and Boston an opportunity to flirt with them and become amused by their (delightfully) broken, conversational English.

Many American students know that once Tocqueville had returned to France in 1832, he would start writing Volume I of his *Democracy in America*, publishing it in 1835. He would also write–but not publish–a shorter work, "A Fortnight in the Wilderness." In 1840, Volume II of Tocqueville's *Democracy in America* was published. After his death in 1859, yet a second Tocqueville work about America turned up: the unpublished "Excursion to Lake Oneida." Ever since the late 20th century, Tocqueville's work has become standard fare in courses on American history. That Tocqueville, as a writer, would rely on the letters he sent back to France in 1831 is testified to by at least four of the postscripts in his letters: "Remember to save my letters."[127]

What is less well known is that Gustave de Beaumont was also busy writing, and in his case, it was a short novel plus matter-of-fact Appendices, numbered A through L. These Appendices describe, in straightforward language, particular facets of American life as Beaumont had found them. His short novel, however, is openly titled *Marie or Slavery in the United States*. (See Section E-4-a below.)

By the time Beaumont and Tocqueville returned to France from their trip to America in 1832, both oral and written English had ceased to be a problem for them, and Beaumont is to be credited for sitting down to read Mrs. Trollope's *Domestic Manners of the Americans*, published as recently as 1832. If Beaumont's 1835 *Marie* is excruciatingly sentimental for today's reader, its attached appendices are superb and better reveal what the two men actually found in America. In those 1835 appendices to *Marie*,

---

[127] Tocqueville, *Letters* 28, 99, 122, and 220.

Beaumont does refer to Mrs. Trollope's book on America, both agreeing and disagreeing with what she had written in 1832.

The English system of inheritance–which those first colonial English settlers had, of course, brought with them from England–was based on "primogeniture": this critically important Latin word essentially means "Firstborn *Son* Inherits Everything: Title, Land, and Money."

In their letters back to France from America, there is a moment when both Tocqueville and Beaumont first understood that *the single key factor* encouraging the new emphasis on money-making was–in common now with post-Revolutionary France–the complete disappearance of "primogeniture." In this new America, a man now had no aristocratic title, and–ultimately–he could divide his assets equally (if he wished to) among all his children, perhaps even going so far as to decide that he wanted to leave them nothing.

For Tocqueville and Beaumont, this lack of primogeniture was the most significant realization of America's newly-chosen economy–comporting well with the ideals of the French Revolution and Napoleon's Civil Code of 1804. Only England still clung to her old laws of primogeniture, while France and America–through their recent revolutions–were now able to opt for equal distribution of parental assets.[128]

In late June 1831, Tocqueville wrote the following to his cousin, Louis de Kergorlay: "Do you know what, in this country's political realm, makes the most vivid impression on me? The effect of laws governing inheritance. . . . Primogeniture gave way to equal division, with almost magical results. . . . Family spirit disappeared. The aristocratic bias that marked the republic's early years was replaced by a democratic thrust of irresistible force. . . . *There can be no doubt that the inheritance law is responsible in some considerable*

---

[128] In England, money had always been inherited. Under primogeniture, the firstborn son inherited most of his father's estate: money, land, title. If the firstborn child of an English aristocrat was so unfortunate as to be a daughter, she needed to marry a family member of the aristocracy who would, by virtue of that marriage, inherit both the title and lands of his new father-in-law. Younger daughters, left out in the cold, tried to marry men of title, and if that was not possible, at least to marry men of "good" background. This is what the television series "Downton Abbey" is all about.

measure for this complete triumph of democratic principles."[129] Earlier in June, Tocqueville had also written the following to his sister-in-law, Émilie: "There are no chateaux here; fortunes aren't large enough, what with patrimonies being divided too many ways for any one heir to contemplate a vast and very durable establishment."[130]

Thus, our new American man was going "to make it" (or not) on his own two feet. Tocqueville admired this new "democracy," and, as he would write later to his cousin, Louis de Kergorlay: "You can hardly conceive of the universal satisfaction with which the existing government is regarded. The common man undoubtedly stands on the higher moral ladder than his counterpart in France: he abounds in a sense of his independent position and individual dignity . . . it definitely prompts him to respect himself and others."[131]

Tocqueville was also adapting to other American ways: he noted to two of his correspondents that he had shaken hands with President Andrew Jackson, observing that he had been required to address the American president not as something equivalent to "Your Majesty," but simply and forthrightly as "Mister" Jackson."[132]

Masses of people were now pouring into America from Britain and Europe (generally "in steerage" or "under the bow"). Their ambition was straightforward: make money–and in a society without a pre-defined class structure. On July 4th of 1831, Gustave de Beaumont wrote his brother, Jules: "Here everyone is actively involved in commerce and industry. . . . [A]nyone can set up as a trader and make a fortune." He went on to comment that "a man who has devoted his entire life to business seldom retires from it" and that "the man who has made a great fortune by working is disposed to have his children work as if their livelihoods depended on it."[133] (Which they did, and still do.)

---

[129] Tocqueville, *Letters* 93, 93, 93-94, 94 (emphasis added).
[130] Tocqueville, *Letters* 70.
[131] Tocqueville, *Letters* 97.
[132] Tocqueville, *Letters* 264, 266-67.
[133] Tocqueville, *Letters* 103, 103, 103-04, 104.

But: in this new "democracy" there was a major problem, and a serious one at that. Americans bent on money-making had little time for the *actual practice of democracy*: that is, in standing for election. Beaumont wrote his sister-in-law, Eugénie, on July 14th that he and Tocqueville had just met Enos Throop, at that time the elected governor of the state of New York. Beaumont wrote that Governor Throop was "a very decent man, but without superior qualities." Mentioning this later to Elam Lynds, creator of the state's penal system, Beaumont was told that "men of great talent would not accept such employment; they prefer commerce and occupations in which one earns more money."

Beaumont summed up for his sister-in-law: "There, in a nutshell, is the American character."[134]

2. Women: household as convent

One learns something about marriage in France by reading what both Beaumont and Tocqueville had to say about marriage in this new America. In brief: marriage in the New World of America seemed to be, actually, quite boring.

Marriage bonds in France were not much different from those in either England or America, but certainly they were more lax, allowing for infidelities. "Drat it!" wrote Tocqueville to his sister-in-law, Émilie."It is clear that one dare not flit about amorously here. . . . Straightforwardness is the rule" (when dealing with couples who were engaged to marry).[135]

Both men paint a stable but grim picture of married life. They had been in America only three weeks when Tocqueville wrote that "people have little or no time to sacrifice to women who are apparently *valued only as mothers and household managers*." By late June 1831, he was again writing that women "abide strictly by their moral conventions. Above all, the marriage bond is more sacrosanct here than anywhere else in the world."[136]

---

134 Tocqueville, *Letters* 117, 118, 118.
135 Tocqueville, *Letters* 72.
136 Tocqueville, *Letters* 68 (emphasis added), 84-85.

Beaumont saw it a little differently, but it is important to remember that when he wrote his sister-in-law, Félicie, he was talking about girls *before* they married: "[T]hey are gracious and banter with perfect ease. It isn't at all unusual to spend an entire evening conversing with the same person, uninterruptedly."[137]

For his part, Tocqueville had been in America scarcely a month before he wrote his sister-in-law, Émilie: "Here, when a woman marries, it's as if she were taking the veil, except that bearing children, and even many children, is not frowned upon in the *conjugal convent*. Her existence is nun-like: no more balls, almost no society, and a cold, estimable husband for exclusive company. . . . The other day I dared ask one of these recluses to tell me, briefly, what an American woman can devote herself to in her leisure time. She replied with perfect composure: 'To admiring her husband.'"[138]

Months later, and again to his sister-in-law, Tocqueville wrote that "this land is the El Dorado of husbands . . . provided one totally lacks romantic imagination and asks of one's wife only that she prepare tea [supper] and raise one's children."[139]

Tocqueville now went one step further in his analysis which, curiously, pre-dates Sigmund Freud: "But it remains to be understood how such perfect domesticity is accomplished, how these women cease to be coquettes from one day to the next." He goes on to suggest that "the coquetry still exists, though unable to display itself? The fact is, and this has been remarked by all travelers, that married women in America are almost all weak and languishing. For myself, I am tempted to believe that they are ill from repressed coquetry."[140]

But then Tocqueville added, "Why not? Isn't it commonplace to see men green around the gills with repressed ambition?"[141]

---

137 Tocqueville, *Letters* 229.
138 Tocqueville, *Letters* 71 (emphasis added).
139 Tocqueville, *Letters* 233.
140 Tocqueville, *Letters* 234, 234.
141 Tocqueville, *Letters* 234.

3. Religion: rigor and rigidity

"Respect for religion [in America] is carried to a fault," Tocqueville wrote his old friend, Eugène Stöffels, on June 28th. "For example, no one would allow himself to hunt, to dance, or even to play an instrument on Sunday; allowances are not made even for foreigners."[142]

Beaumont had noticed much the same thing: ". . . nowhere are religious ideas honored more than here. All forms of worship are free, but the man who belongs to no church would be considered *a brute*. . . ." He continued, "The Sabbath is observed with the utmost rigor. No one works and the shops are shut tighter than in Paris. The only permissible reading is the Bible."[143]

Tocqueville tried to explain religion in America to his old friend and cousin, Louis de Kergorlay. "Picture if you will concentric circles around a fixed point, which is the Catholic faith; with each successive circle, religion draws that much closer to pure deism."[144] Earlier in the same letter, Tocqueville had written: "Unless I'm sadly mistaken, these external forms [of religion] conceal a reservoir of doubt and indifference," adding that "Religion is observed much the way medicine was taken by our fathers in the month of May: it may not do any good, but neither can it do any harm. . . ."[145]

Tocqueville had little genuine respect for religion, whether Catholic or Protestant. "Protestants of every persuasion–Anglicans, Lutherans, Calvinists, Presbyterians, Anabaptists, Quakers, and a hundred others– form the core of the population," Tocqueville wrote in that same letter to his cousin. "They are practicing and indifferent; they live from day to day, grow accustomed to a peaceful 'middle ground,' in which the proprieties are satisfied, if not much else. These sectarians live and die in the wishy-washy, without worrying about the heart of things; they no longer proselytize. Above them are a handful of Catholics, exploiting the tolerance

---

[142] Tocqueville, *Letters* 85.

[143] Tocqueville, *Letters* 30, 31 (emphasis by Beaumont).

[144] Tocqueville, *Letters* 89. This is not a bad visualization for the religious reformations in both England and France.

[145] Tocqueville, *Letters* 88, 89.

of their former adversaries but themselves remaining as intolerant as ever, intolerant in the way that 'believers' are."[146]

In common with Charles Dickens (who did not visit America until 1842), Tocqueville and Beaumont decided to visit a Shaker community outside Albany in July of 1831. They arrived about ten o'clock on a Sunday morning and were able to witness a traditional service in "the temple," a plain room with no altar. "One of them [the Shakers] made a little speech explaining that the Shaker sect was the only path to salvation and admonishing us to convert." The speech had been preceded by two hours of religiously-oriented contortions and "frightful exercise," leading an American Protestant to comment, "Two more spectacles like that one and I'll become a Catholic."[147]

Today, in the 21st century, religion is still important enough that both houses of Congress begin each day with prayer. Although generally careful not to offend any particular belief or denomination, the Senate has chosen a Roman Catholic priest only once: 1832. Since 1774–and still in the Senate– all one-year terms have been Protestant, but in 1998 Rabbi Levi Shemtov led the opening prayer, followed by Imam Yusuf Saleem in 2001. (Both men, as well as select others, were carefully denoted *Guest Chaplain*.) As for the House of Representatives: since 1789, the House has limited its one-year Chaplaincies to Christian Protestants (but with the exception of two Roman Catholic chaplaincies in the years 2000 and 2011.)[148]

4. Africans and Indians: oppression and genocide

Once back in France, *both* Alexis de Tocqueville and Gustave de Beaumont set about checking their notes and the letters they had sent back to their families–and *both* now set about writing of their experiences in the America of President Andrew Jackson. Both men, of course, wrote in French and published their respective volumes in 1835. For Tocqueville, this would be Volume I of *Democracy in America* (1835), to be followed five years later in 1840 by Volume II.

---

[146] Tocqueville, *Letters* 90.
[147] Tocqueville, *Letters* 123-25.
[148] This chapter was written primarily in 2016.

a. Africans

For Beaumont, this stint of writing would be his novella-plus-foreword-plus-appendices: *Marie; or Slavery in the United States*, also in 1835. That the two men collaborated seems clear: in his "Foreword" to *Marie*, Beaumont wrote that "M. de Tocqueville and I are publishing each a book at the same time, on subjects as distinct from one another as the government of a people is distinct from its mores. Those who read these two works will perhaps receive different impressions of America, and may think that we did not form the same judgments on the country we traversed together... . The true reason is this: M. de Tocqueville has described the institutions; I myself have tried to sketch the customs."[149]

Beaumont's appendices (on "customs") are 12 in number, and cover such topics as women, slaves, equality, Anglophobia, etc. Probably due to the title's subject-matter of "slavery," Beaumont's work was not translated from French to English in America for well over one hundred years (not until 1958): this was four years after America's Supreme Court landmark decision dealing with public segregation in the United States.[150] For Beaumont himself, however, *Marie; or Slavery in the United States* won him the coveted Montyon Prize from the Académie Française way back in 1835. In contrast, Tocqueville's self-appointed work on "institutions" was translated into English in 1838 and, since then, has sometimes been required reading for college students.

Critics in both English and American literature would label Beaumont's novella on "customs" as "uneven." Its best chapters are Nos. 8 and 9, dealing with arguments and counter-arguments concerning racism in America.[151]

Yet Gustave Beaumont, true to his career as a prosecutor, was also a good researcher, and at some point during his travels around Washington and Maryland, he had met Charles Carroll of Carrollton Manor, a signer

---

[149] De Beaumont, Gustave Auguste Bonnin de la Bonninière. *Marie; or Slavery in the United States*. 1835. Baltimore: Johns Hopkins University Press, 1999. 7 (Foreword). Print. Hereafter cited as Beaumont, *Marie*.

[150] *Brown v. Board of Education of Topeka*, 347 U.S. 483 (1954).

[151] Overall, however, the novella is marred by (1) the translator's choice of outdated language, and (2) Beaumont's own sentimental characterization of his white-skinned heroine, Marie, one of whose great-grandmothers had been "colored."

of the Declaration of Independence, who was then in his 90s. Frederick Brown (who translated the letters sent back to France by Tocqueville and Beaumont) entered this introduction on p. 209: "This leg of the journey [through America] lasted from October 12, 1831, to January 3, 1832. Tocqueville and Beaumont spent several weeks in Philadelphia, with an excursion to Baltimore, before heading west again . . ." to Memphis and New Orleans.[152]

It may well have been during this period in Philadelphia and Baltimore that Beaumont incidentally learned of tobacco-production in southern Maryland. On October 26, 1831, Beaumont wrote this in a letter to his sister-in-law, Félicie: "I am trying to assemble as many documents as I can about a variety of subjects."[153] One of those researched items turned up as Appendix A (27 pages attached to *Marie*). In this Appendix on slave labor, Beaumont wrote, "There is only one branch of agriculture in Maryland for which one can still use slave labor without loss, and that is tobacco growing. This crop, which demands much minute care, requires an immense number of hands; women and children are sufficient to the task; the important point is to have a large number of them, and Negro families, generally numerous, fulfill this." But Beaumont then went on to quote Charles Carroll himself (on whose estate at the time there were 300 black slaves): "It is a false notion that the Negroes are necessary for the cultivation of certain crops–such as sugar, rice, and tobacco. I am convinced that the whites could accustom themselves to it easily, if they undertook to do so."[154]

Alone of our five visitors to America, Tocqueville and Beaumont, led by an Indian guide, tramped for several weeks through the untamed wilderness of what would later become Michigan and the Great Lakes region. Thus they did not truly encounter slavery until they left Philadelphia in late October of 1831: now they would tackle not only deep snows but what turned out to be Mrs. Trollope's voyage (only in reverse) *down* the Ohio River to the Mississippi. On November 30th of 1831, Tocqueville wrote his brother, Édouard, that "We are arriving at Cincinnati after a painfully cold, snowy

---

152 Tocqueville, *Letters* 209.
153 Tocqueville, *Letters* 228.
154 Beaumont, *Marie* Appendix A, 206.

voyage."[155] In early December, to his mother, Tocqueville complained that "we are in the same latitude as Sicily, yet it's several degrees below freezing, the earth is covered with snow, the rivers are clogged with ice."[156]

By mid-December 1831, the two men had reached Sandy Bridge, Kentucky, on the road from Nashville to Memphis, and here it was that they encountered slavery for the first time. Beaumont wrote his mother that: "My hosts are very good people, very proud, innkeepers though they are, and lazy, though poor. They are proud because they live among slaves. There isn't a landowner, however down-at-heel, who doesn't own two or three negroes. . . . Here, color is a true mark of nobility. The convenience of being served by slaves renders whites indolent. . . . My host, a small landowner who finds work ignominious, is convinced that [work] should be . . . the exclusive domain of slaves. He has feudal mores; he spends his time hunting, horseback riding, or doing nothing."[157]

By the end of December, the two men (bound for New Orleans, Washington, D.C., New York harbor, and finally a packet back to France) had reached Memphis ("a very small town on the banks of the Mississippi, at the far southwestern edge of the state of Tennessee.") "There, for the first time," wrote Tocqueville to his father (Hervé), "we had the opportunity to observe the social consequences of slavery. The right [north] bank of the Ohio is a scene of animation and industry; work is honored, no one owns slaves. But cross the river and you suddenly find yourself in another universe. Gone is the spirit of enterprise. Work is considered not only onerous but shameful: whoever engages in it degrades himself. The white man is meant to ride horseback, to hunt, to smoke all day long; using one's hands is what a slave does."[158]

---

[155] Tocqueville, *Letters* 231.
[156] Tocqueville, *Letters* 241.
[157] Tocqueville, *Letters* 245.
[158] Tocqueville, *Letters* 249.

b. Indians

Finally, we conclude this chapter with Indians–original inhabitants of the entire American continent.

Beaumont and Tocqueville, of course, had been expecting to see *African* slaves: that is, the forced labor of Africans traded from out of their own continent. Slavery at that time was endemic in France's Caribbean islands, including Guadeloupe, Martinique, St. Barts (Saint-Barthélemy), and half (each) of St. Martin, St. Kitts, and Hispaniola (Haiti). These lands contributed to France's overall economy of sugar and cotton–much as those distant Caribbean islands had added to the overall economy of England.

What the two men knew little of, however, was the American Indian. If they expected to see Indians as they descended the gangplank in New York City in 1831, they would have been disappointed. Tocqueville, in fact, noted in a letter to his cousin that he had not seen an American Indian until the two young lawyers had traveled far enough north that they were between Utica and Syracuse in the State of New York. What they saw was pitiable: on July 14th, Beaumont wrote his sister-in-law Eugénie that "What they [the Indians] get from civilization are its vices and rags."[159]

Indians were not allowed to sell their own land; the U.S. government bought it from the natives, then re-sold it to settlers through a nearby "land office." One such land-agent remarked to the two young men: "Thank God, we have land enough for expanding as far as the Pacific Ocean."[160]

It has long been thought that Native Americans–as they are recently being called–crossed a "land bridge" from Asia to America. Yet actual evidence for this, unfortunately, does not seem to exist in known tribal lore. Oddly enough, however, tantalizing suggestions–for such a land bridge and subsequent settlement on the American continent–do appear in letters written by Tocqueville. Example: women in China have had a long history of binding the feet of female infants, and on October 10th of 1831, Tocqueville wrote a cousin, the comtesse de Grancey: "Would you believe

---

[159] Tocqueville, *Letters* 117.
[160] Tocqueville, *Letters* 163.

it, Indian women undergo the same torture to produce the opposite effect? To have their feet point inward?" Here, Tocqueville was repeating what he and Beaumont had noticed a month earlier, and now he went on to describe this practice to Émilie, his sister-in-law: "The custom among women of the forests is to have their feet pointing inward. I don't know if inward is more unnatural than outward, but our European eyes can't easily adjust to this form of beauty. It is achieved by binding the feet of female infants. By age twenty, a woman walks pigeon-toed, and the more pigeon-toed her walk the more *fashionable* she is thought to be."[161]

"We wanted to see the *wilderness* and *Indians*," Tocqueville complained to a cousin. "But you wouldn't believe how hard it is now to find these two things in America. We walked for more than a hundred leagues [300 miles] in the state of New York following the trek of . . . savages without encountering any. We were told that the Indians had still been there ten years ago, eight years ago, two years ago, but European civilization is advancing like a forest fire and driving them before it. At last we arrived at Buffalo, on the shore of the Great Lakes, without having seen a single one."[162]

Tocqueville and Beaumont scuttled their plans to travel eastward to Niagara Falls once they learned of a two-week cruise through the still-untouched wilderness of the Great Lakes to their north and west. The very word *wilderness* could not be translated into French: "We don't have a term [in French] to convey the idea expressed so well by the English word 'wilderness'" Beaumont wrote to Eugénie.[163]

On May 28, 1830, President Andrew Jackson signed a bill, the Indian Removal Act, which empowered him to "negotiate" with Native American tribes for their removal to federal territory west of the Mississippi River in exchange for their ancestral lands. Perhaps the most widely-known forced relocations are what have become known as the "Trail of Tears" of the Cherokee nation and the "Trail of Tears and Death" of the Choctaw nation (see fn 99 above).

---

161 Tocqueville, *Letters* 204, 179 (emphasis by Tocqueville).
162 Tocqueville, *Letters* 202 (emphases by Tocqueville).
163 Tocqueville, *Letters* 116.

The Indian Removal Act forced American-born Indians to leave their tribal lands in the southeast of the new United States, cross the Mississippi by boat, and disperse, under military guard, into Arkansas. It is important to remember that the events described below took place in December of 1830, the dead of winter, at a time when the Ohio, Tennessee, and Missouri Rivers were all frozen solid. The Mississippi, however, was only partially frozen and therefore capable of transporting the Indians across the river and into Arkansas.

We close this chapter with Tocqueville's own eye-witness account as he watched events unfold from his position at Memphis, Tennessee, in December of 1831, Christmas Day. He is writing to his mother about the forced removal of the Choctaws:

> You will learn that the Americans of the United States, a rational people without prejudices, known for their philanthropy, conceived the idea, like the Spanish before them, that God had bestowed upon them, as an unrestricted gift, the New World and its inhabitants. . . . When the Indians found themselves a little too near their white brethren, the president of the United States sent them a message explaining that, in their own interest naturally, they would do well to retreat slightly westward. . . .
>
> The poor Indians carry their old parents in their arms; mothers hoist their children onto their shoulders; the whole nation begins to march; taking their most cherished possessions with them. They abandon forever the soil on which their forefathers lived for a millennium perhaps and settle in a wilderness where the whites will be harassing them ten years from now. . . .
>
> The Chactas [Choctaws] form a powerful nation occupying the border country of Alabama and Georgia. This year, after protracted negotiations, they were persuaded to leave their homeland and emigrate to the west bank of the Mississippi. Six or seven thousand Indians have already crossed the great river; those appearing in Memphis came there with the intention of following their compatriots.

The Indians advanced mournfully toward the riverbank; first came the horses... Then came the men, who, in the customary fashion, bore nothing but their weapons. The women followed, carrying children tied to their backs or swaddled in blankets.... Last of all came the old folk. Among the latter was a woman 110 years old. I have never seen such a horrifying figure. She was naked, except for a threadbare blanket revealing, here and there, the scrawniest body imaginable.... When everyone had passed, the dogs approached the bank but refused to go further and protested with hair-raising yelps. Their masters dragged them aboard.

This whole spectacle had an air of ruin and destruction; it spoke of final farewells and no turning back....[164]

And then they were gone.

---

[164] Tocqueville, *Letters* passim, 251-56.

Chapter 8

St. Mary's County: Catalyst for John LaFarge's Mission Against Racism –and the Disappeared Encyclical

("The Child is father of the Man"
William Wordsworth, "My Heart Leaps Up," 1802)

A. PRÉCIS

John LaFarge (junior) was born in Newport, Rhode Island in 1880, the eighth and last child of John LaFarge, Sr. (a famous muralist) and Margaret **Perry** LaFarge (descended directly from Commodore Perry and Benjamin Franklin).

Since his birth, John LaFarge would prove sickly, but–curiously–not so during his 15 years as a Jesuit missionary in St. Mary's County, Maryland (1911-1926). Perhaps it was the enthusiasm with which he attacked County problems, or perhaps it was simply his relative youthfulness (age 30 when he first arrived in the county seat of Leonardtown). In 1926, when he was 45, he finally had to leave Maryland and the Catholic mission-schools which he had founded–schools for both whites *and blacks*.

From 1926 on, he would take up the position as "associate editor" at Campion House in New York City, headquarters of the weekly Jesuit magazine, *America*. He would live and die in Campion House, at 329 West 108th Street.[1]

John LaFarge lived until the age of 83 and died on November 25th, 1963, shortly after watching the televised funeral cortège of President John F. Kennedy.

With the above as an introduction to John LaFarge, it will now help the reader to understand that there were four distinct periods in his life. (There is some overlap with Chapter 4-B.)

First: his boyhood in Newport. (See Section 8-B below.)

Second: his education. This spans 15 years: whether at Harvard (graduating with the class of 1901); at theological seminary in Austria (1901-1905); and back in America, his final training to become a Jesuit, both at St. Andrew-on-Hudson (Hyde Park, New York; 1905-1909) and at Woodstock College (outside Baltimore; 1909-1911). (See Section 8-C below.)

Third: the 15 years he spent as a missionary in St. Mary's County, Maryland (September 1911 to August 1926). (See Section 8-D below.)

Fourth: his subsequent life in New York City, when he lived and functioned as editor of the news-magazine, *America*.

We confine ourselves to the first three periods in John LaFarge's life (and a quick foray into the Encyclical during World War II). We do not cover his "New York years": when the words "Father LaFarge" became a byword for his unceasing work on racism; and when his "pulpit" became the Jesuit publication, *America*.

---

1 About two weeks before John LaFarge's death in 1963, the Jesuits moved their editorial offices from the Campion House at 329 West 108th Street to "a nine-story building at No. 106 West 56th Street" (before 1926, it had been located at 39 West 86th Street). However, the Campion House still retained its living quarters on the Upper West Side (by Riverside Drive). In 1984, about 20 years after John LaFarge's death, the Campion House was converted into apartments. Miller, Tom. "Campion House–327 and 329 West 108th Street." *Daytonian in Manhattan* (June 12, 2018). Web. 17 Dec. 2021. <https://daytoninmanhattan.blogspot.com/2018/06/campion-house-327-and-329-west-108th.html>.

America is still published today, a twice-monthly magazine produced and edited by Jesuit clergy and currently published by American Media, located at 1212 Sixth Ave in New York City.

That fourth period lies outside our present focus, which is on John LaFarge as he lived and worked in St. Mary's County.[2] The "New York years" lasted from 1926 (age 46) until his death in 1963 (at age 83). In various positions as editor of the weekly magazine, *America*, John LaFarge fulfilled his years as Associate Editor (1926-1941), Executive Editor (1942-1944), and then Editor-in-Chief (1944-1948). In 1948, however, after extensive surgery, he stepped back into his original position as Associate Editor. By this time, he was 68.

It was also during his later time in New York–in his weekly writings for *America*–that he was able to marshal arguments against the racism that had so struck him during his missionary years in lower St. Mary's County, Maryland. In 1934 (during the New York period as Associate Editor of *America*), he founded the anti-racist Catholic Interracial Council of New York (CICNY), and also found time to write his many books, at least ten.[3]

It should also be said that, spiritually, John LaFarge never quite left St. Mary's County–in spite of his departure in 1926. It is likely that he had a hand in choosing his Jesuit successor at Ridge, Horace McKenna (in St. Mary's County from 1931 to 1953).

Over their long, no-holds-barred correspondence, what did these two men *talk* about? Fathers LaFarge and McKenna exchanged a multi-year correspondence which is now part of what has recently been found in the former convent at St. Peter Claver Parish, in Ridge, Maryland. (But even letters can betray the cautious writer, and as a consequence, we will never be privy to what those two priests actually *talked* about.)

---

[2] John LaFarge's work within the County extended from 1911 to 1926, and the date of his creation of the Cardinal Gibbons Institute (a ground-breaking high school for black students) was 1924. About two years later, he was forced to leave St. Mary's County (on Jesuit orders) for New York City.

[3] He began with *The Jesuits in Modern Times* (1928). His book on *Interracial Justice* (1937) was sent to Pope Pius XI (with consequences unimagined–and unimaginable; see Section 8-E below). More books followed: *The Race Question and the Negro* (1944); *No postponement; U. S. moral leadership and the problem of racial minorities* (1950); *The Manner Is Ordinary* (1954); *The Catholic Viewpoint on Race Relations* (1956); *A Report on the American Jesuits* (with photographs by Margaret Bourke-White in 1956); *An American Amen; a statement of hope* (1958); *On Turning Seventy* (1962); and *Reflections on Growing Old* (1963). And, back in 1956, Fathers Thurston Davis and Joseph Small published *A John LaFarge Reader*, a helpful book in which those two men chose specific topics to re-print from LaFarge's extensive writings.

Although Father LaFarge's former parishioners in the County probably never knew it, at least once a year–from New York City (where, since 1926, he had lived and worked)–he would contact Father Horace McKenna and notify him that he wanted to spend his quiet yearly "retreat" down in Ridge, where the Chesapeake Bay empties into the Atlantic.

This trip was by no means easy: it always involved an hours-long train-ride from New York City down to Washington, followed by a two-hour bus-ride to Patuxent River. In addition to these annual "retreats," John LaFarge also discovered that he could work on his books–one by one–in the peace and quiet that was St. Mary's County. But aside from those two exceptions (religious retreats and book-writings), the McKenna-LaFarge correspondence never faltered, and today it makes for reading that is both interesting and informative.

The two men were of one mind in their understanding of the cultural mores of Southern Maryland. There is a letter (presumably kept in the archives at St. Peter Claver Church, Ridge) dated April 30, 1951, where the author (probably Father McKenna) asks Father LaFarge to help him with a crisis: "the lid blew off the interracial situation at St. Michael's." It is worth noting that after Father Horace McKenna was quietly transferred to Washington in 1953 following his stand against a racial episode at St. Michael's Church, Ridge (surely related to the "lid-blew-off" crisis), John LaFarge seldom travelled down to St. Mary's County.

By 1954, LaFarge was in his mid-70s, and younger men were now taking up the struggle for race relations. In May of 1954, the U.S. Supreme Court handed down its landmark decision of *Brown v. Board of Education*, and it would be a matter of only nine years before the March on Washington would take place on August 28, 1963.

By the time of the March on Washington, John LaFarge was 83 and quite frail. Seated immediately behind the speakers (most memorable of whom was Martin Luther King, Jr., who delivered his "I Have a Dream" speech), a select group of people had been provided with reserved "honoree" seating on this raised platform, *behind* the speaker, and therefore they were able to look out over the vast crowds below.

As such an honoree, John LaFarge was thus able to survey the 200,000 people gathered along the edges of the Reflecting Pool. According to his careful biographer and critic, David Southern, "The story goes that A. Philip Randolph [the prominent Negro who had organized the March on Washington] had several young black men lift the aged Jesuit above the crush of the crowd and put him in position to observe the speakers' platform."[4]

John LaFarge died three months after the March on Washington. Known affectionately as "Uncle John" at Campion House (on the Upper West Side), with fellow Jesuits he had been watching–on a small television set up in their living-room–the funeral cortège of President Kennedy as it crossed over Memorial Bridge to Arlington National Cemetery. That date was November 25, 1963. John LaFarge left the group watching television for an afternoon nap, and he died alone in his bedroom. His body was not discovered until an hour or so later.

What did he leave behind?

B. GROWING UP

This first period (1880-1897) encompasses his boyhood in Newport and two mid-high-school years in New York City.

Even when he was young, John LaFarge had often been ill, not altogether surprising since, as last-to-be-born, he was "the runt of the litter," a litter composed of seven far-older brothers and sisters. Beginning in his teens and lasting through his 60s, he was often ill, requiring hospital-stays. Interestingly, he was *never* ill during the 15-year period while working as a missionary in St. Mary's County.

---

4 Southern, David. *John LaFarge and the Limits of Catholic Interracialism, 1911–1963*. Baton Rouge: Louisiana State University Press, 1996. 352. Print.

Father LaFarge described the historic March for Jobs and Freedom "as tranquil and inevitable as God's providence itself, with the majesty and power of an apocalyptic vision. . . . The Aug. 28 March was but a beginning, a summons to unceasing effort. The hour is bound to come–and the less delay the better–when North and South alike will set a final seal upon its simple goal of jobs and freedom for all citizens-yes for *all*." Editorial By Matt Malone, S.J.(citing Father LaFarge). "Of Many Things." *America*, Vol. 209, No. 6 (Whole No. 5021) (Sept. 9-16, 2013). 2 (emphasis in original). Print.

Yet he was gifted, and these "gifts" almost always triumphed over any physical problems. Moreover, it is difficult–in fact, impossible–to rank these three "gifts" in any order of importance. Therefore, as previously discussed in Chapter 4-B, the following aptitudes are "scrambled" in the sections below: (1) languages; (2) reading/writing; and (3) music. Taken as a whole, those three "gifts" go far in making up the man remembered as John LaFarge.

1. Languages

Young John's mother, although a convert to Catholicism, decided *not* to send her son to Newport's parish school (Catholic). Instead he was sent to Newport's public school, Coddington, where teaching was strict, "of the good old New England variety," as LaFarge later wrote.[5]

In the second year of his Newport high school, however, John spent an entire year in bed (thus delaying his graduation from Rogers High until the late spring of 1897). His mother took him to New York City for surgery on his appendix, and he spent what amounted to the following two years generally enjoying New York City and its offerings (1895-1897).

As set forth in Chapter 4-B-3, during his boyhood, John had learned English, French, smatterings of Latin, Danish, and Icelandic (Nordic languages), and Gaelic (a Celtic language.)

2. Music

Unlike his very famous father, young John was not artistic. He was, however, musical. As a boy, he approached his non-musical father one day and asked him what music he liked best. Something of a wit, the senior LaFarge replied, "The music that makes the least sound."[6]

Young John's enjoyment of music came instead from his mother: "When she observed how much I enjoyed listening, she said I might take piano lessons . . . I was so eager to begin that I struggled to attend my first lesson through drifts of snow on the day of the worst blizzard that, to my

---

[5] LaFarge, John. *The Manner Is Ordinary*. New York: Harcourt, Brace and Company, 1954. 37. Print. Hereafter cited as LaFarge, *Manner*.

[6] LaFarge, *Manner* 7.

knowledge, Newport had ever known. When we spent two winters in New York, 1895 to 1897, I took piano lessons from an excellent teacher . . . who at once set me studying for perfection on a relatively easy piece–Chopin's *Nocturne* in E-Flat Major. . . ." [7]

3. Reading and Writing

Before young John had gone to New York in 1895 for treatment of his appendicitis, he was already well on his way in both reading and writing. (In common with most languages, English literature has certain rhythms, and these can be instilled at a surprisingly early age. Nursery rhymes, for example.)

When John LaFarge was finally persuaded to write his autobiography at age 74, he wrote, "At home, we observed the happy practice, so little in vogue now, of reading aloud . . . . my mother would read aloud most of Dickens, Trollope, and Jane Austen. Mother's memory was so clear and her imagination so vivid that the characters in these books became part of our daily life . . . . The signal to end the reading came, a signal not always obeyed, when the curfew rang from the Pelham Street Church at nine o'clock."[8]

Being read-*to*, led, quite naturally, to writing. At around the age of ten, young John LaFarge–with two friends–created and wrote a monthly magazine which they titled "The Sunlight." Surprisingly, it lasted for "ten or twelve issues," and featured what purported to be life on the planet Mars.[9] See Chapter 4-B-1.

C. EDUCATION

1. Harvard (1897-1901)

a. Music

John LaFarge graduated from Harvard College with the Class of 1901– along with the poet Robert Frost. For young John LaFarge, Harvard was an unwelcome drop into Protestantism, and the reader senses that he was

---

[7] LaFarge, *Manner* 47.

[8] LaFarge, *Manner* 40-41.

[9] LaFarge, *Manner* 44.

often on tenterhooks–that is, on the lookout for religious and social snubs which, however, never materialized. (He was afraid of being Catholic in what he took to be a Protestant college.)

By this time in his life, John LaFarge already knew (and had known since about the age of sixteen) that he wanted to become a priest. He might have gone to Georgetown if he had not been told (by a prankster) that the food there was bad: "This touched a very sensitive point, for at the time I was laboring with a sort of recurrent nausea and immediately Georgetown became associated in my mind with certain physical sensations."[10]

Although none of his brothers had gone to Harvard, this was the undergraduate college that John's older brother, Grant LaFarge (and Grant's good friend, Theodore Roosevelt) had urged young John to attend.

In his autobiography, LaFarge later wrote, "For the four years of my college life I still found it impossible to shake off a constant feeling of physical weakness." He tried rowing (on the Charles River), skating (on Spy Pond), and bike rides, "but always the same helpless feeling returned, and I found myself again on the flat of my back."[11]

What to do? LaFarge turned to music, going so far as to *rent a piano* for his college room. This piano was an upright Ivers & Pond.[12] (Where is this piano today? See Section 8-C-1-c below.)

In his chapter on Harvard, LaFarge continues with the subject of music: "The happy discovery that music was an elective led me to enroll in the courses of harmony and counterpoint. . . . More fruitful were my private lessons in piano and organ with Walter Spalding, and it was grand fun practicing the organ in Appleton Chapel."[13]

> I had picked up enough to read off a score of a quartet or symphony and hear it in the mind just as if the instruments were playing. This to me was a great satisfaction and joy.[14]

---

10 LaFarge, *Manner* 49.
11 LaFarge, *Manner* 70.
12 LaFarge, *Manner* 83-84.
13 LaFarge, *Manner* 63-64.
14 LaFarge, *Manner* 47.

b. Languages

Grant LaFarge (young John's far older brother) was a close friend and traveling companion of Theodore Roosevelt, who did not become president until September of 1901, shortly after young John LaFarge–Harvard degree in hand–had already left the United States for Austria.

Theodore Roosevelt, a Harvard grad, "urged me very strongly to carry right through the entire four years with Greek and Latin," and that is what young John LaFarge did. In addition, he decided to study the Semitic languages of the Bible and therefore took elective courses in Hebrew, Syriac, and Aramaic.[15]

Language count for John LaFarge's years at Harvard: English, French, Latin, classical Greek, plus a reading knowledge of three Semitic languages.

c. Reading and Writing

At Harvard, John LaFarge began to come into his own–although he found it difficult to admit this in what was, for him, the bastion of Protestantism. "The English department" he wrote in his autobiography "was one place in the university where you could find good teaching, as contrasted with mere academic lecturing in the German style [this was in the very late 1800s]. Luckily for my needs, freshman English was obligatory, and [Charles] "Copey" Copeland submitted me to his rigors. . . . I don't know of any American English teacher in our time who inspired and helped young writers more; I know he encouraged me to try some writing, and as a result I was elected to the editorial board of the Harvard monthly."[16]

Young LaFarge also became a member of Harvard's Hasty Pudding Club. Yet the most moving moment of his time at Harvard did not come until two decades later.

In 1921, "Members of the [graduating class of 1901] astonished and moved me more than I could say by collecting a substantial sum to aid in building my church of St. Nicholas in St. Mary's County near Patuxent,

---
15 LaFarge, *Manner* 59, 61.
16 LaFarge, *Manner* 61-62.

Maryland."[17] Following this astonishing gift, he dedicated his last book (*Reflections on Growing Old*, 1962), to this group of Harvard alumni one year before his own death at 83: "To Jim Lawrence, Joe O'Gorman, Bill Reid, and other honored survivors of H.C. [Harvard College] '01, the first class of the century."[18]

Getting back to LaFarge's upright Ivers & Pond piano that he played throughout his years at Harvard, decades later, it was tracked down and sent to him to be used at this very same mission chapel of St. Nicholas in St. Mary's County, Maryland.

2. Austria (1901-1905)

a. Reading and Writing

Question: why did John LaFarge *choose* to go to Austria? Answer: during his four years at Harvard, he had decided to make a weekly confession-plus-visit, always to Father Thomas Gasson, his Jesuit confessor (based in Boston):

> Father Gasson had suggested that I should pursue my studies at the University of Innsbruck in Austria . . . . This greatly appealed to me . . . . the idea of studying abroad, particularly of studying in a university of the German type, and in the Alps, had its special attraction. The decision meant no small sacrifice on Father's part, and once more the same persons came to my assistance as had presided at my entrance into college–my brother Bancel and Theodore Roosevelt.[19]

In his autobiography, John LaFarge writes that when he bade his mother goodbye in July of 1901, she begged him, "Don't let them make you a Jesuit!" To which LaFarge replied, "Mother, dear, nothing can ever make me a Jesuit."[20]

---

17 LaFarge, *Manner* 75.

18 LaFarge, John. *Reflections on Growing Old*. Garden City, New York: Doubleday & Company, Inc. 1963. Dedication. Print.

19 LaFarge, *Manner* 76.

20 LaFarge, *Manner* 76-77.

Margaret LaFarge's fears, however, *did* have a basis in her beloved English literature. Before her marriage to John LaFarge (senior) in 1860, she had been thoroughly schooled in English literature: witness her enjoyment in reading aloud to her own young children from Dickens, Trollope, and Jane Austen. Those particular English writers had avoided the temptation of indulging in virulent anti-Catholicism–but in her educational background (as young "Margy" Perry), and as a Protestant she would have been exposed to at least a *reading* knowledge of such supposedly corrupt figures as monks, nuns, and abbesses (at one time the titillating staple of literature in English novels of the very early 1800s.)[21]

Harvard degree in hand, young John LaFarge left the United States for the Austrian Alps in July of 1901. He had not been sure whether he would conduct his seminary studies at Innsbruck (which would have meant learning German), or going farther south to Rome (where he would have had to learn Italian). While waiting to decide, he chose to live at an ordinary boarding house in Innsbruck during the first semester of his first year, and during this period he would probably have been listening to and picking up enough German to just "get by."

In January of 1902, he ultimately made the decision to study theology at Innsbruck's four-year seminary program, rather than in Rome. Now he entered into the Canisianum (an unheated dormitory for theological students), thus becoming a full-fledged seminarian. In winter, the Alps are, of course, cold, and no heat for the buildings was provided.

> In the chapel the holy water froze solid in the bronze fonts, and an acolyte serving Mass had to beware lest he freeze his fingers on the heavy eighteenth-century silver cruet trays.
>
> . . .
>
> [The lecture rooms were also unheated, and] "In class I swathed myself in cloak and galoshes as for an old-fashioned sleigh ride.[22]

---

21 For the curious, see the Wikipedia article, "Anti-Catholicism in literature and the media." <https://en.wikipedia.org/wiki/Anti-Catholicism_in_literature_and_media>.

22 LaFarge, *Manner* 92.

As a seminarian, his classes were all in Latin, except for church history (in German), and any papers he might have written would have had to be in one of those two languages.

> German was the universally prescribed language, for most of the foreign bishops had their students there to learn German, and each seminarian once during his four years had to preach a German sermon in the dining hall to the tune of rattling plates and clattering knives and forks.[23]

But finally–finally–John LaFarge was happy. "Once within the seminary walls, I found myself, in every sense of the word."[24]

b. Music

One thing needs to be said about John LaFarge's first arrival at Innsbruck. He had been homesick during that first semester while he lived at the boarding house in town. "My homesickness led me to desperate measures: I rented a grand piano, a Blüthner, for less than I had paid at Harvard for an upright Ivers and Pond."[25]

It was during the second semester of his first year that he became a full-fledged seminarian and at last moved into a dormitory. His account is silent as to whether he was accompanied by the Blüthner.

c. Languages

Today, would any student choose to do his graduate work in a foreign language he couldn't begin to understand?

Yet this was exactly what young John LaFarge did when he decided to go to theological seminary at Innsbruck, Austria (rather than to an English-language seminary in the United States). Between his graduation from Harvard in June of 1901 and his arrival at the Jesuit seminary in the Austrian Alps one month later, he would have to learn just enough German to "keep up." (Later, while still at the seminary, he would become proficient in

---

23 LaFarge, *Manner* 93.
24 LaFarge, *Manner* 91.
25 LaFarge, *Manner* 84.

German.) His course of theological study covered four years, and he didn't leave Innsbruck, theological degree in hand, until 1905.

In his autobiography, LaFarge wrote that, while still at the seminary in Innsbruck,

> On regular class days the names of one's walking companions were posted . . . on the sign-board by the door, always of different nationality: a Swiss, for instance, with a couple of Americans, and a North German and a Bavarian with a Pole.[26]

This was undoubtedly not only a way for requiring students to learn German, but also a way for them to avoid any tendency toward cliquishness.

Aside from German, however, John LaFarge was also picking up a *non-Germanic language*, a language he would cultivate years later while working as a missionary in lower St. Mary's County, Maryland. That language was Polish, a *Slavic* language remotely related to the East Slavic languages of Russian and Ukrainian. In spite of the seminary's rule to practice German, John LaFarge occasionally practiced this new Slavic language on his walks with the Polish seminarians.[27]

Nor had LaFarge forgotten his boyhood interest in Gaelic, and when his mother and sister journeyed to Innsbruck during LaFarge's summer vacation in 1903, they made their way to Brittany, at that time the home of several LaFarge relatives. LaFarge writes that at the town of Huelgoat, "I struck up the acquaintance of a curé and picked up a few phrases of the Breton language" (a form of Gaelic).[28]

Language count for John LaFarge's four years at the seminary in Austria: English, French, German, Latin, Greek, Polish (somewhat), Gaelic (somewhat), plus a reading knowledge of three Semitic languages.

---

26 LaFarge, *Manner* 93.
27 LaFarge, *Manner* 103.
28 LaFarge, *Manner* 109.

3. Becoming a Jesuit Priest (1905-1911): "Poverty, Chastity, and Obedience"

Following his graduation from seminary in 1905, John LaFarge was ordained to the priesthood on July 26th, "along with others of my [seminary] classmates." By now, he was 25. A few members of his family traveled to Austria for his ordination. "At my first Mass my mother, my sister Margaret . . . and several others were present. I consecrated the Body and Blood of the Good Lord and held Him in my trembling hands for the first time . . . in the tower of the University church."[29]

A scant seven months earlier (January, 1905) he had already decided to become a Jesuit priest rather than a Diocesan:

> It was not that I lacked appreciation for the sanctity of the diocesan priesthood . . . I simply saw with extraordinary distinctness that my personal concept of a priest's life was of one bound by poverty and obedience, in addition to the priestly chastity. . . . The idea of being a priest and not sharing the poverty of the great High Priest seemed to me intolerable. I could not reconcile myself to the idea of owning property, having anything of my own when He Himself was without a place to lay his head.[30]

And, in this way, Father John LaFarge decided to become a Jesuit.

By mail, John LaFarge secured permission from his American bishop to enter the four-year Jesuit training program at St. Andrew-on-Hudson, in Hyde Park, just outside Poughkeepsie, New York. There he would study for two years, followed by two more years in supervised fieldwork (what today we might call "internships"). By the time he had finished his education for the Jesuit priesthood in 1909, he was almost 30.

Probably neither "poverty" nor "chastity" would have been extraordinarily difficult for John LaFarge. "Obedience," however, was going to prove somewhat more difficult. Ignatius Loyola, the founder of the Jesuits, and himself a former military man, had insisted that "obedience" be one of the

---

[29] LaFarge, *Manner* 125.
[30] LaFarge, *Manner* 119.

three vows made by an ordained priest. LaFarge maintained this notion of "obedience" up until the very end–when he disclosed his silence just before he died. See Section 8-E below. (Obedience, however, is predicated on the notion that the person demanding obedience is–himself–usually in the right.)

John LaFarge's first instance of "obedience" would have been humiliating. Insulting, in fact. This, as he writes in his autobiography, is how *his ouster from the Ph.D. program* from Woodstock actually took place.[31] Those two years at Woodstock," LaFarge wrote of the M.A. program, "were for me the time of the greatest natural satisfaction that I have ever experienced. Once I grasped a bit of the essence of Thomism [the writings of Thomas Aquinas] it was intensely interesting to me to review some of the modern philosophical theories that I had glimpsed during my Harvard and Innsbruck years. . . ."[32]

But his days of "the greatest natural satisfaction that I have ever experienced" (at Woodstock) were doomed to end–and his doctoral studies (the Ph.D.) along with them. The following is LaFarge's own account of his rejection and dismissal from Woodstock's doctoral program in early 1911:

> At Woodstock after my return [from his father's funeral] I tried to get what refreshment I could by long walks, rest, and so on, but with no success. Finally the Rector [Anthony J. Maas] called me to his office and in his own homely way he put the matter up to me: "You have the choice, Father LaFarge, of being a live jack-ass or a dead lion. Personally," he said, "I think it is better to be a live jack-ass." . . .
>
> This meant, in less metaphorical language, that *the time had come to give up the idea of pursuing a strictly intellectual speculative career*. The Rector judged, as did Father Provincial, that I would recover my strength better if I were in some active work which would not be too much of a strain. So I said goodbye to my classmates at Woodstock. For the time being

---

[31] At Woodstock, outside Baltimore, he had already received his M.A. degree and, at age 31, was beginning to work on the Ph.D., a prerequisite for anyone wishing to teach beyond the two-year level at any college.

[32] LaFarge, *Manner* 142.

> I was assigned to St. Thomas' Manor, St. Ignatius Church, in Charles County, Maryland.[33]

Ultimately, John LaFarge had failed–and at something crucially important to him. Packing his bags, he left Woodstock–and academic life–behind.

Now what?

No longer was he a student at Woodstock. Nor, for that matter, was he even in academic life.

For the following three weeks, he worked briefly at St. Ignatius Church in Charles County, Maryland, and then was assigned to become an assistant at Old St. Joseph's Church in Philadelphia.

These appear to have been stop-gap measures until he was called (for eight months) to serve as assistant on Blackwell's Island in New York harbor, later called "Welfare Island" (since 1973, Roosevelt Island). This island was "home" to the mentally ill and indigent poor.

Surprisingly, Blackwell's Island proved to be Father LaFarge's salvation.

This was the first time in John LaFarge's entire career that he found himself in a setting that was *non-academic*. He loved it. "In this capacity," he later wrote, "I experienced eight of the most tremendous months of my life, for they opened up to me a vast vision of the tragic as well as the human side of life. I had had a glimpse of this in Poughkeepsie State Hospital, but Blackwell's Island was the real thing."[34]

> One had the distinct feeling of living in a great and rather jovial family. The nurses were a wonderful group .... Even the women prisoners with their bedraggled careers revealed to me much of the hopefully human beneath a forlorn exterior.[35]

Which leaves us to wonder: Had Father Maas been right? Had Maas sensed in John LaFarge a humanizing quality that needed further developing?

---

33 LaFarge, *Manner* 147 (emphasis added). See fn 88 below.
34 LaFarge, *Manner* 148.
35 LaFarge, *Manner* 151.

By the time he wrote his autobiography at age 74, John LaFarge apparently thought so, too. "Innsbruck and Woodstock," he commented in the autobiography he wrote in his 70s, "were schools of knowledge, but Blackwell's Island was a school of life and death."[36]

D. KNOWLEDGE AND WORK (1911-1926)

1. Assistant Pastor in Leonardtown

Continuing with his training in non-academic knowledge, in September of 1911, John LaFarge, now age 31, was assigned to serve (as one of *six* assistant pastors) at St. Aloysius in Leonardtown (the administrative seat of St. Mary's County, Maryland).

He was there for four years (1911-1915), years that provided him with the routines of ordinary parish life. Still relatively young, he functioned as one of five priests at St. Aloysius, aided by "Miss Madge," and under the supervision of Father Lawrence Kelly. Here, Father LaFarge would remain for four years, from 1911 to 1915.

He began to learn the nitty-gritty of parish life and considered himself fortunate to be working–both with and for–Father Kelly, who was "young, energetic, broad and apostolic in his outlook, patient and human, with a good sense of humor . . . a model pastor."[37] For the next four years, Father LaFarge baptized infants, established catechetical centers (separately, for white and "colored"), trained the catechists, visited the sick and dying, performed marriages, and said Mass.

Much later, while in his early 70s and working on his autobiography, LaFarge realized that he had been following the advice that Father Heuser had given him in his boyhood: "that my heart and not my head must find its due place." "It meant that I renounced some congenial intellectual pursuits, but the book of life compensated."[38]

---

36 LaFarge, *Manner* 152.
37 LaFarge, *Manner* 158.
38 LaFarge, *Manner* 56, 159.

On the one hand, he reverted to type (as an intellectual) and requested–from the Library of Congress–*reading material* about St. Mary's County:

> When stationed at Leonardtown I did borrow a case of books on some of these topics [sociology, social ethics] from the Congressional Library in Washington, through the kindness of its librarian, Mr. Herbert Putnam.[39]

But also, John LaFarge noted that his life as a parish priest "had certain hardships, chief of which was the sense of separation from intellectual companionship.[40]

On the other hand, however, he was beginning to "open up"–*emotionally*–to other people, and for this he had Morgan to thank. Morgan? His horse.

In those early years of the 20th century, travel in rural St. Mary's County was by horse and buggy over "roads" of clay and mud–as far north as Mechanicsville. "Morgan" was the horse that had pulled the buggy belonging to a previous Jesuit, Father Clem Lancaster, but which now belonged to Father John LaFarge.[41]

As set forth in Chapter 4-C, LaFarge wrote that Morgan "would come to a dead stop when we met anyone, expecting a little conversation to be started up" because it "had been stone-deaf Father Lancaster's habit to stop and speak . . . if he met anyone travelling in the opposite direction." And as a result, Father LaFarge not only greeted people passing by when Morgan stopped in his tracks, he also ended up "conversing with half the countryside."[42]

And almost certainly John LaFarge was *not* discussing the "textbooks" he had borrowed from the Library of Congress.

His conversations now would have been focused on the people themselves that he (and Morgan) met along the dirt roads that defined St. Mary's County. For John LaFarge, these conversations would have

---

39 LaFarge, *Manner* 301.
40 LaFarge, *Manner* 158.
41 LaFarge, *Manner* 169.
42 LaFarge, *Manner* 169-70.

opened up an entire world to him, a world he had not known since his days on Blackwell's Island, a world of everyday human joy–but also human suffering.[43]

He was–finally–becoming "Father LaFarge."

2. Slavs!

Father LaFarge just might have exclaimed "Slavs!" aloud to himself while still working at St. Aloysius in Leonardtown.

At the mere pronunciation of "Slavs," Father LaFarge would have been transported back to his student days–well over a decade earlier–at the seminary in the Austrian Alps. While there, he had been busy absorbing the languages of his courses, always delivered in Latin or German (never in English). *But*, in the required afternoon walks of this Alpine seminary, he had befriended three Poles who spoke no English–only German–as well as Polish, one of the Slavic languages. These Poles were the future Fathers O'Rourke (not Irish), Korzonkierwicz, and Matzura. John LaFarge had been immediately curious: what were the features of a *Slavic* language? (There are several, Ukrainian and Russian among them.) He had practiced Polish with his new-found seminarian friends (and thereby continued cultivating his abilities as a linguist.)

However, now it was 1914, and he had been working in St. Mary's County since 1911. And just who were these new Slavic immigrants that had suddenly arrived in the County? Did they (or their children) need help in understanding English? If so, *how* might they be helped? Linguist that he was, John LaFarge now decided to speak to them in the little he already knew of Polish, just *one* of the Slavic languages.

He was introduced to the Slavs by the James H. Carroll family, who soon arranged for John Balta to drive Father LaFarge through the Slavic community, meeting and greeting Slavs (via horse and buggy). All of these

---

[43] In his autobiography, Father LaFarge recalled his years in St. Mary's County, Maryland. "The older Negroes, like old folk everywhere, liked to talk of bygone days, even the days of slavery before the Civil War. They referred to the slave days usually as 'the bad times,' spoke with great affection of benevolent masters, and recalled unkind, even vicious masters, who inflicted long and painful hours of work and harsh treatment." LaFarge, *Manner* 183-84.

new Slavic immigrants had bought plots of land, smack-dab in the very middle of St. Mary's City, generally centering on St. John's Pond. (These plots are all on land currently owned by St. Mary's College of Maryland.)[44]

> Many of them [the Slavs] did not speak English, and there were many Catholics among them. As I had already acquired some facility in speaking Polish [a western branch of the Slavic languages], I concluded that the Slav language [spoken by the immigrant group from Slovenia] could not be difficult to master.... Father Emerick and I arranged a Mass at the little chapel, which he had baptized St. James Chapel, after Father James Brent Matthews, who was superior of the St. Inigoes Mission. The Slavs were welcomed and responded generously. I preached a Slav sermon as best I could, heard confessions, and gave them Holy Communion.[45]

The Slavs were perhaps the first white "furriners" (foreigners) in St. Mary's County, and as such "they were looked upon with some suspicion as foreigners out of another world. [But] as people got to know the Slavs, feelings became more friendly. Storekeepers commented that Slavs paid their bills at once, in cash, and fulfilled all their business agreements."[46]

To no one's surprise, Father LaFarge, was *transferred away* from Father Kelly's Leonardtown parish of St. Aloysius, where he had been ministering for four years. (Let us make no mistake about it: in a far-different life, Father LaFarge might have remained under Father Kelly's leadership in Leonardtown. It was the Slavic population that now enabled him to reposition himself farther to the south. The Slavs–and their plight with the English language–provided him with good reason to move to the lower section of St. Mary's County).

---

44 LaFarge, *Manner* 179. Regina **Combs** Hammett provides an excellent diagram of the plots held by the Slavs in her *History of St. Mary's County, Maryland: 1634-1990*. 2nd printing. Ridge, Md: R.C. Hammett, 1994. 441. Print. Hereafter cited as Combs, *History*. See St. John's Pond at https://tinyurl.com/Historical-Tapestry or at https://www.scribblemaps.com/maps/view/Overview-FINAL-locked/Overview-FINAL-locked

45 LaFarge, *Manner* 179.

46 LaFarge, *Manner* 179.

As a Jesuit, Father LaFarge was thus sent farther south on the St. Mary's peninsula to St. Inigoes.[47] "Iñigoe," by the way, was the childhood name of St. Ignatius, founder of the Jesuits.

Beginning with his transfer on September 2, 1915, he began working at St. Inigoes with both Fathers Abraham Emerick and James Brent Matthews (the latter being "superior" or "director," and both men being perhaps almost a generation older than LaFarge).[48] LaFarge was now 35, in good health, and in what is sometimes known as "the prime of his life."

Three months after his arrival at St. Inigoes, on Christmas Day of 1915, Father LaFarge celebrated a Latin Mass for the Slavs at the "new" parish church of St. James. The Slavs had helped create a "narrow red clay road" that ran from "the Manor residence" (at Priests' Point) to St. James Chapel, going through "a dense and lonely forest."[49]

Perhaps Father LaFarge also tried conversing with his Slavic congregants in their own language? As to the services, apparently the mass and the hymns were in English. A patriarch in the church, a "weary Negro farmhand . . . claimed he knew by heart 125 hymns. He sang with the fervor of an angel and the voice of a foghorn."[50]

Since the congregation at St. James Chapel was mixed not only "racially" but also ethnically, the logistics of separating persons was intricate. By conforming with Slav custom, the seating arrangements seem to have verged on the bizarre. Six groups had to be accommodated: Slav men, Slav

---

47 Names can be confusing inasmuch as the same name applies to different places and/or institutions. For example, St. Inigoes is an unincorporated community, and it is also the name of a Catholic mission with both a parish and a church. Similarly, churches and schools often share the same name, such as St. James. (See also fn 88 below.)

Please see maps in this chapter showing locations of churches and schools in Southern Maryland during the first part of the 20th century. And a more comprehensive GIS map is at: https://tinyurl.com/Historical-Tapestry or at https://www.scribblemaps.com/maps/view/Overview-FINAL-locked/Overview-FINAL-locked

48 LaFarge Collection, Box 25, Folder 3, "Items from My Diary: August 1915 to 1926," Georgetown University Library; pp.1-24 (of what appears to be a typed transcription of a taped recording, p.8). Hereafter cited as LaFarge, *Desk Diary*.

49 LaFarge, *Manner* 195, 195. See fn 55 below. See photo of John LaFarge & congregation of St James Church displayed after the maps.

50 LaFarge, *Manner* 384 (Appendix I).

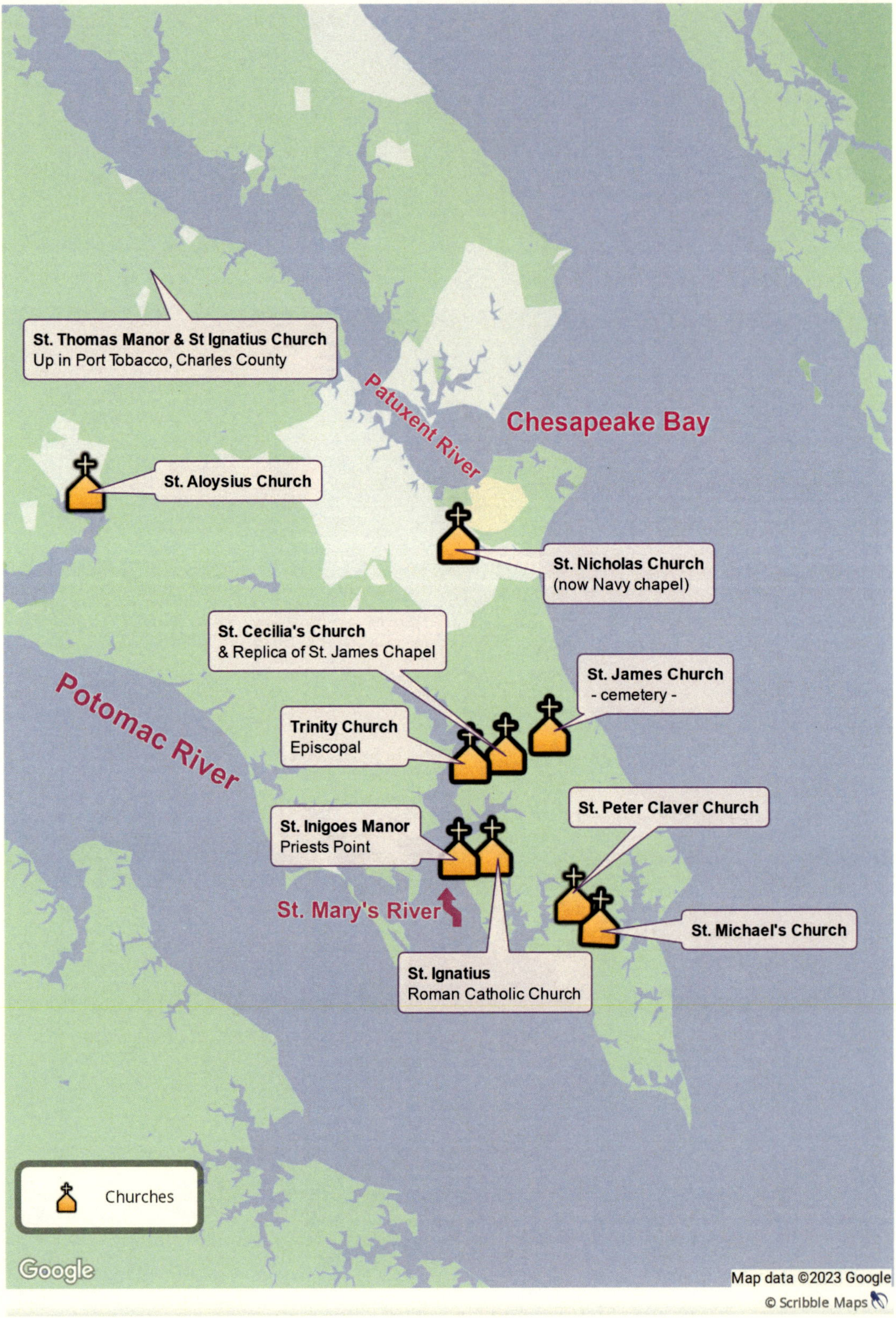
St. Thomas Manor & St Ignatius Church
Up in Port Tobacco, Charles County
Patuxent River
Chesapeake Bay
St. Aloysius Church
St. Nicholas Church
(now Navy chapel)
St. Cecilia's Church
& Replica of St. James Chapel
St. James Church
- cemetery -
Potomac River
Trinity Church
Episcopal
St. Peter Claver Church
St. Inigoes Manor
Priests Point
St. Mary's River
St. Michael's Church
St. Ignatius
Roman Catholic Church
Churches
Google
Map data ©2023 Google
© Scribble Maps

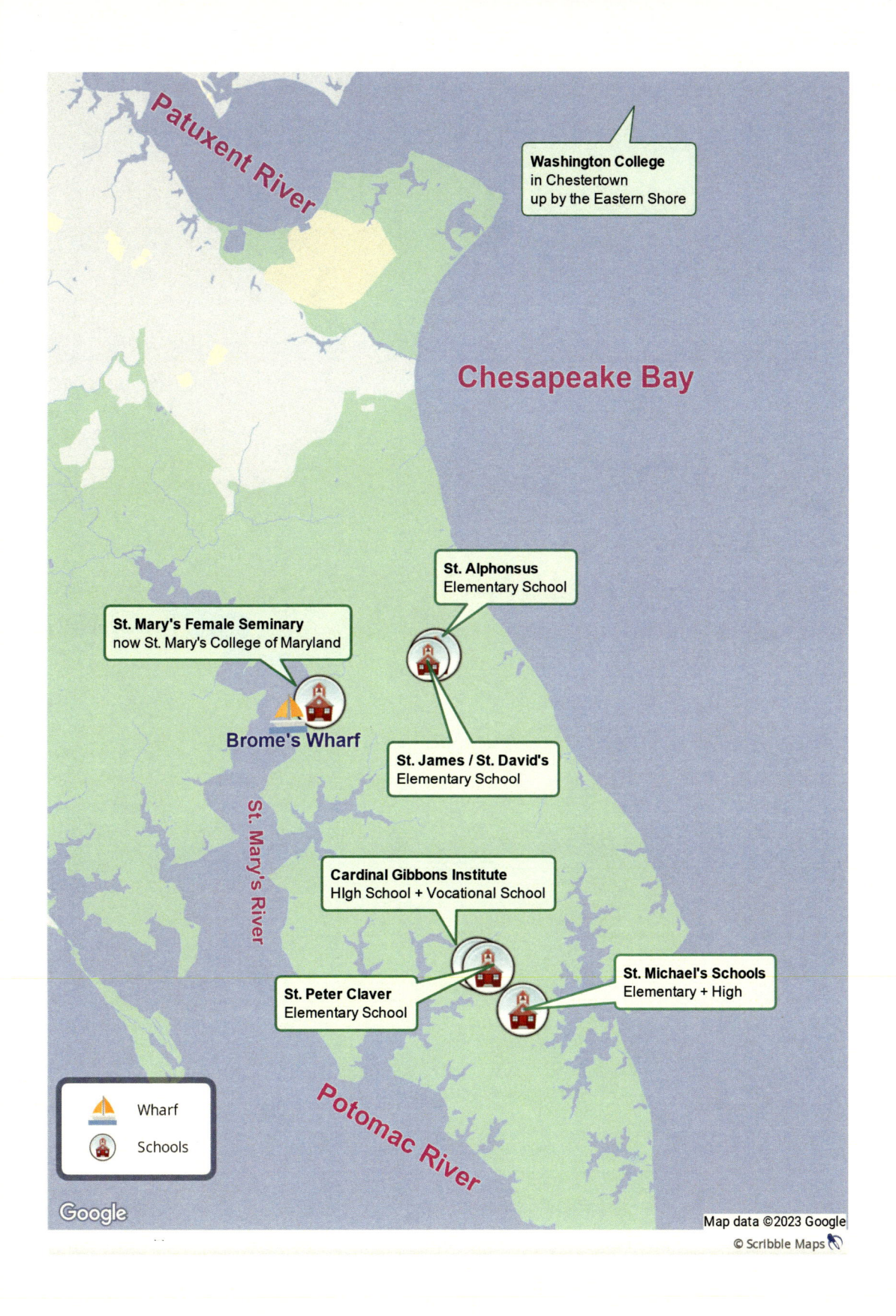

Washington College in Chestertown up by the Eastern Shore

Chesapeake Bay

Patuxent River

St. Alphonsus Elementary School

St. Mary's Female Seminary now St. Mary's College of Maryland

Brome's Wharf

St. James / St. David's Elementary School

St. Mary's River

Cardinal Gibbons Institute High School + Vocational School

St. Peter Claver Elementary School

St. Michael's Schools Elementary + High

Wharf
Schools

Potomac River

299

John LaFarge & congregation of St James Church. "Courtesy of the St Mary's County Historical Society"

women, Slav boys, Slav girls, local white parishioners, and local colored parishioners.[51]

However, tending to the Slavs was not all that Father LaFarge was doing. At St. Inigoes, he was now surrounded not only by "whites" but also by "coloreds"–many of whom were Catholic–but some of whom could not write their own names.

Father LaFarge referred to this as "the rural life problem." Could it be fixed?

Yes and no.

"Yes": if you were white, of certain economic means, and lived in or near Leonardtown, "The [white] girls, again of the 'better' classes, attended St. Mary's Academy in Leonardtown."[52]

---

51 LaFarge, *Manner* 384 (Appendix I).
52 LaFarge, *Manner* 177.

But also, "No": "Strangely enough, after 300 years there were no Catholic *parish schools*" as there had been in Father LaFarge's native Newport. "At Leonardtown itself, Saint Mary's Academy for girls, and Leonard Hall School for boys fulfilled some of the functions of a parish school. *But they charged tuition and many children could not attend them.*"[53] (And most certainly, these schools would never have accepted "the coloreds.")

The Supreme Court had proclaimed on May 18, 1896, in *Plessy v. Ferguson* the ruling of "separate but equal" (which would not be overturned until 1954 with *Brown v. Board of Education*, yet the full implementation of *Brown* in St. Mary's County would be delayed 13 more years, till early Fall of 1967; see fn 84 below). Father LaFarge took it upon himself to see that "the coloreds" were given an "equal" education.

But what would (or could) such an overall education look like, still taking into account that the "coloreds" were a rigorously suppressed population?[54]

3. Establishing Mission Schools

The Desk Diary which Father LaFarge kept during his days at St. Inigoes (and somewhat later, at St. Michael's) was always open and available for review and for recording of entries by Fathers Emerick and Matthews. It is currently archived at Georgetown University. Although LaFarge's notes are brief, this diary contains a good deal of information and was sufficient for the other two priests to have understood.

---

53 LaFarge, *Manner* 177-78 (emphasis added).

54 "Coloreds" have lived as an underclass in St. Mary's County, and a 116-page book (*In Relentless Pursuit of an Education*) provides an account of blacks-only education in the 20th century (well before the decade of required integration of public schools–in full–which was announced by the St. Mary's County public-school board in 1967). Donald M. Barber and Steve Hawkins, *et al*, eds., Unified Committee for Afro-American Contributions of St. Mary's County. *In Relentless Pursuit of an Education–African American Stories from a Century of Segregation (1865-1967)*. Lexington Park, Maryland: UCAC, 2006. Print. Hereafter cited as UCAC, *Relentless.*

Additionally, LaFarge provides an account (historical in nature) that runs for several pages and contains portions (not always within quotation marks) written in a style typical of uneducated persons in the year 1920. These include sentences of ungrammatical "double negatives" and a couple with the word "ain't." LaFarge, *Manner*,183-190.

Decades later, Father McKenna wrote in retrospect: "The coming of Father John LaFarge to the old manor on St. Inigoes Neck marked the sunrise for the Catholic schools of St. Mary's County."[55]

In the late teens and early 1920s, six schools were created by Father LaFarge and–to a somewhat lesser extent–by Father Emerick.[56] Four of these schools were established during World War I (1914-1918). And three were established during the Great Influenza Pandemic (1918-1920).[57]

	Date	School	Location
1.	1916	St. Alphonsus (black elementary)	near St. Mary's City
2.	1916, 1918	St. James School, later dubbed St. David's School (white elementary)	near St. Mary's City
3.	1916	St. Peter Claver (black elementary)	Ridge
4.	1918	St. Michael's (white elementary)	Ridge
5.	1923	St. Michael's High School (white high school)	Ridge
6.	1924	Cardinal Gibbons Institute (black high school)	Ridge

---

55 McKenna, Horace B., S.J.. "Colored Catholics in St. Mary's County." *Woodstock Letters*, Vol. LXXIX, No.1 (Feb. 1950). 58-68; 64. Web. 29 July 2021. <https://jesuitonlinelibrary.bc.edu>. Hereafter cited as McKenna, "Colored Catholics." Jesuit priests lived in St. Ignatius Residence, also called **St. Inigoes Manor**, on St. Inigoes Neck, also known as **Priests' Point** (where the Saint Inigoes Creek meets the St. Mary's River) from 1704 until May 1918 "and lived thereafter at St. Michael's Residence at Ridge, five miles out on the state road." McKenna, "Colored Catholics" 56, 60, 64. This account is similarly reflected as follows: the priests' residence at St. Inigoes Manor at Priests' Point was eventually moved in 1918-19 "to St. Michael's at Ridge, and activity at St. Inigoes Manor decreased." "St. Inigoes Manor." *Southern Maryland Wiki*. Web. 18 July 2022. <https://www.wiki.somd.com/index.php/St._Inigoes_Manor>. Nonetheless, "the Jesuits held on to their land at Priest Point until 1942, when they sold 800 of the 2,000 acres to the U.S. War Department. The Navy established Webster Field in 1943. The Jesuits still own the rest." Roylance, Frank D. "1600s Jesuit mission found in Maryland." *The Baltimore Sun,* 5 Oct. 2000. Web. 30 Aug. 2022. <https://www.baltimoresun.com/news/bs-xpm-2000-10-05-0010050064-story.html>. See also fn 88 below.

56 Father Emerick had been a missionary in Jamaica for several years, and it was his personal belief that he understood black people well.

57 Although well over 50 million people died worldwide, it is estimated that around 10,000 people died in St. Mary's County from the influenza. Schools and churches were ordered to close; and there was a ban on social gatherings until April 1919. "[A]bout 70% of people here were affected." Babcock, Jason. "A century ago, St. Mary's fought another global pandemic." *Southern Maryland News* 12 April 2020. Web. 15 Sept. 2021. See also Combs, *History* 428.

a. St. Alphonsus School

Father LaFarge's first (and abiding) interest was always in the education of "the coloreds." According to his Desk Diary, he opened a small school for blacks on February 1st of 1916, naming it "St. Alphonsus."[58]

How and when he and Father Emerick initially built St. Alphonsus school (whether "from scratch" and/or by modifying an existing structure), we do not know with certainty, although it appears probable that *both* schools (St. Alphonsus and also St. James, the latter re-named St. David's) were operating within the St. James Mission (or Parish), near St. Mary's City.[59]

The actual building of St. James Chapel "was a wooden structure erected in 1915" by Fathers LaFarge and Emerick.[60] By early 1916, Fathers LaFarge and Emerick had already "built St. Alphonsus School" nearby.[61]

There was still a fundamental problem, however.

According to his Desk Diary, by very late July of 1916, Father LaFarge learned that the property on which St. Alphonsus School and St. James Chapel sat did not actually *belong* to the Catholic Church. He set out to remedy this situation.

---

58 LaFarge, John. *Desk Diary*, p.2. There is a disconcerting tendency towards confusion in some of his dates, such as in this diary, which was kept not only by Father LaFarge, but also by others in his absence. *Desk Diary*, p.4. Readers of *The Manner is Ordinary* may notice this discrepancy as to when his schools opened for the first time. Chalk this up to multiple narrators, increasing distance with age, and/or to not double-checking this daily "diary" (which apparently was recorded on tape at some point). For example, see discrepancy in this "school-opening" date as "1917" at LaFarge, *Manner* 196-97. However, Regina **Combs** Hammett also dates the opening of St. Alphonsus School as 1916. Combs, *History* 368. See also fn 74 below re "school-opening" dates.

59 McKenna, "Colored Catholics" 64, 65. Beitzell, Edwin W. *The Jesuit Missions of St. Mary's County, Maryland*. 2nd ed. Abell, MD: sponsored by St. Mary's County Bicentennial Commission, 1976. 277, 288, 303. Print. Hereafter cited as Beitzel, *Jesuit Missions*. And see fn 71 below as to St. James Chapel. St. James Parish also provided a "horse-drawn 'school bus' . . . to provide transportation for the children." Beitzel, *Jesuit Missions* 303. There is no indication as to whether this "horse-bus" was segregated or not. See also fn 95 below.

60 Beitzel, *Jesuit Missions* 303. St. James Chapel was six miles north of St. Michael's Church "opposite the intersection of Three Notch Road and Mattapany Road." Combs, *History* 362.

61 Beitzell, *Jesuit Missions* 288. "In 1916 St Alphonsus School was established at St. James on Route 235 [aka Three Notch Road], six miles north of Ridge [where St. Michael's was located]." Combs, *History* 368, [362]. St. Alphonsus School was "located to the east of the church (later the site of St. James' Hall)." Conley, Rory T., Rev. "The Church of St. James, 1914-1934." *Chronicles of St. Mary's*, Vol. 57, Issue 1 (Winter [2008]-2009). 570. Print. There is a photo of St. Alphonsus School in *Manner* (at 4th page of photos).

By open boat (without so much as a bench), he and the boat-operator made a somewhat harrowing trip across the Chesapeake Bay to the Eastern Shore "to purchase property for schools [note the plural] at St. James' [Parish] . . . from William H. Leonard and Company, who owned most of the land in that vicinity . . . and consent was obtained in an hour's time to transfer to Cardinal Gibbons the following pieces, etc."[62] (Unfortunately, those "pieces" are not specified in Father LaFarge's autobiography.)

St. Alphonsus was successful, largely owing to Mrs. Jenny Beale, who "had attended the convent school of the colored Sisters, the Oblates of Providence" in Baltimore. She had a "gentle voice and a fine sense of humor."[63]

> On the following January 2, 1917, I opened the Negro school, for which I had obtained five and a half acres of property from a firm on the Maryland Eastern Shore. It was a rainy day and the teacher, Mrs. Jenny Beale, had but one pupil. Anyone else would have been discouraged or depressed under those circumstances, but not so Mrs. Beale. With unfailing instinct she knew that once the school was started it could not help but grow. She was placid, imperturbable in her manner . . . and had never lost her love of culture and her boundless belief in the capacities of the colored children.[64]

Less than a year after the St. Alphonsus School had first opened with just one black student, Father LaFarge was able to hand-write in his diary: "Opening of St. Alphonsus School, at 18 [students]" on January 3rd of 1917.[65] St. Alphonsus was financially provided for by the Indian-Negro Fund, administered by Mother Katharine Drexel of the Sisters of the Blessed

---

62 LaFarge, *Desk Diary*, pp. 2, 2, 3. See also LaFarge, *Manner* 196-97.

63 LaFarge, *Manner* 197, 197. "Oblates" suggests that some of the women had not yet taken their final vows.

64 LaFarge, *Manner* 196-97.

65 LaFarge, *Desk Diary*, p.5 (handwritten NB). It is not clear whether St. Alphonsus was operating in the same place/building or perhaps in another structure. See also: Walsh, Francis Michael. *Resurrection: the Story of the Saint Inigoes Mission: 1634-1994*. 1997. Part II, Chapter 14 [titled "The Move to Ridge (1910-1919)"], pp.118-125/191. Web. Available online at The Wayback Machine. <https://web.archive.org/web/20160304205306/http://www.reocities.com/RainForest/vines/6480/inigoes1.html>. Hereafter cited as Walsh, *Resurrection*. This book is dedicated in part to "Mary Ellen **Whalen** Jones, "Aunt Pigeon" (1829-1937)." See Chapter 9-C-2-b at fn 58.

Sacrament, as well as by the Board of Colored Missions (New York).[66] Local historian Beitzell indicates that Mother Katharine Drexel "donated the St. Alphonsus School Building."

St. Alphonsus School closed in 1922.[67] However, at some point, it was consolidated with St. Peter Claver School. (See fn 95 below.)

b. St. James School, later dubbed St. David's School

Having already established a small school for *blacks* (St. Alphonsus), seven months later, LaFarge opened a similar school for *whites* at St. James Chapel (on September 18th of 1916). He noted that "the school was held in the chapel with canvas curtains which could be rolled up and down in front of the sanctuary."[68]

Fifteen white children (Slavs included) showed up on the same day, and by November 15th, 1916, he could boast that enrollment had increased to 55. The teachers were Miss Nanny K. Hebb and Miss Clementine Clarke.[69]

The instruction was, of course, all in English, and for at least one generation, the white Slavic children must have been bilingual: Slavic at home, but English at school. Gradually, however, the Slavic children would have become increasingly proficient in English.[70]

With the two St. Mary City schools now under his belt (one black, the other white; and yet another black elementary school at St. Peter Claver, as described in Section 8-D-3-c-i below), Father LaFarge presumably realized that his little "school" at St. James Chapel just might be fraught with problems: it was a confusion of church (mixed race) *and* school (whites-

---

66 LaFarge, *Desk Diary*, p.20. LaFarge, *Manner* 198. Beitzell, *Jesuit Missions* 303. Combs, *History* 363.

67 Beitzell, *Jesuit Missions* 288, 303. Combs, *History* 368.

68 LaFarge, *Desk Diary*, p.3. LaFarge, *Manner* 196. See also: Combs, *History* 362, 464; McKenna, "Colored Catholics" 65; and Beitzell, *Jesuit Missions* 277, 303.

69 LaFarge, *Desk Diary*, p.3.

70 One of these Slavic students graduated from the High School at St. Mary's Female Seminary in 1926, and another graduated from St. Mary's Junior College in 1931.

only).[71] The little "white" school, held in St. James Chapel, thus excluded children who were black. While white students learned their ABCs in the school-in-the-church, black students could attend church–but not the school-in-the-church. This appears to have been a mirroring of public–and private–education for children in Maryland.[72]

Thus, what was needed was a *separate* school-building for the white children–as there was already a school-building, St. Alphonsus, for the (segregated) blacks. Perhaps worse: the church at St. James was just a bit too splendid. It boasted an ample sanctuary, plus a tiny upstairs bedroom for Father LaFarge, plus a stable (and corn) for the horse.[73] It was obviously "fancier" than the little one-room black school at St. Alphonsus, and any comparison between the two would have been unfortunate.

Was it possible that there ought to be a school–just a *school*–for the white children?

Father LaFarge thought he knew whom to ask for money for such a school: Mrs. David McCarthy of Washington, D.C.. In April of 1917, Mrs. McCarthy made a donation to build a one-room school for whites in St.

---

[71] Although St. James Chapel was torn down in 1975, a "tiny replica of old St. James [Chapel/Church], furnished with its old pews and altar, etc. cut to size, is in a small annex called St. James Chapel." Beitzell, *Jesuit Missions* 303, 309. This annex, St. James Chapel, is now part of St. Cecilia's Church in St. Mary's City, which was built in 1974 to take the place of St. James Chapel. Beitzell, *Jesuit Missions* 308. In 1975, the Art Department at St. Mary's College "presented St. Cecilia's Church with a beautiful historical tapestry commemorating the landing of the Ark and the Dove." Beitzell, *Jesuit Missions* 309. The cover of this book focuses in on the two ships woven in this tapestry.

However, Father LaFarge used the term "St. James Chapel" to refer to what McKenna and Beitzell identified as "St. James Church." LaFarge, *Manner* 383, 384. Thus, in order to avoid confusion, the *original* St. James may be referred to both as a "Chapel" as well as a "Church," whereas the *replica* chapel-annex at St. Cecilia's will be called "St. James Chapel replica." See also Combs, *History* 362-63.

[72] Under Chapter 18 titled "Schools for Colored Children," Sections 96 through 99 of Article LXXVII of the 1888 statutes in effect legalize segregation of public schools (Maryland Code, Public General Laws 1888, Vol. 389, Art. LXXVII titled "Public Education"; Maryland State Archives. Web. 10 Dec. 2021. <https://msa.maryland.gov/megafile/msa/speccol/sc2900/sc2908/ 000001/000389/html/am389--453.html>). Amendments to this statutory scheme in 1914 include an amendment to Section 43, which provides in part that all public schools "shall be free to all white youths" between 6 and 21 years of age (Annotated Code of the Public General Laws of Maryland, 1914, Vol. 373, Art. LXXVII titled "Public Education," Chapter 7 titled "Schools"; Maryland State Archives. Web. 10 Dec. 2021. <https://msa.maryland.gov/megafile/msa/speccol/ sc2900/ sc2908/000001/000373/html/am373--808.html>). Throughout this chapter, there are numerous references to records provided by the Maryland State Archives or the MSA, and each should be read as including: "Courtesy of the Maryland State Archives."

[73] LaFarge, *Manner* 195-96. Walsh, *Resurrection* 121/191.

James Parish. She asked only that it be named for her late husband, David. Thus was born "St. David's School" (for white children) in 1918.[74]

Its companion school (black, and already built) was St. Alphonsus. These two schools were separated by half a mile or more. St. David's School was located on Three Notch Road (now Route 235) near St. Mary's City.[75]

St. James Chapel was now freed up to be, once again, simply a *church*. Church records indicate that its congregation was racially "mixed."[76] Better

---

[74] LaFarge, *Desk Diary*, p.5. LaFarge, *Manner* 222. Beitzell, *Jesuit Missions* 303. McKenna, "Colored Catholics" 64. Combs, *History* 363. Considering LaFarge's statements in his *Desk Diary* at pp. 14 and 20 that St. David's School "opened" in September 1918 and also in September 1922, presumably the term "school-opening" refers to the beginning of the academic year–and not to the establishment of the school itself. See also fn 58 above re "school-opening" dates.

[75] McKenna, "Colored Catholics" 64.

[76] In 1896, the U.S. Supreme Court ruled that "separate but equal facilities" did not violate the Fourteenth Amendment (ratified in 1868). *H.A. Plessy v. J.H. Ferguson*, 163 U.S. 537 (1896). Nevertheless, this ruling did not preclude integration. Some schools that were then private were already integrated, for example, Maryland Law School in 1888. Bogen, David S. "The First Integration of the University of Maryland School of Law" (1989). *Faculty Scholarship*. 712. Web. 29 April 2022. <https://digitalcommons.law.umaryland.edu/fac_pubs/712>.

In Maryland, some congregations were "racially" mixed, and churches had long made their own rules. For example, under the sub-heading of "Religious Corporations," Sections 205 and 207 of Article XXIII of the 1888 statutes allow for the election of persons to establish a "body politic" or to act as trustees in the name of the religious organization in accordance with "known custom and usage of their respective denominations" (Maryland Code, Public General Laws 1888, Vol. 389, Art. XXIII titled "Corporations"; Maryland State Archives. Web. 9 Dec. 2021. <https://msa.maryland.gov/ megafile/msa/speccol/sc2900/sc2908/ 000001/000389/html/am389--453.html>). However, the Maryland Legislature *did* exercise jurisdiction over marriage. In 1884, the Maryland Legislature prohibited interracial marriage, shortly after Frederick Douglass married a white suffragist and abolitionist (a couple of years after his first wife died). Under the sub-heading of "Marrying Unlawfully," Section 200 of Article XXIII of the 1888 statutes prohibits interracial marriage (Maryland Code, Public General Laws 1888, Vol. 389, Art. XXVIII titled "Crimes and Punishments"; Maryland State Archives. Web. 10 Dec. 2021. <https://msa.maryland.gov/megafile/msa/speccol/sc2900/sc2908/000001/ 000389/ html/ am389--453.html>). The Legislature's asserted jurisdiction over marriage dates back to at least 1715, imposing a fine on any person (including ministers and pastors) who is convicted of "any pretence [to] join in marriage any negro with any white person" (Vol. 389, Art. XXVIII, Section 194, also under the sub-heading of "Marrying Unlawfully"). Furthermore, because of the predominant role that common law has played in Maryland, it is possible that there may be case law with holdings on "racially" mixed congregations. See Liebmann, George. Rev. of *The Common Law in Colonial America: Volume I: The Chesapeake and New England, 1607-1660*, by William Nelson (Oxford University Press, 2008). *Law and Politics Book Review*, Vol. 19 No. 2 (2009):148-50. Web. Last accessed 17 Dec. 2021. <http://www.lpbr.net/2009/02/common-law-in-colonial-america-volume-i.html>. See: Chapter 1-B at fn 6; and fn 84 below.

yet, the two schools were finally legal: St. Alphonsus and St. David's were finally now simply that–*schools*.[77]

St. David's School closed in 1926 due to lack of funding, poor road conditions, and the "division of the people in the [St. James] parish since the Slavs had withdrawn many of their children . . . ."[78]

c. Ridge: Dichotomy of Place

In 1916, Father Emerick built a two-room elementary school (for black students) further up the hill from St. Peter Claver Church in Ridge: St. Peter Claver School.[79]

Two years later, in September 1918, Fathers Emerick and LaFarge founded St. Michael's Parochial School. This was an elementary school (for white students) a few miles down the road (south) of St. Peter Claver, at St. Michael's Church (in Ridge).[80]

We might call this "a dichotomy of place"–but apparently it worked. (And it was Maryland law.)

In addition to acquiring buildings and funding for the mission schools, teachers were also needed. Father LaFarge tenaciously invested years and years of effort trying to find teachers. Back in 1915, he embarked on his campaign of trying to persuade Mother Josephine of the Congregation of the Sisters of St. Joseph (New Hartford, Connecticut) to provide teachers "not only [for] the white children but the even more neglected colored ones."[81] Referring to the parish in Ridge, Father LaFarge told Mother Josephine: "It is the *oldest parish of an English-speaking congregation in the new world*. In fact,

---

[77] During the nine months that Father LaFarge had been in Poughkeepsie, N.Y. on his "Tertianship," Father Emerick had taken over both schools: (the white) St. James and (the black) St. Alphonsus. Once Father LaFarge returned in June 1918, he increasingly used the word "We" (in his autobiography) to indicate the forward thrust of both the white and black schools that he–and Father Emerick–were together creating.

[78] LaFarge, *Desk Diary*, p.24. See also: Combs, *History* 363; and Beitzell, *Jesuit Missions* 303.

[79] McKenna, "Colored Catholics" 66. "Our History" and "The St. Peter Claver Elementary School." *St. Peter Claver Catholic Church*. Web. 29 July 2021. <https://www.stpeterclaverchurch.org>.

[80] LaFarge, *Desk Diary*, p.7. See also "History." St. Michael's School. Web. 29 July 2021. <http://www.saint-michaels-school.org>.

[81] Burton, Katherine. *Mightily and Sweetly*. Paterson, New Jersey: St. Anthony Guild Press, 1948. 220. Print. Hereafter cited as Burton, *Mightily*.

it was there that the Jesuits opened the first Catholic schools, even before Bishop Carroll's day. . . ."[82] (See fn 88 below.)

By 1920, however, both St. Peter Claver School and St. Michael's School had fallen on hard times financially. Yet,

> One bright spot remained: Mrs. Beale continued quietly with her little colored school [St. Alphonsus], placid and competent as ever. It would have been more sensible for me to have transferred Mrs. Beale to one of the white schools and I believe that, after the first shock, they would have been grateful to have her teach.[83]

This would have been difficult. Segregation was perceived to be the "law of the land."[84]

Question: Why had these two men (Fathers Emerick and LaFarge) been creating so many schools?

Father LaFarge answered this question in his early 50s, simply by thinking back to his seminary days of "custom Catholicism" in Austria: that is, Catholicism, *required by the political state*:

> I had seen personally the effect of mere custom Catholicism in the Old World, how the Faith had decayed under routine and the devastating influence of a state-controlled Church. *I wanted to see our Catholics intelligently believing and able to stand on their own feet.*[85]

---

82 Burton, *Mightily* 219 (emphasis added). Seven years later, in 1922, Mother Josephine finally provided five Sisters to teach in Ridge. They were disappointed that the "plan to teach colored children had not worked out," although they did provide religious teaching on Saturdays. Burton, *Mightily* 235. They lamented the "unfair treatment" experienced by colored children. One of the Sisters told Mother Josephine that a little boy came up to her after class and asked her "in a hoarse whisper, 'Sister, if I am a very good boy, will I really go to Heaven just the way a white boy does?'" Burton, *Mightily* 236, 236.

83 LaFarge, *Manner* 201.

84 Almost 35 years later, on May 17, 1954, the Supreme Court would hand down its decision that all public schools were to become racially integrated. *Brown v. Board of Education of Topeka*, 347 U.S. 483 (1954). This ruling was particularly difficult to enforce in racially divided St. Mary's County, and piece-meal implementation and civil-rights lawsuits would take up 13 more years. See, for example, *Bd. of Educ. of St. Mary's County v. Groves*, 261 F.2d 527 (1958). At long last, racial integration of all public schools became the norm–but not until the Fall of 1967. For a local newspaper account, see article by Babcock, Jason. "St. Mary's public schools fully integrated 50 years ago." *Southern Maryland News* 6 Sept 2017. Web. 10 Dec. 2021. See: Chapter 1-B at fn 6; and fn 76 above.

85 LaFarge, *Manner* 204 (emphasis added).

Those had been the negative effects of "custom Catholicism." But, just possibly, could there also be better effects in the religiously-plural United States? Father LaFarge would later find it in the congregation at St. Nicholas (the new church was built in 1916): "three-quarters colored, one-quarter white, and all services were held in common."

> I was impressed by the two races' common interest in the community, especially in the preservation of the life of the community. . . . If the home forces for good were divided, whether in the church or the civil community, it would bring only weakness at home. It seemed to me that some basis could be found in which all groups would work together in the community for defending the best traditions of the past. Everyone in the community, the white people and Negroes alike, had a common stake in the future *and at some point they could no longer work separately but would need to recognize their new type of interdependence.*[86]

"Interdependence" between black and white? This has not (yet) been recognized, but it was Father LaFarge's vision of simple amity between what society categorized as two "races": one marked as "black," the other marked as "white." But underlying the stark division of a community into "races" is the very notion of "race" as if it were a legitimate categorization of humankind, instead of acknowledging *the* human race, *Homo sapiens*, as a species of primate.

Unbeknownst to Father LaFarge, however, he was nearing the end of his time in St. Mary's County.

By 1925, he had already submitted an article on racism to the powers-that-be at the then-weekly Jesuit magazine, *America*, and he was being seriously considered for a position as its "associate editor." But for the general public in St. Mary's County, he would delay any acceptance of this news until the summer of 1926.

i. St. Peter Claver Elementary School

In 1902, about nine years before Father LaFarge arrived in St. Mary's County, the Biscoe family donated land to Cardinal Gibbons, that is, to

---

[86] LaFarge, *Manner* 207 (emphasis added).

the Roman Catholic church.[87] This land was located up a steep hill, at St. Inigoes, on top of one of the "ridges" for which the present town of Ridge is named.[88] It's a small wonder that Father LaFarge's "tin Lizzie" could actually make it up to the top of that hill. A photo taken in 1920 shows a smiling John LaFarge in his cassock sitting on the running board of his old Ford (see Walsh, Francis, comp. *A Pictorial History of the Saint Inigoes Mission: 1634-1984*. Hollywood, Maryland: St. Mary's Press, 1984. 57. Print.)

So when Father LaFarge arrived, the St. Peter Claver Sodality Hall–the first "black church"–was already there, sitting on land that belonged to the Catholic Church (while the "white" sodality had St. Michael as its patron).[89]

---

[87] McKenna, "Colored Catholics" 66. Beitzell, *Jesuit Missions* 287.

[88] LaFarge, *Manner* 198, 199. St. Inigoes, an unincorporated community, is less than three miles north-west of Ridge, also an unincorporated community. The parish at **St. Inigoes**, near Ridge, is the *"oldest continuously operating* U.S. Catholic parish in English speaking North America" evolving from the first Roman Catholic church at St. Mary's City. Rebuilt in 1785, the **St. Ignatius Roman Catholic Church** "contains relics from the original *Ark* and *Dove* sailing ships which bore the first settlers to the Maryland colony." "St. Inigoes, Maryland." *Wikipedia*. Web. 31 Aug. 2022. <https://en.wikipedia.org/wiki/St._Inigoes,_Maryland> (emphasis added).

The vast lands that Lord Calvert gave to the Jesuits in 1637, known as the St. Inigoes plantation, would eventually encompass not only the church but also the priests' residence called **St. Inigoes Manor** at **Priests' Point** which was eventually moved (in 1918-19) to St. Michael's at Ridge. See fn 55 above. McKenna, "Colored Catholics" 56, 60, 64. In an article written by Father LaFarge about that move, he stated that St. Inigoes "is the oldest Catholic foundation with permanent existence and activities within the limits of the original thirteen States; it is certainly the most ancient Jesuit establishment in the United States, and probably the oldest in the world that has remained in continuous possession of the Society [of Jesus]." Emblematic of the Venice-like travel conditions from the 17th Century up through the early 20th Century in Southern Maryland, the location at "Priest's Point was unparalleled" because it was approachable by many water-travel passages. Yet, although the Manor was rebuilt after a fire in 1872, its construction was deemed "odd" because it "was full of rooms, with few rooms in which to live." LaFarge, John, S.J.. "The Transfer of the St. Inigoes Residence." *Woodstock Letters*, Vol. LI, No.2 (Jan. 1922). 192-93, 194, 195. Web. 1 Sept. 2022. <https://jesuitonlinelibrary.bc.edu>.

A word of caution: the **St. Ignatius Roman Catholic Church**, located in St. Inigoes, is to be *distinguished from* the **St. Ignatius Church** at **St. Thomas Manor**, also known as St. Ignatius Chapel Point, located in Port Tobacco in Charles County. The parish at St. Ignatius Chapel Point has, also, been described as "the *oldest continuously active* Roman Catholic parish in the American Thirteen Colonies." That "mission settlement" was founded in 1641 by Father Andrew White, S.J. (see Chapter 6-F), and the parish was established in 1662. "St. Thomas Manor." *Wikipedia*. Web. 6 Sept. 2022. <https://en.wikipedia.org/wiki/St._Thomas_Manor> (emphasis added). See fn 47 above about confusion as to names.

[89] That "sodality hall church" was later replaced by Father Emerick's hand-hewn St. Peter Claver Church, reportedly capable of seating some 300 people, which was finally "dedicated" in 1918 (after four years of construction). "Our History." *St. Peter Claver Catholic Church*. Web. 29 July 2021. <https://www.stpeterclaverchurch.org>. However, LaFarge's *Desk Diary* (at p.9) notes that there was a "dedication" for the new church on October 19, 1919, with a sermon by Father LaFarge, as well as a reception for the bishop by the students that same day.

The LaFarge and Emerick team continued with their quest to educate black children. Father Emerick built–by hand–a wooden *two*-room school for elementary-school children who were black.[90]

And in 1916, St. Peter Claver Elementary School opened its doors. For eight years, between 1916 and 1924 (under the directorship of Father Emerick), the school would be put into the hands of black teachers who were willing and able to help out, including three women from the Biscoe family. These teachers were Mrs. Ruth Green, Mrs. Cecilia **Biscoe** Jackson, Mrs. Ellen **Biscoe** Grayson, Mrs. Ethel Brown, Mrs. Lulu **Harper** Brown, Mrs. Sadie Biscoe, and Mrs. Gertrude **Williams** Davis.[91]

Finally, in 1924 (Father Emerick having already departed for Woodstock), Father LaFarge persuaded the (black) Oblate Sisters of Providence to run the little school on what had originally been the Biscoe property.

> The day following their arrival, the Sisters opened school at one o'clock, p.m. *Seventy-five children were present*. Mrs. Sadie Biscoe, who conducted all classes until the arrival of the Sisters, was released with honors.[92]

After a fire in May 1928, St. Peter Claver Elementary School would be replaced–but not until December 1928–by the still-standing, single-story building made out of very durable brick and mortar.[93]

---

[90] Combs, *History* 369. McKenna, "Colored Catholics" 66. It was the last building that Father Emerick completed, as he retired to Woodstock in 1923 and died there in 1931. "Abraham J. Emerick, SJ, Collection." "Biographical Notes (p.3). *Georgetown University Archival Resources*, 15 May 2017. Web. <http://findingaids.library.georgetown.edu/repositories/15/resources/10470/>.

[91] McKenna, "Colored Catholics" 65. Combs, *History* 369. However, Beitzell indicates (without identifying his source) that it was established in 1920. Beitzell, *Jesuit Missions* 277. Yet the "1920" date may be a mis-print as it is not consistent with the date of "1916" he identifies (supported by a source) in another entry of his book. Beitzell, *Jesuit Missions* 288.

[92] McKenna, "Colored Catholics" 66 (citing an account written by the Superioress of Ridge, Mother Mary Cyprian, O.S.P., and her assistant, Sr. Mary Margaretta, O.S.P.) (emphasis added). LaFarge, *Desk Diary*, p.20.

[93] McKenna, "Colored Catholics" 66, 67. Like St Alphonsus School, St. Peter Claver School also received financial support from Mother Katharine Drexel of the Sisters of the Blessed Sacrament. McKenna, "Colored Catholics" 64. Via a "monthly allowance." LaFarge, *Desk Diary*, p. 20.

After closing in 1967, this well-built school-building was turned to other purposes by the Catholic Church. Now known as "McKenna Hall" it is used for the benefit of the parish of St. Peter Claver Church. The top floor has a music room, a video-conference room, archives, and a soon-to-be-inaugurated museum!

As discussed above, although the first black school, St. Alphonsus, had also been founded in 1916, it apparently closed in 1922.[94] Yet, eventually, St. Alphonsus was consolidated with St. Peter's, thus avoiding a gap in elementary-school education (provided by Jesuits) for many of the black children who lived near St. Mary's City.[95]

St. Peter Claver School remained open for the 1st through 8th grades until June 1965; while for the academic years of 1965-66 and 1966-67, it only gave classes for the 7th and 8th grades.[96] It closed in 1967, when full racial integration of all public schools became the norm in St. Mary's County.[97]

ii. St. Michael's Schools

St. Michael's schools met a need for students who were white. In 1918, St. Michael's Parochial School opened (within a two-story wooden building built in 1911 that also served as a social hall), and instruction was given by Sisters and nuns until 1920. However, discipline and teaching skills were not up to par. In 1919, Father LaFarge noted that "I applied to at least sixteen religious communities with regard to this work."[98]

In 1919 and 1920, Fathers LaFarge and Emerick mitigated the discipline challenges by teaching some of the classes themselves to "the boys." In 1920, Father LaFarge was appointed to be priest-in-charge at St. Michael's

---

[94] Beitzell, *Jesuit Missions* 288, 303.

[95] The written accounts are not consistent date-wise. On the one hand, Father McKenna states: "St. Alphonsus [School] continued for six years [thus, 1916-1922]. Since 1928 the St. James [parish] colored children have been brought by bus to St. Peter Claver's [School]. *Likewise* the St. David School was *consolidated* with St. Michael's [School] under Father Gregory Kiehne in 1932." McKenna, "Colored Catholics" 65 (emphases added). Further, a letter on St. Peter Claver's Mission letterhead, dated December 1935, and addressed to the Archbishop of Baltimore acknowledges receipt of "$475.00 for St. Peter Claver's School, and $250.00 for St. Alphonsus School *consolidated* with St. Peter's." One-page letter dated 26 Dec. 1935; presumably kept in the archives at St. Peter Claver Church, Ridge, Maryland (emphasis added).

On the other hand, Father Walsh states that, in September 1925, "the dwindling number of children at St. Alphonsus prompted Father LaFarge to close that school and transfer the children by bus to St. Peter's. The busing of the children from St. James enlarged the enrollment. From this time on, for purposes of diocesan aid, *St. Peter's was considered a consolidated school* incorporating within itself the old Saint Alphonsus School." Walsh, *Resurrection* 133/191 (emphasis added).

[96] Combs, *History* 370.

[97] Combs, *History* 370. Beitzell, *Jesuit Missions* 293. See fn 84 above.

[98] LaFarge, *Manner* 199. LaFarge, *Desk Diary*, pp. 7, 9, 9. Beitzell, *Jesuit Missions* 277. Combs, *History* 362, 363. Regarding his "long and arduous struggle for funds," see LaFarge, *Manner* 198-201.

Parish–of both its (white) church and its (equally white) elementary school. Finally, in November 1920, Father LaFarge secured the long-awaited promise of the Sisters of St. Joseph to arrive in 1922 and help out with the schooling of parish children.[99]

But there would have to be two "empty" years before their arrival (1920 to 1922). So there was a problem: how to handle this somewhat distressing situation?

In his autobiography, Father LaFarge credits Dr. Caroline Martin (a *medical* doctor) who organized several young (white) women to help out until the (white) Sisters of St. Joseph could actually arrive and take over–but not until 1922:

> [Dr. Martin] was a vigorous personality, who knew the people of the County well. From local families she invited several girls to form a little teaching community. The girls led a quasi-religious life, with meditation and Mass in the morning, preparing their lessons for the following day each evening and keeping silence after night prayers. So Dr. Martin, with her girls, staffed my two white schools from September 1920 to June 1922.[100]

Dr. Martin's teachers were dismissed following the arrival of the Sisters of St. Joseph in August of 1922:

> For the [white] St. Joseph sisters, pioneering at Ridge was particularly difficult. Nothing could be less like busy, noisy Hartford, Connecticut, than this remote country side where they heard no sound at night save the chirping of crickets and the occasional yell of a screech-owl. . . . But theirs was love at first sight for the country children, who lost no time in reciprocating.[101]

Thus, in 1922, St. Michael's Elementary School finally opened with classes taught by the Sisters of St. Joseph, so long pursued by Father LaFarge.[102]

---

99 LaFarge, *Desk Diary*, pp. 9, 10. See fn 82 above.
100 LaFarge, *Manner* 202. See also: LaFarge, *Desk Diary*, p.12; and Combs, *History* 363.
101 LaFarge, *Manner* 202.
102 Combs, *History* 363.

In 1932, St. Michael's School took under its wing students from St. David's School via consolidation. And decades later, with de-segregation, after St. Peter Claver School closed, some of those students enrolled in St. Michael's School.[103]

Beginning In 1923, St. Michael's added a first year of high school, and gradually, added the 10th, 11th, and 12th grades. In 1931, St. Michael's High School was built; yet in 1967, it was "discontinued."[104]

Whereas St. Alphonsus was simply abandoned and later destroyed, and St. Peter Claver closed its school in 1967, only St. Michael's elementary and middle school (a private, Catholic school) was left, and it is now racially integrated.

d. Cardinal Gibbons Institute

On a Sunday afternoon in November 1916, "[o]ccurred the memorable meeting, which was the birthplace of the Cardinal Gibbons Institute and in a way the birthplace of the entire Catholic interracial movement." What Fathers LaFarge, Emerick and Matthews had envisaged was the creation of a "colored industrial school for boys for 11 or 12 years [thus elementary through high school]." Subsequently, meetings were held with church "Superiors" and plans were made to form a corporation and visits were made to prospective sites.[105]

By May 1917, farm-land opposite St. Peter Claver Church "belonging to Mrs. Luther Calloway" was in their sights.[106]

Although the institute was initially presented as a reformatory, it must have been tantalizing for those priests to imagine just what *could* be on the Galloway property if indeed the Society of Jesus (the Jesuits) could be persuaded to *buy* the farm within a month's time:

---

103 Beitzell, *Jesuit Missions* 303, 278. Combs, *History* 363, 370. McKenna, "Colored Catholics" 65.

104 Beitzell, *Jesuit Missions* 277, 278. Combs, *History* 363-64. LaFarge, *Desk Diary*, pp.16, 22. LaFarge, *Manner* 203.

105 LaFarge, *Desk Diary*, pp. 3, 4, 5. LaFarge, *Manner* 209.

106 LaFarge, *Desk Diary*, pp. 5, 6. A handwritten interlineation on p.5 purportedly corrects the transcription from Mrs. Luther "Galloway" to "Calloway" (from a "G" to a "C"). However, as described below, real-property deeds show that it was actually "Galloway" with a "G."

There might be an elementary school!

There might even be a high school!

In their excitement, and on the strength of what they were now imagining, this group of three (Fathers Emerick, LaFarge, and Matthews) decided to drive all the way up to Leonardtown, along a muddy highway. They would celebrate with a drink–perhaps even over a meal–the possibilities now stretching out before them.[107]

In the end, the Society of Jesus (the Jesuits) *did* buy the Galloway farm. It was too good to pass up–and eventually it would be put to good use. Cardinal Gibbons donated $8,500 dollars to buy the land, hence the Institute was later named after him.[108] Although the land-purchase was Catholic in origin, title to the land itself would be vested in a non-sectarian corporation.

As detailed in footnote 108, varying accounts of this land-purchase bring to light many discrepancies in the name of the property, the year when it

---

107 LaFarge, *Desk Diary*, p.6.

108 The Cardinal Gibbons Institute in Southern Maryland is to be distinguished from the "Cardinal Gibbons School" up in Baltimore.

There are over half-a-dozen different accounts as to this land-purchase. For example, Father LaFarge refers to a 70 or 80 acre estate abutting Smith's Creek (referred to as either the Calloway farm or the Galloway farm) which was bought in 1917 for $8,000 (donated by Cardinal Gibbons) and subsequently held in a corporation named the "St. Peter Claver Institute" with the help of a white parishioner, Lawrence P. Williams. Others describe an estate of 180 acres called the "old Pembroke Farm" on Smith's Creek. Father McKenna and historian Beitzell indicate it was bought in around 1916 for $8,000. LaFarge, *Desk Diary*, pp.5, 6. LaFarge, *Manner* 209. McKenna, "Colored Catholics" 69. Beitzell, *Jesuit Missions* 290. Combs, *History* 371 (citing McKenna in another publication titled "Twin Silver Jubilees 1924-1949"). Father McKenna states that "title to the property was vested in a corporation known as St. Peter Claver's Institute." McKenna, Horace B., S.J. "Founding of the Cardinal Gibbons Institute." *Twin Silver Jubilees–Three Centuries of Catholic Negro American Life at Ridge, St. Mary's County, Maryland 1924-1949* (1949). 25. A doctoral dissertation about the Cardinal Gibbons Institute indicates that there are further varying accounts, including a purchase in 1916 of 200 acres near Smith's Creek for $3,000. Moore, Cecilia Annette. "A Brilliant Possibility: The Cardinal Gibbons Institute: 1924-1934." Diss. U. Of Virginia. 1997. 55-56. Print. See also Crowley, Francis M. "A Great Cardinal's Memorial." *Columbia* (New Haven, Feb. 1928). 20. Print.

There's more! The Maryland Provincial Archives (MPA) at Box 142, Folder 3, contains an article titled "Historia Domus" *written in Latin* about the Residence History of St. Inigoes/Ridge; it refers to the "St. Peter Claver's Industrial School, Inc." at p.3. And MPA Box 28, Folder 4 contains an article titled "A Fund-Raising Survey, Analysis, and Plan for the Cardinal Gibbons Institute" as well as a promotional booklet titled "The Cardinal Gibbons Institute: a National School for Colored Youth." Archives of the Maryland Province of the Society of Jesus, GTM-000119. Booth Family Center for Special Collections, Georgetown University, Washington, D.C.

was purchased, the purchase-price, and its acreage. (Details of these events were probably obscured by the haze of World War I.)

However, real-property records kept at the Land Records and License Department in the Clerk's Office of the Circuit Court for St. Mary's County (in Leonardtown) disentangle these discrepancies. The grantor-grantee indexes reveal that there are *two* deeds, not just one.[109]

The first deed, dated June 19, 1917, appears to have conveyed two tracts summing 361 acres, including 186 acres (a farm comprised of five parcels) from Edith E. Galloway and Luther H. Galloway to Lawrence J. Kelly for the sum of $8,500. Presumably, this was *Father* Kelly.[110]

Ten months later, a corporation was formed to hold title to the Galloway farm. "The Claver Industrial School, Incorporated" was formed on April 2, 1918.[111]

Then, on May 27, 1918, less than two months after this incorporation, the second deed appears to have conveyed the same land as the first deed, including the 186-acre farm, from Lawrence J. Kelly to The Claver Industrial School, Incorporated for a proverbial "peppercorn" of ten dollars.[112]

The first World War delayed the creation of the Institute, which ended up evolving into an ambitious *national* plan. In 1923, the Archbishop approved of a revised plan that would offer industrial, academic, and agricultural

---

[109] There is further confusion due to clerical errors made when key identifiers in manuscripts of record were transcribed into typed entries for the indexes. For example, upon deciphering the ambiguous handwritten name of "The Claver Industrial School, Incorporated," the transcription was erroneously typed as "*Clovers* Industrial School." See Land Records and License Department, Clerk's Office of the Circuit Court for St. Mary's County, Leonardtown (hereafter cited as Leonardtown LRD), Liber EBA # 17, Folio 377 (emphasis added).

[110] Leonardtown LRD, Liber EBA # 16, Folio 261. John LaFarge had worked at Father Lawrence Kelly's Leonardtown parish of St. Aloysius from 1911 to 1915. See Sections 8-D-1 & 8-D-2 above.

[111] The Maryland State Tax Commission has an Index of the Charter Record from 1908-1965, archived at SM81-6 of the Maryland State Archives. Page 3864 of the pdf is an image of an index "master card" (categorized as Liber 14, Folio 644) for "The Claver Industrial School, Incorporated" which shows its date of incorporation as well as the date when it was forfeited: October 25, 1943. STATE TAX COMMISSION (Charter Record, Index) The Claver Industrial School, Incorporated, MSA SM81-6, SR 658. Courtesy of the Maryland State Archives.

[112] Leonardtown LRD, Liber EBA # 17, Folio 377.

classes to Catholic and Protestant students alike with an exclusively black faculty.[113]

This top-of-the-ridge "farm" proved ideal, and pre-Depression Era money (Catholic money) eventually became available so that a high school–to be named the Cardinal Gibbons Institute–could be built on the former Galloway property.[114]

That meant that, after 1924, black students could now go straight from their elementary school (St. Peter Claver) to the Institute (Grade 7 on up). Both the elementary school and the Institute were run by the Jesuits. In addition to teaching at St. Peter Claver Elementary School, the Oblate Sisters (on loan from their mother-house in Baltimore, Mrs. Beale's former school) also "made significant contributions" to the high school at the Cardinal Gibbons Institute.[115]

Yet this former "Galloway" farm, up the steep hill–less than three miles south of St. Inigoes–would experience "unfortunate" consequences to its decision to provide education for "colored" people: (1) a tenant farmhouse *was burned* in November 1917;[116] (2) the original St. Peter Claver elementary

---

[113] LaFarge, *Desk Diary*, pp. 12, 13, 16, 17. LaFarge, *Manner* 210-11. McKenna, "Colored Catholics" 69-70. Beitzell, *Jesuit Missions* 290. Combs, *History* 371.

[114] McKenna, "Colored Catholics" 69. Beitzell, *Jesuit Missions* 290. Combs, *History* 371. LaFarge described the land as "extending from the high plane of the ridge down to the salt-water front of Smith's Creek, which empties into the Potomac." LaFarge, *Manner* 209.

[115] Combs, *History* 373. Beitzell, *Jesuit Missions* 292. McKenna, "Colored Catholics" 78. LaFarge, *Manner* 210-12, 214.

[116] LaFarge, *Desk Diary*, p.6.

school *was burnt to the ground* in May 1928;[117] and (3) in March 1934, St. Peter Claver Church *was burnt to the ground*.[118]

The new school, the Cardinal Gibbons Institute, was an imposing structure, rising as it did at the end of an elegant, circular drive. Eventually it would have two "wings": one for (black) resident boys from mid-United States; and at the other end of the building, one for resident girls (also black, and from equally far away). In addition, of course, there were also day-students, black as well. And adult education was provided–including courses provided by Mrs. Jenny Beale (of St. Alphonsus fame)![119]

> The 1924-25 enrollment was 28 students; in the Boarding Department seven boys and six girls, and in the Day School Department four boys and eleven girls. . . . Despite recurring financial difficulties the growth of the Institute was constant.[120]

After opening its doors in October of 1924, the Cardinal Gibbons Institute was an obvious success, owing much to Victor Daniel, recently from Bordentown (New Jersey), but raised by a well-educated and affluent family in the Virgin Islands. As headmaster, he was a Tuskegee graduate, class of 1909.[121]

---

117 Combs, *History* 369. Beitzell, *Jesuit Missions* 288. McKenna, "Colored Catholics" 66 (citing an account written by the Superioress of Ridge, Mother Mary Cyprian, O.S.P., and her assistant, Sr. Mary Margaretta, O.S.P.).

118 Beitzell, *Jesuit Missions* 290, 345. Combs, *History* 369. McKenna, "Colored Catholics" 67, 68. "Nothing was saved except the tabernacle key and the pastor." McKenna, "Colored Catholics" 68.

A letter on St. Peter Claver's Mission letterhead, dated Easter 1935, and addressed to "Dear Friend," requests financial help for the re-building of a church "which as a mission, goes back to the days of Lord Baltimore in 1634." This letter states that: on May 28, 1928, the mission school was "burnt to the ground" by a fire of "incendiary origin" (a new school was later built with Father LaFarge's help); and on March 12, 1934, "shortly after midnight, . . . the mission church with all its contents was completely destroyed by a fire, also of a mysterious origin." One-page letter dated Easter 1935; presumably kept in the archives at St. Peter Claver Church, Ridge, Maryland.

In 1938, the "new" St. Peter Claver Church, this time built with brick and mortar, opened its doors. The St. Peter Claver Church is known as "The Church on the Holy Hill."

119 Combs, *History* 371. Beitzell, *Jesuit Missions* 290. McKenna, "Colored Catholics" 75. LaFarge, *Desk Diary*, pp. 18, 20, 21, 22, 23. LaFarge, *Manner* 211-12. See photo of the Cardinal Gibbons Institute.

120 McKenna, "Colored Catholics" 70.

121 Combs, *History* 371. Beitzell, *Jesuit Missions* 290, 291. McKenna, "Colored Catholics" 71. LaFarge, *Desk Diary*, pp.16, 20, 21. LaFarge, *Manner* 211-13.

Better yet, Mr. Daniel knew about what was then (and even today) known as "the Harlem Renaissance." This was a group of American writers who–in various ways–were exploring (in both poetry and fiction) what it meant to both black and "other" than white. Most of these writers were from Harlem (in New York City).

The late James Forrest has described the course of study at the Cardinal Gibbons Institute (a Catholic school accredited by both the State of Maryland and The Catholic University of America):

> Cardinal Gibbons [Institute] was very structured. He was a disciplinarian, Principal [Victor] Daniel was. If you didn't toe the line, you didn't stay there. [laughs] He'd give you a bus ticket, go back where you came from. . . . But you think about those things and we thought as youngsters, that he was very harsh. But you look at it when you get a little older, he wasn't all that harsh, just something that had to be done. And if you didn't follow it, then you'd get a plane ticket, or bus ticket or some kind of ticket [laughs] 'cause you left there. Yep. Yep, yep.[122]

Victor Daniel also made sure that his students learned about "the Harlem Renaissance." This was clearly inspirational, as Mr. Daniel had intended it should be:

> He [Mr. Daniel] told us [the students] about Socrates, Plato, Aristotle, and all those philosophers. He wanted you to broaden your scope of knowledge. We studied quite a bit about Negro history: men who had made a mark in life, Paul Lawrence Dunbar, Phyllis **Wheatley**, and . . . a whole host of others that I recall very well. I had a lot of interest in black history. And he gave me that. He opened that little window. He said, "There is people in your race that has made progress in life. You ought to know about them and know their history." . . . He wanted you to know that these people had made certain strides in life . . .

> [Mr.] Daniel said, "You can do anything you want to do, if you put your mind to it." . . . And I think we need to know that and that gives you a pride in your race. Look, there's a man just

---

[122] UCAC, *Relentless* 54-55.

Dedication Day at the Cardinal Gibbons Institute, October 18, 1925

Cardinal Gibbons Institute. "Courtesy of the St Mary's County Historical Society"

like you, same color same features and everything, and look what he's done; he's made progress in life. Instead of being a nobody, he becomes somebody.[123]

During the Great Depression, despite the fact that the high school had closed in 1933, the Institute provided skeleton programs of extension and welfare work. And after the high school re-opened in 1938, it continued to flourish.[124]

Although the Institute was tucked away in Ridge, Maryland, its purview was strikingly ambitious. It not only provided academic, vocational, and religious instruction to black students from across the United States, it also provided a night school for adults, and it organized group agricultural and health goals (such as sanitation and disease prevention) for the region.[125] Father McKenna remarked: "So the Cardinal Gibbons Institute is for the

---

123 UCAC, *Relentless* 67.

124 Combs, *History* 371-73. Beitzell, *Jesuit Missions* 293. McKenna, "Colored Catholics" 70-78. LaFarge, *Manner* 214-15.

125 McKenna, "Colored Catholics" 78.

lower St. Mary's County a Catholic high school, and for the whole country it is an extension and adult education, health and cultural center."[126]

The last graduating class of the Cardinal Gibbons Institute held its commencement in June 1967. The building itself was demolished in 1972, almost two decades after the 1954 *Brown* decision that paved the way for integration of all public schools, which implementation was delayed in St. Mary's County until the early Fall of 1967.[127]

4. Public Schools of St. Mary's County

At this juncture, however, we need to pause for a minute and ask a question: for the black children, were these *Catholic schools* any better than *the public schools?*

If you were a black who was not Catholic, the public schools, just like the private schools, were also racially segregated.[128]

Fortunately, St. Mary's County has saved one of these one-room schoolhouses in which young black children learned the basics of reading and arithmetic–but little else. The education of those children could best be described as "minimal."[129]

In the year 2006, Janice **Talbert** Walthour–aided by a phalanx of black readers and writers–published a book describing what those black-only, one-room *public* schools had actually been like. She (and her like-minded committee) titled this book *In Relentless Pursuit of an Education*, available

---

126 McKenna, "Colored Catholics." 70-72.

127 Combs, *History* 373. Beitzell, *Jesuit Missions* 290-92. McKenna, "Colored Catholics" 70-78. "The Cardinal Gibbons Institute." *St. Peter Claver Catholic Church*. Web. 29 July 2021. <https://www.stpeterclaverchurch.org>. See fn 84 above. There is a historical marker monument dedicated to the Cardinal Gibbons Institute (in a slightly different location nearby). *Hmdb.org*. "Cardinal Gibbons Institute." Web. 18 Sept. 2022. <https://www.hmdb.org/m.asp?m=128947>

128 It was not until the Fall of 1967 that full racial integration of all public schools became "the law of the land" in St. Mary's County. See fn 84 above.

129 The 1920 census revealed that of the 53 public elementary schools in the County, 43 of them had just *one room* and *one teacher*. And it would not be not until 1927 that the County would open its first public high school (Great Mills). Fausz, J. Frederick. *Monument School of the People: A sesquicentennial history of St. Mary's College of Maryland, 1840-1990*. St. Mary's City, Md.: St. Mary's College of Maryland; 1st Ed., 1990. 66. Print.

today in the bookstore of St. Mary's College, and also on the second floor of the St. Mary's County Historical Society in Leonardtown (see fn 54 above).

If you were black–but *not* Catholic–and you sent your child to a school that was "public," how much "education" could you get?

Probably not much.

What follows is a pastiche of the "education" which black students were receiving in the early-to-mid 20th century in those one-room public schoolhouses.[130]

> "In a one-room school you might have forty with a seat about two feet wide. A big one here and a big one here and a little one in the middle." (Pearl **Thompson** Furey; p. 30.)

> "The black schools were pitiful because we got all the cast-offs, the junk, the broken-down desks, . . . the books with pages tore out. . . . You got blackboards that was chipped. You got erasers that was wore out. You did not get any new equipment in black schools. . . . Everything else was hand-me-downs and stuff that a lot of it should have been thrown in the dump. But here again, it was better than what we had because without that we had nothing." (Clarence Carroll Smith; p. 30.)

> "[T]he whites would have a nice school, and we'd have a terrible old school–an old shanty school. You know, no water, no toilet, and some of the people would have to go build a toilet if they wanted us to have it." (Pearl **Thompson** Furey; p. 16.)

> "[A]t that time the whites called blacks, you know, "Aunt" and "Uncle." My father was always known as Uncle Bunton. . . . Miss Dent, who was superintendent of schools, was introducing Mrs. Mack to someone and she started to call her Aunt Aggie. . . . Before she got it all out, "au-au-aunt–" "Don't you do it, don't you do it. If you can't call me Mrs. Mack, don't you call me nothing!' . . . So then after that I think Miss Dent began to recognize the teachers as Mr. or Mrs." (Leroy Thompson; p. 21.)

---

130 All ten quotations are to be found in the book *In Relentless Pursuit of an Education*, at the pages cited at the conclusion of each such excerpt. UCAC, *Relentless* 30, 30, 16, 21, 27, 27, 29, 30, 31, 91.

> "Back then some of those children came to school with nothing to eat. So, how were they going to learn?" (Elvare **Smith** Gaskin; p. 27.)

> "When we were in the 4th and 5th Grade, Miss Ella [Thompson] let us teach the 1st Grade 'cause she had seven grades every day. Can you imagine that? In a one-room school?" (Angela Marie **Thomas** Maddox; p. 27.)

> "My favorite teachers when I was in school turned out later to be not my favorite teachers. The ones that let me play and have a good time, now, they didn't help me too much at all. It was the ones that I did not like that had the positive influence. And, I suppose that's [true] with all kids." (James W. Neal; p. 29.)

> "There were, I'd say, about thirty or forty kids going to that same one-room school. . . . We got to Jarboesville [a new location] and we had these bathrooms and all that [good] stuff. I couldn't believe it. We were going to school in a mansion!" (Leon M. Briscoe; p. 30.)

> "It was a one-room school and the teacher had to get there and make the fire and keep it going, and she did just that. . . . The books were used when you got them and you couldn't take them home. . . . The boys made their ball out of old clothing and stockings and paper and stuff, and then they would get a piece of wood out of the woods for their bat. That's what they used." (Viola T. Cutchember; pp. 30-31.)

And finally from Vivian Jordan (secretary to the president of St. Mary's College of Maryland):

> "But we never heard the word 'college.' It was not expected of us. Only the people who were making straight A's were ever talked to about it and encouraged to go. A lot of us missed out on that." (Vivian Rose **Hanson** Jordan; p. 91.)

And that was life in the so-called "public" schools.

The "private" (Catholic) schools were only marginally better. However, the Cardinal Gibbons Institute (the somewhat-private Catholic high school) had enjoyed the considerable benefit of headmaster Victor Daniel, that 2009 graduate from Tuskegee Institute, whose work we have already seen.

Eventually, integration of all public schools became the norm in St. Mary's County, but not until 1967, when "colored" schools were torn down, burned to the ground, or left in limbo for future persons to "discover."

E. THE DISAPPEARED ENCYCLICAL

By early August of 1925, Father LaFarge was told that he had been re-assigned–not, however, within St. Mary's County–but much farther north, to Campion House in New York City. There he was to become Associate Editor of all Jesuit publications. Yet he managed to delay his departure for a year, until early August of 1926.

Following his removal from St. Mary's County in 1926, for the next twelve years, Father LaFarge enjoyed meeting fellow Jesuits in New York City. Here, in the Jesuits' Campion House, he published at least ten books, many on both race and theology (see fn 3 above). He was also earning an enviable reputation as a public speaker.

Additionally, he mailed to Pope Pius XI a copy of his book *Interracial Justice* (published in 1937).[131]

What would become of it? Would the Pope even bother to read it?

(Pope Pius XI *did*.)[132]

In May of 1938–and on assignment from *America*–Father LaFarge now left the United States on board one of several steamers carrying passengers "back and forth" to the United States. (Generally it was "forth" as refugees were already fleeing persecutions from the Nazis.) Father LaFarge made plans to return to the United States by the end of August–but only after he discovered what was happening vis-a-vis the Nazis.[133]

---

[131] LaFarge, *Manner* 274.

[132] The Pope exclaimed to LaFarge: "'Interrracial justice,' *c'est bon*!" LaFarge, *Manner* 273. Murphy, James H., Rev. "John LaFarge, S.J. and The Unity of the Human Race." *John J. Burns Library's Blog*. Blog at WordPress.com, 1 Sept. 2015. Web. 30 July 2021. <https://johnjburnslibrary.wordpress.com>. Hereafter cited as Murphy, *LaFarge and Unity*.

[133] LaFarge, *Manner* 253-54, 260.

This was to be a fact-finding trip to Europe: first to Germany, then Austria, and finally to Hungary. Back-tracking, he would not enter Rome itself until June 5th of 1938.[134] In Rome, however, he was astounded and mystified to receive *a hand-written letter of invitation from Pope Pius XI*. This invitation requested a one-on-one meeting with the Pope (by now in his early eighties, and visibly frail.)[135]

During their June 25th meeting in Castel Gandolfo, south of Rome, Pope Pius XI told Father LaFarge that he wanted him to draft an "encyclical"– to be written in French, German, and English–*but promulgated from the Vatican*. They conversed in French, after first dabbling in English, Italian, and German.[136]

Stunned by this request, Father LaFarge wrote the following to an old friend, Father Joseph A. Murphy. This memorandum was dated July 3, 1938, and labeled as follows:

> *Confidential*: Father Maher may have written to you what really did happen at the audience. What happened was that the Pope put me under secrecy, and enjoined upon me to write the text of an Encyclical for the universal Church, on the topic which he considered is most burning at the present time. . . .
>
> *"Say simply,"* he told me, *"what you would say if you yourself were pope."*
>
> . . .
>
> He then outlined the topic, its method of treatment, and discussed the underlying principles.

---

134 LaFarge, *Manner* 257-70. Eisner, Peter. *The Pope's Last Crusade: How an American Jesuit Helped Pope Pius XI's Campaign to Stop Hitler.* New York: HarperCollins Publishers, 2013. 52. Print. Hereafter cited as Eisner, *Pope's Last Crusade*.

135 LaFarge, *Manner* 272. Eisner, *Pope's Last Crusade* 55-56, 59. Passelecq, Georges, and Suchecky, Bernard. *The Hidden Encyclical of Pius XI*. 1995. Trans. Steven Rendall. New York: Harcourt Brace & Company, 1997. 35. Print. Hereafter cited as Passelecq & Suchecky, *Hidden Encyclical*.

136 Eisner, *Pope's Last Crusade* 58-61. Although Passelecq and Suchecky identify June 22nd as the date of this one-on-one meeting (based upon a micro-fiched admission ticket; *Hidden Encyclical*, 35, fn 39), it seems more likely that Eisner's date of June 25th is accurate because he references both a June 22nd visit "attending a general audience" *and* a private audience on the 25th at 11:45 a.m.. Eisner, *Pope's Last Crusade* 54, 56. See also LaFarge, *Manner* 272-74 (published in 1954), which is silent as to the Pope's request for an encyclical rejecting anti-Semitism and racism.

> He told me he would write–which he did–to the V.R. Fr. [Very Reverend Father] General [Ledóchowski], asking him to give me every facility.[137]

The Pope then told Father LaFarge that no one else in the Vatican knew about this decision–not even Superior General Ledóchowski, the leader of the Jesuit order.[138]

> "Properly, I should first have taken this up with Father Ledóchowski before speaking to you," the pope said. But he had not. "I imagine it will be all right . . . after all, a pope is a pope."[139]

In this confidential memo, Father LaFarge continued to express his astonishment to Father Murphy:

> Frankly, I am simply stunned, and all I can say is that the Rock of Peter has fallen on my head. Had I anticipated such a terrific development, nothing would have persuaded me even to go to Rome, much less see the Pope. As it is, nothing to do but go through with the whole thing, as Fr. General says. ....

---

[137] Passelecq & Suchecky, *Hidden Encyclical* 36-37 (italics in original). If "Father Maher" refers to Zacheus Maher, then apparently around 1932, "he moved to the Vatican and became the assistant for North America to Wlodimir Ledóchowski, 26th Superior General of the Society of Jesus." "Zacheus J. Maher" *Wikipedia*. Web. 15 August 2022. <https://en.wikipedia.org/wiki/Zacheus_J._Maher>.

[138] Ledóchowski was a powerful figure at the Vatican. Eisner, *Pope's Last Crusade* 76-78. According to a Wikpedia article on Father Ledóchowski, the "Very Rev. Wlodzimierz . . . Halka Ledóchowski, S.J. (7 October 1866 – 13 December 1942) was a Polish nobleman who was the twenty-sixth Superior-General of the Society of Jesus from 11 February 1914 until his death. Prior to taking holy orders, he was briefly a page in the Habsburg Court." "Wlodimir_ Ledóchowski" *Wikipedia*. Web. 30 July 2021. <https://en.wikipedia.org/wiki/Wlodimir_ Ledóchowski>.

[139] Eisner, *Pope's Last Crusade* 61. On July 17th, 1938, Ledóchowski sent a letter to LaFarge urging him the utmost discretion as to this secret mission. And LaFarge's co-drafter, Gustav Gundlach, also warned him about the Gestapo. Eisner, *Pope's Last Crusade* 96-100.

It appears that the archives at St. Peter Claver Church may have some of the postcards sent by Father LaFarge to Father McKenna in 1938. For example, there were two handwritten postcards mailed from France addressed to Father McKenna simply at "Ridge, St. Mary's County, Maryland, États-Unis d'Amérique" (postmarked August 22 and September 19). There is also a letter from Father LaFarge's secretary at *America* dated September 7th, informing Father McKenna that Father LaFarge would not be back until the beginning of October at the earliest. Two postcards and a letter, all dated 1938; presumably kept in the archives at St. Peter Claver Church, Ridge, Maryland.

In these archives, there was also a document that was discovered that states that Father LaFarge was being sent by the U.S. State Department. So [the plot thickens], was LaFarge *also* acting as a spy?

And when did LaFarge become aware of what Fathers Maher and Ledóchowski had–or had not done–with his encyclical?

> The very day of the [Papal] audience, I was all ready to engage passage back on the *Staatendam*, which should bring me to the States August 27.[140]

Thus, altering his travel-plans, during the Summer of 1938, LaFarge worked in Paris, assisted by two other Jesuits, Gustav Gundlach and Gustave Desbuquois, secretly drafting the encyclical requested by Pope Pius XI.[141]

In late September 1938, LaFarge hand-delivered the draft encyclical (translated into the requisite French, German, English, and Latin) to Father Ledóchowski in Rome.[142] The opening words in Latin were *Humani generis unitas*–thus it would be titled "The Unity of the Human Race."

Father LaFarge did make it back to the United States, but not until early October of 1938.

And after that–nothing.

As noted by professor James O'Toole: "If issued, the encyclical would stand as an unequivocal denunciation of Hitler and his plans for the Holocaust."[143]

However, after their confidential meeting in Castel Gandolfo in June of 1938,[144] it appears that LaFarge did not have any further meetings with Pope Pius XI, who by the time of LaFarge's delivery of the draft encyclical to Superior General Ledóchowski (September 1938), was in delicate health and would die on February 10, 1939.

In a coded letter dated October 16th to LaFarge, Father Gundlach let him know that Ledóchowski had essentially played him and had thus far managed to "sabotage" the Pope's plan to issue the encyclical. Two weeks later, LaFarge wrote a letter to the Pope, informing him that he had delivered the draft encyclical to Ledóchowski in late September, and he asked the apostolic delegate in Washington to ensure that this letter reached the

---

140 Passelecq & Suchecky, *Hidden Encyclical* 37, 38.
141 Passelecq & Suchecky, *Hidden Encyclical* 57-65. Eisner, *Pope's Last Crusade* 89-115.
142 Passelecq & Suchecky, *Hidden Encyclical* 64-65. Eisner, *Pope's Last Crusade* 115-117.
143 Murphy, *LaFarge and Unity*, citing professor James O'Toole.
144 Murphy, *LaFarge and Unity*, citing professor James O'Toole.

Pope's hands. However, it is not clear whether, in fact, the Pope did actually receive LaFarge's letter.[145]

In mid-January 1939, after having recovered from heart problems, Pope Pius XI demanded that Ledóchowski give him the draft encyclical delivered by LaFarge. Thus, barely four months after LaFarge's delivery, the encyclical was finally in the Pope's hands. Accompanying the encyclical was a cover letter from Ledóchowski, who proposed scrapping LaFarge's version and replacing it with a version that *he* would draft.[146]

The Pope's meeting–scheduled for February 11th–to discuss the publication of the encyclical was balked by his own death on February 10th.

> Pius XI planned to issue the [LaFarge] encyclical following his meeting with bishops on 11 February, but died [just one day] before both the meeting and encyclical's promulgation could take place.[147]

According to *Time* magazine, the Pope's last words had been: "'I still have so many things to do.'"[148]

On March 2, 1939, Eugenio Maria Giuseppe Giovanni Pacelli was elected to assume the Papal throne, and–as Pope Pius XII–ruled until October 1958.

So, whatever happened to the draft encyclical and its translations?

On the one hand, the encyclical condemning anti-Semitism and racism was never issued. It had disappeared. Or, perhaps more correctly, it had been disappeared. Presumably in the vast archives of the Vatican.[149]

On the other hand, some of LaFarge's arguments condemning racism were promulgated in another encyclical, "*Summi Ponfiticatus*," issued by Pope Pius XII in the Fall of 1939:

---

145 Eisner, *Pope's Last Crusade* 136-37, 145-46, 165.

146 Eisner, *Pope's Last Crusade* 170-71.

147 "Pope Pius XI." *Wikipedia*. Web. 30 July 2021. <https://en.wikipedia.org/wiki/Pope_Pius_XI#cite_note-101>. See Passelecq & Suchecky, *Hidden Encyclical* 151.

148 Eisner, *Pope's Last Crusade* 183, citing "Religion: Death of a Pope." *Time* February 20, 1939.

149 Passelecq & Suchecky, *Hidden Encyclical* 151-52.

According to the authors, Pius XII was not aware of the text before the death of his predecessor. . . . He chose not to publish its specific statements regarding Judaism and regarding persecution of Jews. However, his first encyclical *Summi Pontificatus (On the Supreme Pontificate*, October 12, 1939), published after the beginning of World War II, has an echo of the previous title in its title: **On the Unity of Human Society** and uses many of the general arguments of the text. *Summi Pontificatus* sees Christianity as universalized and opposed to every form of racial hostility and every claim of racial superiority. There are no real racial differences: the human race forms a unity, because "one ancestor [God] made all nations to inhabit the whole earth".[150]

As to Father LaFarge, he did not refer to the hidden, or disappeared, encyclical until shortly before his own death in 1963–at which time he told the full story to his fellow Jesuits at Campion House.[151]

In December 1972, the *National Catholic Reporter* revealed that LaFarge had drafted an encyclical against anti-Semitism, which "'would have broken the much criticized Vatican silence on the persecution of Jews in Europe, before and during the Second World War.'"[152]

In 1995, *L'Encyclique Cachée de Pie XI*, written by Georges Passelecq (a Benedictine monk) and Bernard Suchecky (a Jewish historian) was first published in France, including the text of the abridged French version of the draft encyclical.[153]

---

[150] "*Humani generis unitas.*" (Emphasis in original.) *Wikipedia*. Web. 30 July 2021. <https://en.wikipedia.org/wiki/Humani_generis_unitas>.

[151] Eisner, *Pope's Last Crusade* 227.

[152] Eisner, *Pope's Last Crusade* 225-226, citing *National Catholic Reporter* associate editor Jim Castelli.

[153] In 1997, the English version was published, *The Hidden Encyclical of Pius XI*, translated from the French by Steven Rendall. A translation of the abridged French version of the draft encyclical by S. Rendall is at pp. 176-275.

However, it was not until 2006 that the silence of Pope Pius XI's archives was finally dispelled.[154]

Although the draft encyclical and related historical documents had, or were, "disappeared" for over half a century, they have now seen the light of day.[155]

One can only speculate as to how the currents of history may have shifted if Pope Pius XI had lived on this Earth just one more day.

---

[154] Eisner, *Pope's Last Crusade* 228. This finally happened: "In June 2006, [when] Pope Benedict XVI ordered all documents from the reign of Pius XI in the Vatican Secret Archives to be opened,[6] and on September 18, 2006 over 30,000 documents were made available to researchers.[7]" "*Humani generis unitas.*" Wikipedia. Web. 16 June 2022. <https://en.wikipedia.org/wiki/Humani_generis_unitas>

[155] However, the draft encyclical has been the subject of criticism: "Although the draft clearly condemned racism and anti-Semitism, the document is deeply grounded in anti-Judaism.[2] The draft criticizes the majority of post-Messianic Jews for not acknowledging Jesus Christ as the true Jewish Messiah.[8]" "*Humani generis unitas.*" Wikipedia. Web. 30 July 2021. <https://en.wikipedia.org/wiki/Humani_generis_unitas>.

Chapter 9

Adele France: Ornaments No Longer [1]

In a tapestry, if one examines closely, certain "guiding" threads create story-lines and unfolding scenes. With her gumption and goals, Adele France wove with strong, vibrant threads to revitalize Maryland's "living monument." Calmly and relentlessly, she led St. Mary's through existential crises. She used bold innovation.

The story-line evolved from a "Female Seminary" that offered elementary and high school education for girls and young women (most of whom boarded there) to a "Junior College" for both women and men, thus wefting

---

[1] Sources for this Chapter (especially those before 2023) include the following entities: the Historical Society of Kent County, Maryland; Washington College Archives; The Woman's Literary Club of Chestertown; Kent County Public Library; Kent County News (on microfilm); Kent County Land Records; Chester Cemetery, Chestertown; Chestertown Volunteer Fire Department; State of Maryland Archives and census records; Columbia University Archives and Alumni Center; St. Mary's County Historical Society; and St. Mary's College of Maryland Archives. See Acknowledgments section thanking individuals who provided valuable assistance

Although correspondence in the Archives at St. Mary's reveals a picture of a woman who had energy, ideas, and unrelenting determination, there are not many written accounts about Adele France. And Time has not permitted this researcher to continue delving into further burrows and tunnels to uncover more documents, as she did with the Horsey Collection and the Chestertown time-capsule. See Chapter 4-A-2 & 4-A-3.

and warping the tapestry for St. Mary's College to be later designated as a National Public Honors College by the Legislature of Maryland in 1992.

A. ADDIE AND THE CHESTERTOWN YEARS

Mary Adele France was born on the Eastern Shore of Maryland, in Quaker Neck, on the outskirts of Chestertown, on February 17, 1880. Four years later, her parents, Emma Price ("Pricie") DeCorse and Thomas Dashiell France, moved into their new home in Chestertown, known as the Dougherty-Barroll house on High Street.[2] Tom France had left farming to instead run a wood-and-coal business with his brother-in-law, James DeCorse, near the corner of Cannon and Queen Streets.

Adele's family and friends called her "Addie."

Addie would focus on education throughout her lifetime.

At the age of 14, she entered the public preparatory school for Washington College. Fortunately for Addie, those prep-school courses were taught by college faculty, and Washington College was just up the road from her childhood home in Chestertown. (Three years earlier, in 1891, when she was 11, Washington College had begun to admit women as college students.)

When she was 16, Addie was admitted to the four-year liberal arts program at Washington College (1896). Once enrolled, she and her female friends started wearing their long hair piled high on top on their heads, just like their mothers. (The concept of "teenager" would not emerge until World War II.) Even at 16 or 17, they were described as "ladies" and would have been tightly corseted, their skirts sweeping the ground. They were always chaperoned.

---

[2] Today, this building is two separate residences (Nos. 108 & 110). However, at the time of the purchase, it was a single residence, sold to Tom and Pricie France by Joseph Wickes and his wife, A.R. Wickes. It was Pricie, not Tom, who had enough money to make the down-payment, but the mortgage was signed by them both as husband and wife and paid off early–in six years. See Chapter 4-A-1, fn 6.

Addie majored in what would have been intrepid fields for a woman at that time–math and physics. Ever practical, Addie also studied on a parallel track to get a Teacher's Certificate from Washington College.[3]

Addie was not what we today would call a "nerd." She enjoyed extracurricular and social activities. In addition to her academic responsibilities, while at college: she started an athletic club for women;[4] she was president (and later vice-president) of the avant garde women's debating society, the Pieria Literary Society; and she was able to maneuver herself onto the all-male editorial board of the college newspaper, *The Washington Collegian*, from Fall 1898 through Spring 1900.[5]

When she was just 20 years old, on June 20, 1900, Mary Adèle France earned a Bachelor's degree from Washington College.[6] She had majored in math and physics.[7] She was the fourth woman to receive a B.A. from

---

[3] Professional opportunities for women–who did not even have the right to vote–were paltry and generally limited to teaching and nursing. "Between 1900 and 1910, 70 percent of the graduates of St. Mary's Female Seminary (fifty-seven out of eighty-one) adopted teaching as a profession." Fausz, J. Frederick. *Monument School of the People: A sesquicentennial history of St. Mary's College of Maryland, 1840-1990*. St. Mary's City, Md.: St. Mary's College of Maryland; 1st Ed., 1990. 55. Print. Hereafter cited as Fausz.

[4] "Feminine Athletic Club – Organized By The Young Lady Students of Washington College-Joint Literary Debate." *The Sun*, 21 March 1898. Web. GenealogyBank.com. Copyrighted by NewsBank and/or the American Antiquarian Society, 2004.

[5] As an alumna, she again inserted herself onto the male-run board of the [Washington] College Alumni Association, probably from 1900 through 1904. Her title was Secretary. See Chapter 4-A-1 at fn 8.

[6] Dumschott, Fred W. *Washington College*. Chestertown, MD: Washington College, 1980. 223. Print. Hereafter cited as Dumschott, *Washington College*. Landskroener, Marcia C., ed. and Thompson, William L., comp. *Washington: The College at Chester*. Chestertown, MD: The Literary House Press at Washington College, 2000. 72, 81. Print. Hereafter cited as *Washington College at Chester*.

She signed her name with the French "grave accent" for Adèle on a page signed by her fellow classmates for the invitation for the Class of 1900 Graduation Exercises.

Professionally, she would later sign her name as "M. Adele France."

[7] Fausz 61. At the time, Washington College had three "courses of study": Classical, Scientific, and Modern Language. In all likelihood, Addie enrolled in the "Scientific Course of Study" (this is merely a hunch). See archives at Washington College, although the fire of 1916 destroyed many of the college's records.

Washington College.[8] She also earned a Teaching Certificate.[9] Ranked second in her class, she delivered one of two orations at the graduation ceremony for the Class of 1900.[10]

Three years later, at age 23, she earned a Master's Degree–probably in the "Scientific Course of Study" since her forte was math and physics–from Washington College in 1903.[11]

Undaunted by subtle (and not so subtle) constraints imposed on women, Addie opened her own school in Chestertown in 1903 and ran it until 1909, when she left her hometown to accept a paid teaching position at St. Mary's Female Seminary.[12]

In the early 1900s, probably 1903, Addie established The Woman's Literary Club of Chestertown ("WLC"), which continues to thrive to this day. But this was not a mere social club. No, not at all. Addie planned to use the WLC as a *vehicle to provide education* for women. And in 1904, the WLC was formally incorporated so that it could participate in, and pay tuition for, the "Correspondence-Study Department" of the University of Chicago. These correspondence courses lasted at least into the 1930s. Today, the WLC

---

[8] The 1942 (second quarter) publication of the *Washington Alumnus* states that: "She graduated with the A.B. degree in 1900, the *fourth woman* to have received a degree from the College." "Three Women Will Receive Degrees at Commencement Exercises May 25." *The Washington Alumnus* XII.2 (1942): 1 (emphasis added). Print. Hereafter cited as 1942-2Q Issue *Washington Alumnus*. However, other sources indicate she was the fifth woman to have received a degree from Washington College.

[9] "Washington College–Graduates in the Collegiate and Normal Departments." *The Sun*, 19 June 1900. Web. GenealogyBank.com. Copyrighted by NewsBank and/or the American Antiquarian Society, 2004.

[10] "The Commencement Proper." *The Washington Collegian* [a monthly student paper] Vol. 3, No. 5 (June 1900): 9. Print. Chestertown, MD: Washington College.

[11] Dumschott, *Washington College* 223. *Washington College at Chester* 72. 1942-2Q Issue *Washington Alumnus* 1. See also archives at Washington College; unfortunately, the fire of 1916 destroyed many of the college's records. However, there *is* a graduation photo of Adele wearing a master's gown with the typically long sleeves.

[12] We do not know what kind of school it was or even where it was located. Speculating, it is possible that she could have run it from the ample family home on High Street. See also Chapter 4-A-1 at fn 10.

has again become a reading club, but it sprang from remarkable origins: Chestertown's first experiment with adult education in the early 1900s.[13]

Addie also pioneered what would become the Public Library in Chestertown–founded by the WLC In 1907. When the Young Men's Club of Chestertown disbanded in 1907, they gave their book collection to the WLC, which promptly donated it to the library.[14] Addie has been recognized as "instrumental in starting the Public Library [of Chestertown] which has grown, affording pleasure to thousands."[15] In the 1909 Time Capsule, Addie noted that the library was "under the direction of the" WLC, and that members of the WLC "act as Librarians, one each week."[16]

For the first two or even three decades of the twentieth century, an entire generation of Chestertown women was provided with the possibility of education at the hands of the WLC. They were also provided with this fledgling library that welcomed them for pleasure reading. Theirs was a generation in which men (white men) were routinely supported with a college education and the start in a profession–but what was the point (so went the argument) of wasting college money on a woman who was only going to marry and raise one baby after another, year after year after year?

---

13 See Chapter 4-A-2 & 4-A-3.

After the Revolutionary War, there was a sense of self-awareness and pride which fomented great interest in "adult education" in the United States. About a generation before the Civil War, "lyceums" had sprung up–sites that sponsored public lectures on literature, science, and sometimes, political causes. Although lyceums withered during and after the Civil War, beginning in the 1870s, "Chautauquas" (named after Methodist retreats at Lake Chautauqua in western New York state) became popular. Chautauquas offered concerts, plays, and perhaps magic shows, in addition to lyceum-type lectures. By the 1920s, Chautauquas faded because of the arrival of radio entertainment. See Chapter 3-B-2.

For those who could not travel to New York in the summer or did not have traveling Chautauquas nearby, in the late 19th Century, the Chautauqua Institute experimented with what we would today call "distance learning," but which they called "correspondence courses." It was not long before universities realized that they could charge tuition for rigorous correspondence courses that would be overseen by bona fide faculty scholars, as did the University of Chicago in 1898.

14 In order to learn procedures for printing up library jackets and cards, Addie corresponded with a library in Philadelphia in 1909. This correspondence is some of the evidence from the water-logged collection that Joan Horsey of Chestertown saved. See Chapter 4-A-2 & 4-A-3.

15 Luckett, Margie H. *Maryland Women*, Vol. 2. Baltimore, Md: King Bros.,Inc., Press, 1937. 120. Print. Hereafter cited as *Maryland Women*.

16 See Chapter 4-A-2.

That generation of women–which could not yet vote–would be followed by one that was beginning to take women's higher education for granted and that could keep up with current events not only by newspaper but also by listening to that new invention, the radio. The WLC took the cultural cue, answered the need, and developed into the reading club that it is today, well over a century later.

Why has Adele France gone without recognition?

First, both of her parents died by the time she became Principal at St. Mary's Female Seminary in 1923. Her only sibling, a younger sister, had married and gone to live outside New York City, on Long Island. As a result, the France name became increasingly unknown in Chestertown.

But the greater reason is that Adele France never sought personal recognition. In Chestertown, as later at St. Mary's, her focus was entirely on the job at hand, be it her little private school, the WLC, or the Chestertown Public Library. And in all these cases–as later when she became head of St. Mary's–she urged girls and women to take stock of themselves and take steps to achieve their full potential.

She did all this before she was 30 years old–and before she ever left town.

If Adele France's life were to be summed up in one sentence, it would look something like this: The goal of her entire life was to educate girls and women to recognize their inborn abilities and cultivate their skills. (As the U.S. Army's advertising slogan would much later proclaim, "to be all that they could be"). Adele's thinking echoed that of women's-rights pioneer Elizabeth **Cady** Stanton, who wrote the following at the age of 45, while married with seven children.

> Men think that self-sacrifice is the most charming of all the cardinal virtues for women, and in order to keep it in healthy working order, they make opportunities for its illustration

as often as possible. I would fain teach women that self-development is a higher duty than self-sacrifice.[17]

Self-development for women–eclipsing self-sacrifice. Even today, this concept rings revolutionary. Instead of "parlor arts" imbued by finishing schools for young women, Adele France focused on academic learning. Not that they had to be academically brilliant. They only had to respect their individual talents–and to not submit to any stereotype of feminine inferiority. The key to this awakening was to be education.

The time is past when we educated our daughters for ornaments only; woman has an economic place in the world, which it is her duty to fulfill to the best of her ability.[18]

Throughout her life, Adele France never modified nor wavered from this strong belief.

B. ADDIE BECOMES "MISS FRANCE"

In 1909, Addie closed down her little school in Kent County in order to take on her first paid teaching position at the Female Seminary ("seminary" being an older name for "school" or "academy") in St. Mary's County.[19] But running her Chestertown school had given her an opportunity, while still in her early 20s, to put into practice the educational theories she had learned at Washington College.

Adele France built up her career in education by teaching and by taking on management roles.

---

17 **Cady** Stanton, Elizabeth. *The Woman's Bible*. 1895. Project Gutenberg. 1950. Chapter VII, Exodus xxxii. Posting Date: November 3, 2011 [EBook #9880] <www.gutenberg.org.> See also Chapters 1-A and 5-A.

18 France, M. Adele. *Annual Prospectus for St. Mary's Female Seminary for 1924-1925*, at p.12. May 1924. Office of the Provost. Catalogs. RG 3.4.1, Box 1 "Prospectus 1924/1925." St. Mary's College of Maryland Archives. Hereafter cited as *1924-25 Prospectus*.

19 Addie's father, Thomas Dashiell France, had roots in St. Mary's County. His mother's family (Addie's grandparents) had been St. Mary Countians since colonial times. And her father's death certificate shows that he died in Mechanicsville, St. Mary's County.

In the Introduction: there are two maps depicting towns (local and regional with local inset). And a more comprehensive GIS map is at: https://tinyurl.com/Historical-Tapestry or at https://www.scribblemaps.com/maps/view/Overview-FINAL-locked/Overview-FINAL-locked

She taught math and physics at St. Mary's Female Seminary from 1909 to 1913 and also from 1917 to 1918.[20] When Adele crossed the Chesapeake Bay in 1909 to teach at St. Mary's, she would have found it a pleasure but perhaps also a frustration. Certainly it would have been an eye-opener.

As for the pleasures: she was now 29, and for the first time in her life, she would be teaching what we may assume were her favorite subjects–science and math. Moreover, even if she had never crossed the Bay as a child to visit relatives, now she would be in St. Mary's County where her paternal grandmother (Sarah Sanner) and perhaps even her grandfather (John France) had been born before moving to Baltimore. Also, she would now be in the "disappeared" city of St. Mary's, Maryland's first capital, and here she would be sure to learn of old religious battles–quite bloody battles–that had been waged in colonial times for political control. (The equivalent in our own times would be the hatreds in Northern Ireland; see Chapter 2.)

Yet above all, Adele would find herself in a school–a girls' boarding school, *not* a college–which had been founded in 1840 with the unusual mission of dealing with (and eradicating) that old religious bitterness.[21] This was something new in her experience, and her curiosity surely would have been piqued.

But if Adele was intrigued with the founding ethic of this female seminary, and if she was pleased that she was finally teaching math and science, nevertheless she was no longer in a position where she could make innovations. Whereas in Chestertown, she had been a trail-blazer by starting her own private school, founding the WLC, and launching the Public Library, here at St. Mary's she was only one among several teachers. Her innovative skills would be limited to how she managed her own classroom.

Adele was now living in a remote area of Southern Maryland, known chiefly for tobacco farms and ox-carts. She was now without the cultural resources of Chestertown, without the stimulus of Washington College,

---

20 Addie's mother died in 1914, and her father died in 1918.
21 See Chapters 3-C-4, 3-D and 5-B, 5-C, 5-D, 5-E, & 5-F.

and without easy access to Baltimore.[22] Perhaps she felt stranded in time–and place. (The sprawling naval base–and Lexington Park–would not arrive until World War II.)

Like the other teachers and students, her daily existence was confined to the Seminary's one building, the "Main Building" (also known then as the "Seminary Building" and now known as Calvert Hall). True, there was a second small building nearby, but it was used only for athletic games, musical events, and graduation exercises.[23] At that time, the Seminary generally graduated girls from the middle grades through 12th grade.

Everyone (Principal, teachers, and students) studied, taught, slept, and ate in the Main Building. Students wore uniforms, middy blouses and navy blue skirts.[24] For dietary reasons, Catholic girls ate at a separate table. *The Baltimore Sun* arrived by steamboat four or five times a week, but only twice in the winter. And quite striking for Adele would have been the absence of males: only one or two among the few day students (who were not allowed to eat lunch with the girls); and no social dances nor "calling" by young gentlemen on a Sunday afternoon. Absolutely not.

Adele taught in this environment for four years and was evidently well-liked. In 1913, she left to teach math and science at the Bristol School in Washington, D.C., but when her mother died in December 1914, Adele apparently returned to Chestertown. The next three or four years are murky, but she returned to teach at St. Mary's from 1917 to 1918. When

---

22 So, how *did* Addie land at the Female Seminary? Well, her uncle was a highly respected minister in Baltimore–the Reverend Joseph France. At some point during her college education, he asked Addie to chaperone his daughter by steamer back to her studies at the Female Seminary. While there, Addie met the Principal, Lucy **Lancaster** Maddox, who later urged her to join the faculty when she was ready. Then, after she began teaching at the Female Seminary, Mrs. Maddox told her that she wanted Adele to succeed her as Principal. France, M. Adele. "President Anticipates Unusual Commencement." *Signal News* [a monthly student paper]. St. Mary's City, MD: St. Mary's Female Seminary-Junior College, 23 October 1942, at p.3. Print. Office of the Dean of Students. Student Newspapers. RG 6.7.4 Box 1. St. Mary's College of Maryland Archives.

23 Fausz 33. Apparently, these musical events reveled in some glitz. The 1914-15 *Prospectus* touts "a handsome hall of Colonial style, fitted for the special use of the Music Department, with opera chairs, curtains, lights and pianos." Presumably, this was the "Music Hall" (today, St. Mary's Hall). *Annual Prospectus for St. Mary's Female Seminary for 1914-1915*, at p.12. [1914.] Office of the Provost. Catalogs. RG 3.4.1, Box 1 "Prospectus 1914/1915." St. Mary's College of Maryland Archives.

24 See Chapter 5-F, at fn 43.

her father died in 1918, she and her sister Emma (then married and living in New York) sold the family home on High Street in 1919.

Adele then took on management roles in public education.[25] She became Supervisor of Kent County Elementary Schools (on Maryland's Eastern Shore) from 1918-1920.[26] Then she traveled West to work as Supervisor of Shelby County Schools in Tennessee from 1920-1922.[27]

Context: in 1920, the 19th Amendment to the U.S. Constitution was enacted, guaranteeing–finally–women's right to vote.

Adele's next move was from Tennessee to New York City in 1922, where she enrolled at Teachers College, Columbia University, to study educational administration. At that time, Teachers College was Mecca for anyone interested in education, and that one, full year of hers in Manhattan must have been a stimulating experience. She would have become conversant with the latest theories and perhaps imagine how she herself might one day put them into practice.

By 1923, at the age of 43, she had earned yet another Master's degree, this time in Education.

---

[25] In June 2008, this author was introduced to a 90-year-old former schoolteacher in Chestertown who remembered that Addie had always kidded her because she (the schoolteacher) definitely did not want to become an administrator. Carrie Schreiber (retired teacher) in discussion with author (Janet Haugaard) during meeting in June 2008.

[26] 1942-2Q Issue *Washington Alumnus* 1. In the State Board of Education's Annual Report for 1918, M. Adele France is listed as the Attendance Officer for Kent County; and in the 1919 Annual Report, she is listed as the Elementary Supervisor for Kent County. State of Maryland Department of Education. *Fifty-Second Annual Report of the State Board of Education Showing Condition of the Public Schools of Maryland for the Year Ending July 31, 1918*. Baltimore: Baltimore City Printing and Binding Co., 1918. 211. Print. Annual Report for 1919, p.197. Print.

[27] 1942-2Q Issue *Washington Alumnus* 1. Historian Fausz states that Adele France was supervisor of "*secondary* schools in Nashville, Tennessee, and on Maryland's Eastern Shore." Fausz 61 (emphasis added). However, Margie Luckett states that Adele was "supervisor of *elementary* schools in Maryland and Tennessee" and that she co-authored "a course of study for elementary schools in Tennessee." *Maryland Women* 120 (emphasis added). Presumably, this was the *Course of Study for Elementary Grades*, published by the Public Schools of Tennessee in 1921. Holt, Andrew D. *The struggle for a state system of public schools in Tennessee, 1903-1936*. New York: Bureau of Publications, Teachers College, Columbia University, 1938. 324. Web. 05 January 2022. <https://babel.hathitrust.org/...>. Furthermore, although there is evidence that Adele France had worked in Memphis (Shelby County, Tennessee), it is not clear to this researcher whether she had *also* worked in Nashville (Davidson County, Tennessee). See for example, <https://en.wikipedia.org/wiki/Mary_Adele_France>. See also Chapter 4-A-2.

The ink was scarcely dry on her diploma when the trustees at St. Mary's unanimously elected M. Adele France to be the next Principal. At the time, St. Mary's Female Seminary offered classes from elementary through high school.

As described below, Miss France would wage vigorous battles to ensure the survival of the Seminary–and its evolution into an accredited four-year Junior College by the mid-20th Century.

Almost twenty years after she took the helm at St. Mary's, she would receive an honorary doctorate (Litt.D.) from Washington College in 1942. Adele France was in good company: Eleanor Roosevelt, who was standing right next to her, also received an honorary degree.[28] Proud of her honorary Doctorate, Adele France chose to wear her doctoral robe for her portrait, painted shortly after she resigned in 1948.

---

28 In 1942, Washington College celebrated the 50th anniversary of the presence of women at that college by awarding three honorary degrees. This would be the first time since it was founded in 1782 that Washington College had ever given an honorary degree to a woman. The awardees were Adele France, Eleanor Roosevelt, and Sophie **Kerr** Underwood. See photo of Ms. France's portrait.

C. MISS FRANCE BATTLES FOR ST. MARY'S

Barely half a year after stepping into the role of Principal, Adele France, known as "Miss France" at the Female Seminary, begins the first of her battles for what has now evolved into St. Mary's College of Maryland. Remarkably, Miss France also continues to teach the students.[29]

Historian Fausz characterizes her as "an inspired and affectionate leader" and as a "Margaret Brent for the modern age."[30]

1. First Battle – Rising from Charred Ruins

a. Fire Galvanizes Mettle

On the eve of her second semester as Principal: catastrophe. During Adele's first Christmas vacation, in early January 1924, a fire destroys the Main Building at St. Mary's.[31]

Whether or not their paths had crossed yet, by this time, Father LaFarge had already gotten wind of Adele France. He notes in his Desk Diary under the date for January 5, 1924: "St. Mary's Seminary burned down at 5:30 P.M. . . . The new principal, Miss France, heard of the disaster as she returned from her Christmas vacation and found all in ruins."[32] In the words of historian Regina **Combs** Hammett:

> Only the gutted brick walls remained standing. Miss M. Adele France, Principal at the time of the tragedy, began immediately

---

29 In an interview (August 9, 2010), at the age of 97, Dorothy Hope **Hodgkinson** Grace '29 spoke fondly of Miss France: "She was a very nice person, a brilliant mathematician and scientist. She taught me physics. . . . I'm forever grateful to her. And she ran a very good, caring institution for girls." RG 19 SlackWater Oral History collection, SMAO10010. St. Mary's College of Maryland Archives.

30 Fausz 61, 61. With reference to Margaret Brent, see Chapter 5-C, at fn 14.

31 It happened exactly eight years after William Smith Hall had burned down at Washington College. Conjecturing, it is possible that when Adele launched into a rebuilding campaign for the Female Seminary, she used the efforts of her old alma mater as an inspiration. Compare photo of the Main Building before the 1924 fire (in Chapter 4) with this photo of the remains of the Main Building after it was destroyed by the 1924 fire. In 1995, an alumna wrote that: "The Seminary itself is a large, yellow, brick building . . " (Archived photos of the pre-fire Main Building are black and white.) Yellow! This revelation is almost like an archeological discovery. RG 20 Janet Haugaard collection. St. Mary's College of Maryland Archives.

32 LaFarge Collection, Box 25, Folder 3, "Items from My Diary: August 1915 to 1926," Georgetown University Library; pp.1-24 (of what appears to be a typed transcription of a taped recording, p.17). Hereafter cited as LaFarge, *Desk Diary*. (See fn 110 below.)

to make plans for the rebirth of the Seminary. She was aided in this by the full cooperation of the emergency committee of the Board of Trustees of the Seminary.[33]

Yet there are also forces who want to *close down* the Female Seminary–forces whom Adele France vigorously opposes. She tenaciously fights back to keep the school open. Until temporary barracks are ready two months later,[34] everyone lives at either the rectory or at Miss Lizzie's (former Principal, Annie Elizabeth **Thomas** Lilburn) house down the hill. "Exactly four weeks after the fire, the school reopened with full attendance and with a full program in operation. . . . The job of rebuilding had begun immediately."[35]

---

[33] Hammett, Regina **Combs**. *History of St. Mary's County, Maryland: 1634-1990*. 2nd printing. Ridge, Md: R.C. Hammett, 1994. 342-43. Print. Hereafter cited as Combs, *History*.

[34] The caretaker's daughters, Polly and Irvanette Wood, indicated that the barracks were not built on site, but instead were *floated down the Chesapeake* by barge from Fort Meade. Haugaard, Janet B. and Wilkinson, Susan G. and King, Julia A., Eds. *St. Mary's: A "When-Did?" Timeline*. St. Mary's College of Maryland: St. Mary's Press, 2007. Entry for 1924. Print. Hereafter cited as St. Mary's, *Timeline*.

[35] Combs, *History* 343 (emphasis in original). See also Beitzell, Edwin."Early Schools of Southern Maryland." *Chronicles of St. Mary's*, Vol. 5 (March 1957). 34. Print.

b. Building on Heritage

Miss France, trustees, and alumnae enthusiastically raise funds for the rebuilding. Question: how to fund a complete renovation? Answer: Galvanizing the unique heritage of St. Mary's.

Two commemorating events are established: (1) Enactment Day; and (2) women's historical role in Maryland.

A couple of months after the fire, in March 1924, the Female Seminary celebrates its very first "Enactment Day" in observance of the 1840 legislation that had created it. In essence, this is part of Miss France's shrewd public-relations operation to raise funds for the rebuilding.

And in May 1924, the students at St. Mary's begin a tradition of performing for the public a historical pageant that "highlight[s] 'the part that woman has played in the history of Maryland.'"[36]

Four months after the fire, Miss France publishes the *Prospectus* (a catalogue for prospective students and parents) for the following academic year with a broad, bold vision.

> St. Mary's Seminary will undertake increasingly to lay the foundation for every type of work: for college, business, home-making, industry, fine arts, music. . . . The Principal . . . knows, too, the world's need of a self-respecting, humanity-serving, socially and economically efficient womanhood. Her idea is to build of one the other.[37]

Three tracks of curriculum are offered: General, Academic, and Commercial (business). Extra courses include Piano, Vocal, Art, Spanish, and German.[38]

Public enthusiasm for rebuilding is on full display with the Summer 1924 ceremony for the laying of the cornerstone of the soon-to-be-rebuilt Main Building–about 1,500 people attend.

---

36 Fausz 68.
37 *1924-25 Prospectus* 12, 13, 13.
38 *1924-25 Prospectus* 18, 20.

The keynote speaker, A.S. Goldsborough, proclaims that the principles enshrined by St. Mary's Female Seminary are the institutional antithesis of "the bigotry of 'religious fanatics' (like the revived Ku Klux Klan) . . . again threatening the ideal of toleration."[39]

Then, in 1925, barely a year and a half after the fire, a new Main Building-*with a third floor*-opens its doors. This building still stands today and is now called Calvert Hall (see fn 45 below). The new extra floor will allow Miss France to materialize her dream: transform the grade and high school into something new and radical–a public junior college and an increased number of students.

Miss France anchors St. Mary's by providing the local community with a further educational benefit: the Seminary accepts local boys as day students so they can earn a high-school diploma.[40] Clearly however, boys could not board at the Female Seminary. There was an exception in 1934, arising from

---

[39] Fausz 70. See also LaFarge, *Desk Diary*, p.19 (emphasis added), noting "Cecilia Roberts, a Catholic lady who was present at the laying of the first cornerstone *eighty years ago*. Now 87, hale and hearty and active, she well remembered the occasion." See photo of the "new"' Main Building, re-built in 1925.

[40] Combs, *History* 344. "St. Mary's Female Seminary had long accepted local boys as day students and was prepared [in 1924] to provide them with even *more* educational opportunities in the near future. Captain Alexander Kennedy's son had attended the Seminary as early as 1902 . . . ." Fausz 66 (emphasis added).

347

a scarlet-fever outbreak that required a three-week quarantine, which two of the "day" boys described as "a delightful situation."[41]

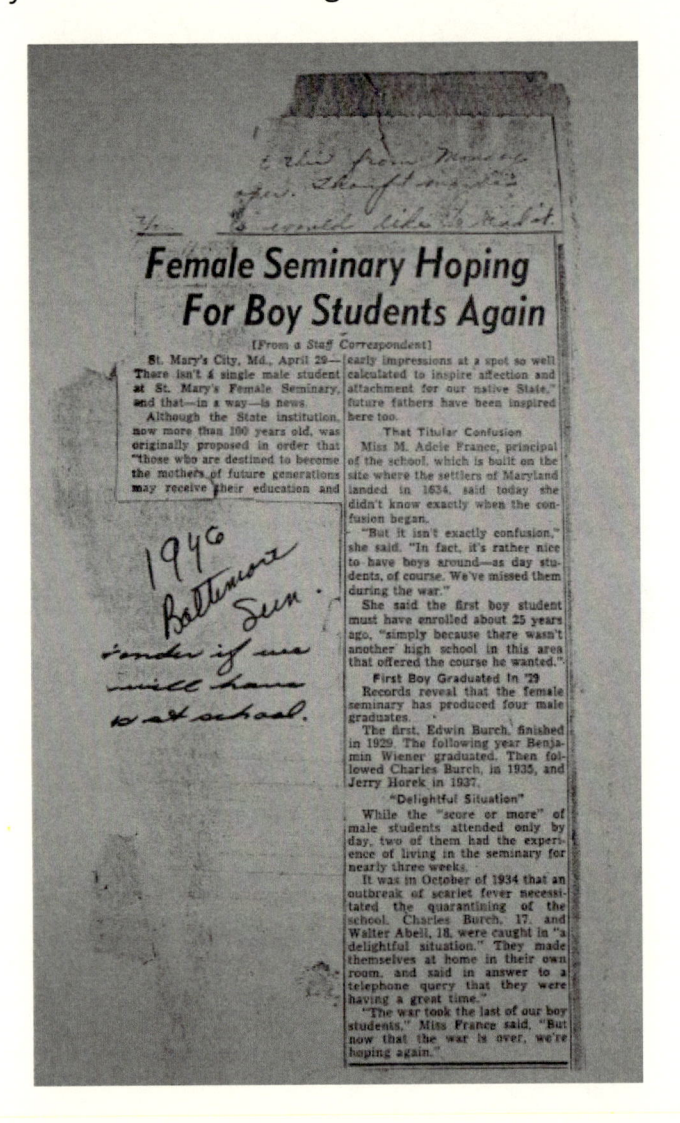

Female Seminary Hoping For Boy Students Again

[From a Staff Correspondent]

St. Mary's City, Md., April 29—There isn't a single male student at St. Mary's Female Seminary, and that—in a way—is news.

Although the State institution, now more than 100 years old, was originally proposed in order that "those who are destined to become the mothers of future generations may receive their education and early impressions at a spot so well calculated to inspire affection and attachment for our native State," future fathers have been inspired here too.

That Titular Confusion

Miss M. Adele France, principal of the school, which is built on the site where the settlers of Maryland landed in 1634, said today she didn't know exactly when the confusion began.

"But it isn't exactly confusion," she said. "In fact, it's rather nice to have boys around—as day students, of course. We've missed them during the war."

She said the first boy student must have enrolled about 25 years ago, "simply because there wasn't another high school in this area that offered the course he wanted."

First Boy Graduated In '29

Records reveal that the female seminary has produced four male graduates.

The first, Edwin Burch, finished in 1929. The following year Benjamin Wiener graduated. Then followed Charles Burch, in 1935, and Jerry Horek in 1937.

"Delightful Situation"

While the "score or more" of male students attended only by day, two of them had the experience of living in the seminary for nearly three weeks.

It was in October of 1934 that an outbreak of scarlet fever necessitated the quarantining of the school. Charles Burch, 17, and Walter Abell, 18, were caught in "a delightful situation." They made themselves at home in their own room, and said in answer to a telephone query that they were having a great time.

"The war took the last of our boy students," Miss France said, "But now that the war is over, we're hoping again."

---

41 "Female Seminary Hoping for Boy Students Again." According to a handwritten note attached to a newspaper clipping, this article appears to have been published in *The Baltimore Sun* on April 29, probably in 1946 (page number unknown). *However*, the actual edition of this newspaper has not been found–yet. Over half a dozen archivists and librarians have searched for this article, exploring many newspapers in addition to *The Baltimore Sun*.

The seeming "ghosting" of this article has a mundane explanation. First, in the mid-1940s, *The Baltimore Sun* printed several editions a day. It is likely that the college received the early edition of the daily newspaper because it would have had to be transported all the way down to rural Southern Maryland. *The Baltimore Sun* printed several editions a day, and some of the "early edition" stories would be replaced later that day with stories that were "newer." Second, not all editions are preserved on microfilm. Thus, it appears that the early edition of the April 29, 1946, newspaper was not microfilmed, although a later edition was microfilmed. In this case, the later edition that was microfilmed had not printed the article with the Adele France interview. (Lesson appreciatively learned, courtesy of the librarian for *The Baltimore Sun*.) See photo of clipping and note.

Thanks to Miss France's foresight, an Alumnae Lodge is also built–on the site of the Old Stable. From the burned-down ruins of the old Main Building, bricks are salvaged and used to transform the old brick stable into a red brick cottage, which in spite of its re-purposing into a residential lodge, would still be referred to as the "Old Stable." And the Old Stable is thus built with colonial-era bricks from *the* first State House that had governed at the now disappeared city of St. Mary's.[42]

c. Two-year Junior College

In 1926, Miss France's spearheading of a Junior College for the Seminary meets its mark with the imprimatur of official approval by the State of Maryland. And St. Mary's Female Seminary changes its name–slightly but significantly–to St. Mary's Female Seminary-Junior College.[43]

With the creation of a junior college, elementary and middle school courses before the ninth grade are phased out. The college now offers: (i) four-year general high school; (ii) college preparatory high school; (iii) a one-year business program; and (iv) and a two-year junior-college program.[44]

In 1929, the northwest wing is finally added to the new Main Building (just as the architect had designed it back in 1924). This riverside wing has a study hall, several classrooms, science laboratories, servants' quarters, and 16 more bedrooms.[45]

Emphasis is placed on the concept of service and a meaningful life, on a duty to the greater good over self. "The organization of the school aims to educate the pupils for rich, purposeful, responsible living." St. Mary's

---

42 St. Mary's, *Timeline*. Entry for 1924. *1924-25 Prospectus* 11. Fausz 68. "The seventeenth-century bricks in the walls of the Alumni Lodge once reverberated with the voices of colonial legislators in Maryland's old capitol building. But these bricks were not discarded due to age; they were reused time and again because they were needed to serve the present and future . . . ." Fausz 146. See Chapter 3-D at fn 75.

43 In 1964, the name would be changed to St. Mary's College of Maryland (in anticipation of becoming a four-year liberal arts college). St. Mary's, *Timeline*. Entry for 1964.

44 St. Mary's, *Timeline*. Entry for 1926.

45 Since 1955, known as Calvert Hall. Fausz 33. *Annual Prospectus for St. Mary's Female Seminary for 1931-1932*, at p.11. Office of the Provost. Catalogs. RG 3.4.1, Box 1 "Prospectus 1931/1932." St. Mary's College of Maryland Archives. Hereafter cited as *1931-32 Prospectus*. The *1931-32 Prospectus* also has photos showing an enclosed tennis court (in front of the Alumnae Lodge). Fausz 81.

"is conducted for service, not profit."[46] Even courses that are advertised by other schools with dreary, industrial-sounding titles are re-imagined at St. Mary's with titles that focus on contributing to society. For example, "Domestic Sciences" is refreshed by St. Mary's as "Household Arts."[47]

2. Second Battle – Overcoming The Great Depression and World War II

Adele France would steer St. Mary's through the Great Depression of the 1930s and then cope with the deprivations of World War II.

a. Stock Market Crash and Revitalization

In 1930, four years after St. Mary's began its junior-college experiment, the first class of Junior College students proudly graduates.[48] It is now less than a year after the stock-market crash of October 29, 1929, ushering in the Great Depression.

In 1931, Miss France turns down a salary-increase of $1,000 due to "the existing business depression."[49] Solidarity indeed.

---

46 *Annual Prospectus for St. Mary's Female Seminary for 1926-1927*, at pp. 28, 9. May 1926. Office of the Provost. Catalogs.RG 3.4.1, Box 1 "Prospectus 1926/1927." St. Mary's College of Maryland Archives. Hereafter cited as *1926-27 Prospectus*. "After careful consideration on the part of the Principal, the Executive Committee of the Board of Trustees, and the whole Board, with the approval of the State Superintendent of Education, it was decided in April of his year to offer for this year 1926-27, on an *experimental basis*, the first year of college work and thus raising the status of the Seminary to that of *Junior College*. Those who are interested in the Seminary feel this to be a move in the right direction and that the school is truly about to enter an *enlarged field of honor and usefulness*. . . . In offering the first year of college work with the intention of adding the second year and thus creating a junior college, St. Mary's Seminary is in position to render *greater service* to the girlhood of the State, and, in consequence, to the State whose founding it commemorates." *1926-27 Prospectus* 8, 10 (emphases added).

47 "The aim of this course [Household Arts] is to fit the students to be homemakers and to view their work as a profession through which they may make their families happy, healthful, and *efficient members of society*." *1926-27 Prospectus* 25 (emphasis added).

48 Additionally, 20 students graduate from the Seminary's high school branch. Fausz 77. Also, in 1931, the high school gains accreditation from the State of Maryland. Combs, *History* 344.

49 St. Mary's, *Timeline*. Entry for 1931. Fausz 80. The equivalent of $1,000 dollars in June 1931 calculated to dollars in October 2021 is $18,317. "CPI Inflation Calculator." *U.S. Bureau of Labor Statistics*. <https://data.bls.gov/cgi-bin/cpicalc.pl?cost1=1%2C000&year1=193106&year2=202110.>

In addition to her responsibilities as Principal, Miss France *also* teaches psychology and philosophy.[50]

Miss France further modernizes St. Mary's by getting it connected to the electric grid. By May 1931, the generation of electricity at St. Mary's progresses from the limited Delco system (a stand-alone generator that provides electric light and mechanical power) to connecting with "city current" provided by the Eastern Shore Power Company. Meanwhile, the "Delco House" at St. Mary's is converted into a science laboratory (fitting since the Delco generator itself–comprised of banks of batteries housed in clear glass cases–resembles a mysterious science experiment).[51]

In anticipation of the hosting role it will play for Maryland's 300th anniversary, St. Mary's also replaces the old windmill with a new water tower, pump house, and chlorinator.[52]

In 1932, while still mired in the Great Depression, the League of Women Voters urges the Maryland Legislature to *close down* the Female Seminary-Junior College, arguing that it is akin to a private boarding school and is not economically viable.[53]

Steadfast, Miss France fights back with a plan to revitalize St. Mary's.[54] By phasing out the ninth and tenth grades, she will strengthen the Female Seminary-Junior College for women by sculpting it over the next half-decade into a focused, four-year institution. Gumption!

---

50 *1931-32 Prospectus* 32. In spite of the Great Depression, the Seminary offered a wealth of academic courses. For example, Hélène Cau taught French, Spanish, and Latin. See letter from Mary Gorman to Ms. Cau, referenced in Chapter 5-D at fn 22.

51 *1931-32 Prospectus* 11. See Fausz 81.

52 St. Mary's, *Timeline*. Entry for 1931. Fausz 81.

53 St. Mary's, *Timeline*. Entry for 1932. Fausz 78.

54 This goal is exemplified in part in a letter that Miss France wrote to a Mrs. Tourtellot in 1933: "[O]urs is known as a 'working school.' I mean by that it is rather the fashion to study and achieve something at St. Mary's. . . . Ours cannot be classed as a 'fashionable finishing school' but our Junior College does serve as a finishing [terminal] school for those girls who do not desire to go through the four year college, while it is possible here to transfer to the Junior class of the four-year college if the regular college course is pursued. We give an excellent and thorough business terminal course as outlined in the catalog." France, M. Adele. Letter to Mrs. Tourtellot. 31 Jan. 1933. RG 20 Janet Haugaard collection. St. Mary's College of Maryland Archives.

b. Maryland's 300th Birthday Celebration

During this sculpting period, there are pivotal historical celebrations that will strengthen St. Mary's bonds to the local community and to the State.

Celebrating its design as a living monument, the Female Seminary-Junior College will host Maryland's tercentenary celebration in 1934 for a full week of festivities.

Miss France knows what she has to do to impress a hundred thousand attendees–meticulous planning and networking.

First, *eight years* before the tercentenary, in 1926, as liaison to the Leonardtown Chapter of the Daughters of the American Revolution, she works with them in laying out the square stones in the cemetery that mark where the first State House stood.

Second, she arranges for an ornamental cast-iron arch gate to be erected at the Seminary entrance, asking sculptor Hans Schuler to cast ornamental medallions for it. Commissioned by the State, Schuler is also sculpting his "Freedom of Conscience" statue for the celebration.[55]

Third, in the midst of the Great Depression, after a two-year undertaking and relentless fund-raising by the alumnae and Miss France, the vegetable plot is transformed by the vision of a landscape-designer into the "Garden of Remembrance." Adorned with a fountain, a pérgola, and benches, this garden is dedicated to commemorate Maryland's 300th anniversary.[56]

Both the Garden of Remembrance and the Freedom of Conscience statue (erected in 1935) are still maintained by St. Mary's College.

Fourth, Miss France, in her dual roles as hostess for the celebration and caretaker for St. Mary's City, turns the Main Building into a hotel for guests and dignitaries. She gives newspaper reporters full use of the Seminary's

---

[55] St. Mary's, *Timeline*. Entries for 1934. Fausz 81.

[56] St. Mary's, *Timeline*. Entries for 1934. This land (next to the Main Building) had been used until then as the Seminary's vegetable plot. Fausz 82.

only telephone, which is in her office: "Great Mills 1" (telephone-numbers back then were based on the name of the city and a number).[57]

On a weekend in mid-June 1934, crammed in the midst of 100-degree heat, thousands of people travel to St. Mary's for Maryland's 300th birthday celebration, with *The Washington Times* proclaiming that 100,000 people had attended. In addition to the construction and paving of a bypass for Route 5, a 10,000-seat stadium is built for the event, which includes an outdoor pageant, "St. Maries, the mother of Maryland." About 500 countians, a few seminarians, and Miss France–all dressed up in seventeenth-century costumes–perform in this pageant. Talk about "heritage"![58]

c. Four-year Junior College

The year after this magnificent celebration, in 1935, the Board of Trustees votes to eliminate the 9th and 10th grades and instead to make St. Mary's a four-year junior college: 11th and 12th grades of high school (the Lower Division) plus the first two years of college (the Upper Division).[59]

By 1937, Miss France's revitalization plan for the Female Seminary-Junior College has culminated. It now offers 11th and 12th grades plus the first two years of college, thus leading to an Associate of Arts degree (A.A). This degree prepares a young woman to *either* go on to a university for the final two years, *or* to enter a field which does not require a B.A. but which answers the wishes and talents of the young woman. For Miss France, both

---

57 St. Mary's, *Timeline*. Entries for 1934. Fausz 83.

58 Fausz 83-84. "One of the most noticed revelers was 102-year-old Mary Ellen **Whalen** Jones ("Aunt Pigeon"), a former Langley family slave who was the cook for the Seminary in the late nineteenth century, as she sat under a shade tree surrounded by dozens of her descendants." Fausz 84.

Jesuit priests, including Father LaFarge, admired Ms. Jones (as shown in at least two of his publications). LaFarge, John. *The Manner Is Ordinary*. New York: Harcourt, Brace and Company, 1954. 168, 185. Print. LaFarge, John. "Aunt Pigeon's Eight Years Plus a Century." *America*, Vol. LVI, No. 22 (Whole No. 1430) (March 6, 1937). 511-12. Print. St. Mary's, *Timeline*. Entries for 1934. See also McKenna, Horace B., S.J.. "Colored Catholics in St. Mary's County." *Woodstock Letters*, Vol. LXXIX, No.1 (Feb. 1950). 59-60. Web. 29 July 2021. <https://jesuitonlinelibrary.bc.edu>. Father Walsh dedicated his book, *Resurrection: the Story of the Saint Inigoes Mission*, to Ms. Jones (see Chapter 8 at fn 65).

59 *Annual Prospectus for St. Mary's Female Seminary for 1938-1939*, at p.6. May 1938. Office of the Provost. Catalogs. RG 3.4.1, Box 1 "Prospectus 1938/1939." St. Mary's College of Maryland Archives. Hereafter cited as *1938-39 Prospectus*. See Fausz 77.

routes are good choices. In the *1938-39 Prospectus*, Miss France illustrates this metamorphosis.

> The period between 1935 and 1938 has been one of *transition*-of thinking thru a maze of suggestions and possibilities, of trying out, of stabilizing opinion. Now however, with confidence, St. Mary's Female Seminary enters upon its latest development to meet the changing State educational needs with earnest belief in the rightness of its action, and with high hopes of *service* to the State and to Youth.[60]

St. Mary's goal of "service" remains as a lodestar. "To glorify work-the task well done-and to keep it, as it now is, 'the fashion' at St. Mary's Seminary."[61]

And St. Mary's itself practices what it preaches. Even during the Great Depression, it continues to provide scholarships to half of the students, including room and board. "Refusing to charge more or to expel delinquent students, despite a five year operating deficit in the mid-1930s, school administrators relied on creative frugality to get them through the tough Depression years."[62]

Almost a century after its inception, St. Mary's *raison d'être* perseveres. Indeed, it thrives. The *1938-39 Prospectus* defines St. Mary's objectives as embracing: "To preserve the Maryland ideal of freedom of conscience-all denominations living together in peace and harmony-in a positive spiritual atmosphere."[63]

Additionally, meeting its further duty to preserve "archives and artifacts related to the early colony," the first archaeological digs in St. Mary's City had broken ground in 1936. Thirty years later, the importance of these

---

60 *1938-39 Prospectus* 6 (emphases added).

61 *1938-39 Prospectus* 4.

62 Fausz 80. Some of these scholarship funds came from sources supplemental to the State's funding, such as the Daughters of the American Revolution. Fausz 80. This followed the Seminary's history of promoting scholarships. The Trustee's Annual Report of 1875 stated that of the 23 students, 13 were on scholarship (10 by the State and three from other sources). "On a consistent basis between the 1860s and the late 1940s, at least half of the annual student body was attending the school on full scholarship." Fausz 47. See Chapter 3-D. See also Chapter 5-C at fn 18.

63 *1938-39 Prospectus* 4.

historical excavations would be formally recognized with the founding of the St. Mary's City Commission in 1966.[64]

With its transformation into a four-year junior college, St. Mary's becomes a regular line-item in the Maryland State budget. Reflecting its metamorphosis from the "seminary" to a junior college, the leadership role, still held by Miss France, changes title from Principal to President.[65] Miss France is the very first President of St. Mary's.

The *1938-39 Prospectus* recognizes the historical role that junior colleges across the country play in the aftermath of the Great Depression– for both women and men. On the one hand, businesses need a better educated workforce. On the other hand, the Depression caused a "dearth of unemployment for youth, a waiting period which brings restlessness and deterioration. Into the picture steps the junior college, to furnish more education and bridge over for young people the waiting time for employment, while they make themselves more ready for employment."[66]

St. Mary's continues to evolve ahead of its time. In addition to being a pioneer in the junior-college movement (years before the Stock Market Crash of 1929), it also devises a new system for grading students with a flexible and pragmatic approach: competition with oneself. This new grading system focuses on a student's efforts, attitude, and *quality* of work, instead of a hierarchical, quantitative assessment (which often favors those who have achieved high grades in the past). "A sincere endeavor is being made to direct the student's attention away from grades, marks, and standings; to encourage her to *compete with herself*."[67]

---

64 St. Mary's, *Timeline*. Entry for 1936. The State legislation of 1840 that established the female seminary "on the site of the Ancient City of St. Mary's" required the seminary to "collect and preserve meaningful archives and artifacts related to the early colony." Fausz, 30, 30. See also fn 68 below.

65 St. Mary's, *Timeline*. Entry for 1937. Fausz 79. In April 1941, St. Mary's Junior College is accredited by the Maryland Department of Education. Fausz 80, 87.

66 *1938-39 Prospectus* 7.

67 *1938-39 Prospectus* 18 (emphasis added). See also Fausz 91.

d. Seminary's 100th Birthday Celebration

As elaborated in Chapter 3-C-4, the Female Seminary had been established in 1840 as a "living monument" to carry out the vision of the now-vanquished St. Mary's City, established in 1634, and its enduring principle of religious tolerance.[68]

In March 1940, about 500 people attend the Enactment Day ceremonies (begun in 1924) for the Female Seminary's 100th birthday. The celebration continues into the Summer. In June, festivities for the "Centenary Commencement" include a historical pageant, dances, music, dinners, and speeches by politicians–all focused on the "ideals of St. Mary's." And Father LaFarge, traveling from New York City, delivers the "baccalaureate sermon" and hosts a "student supper in the Garden of Remembrance."[69]

Also for the Seminary's 100th birthday, Miss France erects a Maryland historical-marker sign, which pronounces that the Legislature established the female seminary "as a <u>living monument</u> to mark the birthplace of the state and of religious liberty."[70]

In 1940-41, before the U.S. would take up arms in World War II,[71] the Gymnasium is built as a gift from the Maryland Legislature to commemorate the 100 years of the founding of St. Mary's Female Seminary as a "living monument" to carry out Lord Baltimore's vision of religious tolerance.[72]

However, the war-years pose new challenges.

---

[68] At the time, Historic St. Mary's City did not exist. The Historic St. Mary's City Commission would not be formed until 1966. And in 1969, Historic St. Mary's City would be recognized as a National Historic Landmark. "About Us." Historic St. Mary's City. Web. 8 Oct. 2021. <https://www.hsmcdigshistory.org/about-hsmc/mission-and-history/>.

[69] Fausz 85, 86, 86.

[70] Emphasis in original. St. Mary's, *Timeline*. Entry for 1940. See photograph referenced in Chapter 1-B at fn 7.

[71] Also in 1941, before World War II, the structure of the Board of Trustees would be changed from its 1858 formation of 15 lifetime trustees from St. Mary's County (of diverse religions) to a Board of 12 trustees who would serve six-year terms, originating from all areas of Maryland–and requiring that *women* serve as well as men. Local lobbying would result in the appointment of six of the current trustees to the new Board. The new Board would keep most of the prior Board's traditions, except–mercifully–the Minutes would now be typed instead of handwritten. St. Mary's, *Timeline*. Entry for 1941. Fausz 89-90.

[72] See Chapter 3-C-4.

e. World War II

Former servants are leaving St. Mary's to take high-paying jobs at the new Patuxent Naval Air Base.[73] There is food rationing. And food is scarce. For example, meat trucks are often empty by the time they rumble all the way down to St. Mary's City. There is no one left to tend to the vegetable garden.

In response, Miss France mobilizes the students–and herself–into cooking and cleaning. On *all* levels, high and low, she persists, undeterred.

> The years of World War II were trying ones for Miss France, Principal. Her biggest problem was the securing and retention of a good faculty. . . . Food was scarce and expensive. There was even a problem in securing heating fuel. . . . Miss France encountered great difficulty in securing haulers to bring it [coal for heating] the nine miles to the Seminary. Despite the many difficulties, Miss France still succeeded in achieving some progress. The tennis courts were completed in 1941 and the bulkhead was built in 1946.[74]

World War II generates new dilemmas with both teachers and students. Competing against war-related jobs offering high salaries, Miss France struggles to keep a qualified faculty, at times having to pay steep salaries to untried teachers, some of whom are unfit. In 1943, "Miss France feared for her life until a particularly unruly instructor was committed to an insane asylum."[75] And the war takes its toll on student conduct. There are numerous disciplinary problems, which lead to the finger-printing of students and instructors in 1946. Because the Board of Trustees no longer

---

73 In St. Mary's Archives are copies of desperate letters Miss France wrote to friends and even students' parents in Washington, asking if they knew of anyone who could come down to clean, cook, etc. Presidential Files, M. Adele France (1923-1948). RG 2.1.1, Box 1. St. Mary's College of Maryland Archives.

In the end, she hired a woman on parole from the House of Correction at Jessup. Further, a questionnaire answered (in December 1995) by an alumna of the Class of 1947, states: "During the war it was difficult to obtain help. Miss France was able to hire women from the state correctional institute at Jessup, Md. due to the fact that her niece, Helen **DeCorse** McArthur, was CEO at that time. I recall one such woman . . . , who was reputed to have murdered someone + was thus incarcerated." Handwritten answers to Questionnaire of an alumna [name redacted], mid-1940s. RG 20 Janet Haugaard collection. St. Mary's College of Maryland Archives. See also Fausz 90.

74 Combs, *History* 345, 345, 345.

75 Fausz 90.

meets on a regular basis, it is Miss France who manages these escalating problems and averts crises.[76]

The *1945-46 Prospectus* recognizes the historical role that junior colleges across the country will continue to play, now in the aftermath of World War II, "to provide suitable education for returning service men and women."[77]

Additionally, St. Mary's maintains an Army Observation Post "manned by students and faculty," a Red Cross Room for making surgical dressings and bandages, and it sets up various committees of faculty and students "to meet the constant and temporary needs of our Government and the United Nations in their prosecution of the war and their preparation for peace."[78]

In the thick haze of wartime conditions, St. Mary's keeps spirits up with social and athletic events: the Dramatic Club, the Glee Club, the French Club, the Art Club, the Athletic Association, and a "lyceum course of artists and lectures."[79]

3. Third Battle – Again Triumphing Over Forces Intent on Closing St. Mary's

a. Marbury Commission

In 1947, in a voluminous report about higher education in Maryland, the Marbury Commission, an investigatory body of the Maryland Legislature, curtly recommends closure of the Female Seminary-Junior College. The Letter of Transmittal of this report (at pp. vi and vi of this 418-page book) is dated February 1, 1947.

> The state is conducting a junior college for women at St. Mary's City. The findings of our survey staff show very clearly that this operation is without economic justification due to the small size of the institution and to its inaccessible location.

---

[76] Fausz 90, 92.

[77] *Annual Prospectus for St. Mary's Female Seminary for 1945-1946*, at p.7. April 1945. Office of the Provost. Catalogs. RG 3.4.1, Box 2 "Prospectus 1945/1946." St. Mary's College of Maryland Archives. Hereafter cited as *1945-46 Prospectus*.

[78] *1945-46 Prospectus* 44.

[79] *1945-46 Prospectus* 47.

...

> As to St. Mary's Female Seminary, it seems to your Commission that the findings of our survey staff permit of but one conclusion. *Apart from sentiment*, there can be no sound reason for continuing the existence of this institution. As a memorial to the founders of the state, it is unduly costly; its inaccessible location, small size, and lack of accredited status make it unfit for inclusion in a well-integrated system of institutions of higher education. To bring St. Mary's Female Seminary up to standard would increase the cost per student, already abnormally high, and would, in our opinion, be an unjustifiable expenditure of public money.[80]

"*Apart from sentiment*"! Miss France must have been appalled at this report. She has devoted her whole life to education, and the last quarter century to St. Mary's. As if history and noble goals may be trivialized as mere "sentiment."

This report is also based on untrue and cavalier statements. For example, the Female Seminary-Junior College *had* in fact been accredited. Six years earlier–back in 1941.[81] In fact, it was *St. Mary's* who had pioneered junior-colleges in Maryland.

And the "inaccessibility" argument is flimsy because, at that time, there are regular bus routes with Washington and Baltimore which had begun after the founding of the town of Lexington Park (where the military base is located) during World War II.[82]

b. Go bust? No: instead, funding boost!

Yet again, undaunted, Miss France fights back with the help of alumnae (which she has wisely nurtured over the years) and trustees. Miss France publishes the college's response, touting St. Mary's Female Seminary-Junior College as the only institution of higher education in both St. Mary's and

---

[80] *Higher Education In Maryland. A Report of a Survey by the American Council on Education With Recommendations of the Maryland Commission on Higher Education 1947*, at pp. 349, 370 (emphasis added). The Survey Staff consisted of seven men and apparently no women (p.iv). The Maryland Commission on Higher Education consisted of eight men and one woman (p.vi).

[81] St. Mary's, *Timeline*. Entry for 1941.

[82] Fausz 94. St. Mary's, *Timeline*. Entries for 1943.

Charles' counties, highlighting that it offers small classes in a liberal arts curriculum. She also emphasizes that smaller colleges can provide a *better* education to students than large institutions.[83]

In the summer of 1947, Miss France travels to Annapolis and testifies before the State Legislature, arguing in part that the State should preserve St. Mary's *and* increase its funding. She wins.[84] And St. Mary's wins, keeping its doors open for future generations of women–and men.[85]

After winning that third major battle, Miss France suffers a heart attack in December 1947 and is carried out of the Main Building on a stretcher. No wonder–during her tenure as Principal, Miss France *never* took vacation nor sick leave.[86] The following Spring, at the age of 68 and after almost a quarter of a century of dedication to St. Mary's, she resigns from her leadership role.[87]

D. OPENING WINDOWS AND MODERNIZING THE LIVING MONUMENT

Since its founding in 1840, the Female Seminary had been going strong for a good 80 years, but Adele France was its first Principal who was college-educated, not to mention the fact that she had two Master's degrees. She brought to St. Mary's an insistence on good education, and she did it with characteristic optimism and high spirits.

Her first job as head of school was to open all the windows, so to speak. Fresh air. Modern ideas.

---

83 St. Mary's, *Timeline*. Entry for 1947. Fausz 92-94. As to the Alumnae Association, see Chapter 5-E.

84 In late 1947, the Legislative Council recommends that St. Mary's continue as an institution of higher education. It would not be until December 1, 1948 (almost a year after Miss France's heart attack) that the General Assembly would completely reject the Marbury Commission's assessment of St. Mary's. Fausz 94.

85 For over 100 years, St. Mary's had accepted local boys as day students. See fn 41 above. It would not be until 1965 that there were male students living on campus. Fausz 111. See St. Mary's, *Timeline*. Entry for 1965.

86 There is a letter dated January 20, 1948, from W.D. Owens (Walter D. Owens was then Commissioner of State Employment and Registration for the State of Maryland), who states in part: "There is no record of any sick or vacation leave that has been taken by Miss France. . . . I am indeed sorry to learn of Miss France's illness and hope that she is able to return soon to the Seminary." Owens, W.D.. Letter to Miss Gill. 20 Jan. 1948. Presidential Files, M. Adele France (1923-1948). RG 2.1.1, Box 1. St. Mary's College of Maryland Archives.

87 However, she stays briefly while her portrait is painted by Colonel James M. Wharton. This portrait now hangs in the Hilda C. Landers Library.

New faculty (many with master's degrees) replaced old.

Even though St. Mary's was a public institution, students wishing to enter were now required to take a battery of tests.

The elementary division was on its way to extinction.

And further non-structural changes were welcomed by the students.

Catholic students no longer ate at a separate table, and *everyone* ate fish on Fridays.

Girls no longer wore uniforms and–wonder of wonders–high school girls were encouraged to give social dances, with male partners! Likewise, they were encouraged to attend dances given by the private boys' schools up in Charlotte Hall and in Leonard Hall. In the 1920s and 30s, these mixers had protocols: chaperones, "bid lists" approved by school administrators, and "dance cards."[88]

There were also rules restricting social interactions with boys and men, such as not leaving school grounds unchaperoned, callers must be approved by parents (who were to provide a list of men approved as callers and dance escorts), and the requirement that all visitors must be seen by the Principal on arrival and departure.[89] Calling hours were from 8:00 to 10:30 on Saturday evenings and from 2:00 to 4:30 on Sunday afternoons, when "Quiet Hour" begins, and all visitors must leave.[90] And without question: "All masculine visitors are to be entertained on the first floor."[91]

---

88 However, Miss France wanted to present her students as "wholesome," and she personally inspected each girl before the dance. Alumnae remember that if Miss France decided that a neckline was too low, then she would provide that girl with a variety of tulle swatches and ask her to choose a color swatch to cover her decolletage. Yet, unbeknownst to Miss France, during the bus ride to the dance, dresses would be re-adjusted and tulle swatches would be stuffed into coat pockets. Haugaard, Janet. "Six Inches Apart: Dancing and Dating in the M. Adele France Years." *Mulberry Tree Papers* (Fall 1998): 6-12. Print. Hereafter cited as "Dancing and Dating." For the period before Miss France's tenure as Principal, see Chapter 5-F at fn 54 & fn 57.

89 *1926-27 Prospectus* 14.

90 *Annual Prospectus for St. Mary's Female Seminary for 1936-1937*, at p.37. May 1936. Office of the Provost. Catalogs. RG 3.4.1, Box 1 "Prospectus 1936/1937." St. Mary's College of Maryland Archives. Hereafter cited as *1936-37 Prospectus*. Five years earlier, the visiting hours were half an hour shorter, from 8:00 to 10:00 on Saturday evenings. So, some progress had been made. *1931-32 Prospectus* 25.

91 *1936-37 Prospectus* 37. *1931-32 Prospectus* 25.

In the *1945-46 Prospectus*, social events were included as a selling point for future students–and their parents.

> Visiting [athletic] teams are always entertained at dinner or tea. . . . [A] great many social affairs are given, formal and informal, all in the cause of pleasure and social efficiency. There are dances, teas, dinners, suppers, garden parties, picnics, and evening parties of all kinds, held at the Seminary, in the neighborhood, and at Charlotte Hall, a boys' school, a short drive away. . . . During the past four years some joint college and community social affairs have been arranged, to the mutual pleasure and advantage of both.[92]

With World War II, Miss France also allowed the college girls to attend dances at the newly built Patuxent Naval Air Station and at Piney Point–with, as was customary, a chaperone.

Why the continued need for chaperoning? Before the 1960s, a college or boarding school acted as parent for the student. This was known as "in loco parentis." Parents would thus be assured that their daughters would never, ever, be left alone with a young man. Birth control was not generally part of a teenage girl's education. "The pill" had not been invented yet.

Miss France's predecessors had avoided the predicament of pregnancies by steering clear of events where girls and boys could mix. Yet Miss France *did* allow dating and dancing–subject to chaperoning and other measures (ultimately aimed at preventing pregnancies). For example, at the 1947 St. Mary's Prom, a chaperone wove her way across the dance floor, warning "Six inches apart, girls! Six inches apart!" and–where necessary–wedged a six-inch ruler between a girl and her uniformed male escort.[93]

Alumnae have recounted rare instances of rebellion that took place under cover of darkness (eluding chaperones, canoeing on the river at night, signaling in Morse code to naval craft out on the river, and sliding down the dormitory walls on knotted bedsheets), while at the same time expressing their respect and affection for Miss France and the College.

---

[92] *1945-46 Prospectus* 46, 46, 47.

[93] "Dancing and Dating," at p.6.

They realized that these restrictions did not arise from mean-spiritedness, but instead from genuine concern for their well-being.[94]

The smoking of cigarettes by *women* was another way for them to assert their independence–a public symbol of equality with men.[95] During the 1920s, 30s, and 40s (when Miss France was Principal), arguments made against women smoking were usually not medical, but rather moral, such as criticizing women for being "unladylike." (It would not be until 1957 that the U.S. Surgeon General reported in a press conference about the causal link between lung cancer and cigarette smoking.)

---

[94] Alumna Elizabeth ("Betty") Jane **Miles** '47 stated: "Miss France wasn't just trying to be a popular president, she took on the role, really, as parent." Ms. Miles added: "Most of all–the part of our lives that we resented the most has become the most dear to us." "Dancing and Dating," at p.12. See photo of Ms. France (taken in the 1930s).

[95] World War I saw young women raising their hemlines above the ankle, throwing off stiff corsets, bobbing their hair, and taking up cigarettes. Haugaard, Janet. "The M. Adele France Years: Women and Smoking." *Mulberry Tree Papers* (Fall 1997): 32-35. 32. Print. Hereafter cited as "Women and Smoking."

As the United States teetered towards World War II, social upheaval rocked every institution in the country, including St. Mary's. As her correspondence shows, Miss France was now faced by an increasingly restless student body.

Perhaps in an effort to reduce tensions, this non-smoking Principal sent out a letter to all parents on March 18, 1940, notifying them that the girls were now to be given smoking privileges. She asked the parents to either give or withhold consent, assuring them that smoking would be done under carefully controlled conditions and only at specified hours. Her reasoning was shrewd. "Personally," she wrote to the parents, "I much prefer to have smoking done in the open than to have my girls do it under cover, breaking a rule, and thus forming the general habit of breaking rules when rules don't suit them–one of the most pernicious habits, I'm sure you'll agree, anyone can form."[96] Thus, students were finally allowed to smoke in a special room in the Gymnasium (with parental permission).

When Miss France retired in 1948, smoking among women was no longer the "moral" issue that it had been when she began her tenure in 1923. As women gradually began achieving more economic and social goals (and in spite of pro-smoking advertising slogans directed at women, such as "You've come a long way, baby" in the 1960s and 70s), the symbolism of smoking as an intrinsically feminist act would fade over the decades.

E. THE JUNIOR COLLEGE AS INSTITUTIONAL CATALYST FOR THE LIBERAL ARTS COLLEGE

However, Miss France's greatest innovation at St. Mary's was her experiment–the creation of a junior college. St. Mary's was the first junior college in all of Maryland. This status would lure well-qualified teachers who otherwise may have been hesitant to move to such a faraway campus.

Remember William Rainey Harper, the first president of the University of Chicago?[97] University-correspondence courses had been innovated by

---

96 "Women and Smoking," at p.34.

97 See Chapter 4-A-2. Discussed at the beginning of this chapter are the "correspondence courses" which The Woman's Literary Club of Chestertown ("WLC") provided to its members in the early 20th Century, which were administered by the University of Chicago. See also Section 9-A, including close of fn 13.

him in 1898. Well, Mr. Harper had *also* launched the first "junior" college in Illinois, inspired by the words of Dean Alexis Lange of the University of California who had said that junior colleges should be created for those who "cannot, will not, and should not become university students."[98]

Adele France agreed only in part with this draconian idea. When she added on the two years of junior college to the Female Seminary, she intended two possible outcomes. First, girls who had no ambition for a four-year college education could, nevertheless, study for a terminal A.A. degree (Associate in Arts). Second, those who did not want such a degree could spend those two junior college years studying the liberal arts before transferring to a university (which they should have no trouble getting into) with the goal of earning a bachelor's degree. Miss France firmly believed that graduates of St. Mary's junior college should be educated to take "an economic place in the world."

In 1941, fifteen years after the State of Maryland had officially approved of the two-year Junior College, the State grants accreditation to the four-year Junior College: grades 11 and 12 of high school and the first two years of college.[99]

In contrast to most other junior colleges, St. Mary's focused on a liberal arts education instead of vocational training. As a further contrast, unlike most junior colleges, St. Mary's president, its faculty, and its student-body were comprised mainly of women.[100]

Six years after Miss France resigned, in May of 1954, the Supreme Court would hand down its decision in *Brown v. Board of Education* that all public schools were to become racially integrated. However, civil litigation would ensue in Maryland courts over the next 13 years. It was not until the Fall of 1967 that racial integration of all public schools was required in St. Mary's County.[101]

---

[98] Hillway, Tyrus. *The American Two-Year College*. New York: Harper & Brothers, Publishers, 1958. 63-64. Print.
[99] St. Mary's, *Timeline*. Entry for 1941.
[100] Fausz 74.
[101] See Chapter 8 at fn 84.

In 1968, the first black student enrolls–formally, as such–at St. Mary's.[102]

Caveat: six years earlier, in 1962, the first black student enrolls at St. Mary's Junior College, Elizabeth "Liz" Barber. However, Ms. Barber was admitted because: (1) she did not answer the "race" question on the application; (2) she did not submit a photo; and (3) she did not name the "colored" school from which she was graduating. And she graduates from the Junior College in 1964–four years *before* the first official enrollment by a black student.[103]

This feat shows gumption. By Ms. Barber. And by St. Mary's, honoring its legacy and its destiny: tolerance, respect for humanity.

Miss France's junior college lasted until the late 1960s, at which time it developed into the four-year college for the liberal arts that we know today.[104]

F. FULL CIRCLE

At the age of 74, Mary Adele France died in a Catonsville nursing home (near Baltimore) in September 1954.[105] She is buried in her hometown, in Chester Cemetery, which is where the research for this book began in the Winter of 2005 (although full attention was not possible until 2009). The inscription on her tombstone is "M. Adele France, Litt.D."

1954 was the same year in which Father LaFarge published his autobiography (*The Manner is Ordinary*) that centered on his transformative fifteen years in Southern Maryland.

---

102 St. Mary's, *Timeline*. Entries for 1954, 1956, 1958, 1964, 1967, 1968, and 1969.

103 St. Mary's, *Timeline*. Entry for 1962. See also Dunlap, Patricia Riley. "She got through: Liz Barber's St. Mary's experience." *Mulberry Tree Papers* (Spring 2001): 10-13. Print.

104 Between 1930 and 1960, students received either a High School diploma or an Associate in Arts degree from the Junior College Division. The last High School diploma was given out in 1960; and from 1961 through 1968, only degrees from the Junior College were awarded. No degrees were given during the transition years of 1969 and 1970. The first baccalaureate degrees (B.A. and B.S.) of the new four-year liberal arts college were awarded in 1971. After academic year 1982-83, only the B.A. was offered. St. Mary's, *Timeline*. Entries for 1960, 1968, 1971, 1983.

105 Adele France's funeral was held a few blocks from her childhood home, in Emmanuel Episcopal Church in Chestertown. The newspapers of the day particularly noted that domestics of the Female Seminary-Junior College drove up for her funeral and burial (today, a two-and-a-half hour drive from St. Mary's College).

Question. Did Adele France and John LaFarge actually know each other?

Yes, they did. However, there is scant documentation of their rapport.[106]

She helped pioneer women's rights to education with her "ornaments-no-longer" approach and her goal of economic independence for women. He helped pioneer blacks' rights to education. Both were dedicated to their vocations. It seems quite likely that they were aware of each other's endeavors for what we now define as civil rights and human rights. Presumably, they felt some sort of kinship towards one another.

Adele France and John LaFarge accomplished their goals–undeterred by their own physical afflictions and undaunted by social constraints.[107]

Wistfully, we have only a few written traces of when their paths crossed. Yet these scarce traces reveal a cordial relationship and mutual admiration.

For example, in a letter dated May 13, 1942, Adele France thanks John LaFarge for his letter. In her reply, she explains that she was able to find the information that he was seeking in the original Minute Book for the Seminary which "was lost for years and then washed up on the shores of the Patuxent!" Alluding to a shared past: "Life in St. Mary's is not what it used to be, alas! The old calm days are gone; but it is still lovely and peaceful here at the Seminary." She cheerfully ends her letter: "I wish you could be with us for Commencement, we love to have you always. And I hope you are very well."[108]

We can presume that this synergetic relationship also lasted for at least a quarter of a century, spanning from about 1923 or 1924 to the late

---

[106] In a historical quirk, Addie France was actually aware of John LaFarge's famous father, the stained-glass artist and muralist John LaFarge (Sr.), years before she ever met John LaFarge (Jr., aka "Father LaFarge") in the early 20th century. Remember the Horsey Collection that contains Addie's handwritten notes for the WLC? (See Chapter 4-A-3 at fn 19 and Appendix C.) Well, it contains a handwritten page dated February 18, 1916, listing the assignments for WLC members. One of these assignments under "2nd Paper" states "LaFarge, Miss Nicholson." (Appendix C, p.5.) It appears that Miss Nicholson was a member of the WLC and assigned to research and make a presentation on John LaFarge (Sr.).

[107] See Chapters 4-A, 4-B, and 8-B.

[108] President of Saint Mary's Female Seminary-Junior College (France, M. Adele). One-page single-spaced letter to Rev. John LaFarge at 329 West 108th Street in NY [the Campion House; see Chapter 8-A at fn 1]. 13 May 1942. LaFarge Collection, Box 25, Folder 2. Georgetown University Library.

1940s, perhaps beyond–and most likely, even *before* Adele France became Principal.[109]

As chronicled earlier, at the beginning of Miss France's career as Principal, Father LaFarge made an entry in his Desk Diary, for January 5, 1924: "St. Mary's Seminary burned down at 5:30 P.M. . . . The new principal, Miss France, heard of the disaster as she returned from her Christmas vacation and found all in ruins."[110]

Father LaFarge also attended the ceremony in the Summer of 1924 for the laying of the cornerstone for the new Main Building, now known as Calvert Hall.[111]

For the Female Seminary's 100th anniversary in 1940 (enhanced with junior-college status since 1926), Miss France heralded to the students:

> Our dear Father LaFarge, who was in the County when I came here [as a teacher] and for several years after, but who is now in New York on the editorial staff of *America* (national Catholic weekly), is coming to give our Baccalaureate sermon–that will be a rare treat. Father LaFarge is a forceful and delightful speaker.[112]

As shown by Miss France's 1942 letter to John LaFarge,[113] they continued to be in contact *long after* he had left St. Mary's County in the summer of 1926. It seems that his regular jaunts down to St. Mary's County after he had been posted to New York City included not only re-connecting with his colleagues at the Missions,[114] but also re-connecting with schools in the county, including St. Mary's Female Seminary-Junior College.

---

109 Before she was elected as Principal in 1923, Adele France had taught at St. Mary's Female Seminary from 1909 to 1913 and again from 1917 to 1918, while John LaFarge had been assigned to missions in St. Mary's County from 1911 until 1926.

110 See fn 32 above.

111 See fn 39 & fn 45 above.

112 France, M. Adele. "President Anticipates Unusual Commencement." *Signal News* [a monthly student paper]. St. Mary's City, MD: St. Mary's Female Seminary-Junior College, 31 May 1940, at p.3. Print. Office of the Dean of Students. Student Newspapers. RG 6.7.4 Box 1. St. Mary's College of Maryland Archives. See also fn 69 above.

113 See fn 108 above.

114 Colleagues such as Father McKenna; see Chapter 8-A.

They both fathomed the importance of the currents of history. World history. Maryland history. Local history.

For example, Miss France spent eight years planning ahead for the celebration of Maryland's 300th anniversary (1934). And just before that tercentenary, Father LaFarge's nephew, Christopher LaFarge, designed a monument that was erected in 1933 at Chancellor's Point to recognize Father Andrew White and the first Catholic colonists in Maryland.[115] As Father Conley points out, John LaFarge explained why this was important: "I was not a professional historian, but I hoped that by making a little noise some attention would be paid to the treasures which we were on the point of losing, and again to some of the great issues which were being ignored."[116]

For the Female Seminary's 100th anniversary (1940), Adele France carefully orchestrated the festivities, and John LaFarge made the long journey all the way down from New York City to the southern tip of rural Maryland to participate as a keynote speaker for St. Mary's College.

Over the years, what *did* Adele France and John LaFarge discuss? Education? Religion? Racial issues? Gender issues?

We can only speculate as to what they talked about. And as to whether they engaged in behind-the-scenes networking in support of each other's goals.

Also, did Adele France and John LaFarge ever converse with each other in a language *other than* English?

Although John LaFarge's linguistic abilities are lauded, Adele France's are unsung.[117] Perhaps because these were not skills she used often in her role as Principal. Yet, Miss France stated in a letter to a parent complaining about his daughter's problems in learning French that she understood the

---

115 Conley, Rory T., Rev. "The Church of St. James, 1914-1934." *Chronicles of St. Mary's*, Vol. 57, Issue 1 (Winter [2008]-2009). 571. Print. Hereafter cited as Conley, "St. James Church." See also Chapter 2-C at fn 11 and Chapter 6-F & 6-H.

116 Conley, "St. James Church" 571, citing John LaFarge.

117 At times she signed her name in the French manner as Adèle. See fn 6 above.

challenges in learning a new language because she herself had "studied four languages and done a little teaching in one or two."[118]

To answer the question: we simply do not know.

If so, then this would have been yet another bridge between two persons who devoted their lives to empowering others.

---

[118] President (France, M. Adele). Two-page typed letter to the father of a student. 6 Nov. 1940. RG 5.2.2 Alumni Student Records, Box 4, 1941. St. Mary's College of Maryland Archives. Miss France also stated that she had told this student that arguing that "why we in the United States do one way and why the French do another" is not productive and that students should "accept their [the French] way of expressing themselves and . . . learn to read and write" their language "their way." Inherent in this advice is the insight that language reflects culture–which should be respected.

Appendix A

Charlotte Hall School was never re-named a military school as such, but its military uniforms and military-style discipline, with "Reveille" at 6:45 a.m., were premised on students boarding from dusk to dawn.

These are the family names that recur in the lists of both Gough and Guyther: Abell, Adams, Alvey, Baden, Blackistone, Bond, Boyd, Briscoe, Budd, Bunting, Chesley, Coad, Combs, Crane, Dawson, Dent, Dorsey, Drury, Edelen, Fenwick, Ford, Forrest, Foxwell, Freeman, Goddard, Graves, Greenwell, Hammett, Hayden, Henry, Herbert, Holmes, Jarboe, Johnson, Jones, Joy, Key, King, Latham, Lawrence, Loker, Love, Lynch, Maddox, Matthews, Mattingly, Mills, Moore, Morgan, Norris, Parsons, Perry, Plowden, Raley, Reeder, Richards, Roach, Russell, Scott, Simms, Smith, Sothoron, Spalding, Stone, Tucker, Wallis, Wathen, Wible, Wilkinson, Williams, Wilson, Wise, Yates, Young.

Appendix B

The following plaque is located on the second floor of the library of St. Mary's College of Maryland, not far from the large window overlooking the river:

>The Reeves-Garner Reading Room
>Named in memory of
>Richard H. Garner, Trustee, 1883-1904
>Lucy Maddox, President, 1900-1923
>Henry G. Garner, Trustee, 1923-1935
>Anna May Russell, President, 1948-1968
>And dedicated to the community spirit of others
>In the Chaptico area who have contributed
>To the growth of St. Mary's College of Maryland
>This tribute is made possible by the generous gift of
>George Bradford and Willma Reeves

Appendix C

The Woman's Literary Club of Chestertown was organized December 2, 1904.

Officers for 1904-1905:
President— Mary Adele France
Secretary & Treasurer— Susiebelle Culp

Members:
Mary Cacy Burchinal. Susiebelle Culp.
Mary Adele France. Hallie Isabelle Toulson.
Mabel Toulson. Hallie Roberts Westcott.
Irma Briscoe Eliason. Ann Burton Smith.
Julia Morris Burchinal. Antoinette Louise Stam.
Rebecca Brown Eliason.

Members 1908-1909
Mary Adele France. Ann Burton Smith.
Hallie Isabelle Toulson. Mabel Toulson.
Jennie Wilkins. Sarah Elizabeth Stuart.
Clara Vickers Perkins. Belle Emory.
Mary Ingram Rogers. Irma Briscoe Eliason.
Bessie Morton McKibbon. Nellie Barwick Jefferson.
Anne Gee Gault. Antoinette Louise Stam.
Mary V. Carroll

Officers:
President— Mary Adele France
Vice President— Ann Burton Smith
Secretary & Treasurer— Belle Emory

The Chestertown Public Library, under the direction of the Woman's Literary Club, was opened to the public February 19, 1907. It has been open every Tuesday since; beginning October 1st from 2 to 5 P.M.; beginning June 1st from 10 to 1.

The subscription price is $.50 (fifty cents) a year, which entitles the subscriber to one book a week. The Club members act as Librarians, one each week. In May 1908, Ann Burton Smith was elected Secretary & Treasurer of the Library to serve one year.

At the present date — January 21, 1909 — there are 140 subscribers & 486 books.

21 January 1909
Time-capsule placed in
Volunteer Fire Company of Chestertown.
Describes both The Woman's Literary Club and
Chestertown Public Library.
Handwriting is Adele France's.
(Courtesy, Joan Horsey)

The University of Chicago
FOUNDED BY JOHN D. ROCKEFELLER

The Extension Division
CORRESPONDENCE-STUDY DEPARTMENT
HERVEY F. MALLORY, SECRETARY

CHICAGO, ILLINOIS

Outline Course of Study for Woman's Literary Club of Chestertown, Maryland.

MEETING ONE: Thackeray.
MEETING TWO: Dickens.
MEETING THREE: Charlotte Bronte.
MEETINGS 4 & 5: Carlyle.
MEETING 6 & 7:   Ruskin (Three meetings included).
Meeting 8, 9 & 10: Browning.
Meeting 11 & 12: Mrs. Browning.
Meeting 13:   Dante Gabriel Rossetti.
Meeting 14:   Christina Rossetti.
Meeting 15:   William Morris.
Meeting 16:   Kipling.
Meeting 17:   Phillips.
Meeting 18:19,20: Stevenson.

February 25, 1905.

I. Paper: The Church and the early drama.
       L. A. Stam.

II. Critical analysis of Hamlet.
1. Sources & Construction of the plot.
       I. B. Eliason.
2. Was Hamlet mad?
       M. A. France.
3. Hamlet as a son.
       M. C. Burchinal.
4. Hamlet as a lover.
       A. B. Smith.
5. Gertrude, Queen of Denmark.
       S. Culp.
6. Claudius, King of Denmark.
       H. Toulson.
7. Comparison of Ophelia & Hero.
       M. Toulson.
8. Comparison of Polonius & Leonato.
       L. A. Stam.
9. Horatio.
       J. M. Burchinal.
10. Laertes.
    (H. Westcott) A. B. Smith.

The Woman's Literary Club,
Assignment Sheet of 25 February 1905.

Handwriting is Adele France's.
(Courtesy, Joan Horsey)

IV.   Feb. 18, 1916
Centennial (1876) & Columbian Exposition (1893) Periods.

1st Paper.   Whistler,
                     Miss Stuart.

2nd Paper.   La Farge,
                     Miss Nicholson.

Class Study,   Miss France
Turning point in History of American Art. Impetus given American Art. City planning inaugurated.

Current Events,   Mrs. B. Jefferson

February 18.

References —

Caffin, Chapter IX. & Pages 313–315
Van Dyke (A History of A. Painting) Pages 267, 268
Isham, Chapter XIX. Pages 390, 396
Pages 563, 564 & Pages 544, 547.

Centennial 1876.

1 — Why is 1876 a turning point in A. art?
2 — What art educational influence preceded the Centennial Exposition?
3 — What sort of native works was exhibited in the period immediately preceding the Centennial Exposition?
4 — Give some concrete results of the Centennial Exposition.
5 — What were the artistic results?
6 — What were the material causes that led up to the stimulated activity in art?
7 — How was the greatest effect upon art accomplished? Results in societies.
8 — Give the ultimate result of the movement on the art of the U.S.
9 — How were the returned A. artists treated by the Academy of Design?
10 — Give some opinions of the works of great artists held by the Academy of Design.
11 — Give a brief history of the beginning of the Society of American Artists.
12 — When & under what circumstances did the Society of A. Artists take

its place as a settled institution?

Columbian Exposition 1893.

1— What phase of painting did the Columbian Exhibition bring to the front?
2— What did it accomplish along this line?
3— Describe the general appearance of the "White City."
4— What lesson did it teach with regard to beauty?
5— Explain the new idea it gave of the value of ensembles.
6— Give the notable effects in Chicago, Philadelphia, New York & Boston.
7— Cite any example of city planning you recall.
8— What has been accomplished in the decade since 1893?
9— Give Isham's vision of the future.
10— How does protective tariff hamper art?

Appendix D

Fund-Publication, No. 28.

THE CALVERT PAPERS.

NUMBER ONE.

With an account of their recovery, and presentation to the Society,

December 10th, 1888.

Together with a Calendar of the Papers recovered,
and Selections from the Papers.

Baltimore, 1889.

THE CALVERT PAPERS.

No. 1.

LORD BALTIMORE'S INSTRUCTIONS TO COLONISTS.

[Indorsement.]

15 Nouem. 1633.
A Coppy of
Instructions to M.[r] Leo.
Caluert, M.[r] Jerom Hawley
& M.[r] Tho. Cornwaleys the
Lo: Baltimores Gouernor &
Comissioners of his prouince
of Maryland.
In the 5.th Article some
directions is giuen con-
cerning Cap. Cleyborne.

Iustructions 13 Nouem: 1633 directed by the Right Hono[ble] Cecilius Lo: Baltimore & Lord of the Prouinces of Mary Land and Avalon vnto his well beloued Brother Leo: Caluert Esq.[r] his Lop.[s] Deputy Gouernor of his prouince of Mary Land and vnto Jerom Hawley and Thomas Cornwaleys Esq.[rs] his Lo.[pps] Comissioners for the gouernment of the said Prouince.,

1. Inpri: His Lo[rp] requires his said Gouernor & Comissioners th[t] in their voyage to Mary Land they be very carefull to preserue vnity & peace amongst all the passengers on Shipp-board, and that they suffer no scandall nor offence to be giuen to any of the Protestants, whereby any iust complaint may heereafter be made, by them, in Virginea or in England, and that for that end, they cause all Acts of Romane Catholique Religion to be done as priuately as may be, and that they instruct all the Romane Catholiques to be silent vpon all occasions of discourse concerning matters of Religion; and that the said Gouernor & Comissioners treate the Protestants wth as much mildness and fauor as Justice will permitt. And this to be obserued at Land as well as at Sea.

2. That while they are aboard, they do theyre best endeauors by such instruments as they shall find fittest for it, amongst the seamen & passengers to discouer what any of them do know concerning the priuate plotts of his Lo[pps] aduersaries in England, who endeauored to ouerthrow his voyage: to learne, if they cann the names of all such, their speeches, where & when they spoke them, and to whom; The places, if they had any, of their consultations, the Instruments they vsed and the like: to gather what proofes they cann of them; and to sett them downe particulerly and cleerely in writing wth all the Circumstances; together wth their opinions of the truth and validity of them according to the condition of the persons from whom they had the information; And to gett if they can euery such informer to sett his hand to his Informa̅con. And if they find it necessary & that they haue any good probable ground to discouer the truth better, or that they find some vnwilling to reueale that w[ch] (by some speeches at randome, that haue fallen from them) they haue reason to suspect they do know concerning that buisness: that at their arriuall

in Mary Land they cause euery such pson to answer vpon oath, to such questions as they shall thinke fitt to propose vnto them: And by some trusty messenger in the next shipps that returne for England to send his Lo^pp in writing all such Intelligences taken either by deposition or otherwise.

3. That as soone as it shall please god they shall arriue vpon the coast of Virginea, they be not perswaded by the master or any other of the shipp, in any case or for any respect whatsoeuer to goe to James Towne, or to come wth in the comand of the the fort at Poynt-Comfort: vnless they should be forct vnto it by some extremity, of weather, (wch god forbidd) for the preseruation of their liues & goodes, and that they find it altogether impossible otherwise to preserue themselues: But that they come to an Anchor somewhere about Acomacke, so as it be not vnder the comand of any fort; & to send ashoare there, to inquire if they cann find any to take wth them, that cann giue them some good informatione of the Bay of Chesapeacke and Pattawomeck Riuer, and that may giue them some light of a fitt place in his Lo^pps Countrey to sett downe on; wherein their cheife care must be to make choice of a place first that is probable to be healthfull and fruitfull, next that it may be easily fortified, and thirdly that it may be convenient for trade both wth the English and sauages.

4. That by the first oportunity after theyr arriuall in Mary Land they cause a messenger to be dispatcht away to James Town such a one as is conformable to the Church of England, and as they may according to the best of their iudgments trust; and he to carry his ma^ties letter to Sr John Haruie the Gouernor and to the rest of the Councell there, as likewise his Lo^rps letter to S^r Jo: Haruie, and to give him notice of their arriuall: And to haue in charge, vpon the deliuery of the said

letters to behaue himself wth much respect vnto the Gouernor, and to tell him th^t his Lo^{pp} had an intention to haue come himself in person this yeare into those parts, as he may perceiue by his ma^{ties} letter to him but finding that the setling of that buisness of his Plantation and some other occasions, required his presence in England for some time longer then he expected, he hath deferred his owne coming till the next yeare, when he will not faile by the grace of god to be there; and to lett him vnderstand how much his Lo^{pp} desires to hold a good correspondency wth him and that Plantation of Virginea, wch he wilbe ready to shew vpon all occasions and to assure him by the best words he cann, of his Lo^{pps} particuler affection to his person, in respect of the many reports he hath heard of his worth, and of the ancient acquaintance and freindshipp wch he hath vnderstood was between his Lo^{pps} father & him as likewise for those kind respects he hath shewne vnto his L^{opp} by his letters since he vnderstoode of his L^{opps} intention to be his neighbor in those parts: And to present him wth a Butt of sacke from his L^{opp} wch his L^{opp} hath giuen directions for, to be sent vnto him.

5. That they write a letter to Cap: Clayborne as soone as conveniently other more necessary occasions will giue them leaue after their arriuall in the Countrey, to give him notice of their arriuall and of the Authority & charge comitted to them by his L^{opp} and to send the said letter together wth his L^{opps} to him by some trusty messenger that is likewise conformable vnto the Church of England, wth a message also from them to him if it be not inserted in their letter wch is better, to invite him kindly to come vnto them, and to signify that they haue some buisness of importance to speake wth him about from his L^{opp} wch concernes his good very much; And if he come vnto them then that they vse him courteously and well, and tell

him, that his L^opp vnderstanding that he hath settled a plantacōn there wth in the precincts of his L^opps Pattent, wished them to lett him know that his L^opp is willing to giue him all the encouragement he cann to proceede; And that his L^opp hath had some propositions made vnto him by certaine m^rchants in London who pretend to be partners wth him in that plantation, (viz) Mr Delabarr, Mr Tompson Mr Cloberry, Mr Collins, & some others, and that they desired to haue a grant from his L^opp of that Iland where he is: But his L^opp vnderstanding from some others that there was some difference in partnershipp between him and them, and his L^opp finding them in their discourse to him, that they made somewhat slight of Cap: Clayberne's interest, doubted least he might preiudice him by making them any grant his Lo^pp being ignorant of the true state of their buisness and of the thing they desired, as likewise being well assured that by Cap: Clayborne his care and industry besides his charges, that plantation was first begunn and so farr aduanced, was for these reasons vnwilling to condescend vnto their desires, and therefore deferred all treaty wth them till his Lo^pp could truly vnderstand from him, how matters stand between them, and what he would desire of his L^opp in it. wch his Lo^pp expects from him; that therevpon his L^opp may take it into farther consideration how to do iustice to euery one of them and to giue them all reasonable satisfaction; And that they assure him in fine that his L^opp intends not to do him any wrong, but to shew him all the loue and fauor that he cann, and that his L^opp gaue them directions to do so to him in his absence; in confidence that he will, like a good subiect to his ma^tie conforme himself to his higness gratious letters pattents granted to his Lo^pls whereof he may see the Duplicate if he desire it together wth their Comission from his L^opp. If he do refuse to come vnto them vpon their invitation, that they lett him alone for the first yeare, till vpon notice giuen to his L[opp] of his answere and behauiour they receiue farther directions from his L[opp]; and that they informe themselues as well as they cann of his plantation and what his designes are, of what strength & what Correspondency he keepes wth Virginea, and to giue an Account of euery particular to his L[opp].

6. That when they haue made choice of the place where they intend to settle themselues and that they haue brought their men ashoare wth all their prouisions, they do assemble all the people together in a fitt and decent manner and then cause his ma[ties] letters pattents to be publikely read by his L[opps] Secretary John Bolles, and afterwards his L[opps] Comission to them, and that either the Gouernor or one of the Comissioners presently after make some short declaration to the people of his L[opps] intentions w[ch] he means to pursue in this his intended plantation, w[ch] are first the honor of god by endeauoring the conversion of the sauages to Christianity, secondly the augmentation of his ma[ties] Empire & Dominions in those parts of the world by reducing them vnder the subiection of his Crowne, and thirdly by the good of such of his Countreymen as are willing to aduenture their fortunes and themselues in it, by endeauoring all he cann, to assist them, that they may reape the fruites of their charges & labors according to the hopefulnes of the thing, wth as much freedome comfort and incouragement as they cann desire; and wth all to assure them, that his L[opps] affection & zeale is so greate to the aduancement of this Plantacon and consequently of their good, that he will imploy all his endeauors in it, and that he would not haue failed to haue come himself in person along wth them this first yeare, to haue beene partaker wth them in the honor of the first voyage thither, but that by reasons of some vnexpected

accidents, he found it more necessary for their good, to stay in England some time longer, for the better establishment of his and their right, then it was fitt that the shipp should stay for him, but that by the grace of god he intends w[th]out faile to be w[th] them the next year: And that at this time they take occasion to minister an oath of Allegeance to his ma[tie] vnto all and euery one vpon the place, after hauing first publikely in the presence of the people taken it themselues; letting them know that his Lo[pp] gaue particuler directions to haue it one of the first thinges that were done, to testify to the world that none should enioy the benefitt of his ma[ties] gratious Grant vnto his L[pp] of that place, but such as should giue a publique assurance of their fidelity & allegeance to his ma[tie].

7. that they informe themselues what they cann of the present state of the old Colony of Virginea, both for matter of gouernment & and Plantacon as likewise what trades they driue both at home and abroade, who are the cheife and richest men, & haue the greatest power amongst them whether their clamors against his Lo[pps] pattent continue and whether they increase or diminish, who they are of note that shew themselues most in it, and to find out as neere as they cann, what is the true reason of their disgust against it, or whether there be really any other reason but what, being well examined proceedes rather from spleene and malice then from any other cause; And to informe his L[opp] exactly what they vnderstand in any of these particulers.

8. That they take all occasions to gaine and oblige any of the Councell of Virginea, that they shall vnderstand incline to have a good correspondency w[th] his L[opps] plantation, either by permission of trade to them in a reasonable proportion, w[th]in his L[opps] precincts, or any other way they can, so it be cleerely vnderstood that it is by the way of courtesy and not of right.

9. That where they intend to settle the Plantacon they first make choice of a fitt place, and a competent quantity of ground for a fort w^{ch}in wch or neere vnto it a convenient house, and a church or a chappel adiacent may be built, for the seate of his L^{opp} or his Gouernor or other Comissioners for the time being in his absence, both wch his Lo^{pp} would haue them take care should in the first place be erected, in some proportion at least, as much as is necessary for present vse though not so compleate in euery part as in fine afterwards they may be and to send his L^{opp} a Platt of it and of the scituation, by the next oportunity, if it be done by that time, if not or but part of it neuertheless to send a Platt of what they intend to do in it. That they likewise make choise of a fitt place neere vnto it to seate a towne.

10. That they cause all the Planters to build their houses in as decent and vniforme a manner as their abilities and the place will afford, & neere adioyning one to an other, and for that purpose to cause streetes to be marked out where they intend to place the towne and to oblige euery man to buyld one by an other according to that rule and that they cause diuisions of Land to be made adioyning on the back sides of their houses and to be assigned vnto them for gardens and such vses according to the proportion of euery ones building and adventure and as the conveniency of the place will afford wch his L^{opp} referreth to their discretion, but is desirous to haue a particuler account from them what they do in it, that his Lo^{pp} may be satisfied that euery man hath iustice done vnto him.

11. That as soone as conveniently they cann they cause his L^{opps} surveyor Robert Simpson to survay out such a proportion of Land both in and about the intended towne as likewise wthin the Countrey adioyning as wilbe necessary to be assigned to the present aduenturers, and that they assigne euery adven-

turer his proportion of Land both in and about the intended towne, as alsoe wthin the Countrey adioyning, according to the proportion of his aduenture and the conditions of plantaçon propounded by his Lo^{pp} to the first aduenturers, wch his L^{opp} in convenient time will confirme vnto them by Pattent. And heerein his L^{opp} wills his said Gouernor and Comissioners to take care that in each of the aforesaid places, that is to say in and about the first intended Towne and in the Countrey adiacent they cause in the first and most convenient places a proportion of Land to be sett out for his L^{opps} owne proper vse and inheritance according to the number of men he sends this first yeare vpon his owne account; and as he alloweth vnto the aduenturers, before any other be assigned his part; wth w^{ch} (although his Lopp might very well make a difference of proportion between himself and the aduenturers) he will in this first colony, content himself, for the better encouragement and accomodation of the first aduenturers, vnto whom his L^{opp} conceiue himself more bound in honor and is therefore desirous to giue more satisfaction in euery thing then he intends to do vnto any that shall come heereafter. That they cause his Lo^{pps} survayor likewise to drawe an exact mapp of as much of the countrey as they shall discouer together wth the soundings of the riuers and Baye, and to send it to his L^{opp}.

12. That they cause all the planters to imploy their seruants in planting of sufficient quantity of corne and other prouision of victuall and that they do not suffer them to plant any other comodity whatsoeuer before that be done in a sufficient proportion wch they are to obserue yearely.

13. That they cause all sorts of men in the plantation to be mustered and trained in military discipline and that there be days appoynted for that purpose either weekely or monthly according to the conuenieney of other occasions; wch are duly

to be observed and that they cause constant watch and ward to be kept in places necessary.

14. That they informe themselues whether there be any convenient place wthin his L^{opps} precincts for the making of Salt whether there be proper earth for the making of salt-peeter and if there be in what quantity; whether there be probability of Iron oare or any other mines and that they be carefull to find out what other comodities may probably be made and that they giue his L^{opp} notice together wth their opinions of them.

15. That In fine they bee very carefull to do iustice to euery man wthout partiality, and that they auoid any occasion of difference wth those of Virginea and to haue as litle to do wth them as they cann this first yeare that they conniue and suffer litle iniuryes from them rather then to engage themselues in a publique quarrell wth them, wch may disturbe the buisness much in England in the Infancy of it. And that they giue vnto his Lo^{pp} an exact account by their letters from time to time of their proceedings both in these instructions from Article to Article and in any other accident that shall happen worthy his Lo^{pps} notice, that thereupon his L^{pp} may giue them farther instructions what to doe and that by euery conveyance by wch they send any letters as his Lo^{pp} would not haue them to omitt any they send likewise a Duplicate of the letters wch they writt by the last conveyance before that, least they should haue failed and not be come to his Lo^{pps} hands.

Acknowledgments

Thank you to all those persons who generously shared their knowledge and insights. Apologies are offered to any persons who helped but may not be listed below (in such case, due solely to the author's or the editor's oversight, not to any lack of merit nor appreciation).

The opinions expressed in this book, as well as any errors that may have been made, are the responsibility of this author and should not be attributed in any way to those persons who graciously bestowed their time.

Special thanks to Lee, Kat, Abby, Joan, and Al.

St. Mary's College of Maryland (SMCM) - Board of Trustees:

Officers
Susan Dyer, chair
Paula Collins, vice chair
John C. Wobensmith '93, treasurer
Nicolas Abrams '99, secretary

Members

Carlos Alcazar

Anirban Basu

John Bell '95

Arthur A. "Lex" Birney Jr.

Peter Bruns

Donny Bryan '73

Peg Duchesne '77

Judith Filius '79

Kate Fritz '04 (Alumni Association)

Elizabeth Graves '95

Kristen Greenaway

Gail Harmon

Sven Erik Holmes

Talib Horne '93

Steny Hoyer

Kimberly B. Kelley

Jesse Price '92

Melanie Rosalez '92

Aaron Tomarchio '96 (HSMC)

Danielle Troyan '92

Raymond Wernecke

Isabella Woel-Popovich '24 (Student Trustee)

SMCM - Governance:

Tuajuanda C. Jordan, President (2014-present)

Katherine Gantz, Vice President for Academic Affairs and Dean of Faculty (2023-present)

Carolyn Curry, Vice President for Institutional Advancement & Executive Director, SMCM Foundation, Inc. (2015-present)

Ian Newbould, Interim President (2013-2014)

Joseph R. Urgo, President (2010-2013)

Larry E. Vote, Acting President (2009-2010)

Jane Margaret O'Brien, President (1996-2009)

Salvatore M. Meringolo, Vice President for Institutional Advancement & Executive Director, SMCM Foundation, Inc. (1996-2009)

Edward T. Lewis, President (1983-1996)

SMCM - Publishing:

Lee Capristo, Director of Writing and Content, Integrated Marketing and Communications Department

Abigale Larsh, Senior Graphic Designer, Integrated Marketing and Communications Department

Topic: Adele France:

Joan Andersen, Historical Society of Kent County

Dawn J. Bielert, Lead Land Records Clerk, Kent County Circuit Court, Chestertown

Diane Daniels, Historical Society of Kent County

Jack Diller, Chester Cemetery

Marge Fallaw, Historical Society of Kent County

Kevin Hemstock, former editor, Kent County News

Joseph L. Holt, Vice President for Administration, Washington College

Joan Horsey, Historical Society of Kent County *and* the Woman's Literary Club of Chestertown

Mark Mumford, Volunteer Fire Department, Chestertown

April Perry, Columbia Alumni Center

Linda Reno, St. Mary's County Historical Society

Carrie Schreiber, Historical Society of Kent County

Topic - John LaFarge, S.J.:

Claudette Bennett and Shirley Dickerson, parish of St. Peter Claver Catholic Church

Rev. Thomas F. Clifford, S.J., Pastor, St. Ignatius Catholic Church, Chapel Point (Port Tobacco)

Rev. Rory T. Conley, Pastor, St. Mary's Catholic Church (Bryantown)

Father Scott Wood, St. Cecilia Catholic Church (St. Mary's City) and St. Peter Claver Catholic Church (St. Inigoes)

Topic - History:

David S. Bogen, Professor Emeritus of Law, Maryland Carey School of Law, University of Maryland

Alfred Gough

Hope Grace, Daughters of the American Revolution (St. Mary's County)

Jennifer Rae Greeson, Chair, Department of American Studies, Associate Professor of English, University of Virginia

Francine Hawkins

Steve Hawkins

Peter Himmelheber, *Chronicles*, St. Mary's County Historical Society

Silas D. Hurry, Adjunct Professor of Anthropology, SMCM

Peter LaPorte, Executive Director, St. Mary's County Historical Society

Jane Miklos, The Bristol Magazine, Bath, U.K.

Henry Miller, Adjunct Professor of Anthropology, SMCM

Carol Moody, *Chronicles*, St. Mary's County Historical Society

Deacon Vito S. Piazza, Sr., St. Mary's Spiritual Center & Historic Site on Paca Street

Barbara Seman, Daughters of the American Revolution (St. Mary's County)

Librarians, Archivists, Information Custodians:

Jennifer Abbott, Maryland State Archives

Wendy Alls, Lead Land Records Clerk, Land Records and License Department, St. Mary's County Circuit Court, Leonardtown, Maryland

Christine E. Alvey, Librarian, Maryland State Archives

Ancestry, Emily, Executive Office

Matthew Andrews, Maryland State Archives

Robert Barnes, Reference Archivist, Maryland State Archives

Mary Baumann, U.S. Senate Historical Office

Cassandra Berman, Archivist, Maryland Province Archives, Booth Family Center for Special Collections, Georgetown University Library

Elizabeth L. Brown, MLS, Reference Librarian, Main Reading Room, Library of Congress

Joanna Colclough, Reference Librarian, Newspaper & Current Periodical Reading Room, Serial & Government Publications Division, Library of Congress

Lois Coryell, Assistant Branch Manager, St. Mary's County Library (Leonardtown)

Megan Craynon, Deputy Director, Special Collections and Conservation, Maryland State Archives

Maria A. Day, Director, Special Collections and Conservation, Maryland State Archives

Alison M. Foley, Reference Archivist, Associated Archives at St. Mary's Seminary & University

Julia Gardner, University of Chicago Archives

Meg Gers, Periodicals Department, Enoch Pratt Free Library

Dr Daniel F. Gosling, Principal Legal Records Specialist, Collections Expertise & Engagement, The National Archives, United Kingdom

Clare "Pat" Ingersoll, Kent County Public Library

DRJ, Reference Specialist, Main Reading Room - Researcher and Reference Services Division, Library of Congress

Stephanie A.T. Jacobe, Director of Archives, The Roman Catholic Archdiocese of Washington

Ann N. Knake, Reference Archivist, Jesuit Archives & Research Center

Claire Lattin, Archivist Trainee, Maryland State Archives

Owen Lourie, Historian, Maryland State Archives

Kim MacVaugh, Research Services Department, Lauinger Library, Georgetown University

Paul McCardell, Librarian, Baltimore Sun

Nate Miller, Reference Archivist, Maryland State Archives

David Miros, Director, Jesuit Archives & Research Center

Jennifer Nesbitt, Miller Library, Washington College

New England Historic Genealogical Society: David Allen Lambert, Chief Genealogist; and Renise

Edward C. Papenfuse, Archivist, Maryland State Archives

Jeffrey Phillips, Kent County Public Library, Chestertown

Marion Quick, Librarian, Washington College

Kent Randell, Associate Librarian, SMCM

Michael Reid, Community Coordinator, Southern Maryland News

Lisa Rutherford, San Diego Public Library

Katherine Ryner, Associate Director of the Library & Head of Collections Support Services, SMCM

Lindsay A. Sheldon, Director of Archives & Technical Services, Library & Academic Technology, Washington College

Ruth Shoge, Miller Library, Washington College

Scott Taylor, Georgetown University Library

Heather C. Thomas, Reference Librarian, Serial & Government Publications Division, Library of Congress

U.S. House of Representatives, Office of the Historian

Jocelyn Wilk, Columbia University Archives, Butler Library, Columbia University

Karen Wood, Volunteer, Research Center, St. Mary's County Historical Society

Assistance:

JulieAnn Engel

Father Peter Giovanoni, Pastor, St. Michael's Catholic Church (Ridge)

Mary (María) B. Haugaard

Laura Lancaster, Accountant, St. Cecilia Catholic Church (St. Mary's City)

Mary Vernon Butler Nickerson

Abigail R. Sivak, Office of Planning and Facilities, SMCM

Reverend Larry Swink, Pastor, St. Cecilia Catholic Church (St. Mary's City)

Barbara Williams, Office of Publications, SMCM

Maps:

Mike Carter, scribblemaps.com

Index

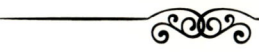

1840 Painting, 2, 18, 19, 20, 33, 35, 39, 86, 115, 130, 252

1st Constitution of Commonwealth, 62

2nd Constitution of Commonwealth, 63

Abbott, William, 228, 236

Abell, James Thomas, 213, 214, 224, 227, 260

Académie Française, 269

Act Against Jesuits ... of 1585, 56

Act Against [Popish] Recusants of 1593, 56

Act Against [Popish] Recusants of 1605, 51

Act Against [Popish] Recusants of 1657, 63

Act Against [Popish] Recusants of 1673, 65

Act declaring England to be a Commonwealth, 61

Act for the better Security of his Majestys Royall Person & Govt, 69, 76

Act for the further preventing the Growth of Popery, 69, 70

Act of Settlement of 1701, 67, 71

Act of Supremacy of 1534, 44, 55

Act of Supremacy of 1558, 56

Act to Preserve the Existence of the St. Mary's Female Seminary, 108

Act to Prevent the Growth of Popery of 1704, 74

Acts of Union of 1707, 72, 78

Adams, Henry, 139

Adirondack Mountains, 83

Adkins, Lesley and Roy, 32, 36, 37

Africa, 29-33, 45, 116, 179, 184-96, 201, 204, 210-12, 250, 254-56, 269, 272

Agassiz, Louis, 92

Airplanes, 135, 320

Alabama, 222, 251, 256-58, 274

Albany (New York), 83, 151, 268

Alexander the Great, 187

Allegheny Mountains, 83, 215, 222, 225-26, 248, 250

Alumnae Association, St. Mary's, 3, 112, 170, 346, 349, 352, 359-60

America magazine, 5, 16, 24, 28, 38, 39, 145-46, 190, 278-79, 281, 310, 325, 327, 353, 368

American Colonization Society, 228

Amherst College, 245

Andersen, Joan, 128

Angles and Saxons, 187

Anglo-Saxon (language), 187

Angola, 189-90, 201, 212

Annapolis, 11, 48, 54, 68, 72, 76, 85, 89, 90, 101, 104, 108, 115, 185, 255, 360

Anne Arundell Towne, 68

Anthony, Susan B., 154, 156

Anti-Slavery Act of 1833, 19, 34-35, 87

Anti-Slavery Convention, 2, 18, 19-22, 33, 35, 39, 86, 115, 130, 151-52, 252

Anti-Slavery Society, 18, 20, 22, 34-35

Antigua (island), 254

Antiques Road Show, 237

Appalachian Mountains, 83

Aquinas, Thomas, 291

Aramaic (language), 141, 285

Archbishop of Canterbury, 45, 47, 66, 193

Aristotle, 320

Ark and Dove, 46, 49, 58, 180, 183-84, 198-210, 212, 306, 311

Arkansas, 274

Aruba, Bonaire, and Curaçao (islands), 184, 185

Athenians, 187

Augusta (Georgia), 222

Austen, Jane, 32, 36-38, 93, 138, 283, 287

Austria, 142, 278, 285-90, 309, 326

Austro-Hungarian Empire, 142

Automobiles, 12, 94, 112, 113, 128, 135, 148-49, 163, 311

Avalon, 49, 181-82

Babcock, Jason, 302, 309

Bahamas, 191

Balta, John, 295

Baltimore, 7, 8, 11, 12, 14, 48, 84, 91, 97, 98, 99, 108, 110, 119, 123, 129, 136, 143, 148, 161, 214, 219, 222, 227, 239, 241, 248, 249, 257, 258, 270, 278, 291, 304, 313, 316, 318, 340, 341, 359, 366

Baltimore (Ireland), 201

Baltimore Academy of the Visitation, 109

Baltimore College, 99

Baltimore Institute of Art, 166

Barbados, 22, 49, 183, 185, 186, 202-09, 211-12, 254

Barbary Coast (North Africa), 201

Barber, Donald M., 301

Barber, Elizabeth, 366

Barber, Ernest, 119

Barge, 222, 223, 230, 345

Barnard College, 123

Battle of the Severn, 61

Bd. of Educ. of St. Mary's County v. Groves, 261 F.2d 527 (1958), 309

Beale, Jenny, 304, 309, 318, 319

Beaumont, Eugénie, 265, 272, 273

Beaumont, Félicie, 266, 270

Beaumont, Gustave, 214, 217-20, 224-25, 260-73

Beaumont, Jules (Jr.), 260, 264

Beaumont, Jules (Sr.), 297

Beaumont, Rose, 217, 271

Beaver, muskrat, deer, 181, 182, 202, 210

Beecher Stowe, Harriet, 164

Beitzell, Edwin W., 52, 77-78, 80, 87-88, 100, 303, 305-06, 312, 316

Bell Tingle, Mina Dirickson, 176

Belvidere (steamboat), 231

Bennett, Claudette, 5

Bennett, John White, 104

Bill of Rights of 1689 - Constitutional Monarchy, 67, 68

Bill of Rights of 1789, 79, 82, 99

Biscoe family, 310, 312

Biscoe Grayson, Ellen, 312

Biscoe Jackson, Cecilia, 312

Biscoe, Fred, 174

Biscoe, Sadie, 312

Bishop of Exeter, 34, 38

Bishop, Emily Clayton, 165-67, 168

Blackistone Lancaster, Priscilla Hebb, 167

Blackistone, Eleanor Grace, 121

Blackistone, George, 91

Blackistone, James T., 85, 87, 88, 91, 100, 102, 104, 107, 118, 158-59, 250

Blackistone, James T. and Ann Thomas, 88

Bladen, Thomas, 75

Bladen, William, 75

Bledsoe, Albert, 93

Board of Colored Missions (New York), 305

Boats, 2, 7, 8, 9, 12-14, 22, 29-33, 37, 46, 49, 81, 82, 83, 92, 97, 105, 117, 119, 128, 135, 139, 141, 143, 148, 157, 164, 180, 183, 186, 187, 189, 192, 194-99, 201-12, 215, 218-23, 228-31, 248, 253-55, 261, 274, 304, 306, 311, 325, 341, 345, 362

Bogen, David S., 307

Boko Haram, 187

Boleyn, Anne, 44

Bolivia, 196

Bonnie Prince Charlie ("Young Pretender"), 70

Borburata, 194

Boston, 31, 79, 97, 98, 164, 202, 219, 222, 227, 236, 238, 257, 262, 286

Boston College, 190

Boswell, James, 95, 138

Boughton, Helen, 114

Bourbon monarchs, 76

Bradford, Augustus, 110

Bradford, William, 98

Bratislava, 145

Brazil, 30, 179, 189

Brennan, S.J., 14

Brent, Margaret, 160, 177, 344

Breton (language), 142, 143, 289

Briscoe, Leon M., 324

Bristol (England), 192

Bristol School (Washington, D.C.), 120, 341

Brittany, 142, 187, 221, 289

Brome, John, 102

Brome's Landing (Brome's Wharf), 7, 8, 9, 12, 105, 119, 120, 299

Brome's Landing Road (Brome's Wharf Road), 25

Brontë, Charlotte, 28, 30, 31, 94, 95

Brooke, Robert, 76

Brown v. Board of Education of Topeka, 347 U.S. 483 (1954), 24, 38, 269, 280, 301, 309, 322, 365

Brown, Ethel, 312

Brown, Frederick, 218, 219, 261, 270

Browne, Thomas, 54, 72

Browning, Elizabeth Barrett, 176

Bruges (northwest Flanders), 78

Bryn Mawr College, 123

Buddhists, 114, 160

Buffalo (New York), 273

Bureau of Indian Affairs, 252

Burns, Robert, 213

Burton, Katherine, 308, 309

Bus, 12, 280, 303, 313, 320, 359, 361

Byrne, Paula, 36

Cabot, John, 190, 192-93, 196

Cady Stanton, Elizabeth, 18, 20, 21, 39, 151-57, 159-60, 338-39

Calais (France), 78

Calloway, Mrs. Luther, 315, 316

Calvert County, 162, 231

Calvert Hall (Main Building), 119, 120, 172, 175, 341, 344-47, 349, 352, 360, 368

Calvert, Cecil, 2, 40, 48, 49, 51-53, 57, 61, 63, 68, 72, 73, 80, 84, 97, 99, 102, 108, 115, 118, 157, 158, 179-81, 182, 197-201, 203, 205-07, 209, 211, 319, 356

Calvert, George, 49, 50, 53, 181, 182, 197, 211

Calvert, George (Jr.), 203

Calvert, Leonard, 40, 48, 49, 58, 72, 97, 102, 103, 115, 158, 160, 169, 179-81, 199-200, 203-05, 209, 211-12, 311

Camalier, Vincent, 85, 88

Campbell, John, 93

Campion House (New York City), 145, 146, 278, 281, 325, 330, 367

Canada, 92

Canary Islands, 191, 194, 202, 204

Canoe, 195, 362

Cape Verde Islands, 189, 195

Cardinal Gibbons Institute, 5, 15, 16, 23, 24, 26, 145, 161, 228, 279, 299, 302, 315-16, 318-22

Cardinal Gibbons School (Baltimore), 316

Caribbean, 30-31, 38, 45, 46, 183-85, 205, 211, 254, 272

Carnegie, Andrew, 92

Carolina, 192, 210, 256, 257

Carroll, Charles, 78, 269, 270

Carroll, James H., 295

Carroll, John, 77, 78, 84, 239, 309

Carrollton Manor, 269

Cartagena (Colombia), 195

Casey, Father, 148

Castel Gandolfo, 326, 328

Castelli, Jim, 330

Catherine of Aragon, 44, 189

Catholic Emancipation Act, 71

Catholic Interracial Council of New York, 279

Catholic University of America, 320

Cau, Hélène, 163, 351

Celts, 187

Ceylon (now Sri Lanka), 255

Champlin, Christopher, 28-30

Chancellor's Point, 369

Channel (aka la Manche), 78, 187, 197, 199

Chaptico, 104

Charles County, 8, 89-90, 110, 214, 231, 292, 311, 360

Charleston (South Carolina), 28, 185, 222, 258

Charlotte Hall, 12, 102, 177

Charlotte Hall School, 89-91, 92, 101, 102, 103, 109, 157, 177, 178, 215, 361, 362

Charlottesville (Virginia), 222, 230, 257

Charter for the Province of Maryland, 48, 57, 72, 73, 203

Chaucer, Geoffrey, 133

Chautauqua Institute, 337

Chautauquas, 91, 337

Cherokee (language), 251-52

Cherokee nation, 251-52, 254, 273

Cherry Fields Plantation, 102, 158

Chesapeake Bay, 2, 7, 8, 9, 10, 11, 12, 13, 14, 49, 79, 82, 116, 117, 126, 157, 208, 280, 298, 299, 304, 340, 345

Chester Cemetery, 333, 366

Chestertown, 4, 11, 14, 26, 79, 116, 123, 124, 128–34, 156, 157, 170, 299, 333, 334-42, 366

Chestertown library, 132, 157, 333, 337, 338, 340

Chestertown Volunteer Fire Department, 124, 132, 333

Chickasaw nation, 253

China, 214, 272

Choctaw nation, 252-53, 273, 274-75

Chopin, Frédéric, 283

Chopin, Kate, 164

Cincinnati (Ohio), 222, 225, 228-29, 231-32, 233-34, 236, 238-39, 241, 246-48, 251, 252, 253, 256, 270-71

Circuit Court for St. Mary's County, Clerk's Office, 317

Civil Code of 1804 (Napoleonic Code), 263

Civil Rights Act of 1964, 24

Civil War (U.S.), 2, 24, 31, 34, 38, 84, 87, 88, 90, 91, 110, 116-17, 190, 215, 217, 219, 226, 232, 239, 259, 295, 337

Claiborne, William, 59

Clark Wetherill, Peggy, 111

Clark-Pujara, Christy, 32

Clarke, Clementine, 305

Clarkson, Thomas, 35, 36

Claver Industrial School, Incorporated, 317

Clay, Henry, 228, 253

Coad Roberts, Cecilia, 111

Coad, William, 102, 104, 111, 118, 158, 159, 250

Code of Hammurabi, 187

Coffin Mott, Lucretia, 18, 20-22, 39, 152, 154-55

Colonial Ball, 177

Columbia (South Carolina), 222

Columbia University, 15, 26, 116, 132, 155, 342

Columbia University Archives and Alumni Center, 333

Columbus, Christopher, 183, 190-91, 196

Combs Hammett, Regina, 53, 80, 83, 296, 303, 344, 350

Combs, Cornelius, 104

Combs, George, 85

Commager, Henry Steele, 95-96, 97, 106

Commonwealth of Nations, 205

Conley, Rory T., 86, 303, 369

Connecticut, 289

Constitution (U.S.), 1, 22, 24, 78, 79, 96, 99, 106, 110, 129, 134, 155, 156, 169, 216, 241, 251, 254, 342

Constitution, Article VI, 79

Constitution, 1st Amendment, 79, 99

Constitution, 13th Amendment, 22

Constitution, 14th Amendment, 24, 110, 307

Constitution, 19th Amendment, 1, 22, 129, 134, 155, 156, 169, 241, 342

Constitution, Three-Fifths Clause, 110

Coode, John Jr., 43, 74, 76

Cool Springs, 89, 90

Cooper, James Fennimore, 93, 96

Copeland, Charles (Copey), 139, 285

Copley, Lionel, 73

Copley, Thomas, 51

Cornwaleys (Cornwallis), Thomas, 180, 199, 203, 205, 209

Cornwall and Devon counties (England), 192-93

Corporation Act of 1661, 64

Cotton, 30, 32, 210, 254, 272

Coughtry, Jay, 32

Cox, Ginny and Tom, 77

Crandall, Ralph J., 83

Creek nation, 253

Creole (language), 191

Criterion (steamboat), 229

Croatia, 145

Cromwell, 47, 53, 60, 62, 63

Crowley, Francis M., 316

Cuba, 122, 184, 191, 192, 202

Curaçao, 184, 185

Cutchember, Viola T., 324

Czar Ivan the Terrible, 187

401

Czar Nicholas, 135

Czechoslovakia, 145

Dances, 3, 12, 109, 177-78, 267, 341, 356, 361-62

Daniel, Victor, 319-20, 325

Danish (language), 141, 282

Darwin, Charles, 92, 243

Darwin, Erasmus, 243

Daughters of the American Revolution, 169-70, 352, 354

Davenport, William H., 176

Davis, Thurston, 279

De las Casas, Bartolomé, 190, 191-92

Declaration for Liberty of Conscience, 66

Declaration of Breda, 64

Declaration of Independence, 72, 96, 152, 229, 270

Declaration of Indulgence, 66

Declaration of Rights and Sentiments, 152-54, 155, 156, 157

DeCorse France, Emma Price, 123, 124, 129, 132, 334, 340, 341

DeCorse McArthur, Helen, 357

DeCorse, James, 124, 334

Delaware, 11, 14

Delco building, 177, 351

Delmarva Peninsula, 11, 14

Denmark, 30, 54, 187, 211

Dent Gough, Lettie, 168, 323

Dent, Helen, 121

Dent, Walter Benjamin, 121

Depression of 1837, 104

Desbuquois, Gustave, 328

Dewey, John, 23

Dickens, Catherine, 226

Dickens, Charles, 93, 132, 138, 215, 217-19, 220-22, 224-27, 230, 233, 235-40, 243, 246, 249-50, 253, 257, 259, 260, 268, 283, 287

Dickerson, Shirley, 5

Dickinson, Emily, 94, 164

Disappeared city of St. Mary's, 97, 99-100, 102, 104-06, 110, 340, 349, 352, 355, 356

Disappeared encyclical, 277, 278, 325-31

Dominica (island), 254

Dominican Republic, 185, 191, 194

Douay (France), 198

Dougherty-Barroll house, 124, 128, 129, 334

Douglass, Frederick, 307

Dover (England), 78

Downton Abbey, 163, 263

Dragon (ship), 201-02, 212

Dragonships (longships), 187

Drake, Francis, 193-97, 212

Du Motier, Gilbert (Marquis de Lafayette), 228

Dumschott, Fred W., 335, 336

Dunbar, Lucy, 110

Dunbar, Paul Laurence (Lawrence), 164, 320

Dürer, 133

Dutch, 53, 66, 96, 184, 185, 197, 234

Dyer, William, 112

East India Company, 212, 255

East Indies, 190, 191

East River (New York), 219

Eastern Shore, 12, 14, 79, 108, 116, 214, 299, 304, 334, 342

Eastern Shore Power Company, 351

Edward (packet-ship), 228

Einstein, Albert, 135

Eisner, Peter, 326, 327

Electricity, 92, 175, 351

Emancipation Proclamation (1863), 34, 84

Emerick, Abraham, 296, 297, 301, 302, 303, 308-09, 311-13, 315-16

Emerson, Ralph Waldo, 93, 238

Emmanuel Episcopal Church (Chestertown), 366

Enactment Day (1840 - Female Seminary at St. Mary's), 346, 356, 368, 369

England, 20-22, 30-31, 33-37, 40, 43-46, 48-51, 53-79, 81, 86-87, 89-90, 96-98, 115, 143, 155, 160, 181-83, 185-87, 192-205, 208-11, 215-19, 224-31, 233-38, 240-44, 246, 248, 250, 252-54, 260, 263, 265, 267, 272

English (language), 51, 78, 90, 95, 100, 109, 125, 131, 133, 139-42, 144, 175, 183, 185, 195, 197, 198, 200, 205, 207, 209, 214, 215, 217, 218, 221, 233, 242, 253, 260, 261, 262, 269, 273, 282, 283, 285, 287, 288, 289, 295-97, 305, 308, 311, 326, 328, 330, 369

English Civil Wars, 47, 51, 53, 59, 60

English Reformation, 40, 44-47, 54-55, 72, 115, 133, 182, 196, 197, 267

English Restoration, 53, 64, 69

Episcopal re-branding, 79, 248

Erie Canal, 83

Exeter (England), 34, 38, 192

Fabergé, Carl, 136

Falmouth (England), 192

Fausz, J. Frederick, 100, 102, 104, 106, 111, 112, 148, 161, 163, 168, 171-76, 322, 335, 342, 344, 347, 349, 352-56, 360

Fawkes, Guy, 50-51

Fenwick, A.F., 85

Fenwick, Charles, 14

Fenwick, Cuthbert, 180-81, 186, 210

Fillmore, Millard, 99

Finland, 189

Florida, 185, 210

Forrest, James, 320

Forster, John, 240

Foster, James, 49, 50

Foxwell, Ben, 88

France, 30, 48, 69, 78, 145, 166, 183, 185, 187, 197, 208, 211, 214, 217-20, 224, 259, 261-65, 267, 268, 270-72, 327, 330, 370

France, Adele, 1-2, 3-5, 7-8, 14-16, 23-26, 27-28, 39, 41, 111, 112, 114-18, 119-34, 135, 148-49, 155-57, 163-64, 167, 170-71, 173, 175-78, 245, 333-70

France, Emma, 338, 342

France, Emma Price ("Pricie"), 123-24, 129, 132, 334, 340, 341

France, John, 340

France, Joseph, 341

France, Thomas Dashiell, 124, 129, 132, 334, 339, 340, 342

Franklin, Benjamin, 92, 137, 277

Fredericksburg, Virginia, 257

Freedom-of-Conscience statue, 352

French, 44, 184, 197, 203, 204, 208, 209, 214, 217, 218, 224, 227, 228, 229, 234, 260

French (language), 90, 109, 140-42, 145, 155, 157, 164, 181, 185, 191, 218, 221, 250, 261, 268, 269, 273, 282, 285, 289, 326, 328, 330, 335, 351, 358, 369, 370

French Revolution of 1789, 132, 218, 261, 263

Fresco, Margaret, 88, 91

Freud, Sigmund, 158, 266

Frobisher, Martin, 196-97, 212

Frost, Robert, 27, 283

Gaelic (language), 141, 143, 187, 282, 289

Galloway Farm, 315-18

Galloway, Edith and Luther, 317

403

Galloway, Mrs. Luther, 315

Gambia Merchants Company, 33

Garden of Remembrance, 352, 356

Gardiner, Thomas, 77

Garrison, William Lloyd, 18, 22

Gasson, Thomas, 286

Georgetown Philodemic Society, 100-01

Georgetown University (College), 4-5, 78, 100-01, 136, 139, 140, 145, 284, 301

Georgetown Visitation, 239

Georgia, 31, 222, 251, 256, 257, 274

German (language), 142, 143, 145, 164, 165, 287-89, 295, 326, 328, 346

Germany, 45, 145, 169, 187, 326

Gestapo, 327

Gibbons, James (Cardinal and Archbishop), 304, 310, 316

Gill, Frances, 28, 360

Glorious Revolution, 47, 66, 72, 190

Gold Rush of 1848, 215

Goldsborough, A.S., 347

Goodheart, Adam, 79

Gorman, Mary, 163-65, 173, 351

Gough, Alfred, 84-89, 91-94, 117, 156

Grancey, comtesse de, 272

Grason, William, 105

Great Awakening, 82

Great Britain, 19, 20, 22, 30, 33, 34, 37-40, 45, 54, 69, 71, 72, 78, 79, 82, 87, 92, 95, 106, 115, 116

Great Depression, 24, 26, 321, 350-55

Great Lakes, 220, 270, 273

Great March on Washington - 1963, 24, 280-81

Great Mills High School, 322

Greece, 166, 187

Greek (language), 90, 141, 242, 285, 289

Greeks, 187

Green, Ruth, 312

Grenada (island), 254

Grew, Henry, 21

Griffith, Dirk, 3

Griffith, Emily Jane, 162

Griswold, Mac, 32

Grube, Jim, 77

Guadeloupe (island), 184, 207, 272

Guinea Coast, 30-32, 189, 194-96

Gundlach, Gustav, 327-28

Gunpowder Plot, 51, 56, 205

Guyana (Suriname), 184

Guyane (French Guiana), 184

Guyther, Roy, 89-91

Habsburg Monarchy, 327

Hagerstown (Maryland), 166, 248

Haiti, 184, 191, 194, 228, 229, 272

Hakluyt, Richard, 194-95

Halifax, Nova Scotia (Canada), 219

Hall, Clayton Colman, 49, 200

Ham (Cham), 188

Hanson Jordan, Vivian Rose, 324

Harlem Renaissance, 320

Harper Brown, Lulu, 312

Harper, William Rainey, 131, 364-65

Harris, Benjamin G., 85

Hart sisters, 109, 130

Hartford (Connecticut), 161, 221, 308, 314

Harvard College, 27, 99, 121, 122, 135, 139-42, 147, 239, 278, 283-86, 287, 288, 291

Harvey, John (Jamestown), 186, 209

Hawkins, John, 193-97, 212

Hawkins, Steve, 301

Hawks, Francis Lister, 207

Hawley, Henry, 203, 204, 205

Hawley, Jerome, 199, 203, 204, 205, 207, 209

Hawley, William, 186, 203, 204, 205

Hawthorne, Nathaniel, 93, 97

Haydon, Benjamin Robert, 2, 18, 19, 33, 35, 39, 86

Hebb, Nanny K., 305

Hebrew (language), 141, 285

Hemstock, Kevin, 124

Hervieu, Auguste, 228

Heuser, Herman, 146, 149, 293

Hispaniola, 184, 185, 191-92, 194, 202, 272

Historic St. Mary's City Commission, 54, 55, 179, 356

Historical Society of Kent County, 128, 333

Hitler, Adolf, 165, 326, 328

Hochschild, Adam, 32

Hodgkinson Grace, Dorothy Hope, 344

Holbrook, Stewart, 83

Holland, 30, 47, 66, 166, 185, 197, 211

Hollywood (Los Angeles), 226, 232

Holocaust, 328, 330

Holt, Andrew D., 342

Horse, 14, 103, 112, 119, 148-50, 163, 174, 181, 221, 222, 223, 235, 236, 248, 257, 271, 275, 294, 295, 303, 306

Horsey Collection, 132, 133-34, 333, 367

Horsey, Joan, 133, 337

Hungary, 142, 145, 326

Hurry, Silas, 55, 108

Hutchinson, Anne, 98

Hutchinson, Thomas, 36

Iceland, 201

Icelandic (language), 141, 282

India, 189, 255

Indian Removal Act of 1830, 251, 273, 274

Indian-Negro Fund, 304

Influenza Pandemic, 302

Ingle, Richard, 51, 59, 77, 180

Ingle's Rebellion, 51, 59, 77, 180

International Eucharistic Congress, 145

Interregnum, 47, 51, 53, 59-63

Ireland, 48, 62, 64, 71, 75, 78, 187, 201, 340

Irish, 74, 75, 90, 141, 144, 184, 193, 201, 207, 234

Irving, Washington, 93, 96, 97, 237

Isle of Wight (English Channel), 199, 201, 207

Italian (language), 145, 287, 326

Italy, 145, 166, 190, 311

Jackson, Andrew, 228, 234, 251, 264, 268, 273

Jackson, Renwick, 114

Jamaica, 36, 254, 302

James Francis Edward Stuart ("Old Pretender"), 66, 69, 70

James, Henry, 129, 136, 164

James, William, 136

Jamestown (Virginia), 185, 186, 208

Japan, 190, 191

Japheth, 188

Jarboe, Francis M., 82, 87, 215

Jefferson, Thomas, 177, 222, 226, 228, 230, 259

Jeffrey, Louisa, 225, 243

Jessup House of Correction, 357

Jesus of Nazareth, 52, 189, 331

Jews, 52, 67, 112, 114, 171, 206, 268, 330-31

Johns Hopkins University, 166

Johnson, Donald F., 210

Jones, Caleb M., 104

Jones, Mary Ellen Whalen, 304, 353

Jordan, Vivian, 324

Kalinago (Caribs), 183

Keane, James T., 39

Keats, John, 19

Kee-Mar Academy, 166

Kelly, Lawrence, 293, 296, 317

Kennedy, Alexander, 347

Kennedy, John Fitzgerald, 146, 278, 281

Kennedy, John Pendleton, 94, 97, 98-101, 105, 106, 118, 158

Kent County, 339, 342

Kent County Board of Education, 132

Kent County Elementary Schools, 342

Kent County Historical Society, 128, 333

Kent County Land Records, 124, 129, 333, 334

Kent County Public Library (Chestertown library), 333

Kent Island, 59

Kentucky, 83, 84, 227, 232, 253, 271

Kentucky Fried Chicken, 232

Kergorlay, Louis de, 263, 264, 267

Kerr Underwood, Sophie, 343

Key, Henry G.S., 85, 88

Kiehne, Gregory, 313

King Charles I, 40, 47, 48, 49, 51, 57-60, 64, 182, 183, 199, 208

King Charles II, 47, 51, 53, 64-65

King Charles V of the Holy Roman Empire, 192

King Edward VI, 47, 50

King Ferdinand the Catholic (Spain), 191, 192

King George I, 72, 75, 89

King George II, 72, 75

King George III, 70-71, 72, 90

King George IV, 71

King Henry VII, 197

King Henry VIII, 44, 45, 47, 50, 55, 183, 194

King James I, 47, 51, 56-57, 163, 194, 197, 203, 204, 205

King James II, 47, 54, 65-66, 68, 69, 70, 73

King Phillip II (Spain), 55, 196, 197

King William & Queen Mary, 47, 53, 55, 66-68, 72, 73, 74

King William III, 47, 53, 55, 66-68, 69, 72

King William's School (later St. John's College), 90

King, Francis V., 92

King, George, 89

King, Jr., Martin Luther, 24, 280

Kingdom of Kongo, 190

Kissel, Susan, 217

Klobusicky Perlman, Eleanor, 114

Korzonkierwicz, canon, 295

Ku Klux Klan, 347

Ladies Improvement Society of Chestertown, 128

LaFarge Collection (Georgetown University), 4, 11, 136, 145, 297, 344, 367

LaFarge, Bancel, 139, 286

LaFarge, Christopher, 369

LaFarge, Grant, 121, 139, 284, 285

LaFarge, John, 2, 5, 7-8, 12, 14-16, 23-24, 26-31, 38, 39, 41, 43-44, 80, 111, 115-16, 118, 119, 122, 127, 128, 135-150, 206, 213, 228, 255, 277-330, 344, 347, 353, 356, 366, 367-70

LaFarge, Margaret (John's sister), 142, 289, 290

LaFarge, Sr., John, 128, 132, 136-37, 139, 277, 282, 287, 367

Laffoon, Ruby, 232

Lalique, René, 136

Lancaster Maddox, Lucy, 111, 167-69, 171-73, 175-77, 341

Lancaster, Clem, 150, 294

Lancaster, John, 167

Landskroener, Marcia C., 125, 335

Lane Patterson, Mary Blair, 12, 127

Lange, Alexis F., 365

Langley, Laurel R., 163, 165-67

Languages (Native American), 251-52, 254

Latin (language), 51, 90, 109, 125, 140, 141, 142, 157, 162, 175, 176, 185, 200, 204, 206, 263, 282, 285, 288, 289, 295, 297, 316, 328, 351

Lattin, Claire, 108

Lawrence, Jim, 141, 286

Le Havre (France), 220

Le Havre (packet-ship), 218, 220

League of Women Voters, 351

Lebanon (New York), 249

Ledóchowski, Wlodzimierz Halka, 327-39

Lee, Charlotte (Lady Baltimore), 177

Lee, John W.M., 180

Lemay, Leo, 198, 207

Leonard Hall School, 149, 178, 301, 361

Leonard, William H., 304

Leonardtown, 8, 9, 10, 14, 15, 27, 82-88, 90-92, 94-95, 100-04, 112-13, 115-17, 119, 129, 143-44, 147-49, 156, 169-70, 174, 215, 244, 277, 293-96, 300-01, 316-17, 323, 352

Leonardtown Library, 84-86, 91-93, 94, 116

Leonardtown Memorial Library, 94

Lewger, John, 207

Lewis, John, 255

Lexington Park, 341, 359

Liberia, 228

Libraries, 14, 37, 84-86, 91-94, 116, 127, 131-32, 138, 139, 141, 156-57, 164, 166, 199, 238, 243, 294, 333, 337-38, 340, 348

Library of Congress, 199, 243, 294

Liebmann, George, 155, 307

Liège (Belgium), 78, 198

Lincoln, Abraham, 34

Little Flower School, 160

Liverpool (England), 219, 220

Living monument, 2, 25, 102, 106, 110, 333, 352, 356, 360

Loker Sowell, Eleanor, 174, 178

Loker, Aleck, 82, 83, 87, 174

London, 2, 18, 19-23, 35-37, 39-40, 44-48, 54, 71, 76, 86, 115, 130, 151-52, 180, 185, 194, 196, 197, 198, 200-01, 207-09, 216, 220, 228-29, 235, 252

Longfellow, Henry Wadsworth, 138

Lord Aberdeen, 20

Lord Mansfield, 36

Lord Morpet, 20

Lottery, 83, 104, 105, 158, 159

Louisiana, 31, 222, 256

Louisiana Purchase of 1803, 226

Louisville, Kentucky, 253

Lowell, Massachusetts, 238, 239

Loyola, Ignatius, 46, 189, 290, 297

Luanda (Angola), 189, 190

Luckett, Margie H., 128, 342

Lusitania, 135, 169

Luther, Martin, 45, 133

Lyceum, 91, 244, 337, 358

Lyell, Charles, 92

Lynds, Elam, 265

Maas, Anthony J., 291, 292

Madame Despommier's French and English Academy, 108

Maddox, George William, 167

Madeira (island), 38

Madison, Dolly, 177

Madison, James, 177, 245, 249, 257, 258

Magna Carta, 67

Maher, Zacheus, 326, 327

Malone, Mary Franceline, 84

Malone, Matt, 281

Manco, Jean, 193

Manhattan, 16, 96, 136, 137, 141, 145, 146, 254, 278, 342

Manners, Dorothy, 177

Marbury Commission, 358-59, 360

Mars, 138-39, 283

Marshall, John, 251

Martanet, Marjorie, 166

Martin, Caroline, 314

Martineau, Harriet, 214, 216-17, 219, 220-25, 227, 230, 233-46, 249-50, 253-54, 256-59, 260

Martinique (island, 184, 185, 207, 272

Maryland, 1-2, 4, 7-8, 9, 10, 14, 23-28, 33, 40-41, 43-55, 57-68, 72-80, 81-84, 87-92, 98-101, 106-07, 110, 114-17, 122, 125, 130, 136, 142, 155, 157, 159, 160, 161, 166-67, 168, 175-76, 179-83, 197-210, 213-15, 227-28, 231, 239, 245, 248-49, 255, 269, 270, 277-80, 286, 289, 292, 293, 295, 304, 306-08, 311, 316, 317, 320, 321, 327, 333-34, 340, 342, 346, 349, 350-56, 358-60, 364-65, 369

Maryland Commission on Higher Education, 359

Maryland Declaration of Rights, 79

Maryland Oath of Allegiance of 1638, 58

Maryland State Archives, 48, 53, 58, 73, 90, 108, 159, 162, 181, 306, 307, 317

Maryland State Highway Commission, 25

Maryland State House of 1676, 112

Maryland Toleration Act of 1649, 51, 52, 53, 60, 62, 63, 206

Matthews, James Brent, 296, 297, 301, 315, 316

Matzura, Michael, 295

McCarthy, Mrs. David, 306

McDermott, Jim, 39

McKenna Hall, 312

McKenna, Horace B., 5, 14, 26, 206, 279-80, 302, 306, 313, 316, 319, 321, 327, 368

Mechanicsville, 11, 14, 149, 294, 339

Medes and Persians (Iranians), 187

Melville, Herman, 93

Memphis (Tennessee), 26, 132, 170, 228, 231, 270, 271, 274, 342

Mesopotamia, 187

Mexican, 144

Mexico, 196

Michener, James, 103, 158

Michigan, 270

Miller, Henry, 54, 55, 210

Miller, Tom, 278

Milton, John, 176

Mississippi River, 13, 215, 222, 225-29, 231, 246, 252, 270-71, 273-75

Missouri, 253

Missouri River, 274

Mobile (Mississippi), 222

Montgomery (Alabama), 222, 258

Montgomery County (Maryland), 127, 162

Monticello (Virginia), 222

Montserrat (island), 207, 254

Moody, Carol, 92-93

Moore, Cecilia Annette, 316

More, Thomas, 55

Moreland Kerby, Bertha, 110, 111, 113, 167, 171-77

Morgan, 119, 148, 149-50, 294

Morris, William, 136

Morse Museum of American Art (Florida), 136

Moryson, Jane, 180-81, 186, 209-10

Mother Josephine (Sisters of St. Joseph), 308, 309

Mother Katharine Drexel (Sisters of the Blessed Sacrament), 304-05, 312

Mother Mary Cyprian (Oblate Sisters of Providence), 312, 319

Mount Holyoke College, 123, 245

Mount Vernon Literary Society, 124

Movies, 85

Mozart, Wolfgang Amadeus, 234

Mulberry Tree Papers, 12, 127, 361, 363, 366

Murphy, James H., 325, 328

Murphy, Joseph A., 326, 327

Murphy, Thomas, 255

Music Hall (St. Mary's Hall), 172, 173, 341

Muslims, 52, 112, 171, 187, 200-02, 207

Napoleon I (Napoleon Bonaparte), 158, 263

Nashoba commune, 228-29

Nashville (Tennessee), 271, 342

National Historic Landmark, 356

National Portrait Gallery (London), 18, 19, 35

National Public Honors College, 1, 334

Nazis, 325

Neal, James W., 324

Nelson, William, 155, 307

New Amsterdam (New York City), 185

New Bedford (Massachusetts), 219

New Hartford (Connecticut), 308

New Haven (Connecticut), 221, 239

New Orleans (Louisiana), 28, 185, 219, 220, 222, 225, 227, 228, 255, 257, 270, 271

New York (state), 20, 21, 27, 96, 109, 130, 151, 154, 219, 244, 249, 265, 272, 273, 278, 290, 337

New York City, 5, 15, 16, 24, 28, 31, 48, 100, 132, 136, 141, 143, 146, 147, 155, 164, 185, 217, 219, 220, 221, 222, 227, 236, 238, 241, 254, 260, 261, 262, 271, 272, 278, 279-83, 292, 305, 320, 325, 338, 342, 356, 368, 369

Newfoundland, 49, 181-92, 192, 196

Newport (Rhode Island), 14, 27-29, 30-32, 116, 135, 137-41, 211, 220, 277, 278, 281-83, 301

Newtown, 78, 213

Niagara Falls, 273

Nicholson, Francis, 77

Nicholson, Miss, 367

Nigeria, 187

Niles' National Register, 19-20, 155

Noah, 188

Norman Conquest (1066), 155

Norse, 140-41

North America, 20, 32, 45-46, 191, 311, 327

North Carolina, 251, 256, 257

North Equatorial Current, 202

Norway, 54, 187

Oath of Abjuration of 1643, 59, 63

Oath of Abjuration of 1657, 63

Oath of Allegiance of 1606, 55, 57

Oath of Allegiance of 1625, 55, 57, 199

Oath of Supremacy of 1558, 56

Oaths of Allegiance and Supremacy, 55, 58, 64, 70, 71

Oaths of Allegiance and Supremacy Act of 1688, 67, 69

Oblate Sisters of Providence, 161, 304, 312, 318

Ohio River, 221, 228, 253, 270, 271, 274

Ohr, Eliza M., 107

Old St. Joseph's Church (Philadelphia), 292

Osgood, James, 232

Overbrook Seminary, 146

Owens, Walter D., 360

Ox cart, 163, 174, 340

O'Conor, Herbert Romulus, 104, 159

O'Gorman, Joe, 141, 286

O'Rourke, Edward M., 295

O'Toole, James, 328

Packet-ship, 219-20, 223, 228, 253, 271

Panama Canal, 135

Papists Act of 1778, 70, 71

Paris, 166, 220, 267, 328

Passelecq, Georges, 326, 330

Patapsco Female Institute, 109, 130

Patric, John, 114

Patuxent, 142, 285

Patuxent River, 10, 11, 280, 298, 299, 367

Patuxent River Naval Air Station, 10, 11, 357, 362

Peabody Institute, 99

Pembroke Farm, 316

Pennsylvania Academy of The Fine Arts, 165-67

Perdue, Theda, 252

Perry LaFarge, Margaret, 28, 136-38, 140-42, 277, 282-83, 286-90

Perry, Oliver Hazard, 137, 277

Persons, Robert, 78

Philadelphia, 21, 48, 82, 145, 166, 215, 219, 221, 241, 257, 270, 292, 337

Phillips, Wendell, 18, 20-22

Philomathean Society, 124

Philpotts, Henry, 34, 38

Piano, 140, 142, 177, 238, 282, 284, 286, 288, 341, 346

Pickrell, Eloise, 94

Pieria Literary Society, 124, 125, 256, 335

Pierre, John K., 25

Pilgrims, 4-5, 46, 98, 106, 185

Piney Point, 13, 362

Pirates (privateers), 51, 59, 193, 200-02

Pitchlynn (Choctaw chief), 253

Plato, 320

Plessy v. Ferguson, 163 U.S. 537 (1896), 24, 301, 307

Plundering time, 51, 59, 179, 180

Plymouth (England), 192

Plymouth (Massachusetts), 46, 97, 101, 185

Plymouth Rock, 97-98, 99, 102, 106

Poe, Edgar Allan, 93, 97

Pogue, Robert, 13, 202

Point Lookout, 10, 11, 14, 15

Polish (language), 142, 144, 289, 295, 296

Pollen, John Hungerford, 76, 77

Pope Benedict XVI, 331

Pope Clement VII, 44

Pope Clement XIV, 76, 77

Pope Pius V, 45

Pope Pius VII, 77, 82, 101

Pope Pius XI, 145, 279, 325-29, 331

Pope Pius XII, 329-30

Pope, Alexander, 124, 256

Popery Act of 1698, 40, 69, 70

Portugal, 30, 38, 179, 189, 190, 193-96, 201, 211, 212

Portuguese (language), 195

Potomac County, 53

Potomac River, 2, 7, 8, 9, 10, 11, 51, 117, 148, 208-10, 212, 214, 259, 298, 299, 318

Poughkeepsie (New York), 290, 308

Poughkeepsie State Hospital for the Insane, 24, 147, 292

Prelacy, 53

Prescod, Samuel Jackman, 18, 22

Priest hole, 77

Priests' Point, 9, 144, 297, 298, 302, 311

Prince George's County, 78, 89-90

Protestant Associators, 68, 72-73

Protestant Revolution of 1689 (Maryland), 68, 72-73

Providence, Rhode Island, 185

Puerto Rico, 184, 185, 202

Puritan Uprising, 51, 61, 77

Puritans, 46, 51, 53, 59, 61, 62, 63, 68, 72, 77, 98, 185, 234

Putnam, Herbert, 294

Quaker Neck, 124, 334

Quakers, 20, 46, 52, 98, 152, 246, 267

Queen Anne, 33, 54, 68, 72, 74, 75

Queen Anne County, 162

Queen Charlotte, 90

Queen Elizabeth I, 47, 50, 56, 183, 194, 196, 197

Queen Elizabeth II, 1, 44-45, 163, 205

Queen Henrietta Maria, 49

Queen Mary I (Mary Tudor aka Bloody Mary), 47, 50, 55, 183, 197

Queen Mary I of Scotland (Mary Stuart), 50, 196, 197

Queen Mary II (co-monarch with William), 47, 53, 66-68, 69, 72

Quonnecticut (Connecticut), 254

Radcliffe College, 123

Radio, 85, 163, 337, 338

Raleigh, Walter, 191

Ramadhan, 202

Randolph, A. Philip, 281

Rappeleye, Charles, 32

Reading Room and Debating Society of Leonardtown, 84-95, 100-02, 107, 117, 156, 215, 244

Recusant, 50, 56, 63, 65

Redwood Library, 138

Reeves, Wilma, 104

Reid, Bill, 141, 286

Rendall, Steven, 326, 330

Revolutionary War of 1776, 30, 36, 40, 41, 45, 47, 72, 76, 78, 79, 81, 83, 89, 90, 92, 98, 100, 116, 170, 215, 216, 219, 226, 227, 255, 337

Rhode Island, 27-32, 116, 211, 277

Rhys, Jean, 38

Rice, 30, 210, 256, 270

Richmond (Virginia), 222, 257

Ridge, 10, 11, 24, 27, 77, 135, 279-80, 302, 303, 304, 308-22, 327

Riordan, Timothy B., 179-81

411

Roberts, Cecilia, 347

Rockefeller, John D., 131

Rocky Mountains, 215

Rodgers and Hammerstein, 103, 158

Rodin, Auguste, 166

Roman Catholic Relief Act of 1791, 40, 46, 71

Roman Catholic Relief Act of 1829, 40, 71

Roman Empire, 187

Romance languages, 131

Romans, 187

Romanticism, 96, 97, 100, 104

Rome, 68, 71, 145, 179, 192, 199, 287, 326, 327, 328

Roosevelt, Eleanor, 4, 343

Roosevelt, Theodore, 121-22, 135, 139, 141, 284, 285, 286

Ropes, John, 147

Rose Hill, 88

Royal Africa Trading Company, 33

Royal Declaration against Transubstantiation, 68

Roylance, Frank D., 302

Rudd, Daniel, 84

Russell, Anna May, 114

Russell, Bertrand, 164

Russia, 87, 135, 187

Russian (language), 289, 295

Rust, Hester, 228

Saint Helena (island, South Atlantic), 255

Saint Paul, 21, 189, 211

Saint-Barthélemy (island), 272

Saint-Domingue, 184, 185, 191, 229

Saleem, Yusuf, 268

Salem (Massachussetts), 98, 185

Salzburg, Austria, 234

Sambula (island), 195

Samoset, 98

Sandy Bridge (Kentucky), 271

Sanger, Margaret, 135

Sanner, Alfred G., 123

Sanner, Sarah, 123, 340

Santo Domingo, 185, 191

Savannah (Georgia), 28, 219

Scholarships, 110-11, 161-62, 165-66, 170, 354

Schongauer, Martin, 133

Schreiber, Carrie, 127, 342

Schroth, Raymond, 190

Schuler, Hans, 352

Scilly Isles (England), 201-02

Scotland, 48, 62, 64, 75, 78, 187, 213, 228

Scots, 234

Scott, Walter, 253

Semitic languages, 131, 141, 285, 289

Seneca Falls (New York), 21, 153, 154

Seneca Falls Convention of 1848, 21, 39, 152, 154, 155

Sergeant, Thomas, 137

Seven Sisters Colleges, 123, 245

Seymour, John, 74, 76

Shakers ("Shaking Quakers"), 249, 268

Shakespeare, William, 81, 107, 132, 166, 194

Shaw, Joseph F., 91, 102, 104, 118, 158, 159, 250

Shelby County Schools (Tennessee), 132, 342

Shem, 188

Shemtov, Levi, 268

Siberians, 187

Sicily, 271

Sierra Leona, 194

412

Silliman, Benjamin, 36

Simon, John, 45

Sister Mary Margaretta (Oblate Sisters of Providence), 312, 319

Sisters of Charity of Nazareth, 160

Sisters of St. Joseph, 161, 308, 314

Sisters of the Blessed Sacrament, 84, 304, 312

Skinner, John, 180

SlackWater Oral History Collection, 113, 167, 344

Slackwater: Oral Folk History of Southern Maryland, 210

Slave Trade Act of 1807, 34, 37, 87, 254

Slavic (language), 144, 289, 295, 296, 305

Slavs, 144, 187, 295-97, 300, 305, 308

Slovenia, 145, 296

Small, Joseph, 279

Smith College, 123

Smith Gaskin, Elvare, 324

Smith, Clarence Carroll, 323

Smith, John Walter, 124

Smith, Suzanne, 166

Smitha, Frank E., 189, 190

Smithsburg, 166, 167

Smithsonian American Art Museum (Renwick Gallery), 165

Smith's Creek, Ridge, 316, 318

Socrates, 320

Sousa, Matthias, 206

South America, 133, 184, 191

South Carolina, 31, 100, 222, 256, 257

South Seas, 137

Southern Maryland, 4, 7-8, 9, 10, 14, 16, 23-28, 40, 43, 78, 81-84, 89-90, 128, 130, 143, 148-49, 158, 160, 231, 270, 277-80, 289, 293, 295, 297, 309, 311, 316, 321, 327, 340 348, 366

Southern, David, 281

Spain, 30, 50, 55, 183-85, 190-94, 196-98, 202, 211

Spalding, George J., 85

Spalding, Walter, 284

Spanish, 184, 193, 206, 274

Spanish (language), 185, 190, 191, 195, 202, 250, 346, 351

Spanish Armada, 196-98

Spartans, 187

Spedden, Lucy, 170

Spedden McDorman, Mildred, 113, 119, 174-75, 177-78

Spiller, Robert, 208

Squanto, 98

St. Aloysius Choral Club, 144

St. Aloysius Church/Parish, 8, 27, 87-88, 102, 103, 113, 143, 144, 148, 149, 293, 295, 296, 298, 317

St. Alphonsus School, 299, 302, 303-08, 309, 313, 315, 319

St. Andrew-on-Hudson, New York, 143, 147, 278, 290

St. Cecilia's Church, 5, 298, 306

St. Christopher Island (St. Kitts), 49, 183-85, 203, 204, 207-09, 254, 272

St. Clement's Island, 49

St. David's School, 160, 299, 302, 303, 305-08, 313, 315

St. Ignatius Church (St. Thomas' Manor), 8, 292, 298, 311

St. Ignatius Roman Catholic Church, 298, 311

St. Inigoes, 10, 11, 97, 297, 311, 318

St. Inigoes Manor, 144, 145, 297, 298, 301, 302, 311, 316

St. Inigoes Mission, 5, 8, 27, 45, 144, 296, 297, 300, 311

St. Inigoes Parish, 144, 311

St. James Chapel replica, 298, 306

St. James Chapel/Church, 144, 296, 297, 298, 300, 303, 305-08, 369

St. James Parish, 297, 303, 304, 308

St. James School, 160, 299, 302, 303, 305-08, 313

St. John's Pond, 296

St. Lucia (island), 207

St. Maarten (island), 184, 185, 272

St. Mary's Academy, 88, 129, 160, 300

St. Mary's Catholic College, 248

St. Mary's City, 7-8, 10, 11, 12-13, 33, 43, 49-51, 53-55, 58-59, 68, 72, 74, 76, 97-99, 100, 102, 104-06, 108, 110, 116, 119, 132, 144, 148, 157-58, 160, 162, 166, 176, 179, 182-83, 185-86, 206, 209, 215, 296, 302, 303, 306, 307, 311, 313, 352, 354, 355, 356, 357, 358

St. Mary's College of Maryland, 1, 4, 5, 7, 12, 23-24, 28, 100, 102, 106, 114, 127-28, 156, 161-63, 166, 167, 170, 173, 176, 177, 296, 306, 323, 324, 334, 344, 349, 352, 366

St. Mary's County, 2, 4-5, 8, 12-16, 23-24, 40, 43, 53, 82-85, 88-90, 94, 98, 101-02, 104, 106, 108, 114-18, 122-23, 135, 142, 143, 148, 150, 158, 160, 163, 168, 171, 202, 206, 215, 227-28, 250, 254, 277-81, 285-86, 289, 293-96, 301-03, 309-10, 313, 316-17, 322, 325, 327, 339-40, 345, 353, 356, 365, 368

St. Mary's County Historical Society, 14, 85, 93, 94, 117, 300, 321, 323, 333

St. Mary's County Memorial Library, 94

St. Mary's County public-school board, 301, 309

St. Mary's Female Seminary, 1, 2, 3, 4, 7, 9, 12, 15, 23, 25-26, 28, 39-40, 91, 101-14, 116, 118-23, 126-28, 130, 132, 148-49, 155, 157-58, 215, 245, 250, 299, 305, 333, 335, 336, 338-41, 343, 344-49, 350-57, 359-61, 365-369

St. Mary's Female Seminary, Fundamental Rules, 112

St. Mary's Female Seminary, Organic Rules, 112, 171, 172

St. Mary's Female Seminary-Junior College, 1, 3, 4, 7, 23, 25, 26, 114, 127-29, 132, 157, 159, 170, 245, 305, 333, 343, 347, 348, 349-55, 357-60, 362-66, 367-69

St. Mary's River, 10, 11, 12, 298, 299, 302, 362

St. Mary's Spiritual Center & Historic Site, 249

St. Michael's Church/Parish, 280, 298, 303, 308, 311, 313

St. Michael's Residence (Ridge), 301, 302, 311

St. Michael's Schools, 160, 299, 302, 303, 308, 309, 313-15

St. Nicholas Church/Parish, 142, 285-86, 310

St. Omer (town in France), 78

St. Omer's College, 78, 92

St. Paul's (Methodist) Church, 103, 113

St. Peter Claver Church, 5, 279-80, 298, 308, 311, 312, 313, 315, 319, 327

St. Peter Claver Institute, Inc., 316

St. Peter Claver Parish/Mission, 5, 279-80, 311, 313, 319, 327

St. Peter Claver School, 161, 299, 302, 305, 308-13, 315, 318

St. Peter Claver's Industrial School, Inc., 316

St. Peter Claver's Institute, Inc., 316

Staatendam (ocean liner), 328

Stanford (Leland Stanford Junior University), 25

Stanwood, Owen, 51, 190

State Normal School (Towson), 168

State University of New York (Stony Brook), 219

Steamboat, 2, 7, 8, 9, 12-14, 82, 105, 119, 143, 148, 157, 164, 215, 220-23, 229, 231, 248, 325, 341

Stoffels, Eugène, 267

Stone, William, 51, 61

Stonyhurst, 78

Stuart "Pretenders", 66, 69, 70

Suchecky, Bernard, 326, 330

Sugar, molasses, and rum, 29-31, 38, 183, 191, 192, 210, 234, 254, 256, 270, 272

Sullivan, Louis, 136

Swann, Thomas, 110

Sweden, 187, 214

Swedish (language), 141

Switzerland, 145

Syracuse (New York), 272

Syriac (language), 141, 285

Taino, 190

Talbert Walthour, Janice, 322

Taylor, Scott, 5

Teachers College (Columbia University), 116, 132, 342

Teenager, 173, 334

Telephones, 163, 353

Television, 146, 278, 281

Tennessee, 26, 132, 170, 228, 251, 271, 274, 342

Tennessee ("Tanasi"), 251

Tennessee River, 274

Tennyson, Alfred, 133, 176

Tercentenary celebration (Maryland), 352-53, 369

Test Act of 1673, 65, 79

Test Act of 1678, 65, 79

Test Oath of 1699, 74, 79

Texas, 20, 129

Thackeray, William Makepeace, 93

Thatcher, James, 98, 99, 101, 106

The American Catholic Tribune, 84

The Baltimore American, 86

The Baltimore Sun, 113, 119, 163, 174, 175, 177, 178, 249, 302, 341, 348

The Catholic Encyclopedia, 76-77

The Century magazine, 164

The Chestertown Transcript, 127

The Chronicles of St. Mary's, 78, 84, 89, 94, 117, 210, 303, 345, 369

The Daily National Intelligencer, 20, 108

The Harper's Magazine, 166

The Kent County News, 333

The Leonard Town Herald, 82, 87, 101, 215

The Liberator, 22

The Lowell Offering, 238

The Messenger (steamboat), 221

The Mulberry Tree Papers, 12, 127, 361, 363, 366

The National Catholic Reporter, 330

The National Geographic Magazine, 114

The New York Times, 45, 167

The Signal News, 341, 368

The St. Mary's Beacon, 82, 87-89, 92, 94, 117, 215

The Sun, 335, 336

The Sunlight, 138, 283

The Time magazine, 329

The Washington Alumnus, 127, 336, 342

The Washington Collegian, 125, 335, 336

The Washington Times, 353

The Woman's Literary Club of Chestertown, 129-33, 134, 135, 156, 333, 336-38, 340, 364, 367

The Young Men's Club of Chestertown, 337

The Youth's Companion magazine, 164

Thomas Lilburn, Annie Elizabeth, 162, 345

Thomas Maddox, Angela Marie, 324

Thompson, Leroy, 323

Thompson Furey, Pearl, 323

Thompson, William L., 125, 335

Thoreau, Henry David, 93

Throop, Enos, 265

Tobacco, 12, 30, 73, 81, 180, 181, 183, 185, 210-11, 230-31, 235, 240, 270, 271, 340, 363-64

Tocqueville, Alexis, 214, 217-21, 224, 225, 260-75

Tocqueville, Édouard, 260-61, 270

Tocqueville, Émilie, 264, 265, 266, 273

Tocqueville, Hervé, 271

Tocqueville, Louise, 220, 221, 261, 271, 274

Toleration Act of 1688 (English Parliament), 46, 67

Tolson Waikart, Jean, 13

Tourtellot, Mrs., 351

Trail of Tears, 251-52, 273

Trail of Tears and Death, 252, 273

Train, 12, 14, 135, 221, 238, 240, 257, 280

Treasons Act of 1534, 55

Treaty of Alcáçovas-Toledo, 189

Treaty of Augsburg, 184

Treaty of New Echota, 252

Treaty of Paris, 72

Trinidad (island), 254

Trinity Episcopal Church, 102, 103, 105, 113, 298

Trollope, 138, 228, 283, 287

Trollope, Anthony, 93

Trollope, Frances, 93, 214, 216-20, 224-25, 227-37, 239-43, 246-53, 255-57, 259, 260, 262-63, 270

Trollope, Thomas Adolphus and Anthony, 225

Trollope, Thomas Anthony, 225, 231, 251

Troy Female Seminary, 109, 130

Trustees, St. Mary's Female Seminary, 1, 15, 101-02, 104-05, 107-12, 121, 123, 132, 157, 159, 161, 170-73, 178, 250, 343, 345, 346, 350, 353-54, 356-67, 359

Tuskegee Institute, 319, 325

Twain, Mark, 93, 164, 232-33

Tyler, John, 237

U.S. State Department., 327

Ukrainian (language), 289, 295

United Nations, 358

University of California, 365

University of Cambridge, 205

University of Chicago, 25, 131, 133, 134, 336, 337, 364

University of Innsbruck (Austria), 142, 144, 146, 278, 285, 286-89, 290, 291, 293, 295, 309

University of Maryland, 99, 307

University of Oxford, 205, 207

University of Pennsylvania, 102

University of the West Indies, 205

University of Virginia, 222, 230, 257, 259

Utica (New York), 272

Van Buren, Martin, 252

Vassar College, 123

Vatican, 326-31

Vatican II Council, 39, 255

Velikovsky, Immanuel, 81

Venezuela, 184, 194, 202, 203

Vespucci, Amerigo, 190, 191

Vikings, 140, 141, 187-88

Virgin Islands, 319

Virginia, 7, 10, 11, 14, 49, 51, 61, 116, 118, 180, 183, 186, 197, 200, 204, 207-10, 212, 214, 231, 248, 256-59

Virginia Company (London), 200, 208

Voltaire (François-Marie Arouet), 249

Voting Rights Act of 1965, 22

Wales, 78, 187

Walsh, Francis Michael, 45, 304, 311, 313, 353

War of 1812, 99, 216, 227, 243, 254

Waring, Basil, 78

Washington and Stonewall Literary Society, 99, 101

Washington College, 4, 14, 26, 39, 79, 116, 123-28, 131-32, 135, 156, 299, 334-36, 339, 340, 343, 344

Washington College Alumni Association, 126, 127, 170, 335

Washington College Archives, 125, 333, 336

Washington County, 166

Washington, Booker T., 164

Washington, D.C., 4, 7-8, 9, 11, 12, 14, 26, 100, 108, 114, 119, 120, 132, 148, 170, 222, 234-37, 239, 251-54, 269, 271, 280, 281, 294, 306, 328, 341, 357, 359

Washington, George, 177, 234

Weatherby, Lawrence, 232

Webster Field (U.S. Navy), 302

Webster, Noah, 95

Weiner, Benjamin, 114

Welfare Island (fka Blackwells Island), 27, 147-48, 149, 282, 292-93, 295

Wellesley College, 123

West Indies, 32, 34, 76, 92, 183-86, 191-92, 195, 197, 202, 203, 205, 208, 211

West Point Academy, 243

Westminster Abbey, 246

Whalen Jones, Mary Ellen, 304, 353

Wharton, James M., 360

Wheatley, Phyllis, 320

Wheeling (Virginia, now West Virginia), 240

White, Andrew, 51, 184, 198-209, 211, 311, 369

Whitman, Walt, 93, 164

Wickes, Adelaide, 129

Wickes, Joseph, 128, 129

Wickes, Judge Joseph and Ann, 124, 128, 129, 334

Williams Davis, Gertrude, 312

Williams, Lawrence P., 316

Williams, Roger, 98

Windmill, 175, 351

Winthrop, John, 98, 202

Wood, Irvanette, 345

Wood, Polly, 345

Wood, Scott, 5

Woodlawn, 77

Woodstock College (near Baltimore), 143, 148, 278, 291-92, 293, 312

Wooton, Turner, 78

Worcester v. Georgia, 31 U.S. 515 (1832), 251

Wordsworth, William, 140, 277

World Columbian Exposition of 1893, 132, 136

World War I, 23, 38, 85, 94, 135, 169, 175, 237, 302, 317, 363

World War II, 24, 38, 145, 237, 278, 330, 334, 341, 350, 356, 357-58, 359, 362, 364

Wright, Frances (Fanny), 217, 228-29

Wright, Frank Lloyd, 136

Yale College/University, 36, 95, 166, 239

Yaocomico (Yaocomaco) people, 58

Zwinge, S.J., 14

About the Author

Janet Butler Haugaard

Janet McKee Butler went to a girls' school run by Quakers in Providence during World War II. When her family moved to Princeton in 1948, she went to yet another girls' school before going on to Bryn Mawr and, later, Barnard. In 1961, she got her master's in English literature at New York University.

In 1962, Janet Butler Haugaard moved to Puerto Rico. She taught literature at the University of Puerto Rico, where she shared an office with five other professors (including Ted Lewis). In the 1970s, the University of Puerto Rico sent her to Cornell, where she specialized in Black American and Caribbean Literature and earned her Ph.D. Janet continued teaching and writing at the University of Puerto Rico until 1987, when Ted Lewis, who was then President of St. Mary's College of Maryland, asked her to revamp writing at the College and to be assistant to the President.

Her curiosity piqued by the College's unique heritage, Janet began interviewing alumnae of St. Mary's to make a record of early-to-mid-century customs before they were lost to time. Archived transcripts and questionnaires provide a cultural snapshot of the 25 years when M. Adele France was Principal, later President, of St. Mary's.

In the mid-1990s, Janet became executive editor and writer for the College. She was designated *Editor Emerita* upon her formal retirement in late 2008. The College provided her with an office where she could work on her until-then-shelved Adele France project. From 2009 through 2019, Janet wrote this book centered on Adele France, after delving into historical-research excursions and chancing upon Adele's contemporary, John LaFarge.